WORK ANALYSIS
AND DESIGN
FOR
HOTELS, RESTAURANTS
AND INSTITUTIONS

SECOND EDITION

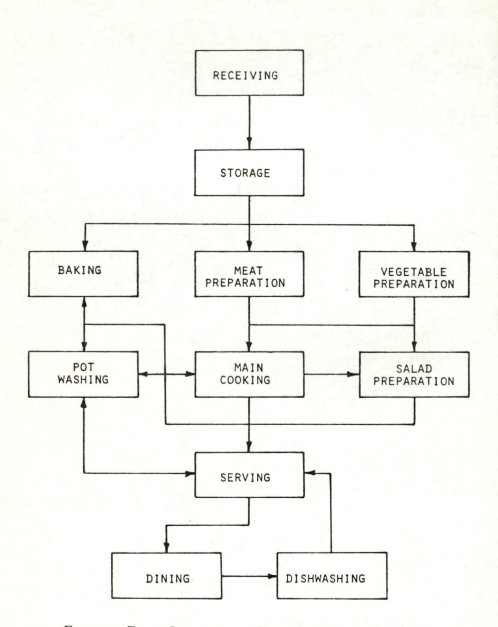

FUNCTION FLOW CHART FOR A FOOD SERVICE OPERATION

WORK ANALYSIS AND DESIGN FOR HOTELS, RESTAURANTS AND INSTITUTIONS

SECOND EDITION

Edward A. Kazarian, Ph.D.

Professor, School of Hotel,
Restaurant and Institutional Management
Michigan State University

AVI PUBLISHING COMPANY, INC.
Westport, Connecticut

©Copyright 1979 by
THE AVI PUBLISHING COMPANY, INC.
Westport, Connecticut

Library of Congress Cataloging in Publication Data

Kazarian, Edward A
  Work analysis and design for hotels, restaurants, and institutions.

  Bibliography: p.
  Includes index.
  1. Hotel management. 2. Restaurant management.
3. Institution management. I. Title.
TX911.3.M27K4 1979   658.5'3   79-10668
ISBN 0-87055-317-8

Printed in the United States of America

Preface To The Second Edition

I have been pleased with the reception this book has received in colleges and universities around the country. It has been suggested that I up-date the book at the first opportunity. This I have now done.

A complete new unit has been added dealing with task sequencing. The sequencing or scheduling of various tasks that have to be performed for a given situation represents a significant problem for management. Satisfactory solutions to these types of problems are necessary in order to assure efficient operation of the business or institution. Of the many types of sequencing and scheduling problems that may be encountered, the case of scheduling several tasks through each of two pieces of equipment or through two work areas are used to illustrate solution procedures. The solution procedures are then expanded to the problem of scheduling of several tasks through three pieces of equipment or three work areas. A necessary prerequisite to the solution of these types of problems is to know the times required to process each task on each piece of equipment or through each work area. Only those problems that involve tasks which are to be processed in the same order can be solved. This means that each task must first be processed on one piece of equipment before being processed on a second piece of equipment. There are many examples of tasks in the hotel, restaurant and institutional field that have to be sequenced and these are dealt with in depth.

In response to requests, a complete new unit has been added presenting problems and exercises for each chapter.

I would have liked to convert the text totally to the metric system. However, such a conversion is possibly premature. Conversion tables will be found in the appendix.

I trust that my decision concerning these additions and changes will be in keeping with the best interests of all those working in the field.

EDWARD A. KAZARIAN

East Lansing, Michigan
January, 1979

Preface To The First Edition

This book deals with the study of work systems that are commonly found in Hotels, Restaurants and Institutions. The primary purpose of the book is to present the principles, knowledge and techniques required to successfully analyze and design such work systems so that they are as efficient as possible. The basic material presented has been primarily drawn from the field of Industrial Engineering; and the only innovations that may be claimed are embodied in the applications of this material to the Hotel, Restaurant and Institutional field.

Recent changes in the labor market as well as increasing wage levels in the Hotel, Restaurant and Institutional area have created difficult problems for management. Problems such as low employee productivity and high turnover rates are created by the fact that a large portion of the manpower required is used to provide personal services which are not very conducive to ordinary methods of automation. Thus management has to consider new and creative methods of increasing their manpower productivity in order to realize an adequate profit. It is my belief that the area of work analysis and design holds great promise as a solution to the problems of increasing the productivity in the Hotel, Restaurant and Institutional field.

It is hoped that this book will serve both as a text for classroom instruction at the University and Junior College level and as a basic reference for managers, administrators and supervisors currently engaged in Hotel, Restaurant or Institutional work. The book should also serve as a source of prerequisite knowledge to the study of layout and design of facilities.

It should be emphasized that the material presented in this book is limited to those areas that are thought to be most applicable to the Hotel, Restaurant and Institutional field, and does not attempt to cover all aspects of Industrial Engineering in great detail.

Grateful acknowledgement is made to those individuals who contributed their ideas, suggestions and materials for this book.

EDWARD A. KAZARIAN

August 1, 1969

Contents

Introduction to Work Analysis and Design

ADVANTAGES

Work analysis and design refers to a program of continuing effort to increase the effectiveness of work systems. Industrial Engineers have been using work analysis and design techniques for many years in the manufacturing industries. Their efforts over the past 30 years have increased the output of manufacturing industries approximately 150%, while the manpower needed for the greater output increased only about 50%. This increase in production is primarily the result of increased productivity of workers, although mechanization and automation have played an important part. An important fact is that this increased output was accomplished with considerable improvements in working conditions, work methods, wages and fringe benefits. The physical effort required by the workers has also been markedly reduced. The latest data from manufacturing industries indicate that employee productivity is still increasing at a rate of approximately three percent per year. This continuing growth in employee productivity has led to record profits and wages for the manufacturing industry.

WORK ANALYSIS AND DESIGN IN HOTELS, RESTAURANTS AND INSTITUTIONS

The use of work analysis and design in the hotel, restaurant and institutional field has been very spotty. Only in the last few years has there been an interest and need for a full-fledged work analysis and design program. The hospitals appear to be the only area that have taken advantage of the benefits of work analysis and design programs. In fact some hospitals employ an industrial engineer to devote full time to work improvement. Very few hotels or restaurants regardless of size have a true work analysis and design program.

The hesitant attitude of the hospitality field to accept and use work analysis and design in the past may be explained from a number of standpoints. Probably the most important factor was the availability of low cost labor in the past. Even until the late 1950's, wages of 25¢ per hour or less were reported for some classes of workers in hotels and restaurants in the southern states (Anon. 1962). Wages of maids rarely went over 85¢ per hour in hotels regardless of their geographic location. Even today, wages for hourly employees in the hotel, restaurant and institutional field are among the lowest of the major classification of industries. This pool of low cost labor is no longer available to the hotels, restaurants and institutions.

Another factor causing the hesitant attitude was that many hotels and restaurants were experiencing high profits and business was generally good until the early or mid 1950's. In those times little thought was given to improving worker productivity because the need was not there. An important point to remember is that employee productivity in the hospitality field is closely related to the sales volume. When the sales volume is high, productivity of the employees will also be high. If sales drop off the employee productivity also drops off. For example, a hotel operating at 90% occupancy will show a higher employee productivity than when it is operating at 40% occupancy. This is caused by the fact that the hotel has to operate with a fixed minimum staff regardless of the occupancy.

The hospitality industry differs from many industries in two important ways. First, the demands for the products and especially the services offered in the hospitality field are highly variable and in most cases instantaneous. A restaurant will probably encounter its greatest demand during the noon or evening meals and, of course, all the customers want to be served the moment they enter. Unfortunately most of the products and services can not be "stockpiled" easily to meet fluctuating demands. The products involved are perishable and the services have to be provided at the will of the customer.

The second important difference exists in the nature of the tasks and jobs encountered in the hospitality field. Most workers are involved in tasks that vary considerably either in their entire content or at least in some of their components during any given work period. This task variability probably led to the feeling that work analysis and design could not be applied as readily or easily as it could for repetitive tasks. Of course, this should not be a deterrent to work analysis and design but instead should act as a stimulant to use new and creative techniques to analyze such tasks. It should be noted that many repetitive tasks can be found in the hospitality industry and these can be easily analyzed and improved.

Another factor that may have played a part in the hesitancy of using work analysis and design in the hospitality field is the education of management and supervisory personnel. Many of these individuals did not have any formal education in work analysis and design. Even more disturbing is that schools, colleges and universities offering work in hotel, restaurant and institutional management, with few exceptions, place too little emphasis on work analysis and design. A thorough understanding and appreciation of work analysis and design at the management and supervisory level is a necessary prerequisite to a satisfactory work improvement program that will lead to increased worker productivity.

The Need for Work Analysis and Design

Various reports identifying the characteristics of the hospitality field point out the need for a work analysis and design program. One report[1] shows that the productivity for eating and drinking places rose at an average annual rate of 1% between 1958 and 1976 as shown in Table 1.1. The trend of labor productivity can be seen to deviate significantly from the long-term average.

During the same period, productivity in the private economy increased an average of 2.8% a year. This comparison would indicate that considerable improvement in the productivity for eating and drinking places might be realized in the years ahead.

Labor turnover is also a critical problem in the hospitality field that contributes to reduced productivity. Many hotels, restaurants and institutions have turnovers of at least one-fourth of their employees each year. Some operations have a turnover rate of over 50%. The costs involved in frequent employee turnover have a very detrimental effect on productivity since the estimated cost of turnover is $200 to $300 per separated worker.

Rising labor costs are another factor indicating the need for work analysis and design. Labor costs, expressed as a percentage of total sales, have been increasing at a rate of 1 to 2% per year in the hospitality industry. This is especially critical for hotels because the labor costs represents 40 to 45% of the operating expenses. Recent minimum wage legislation has been and will continue to be an important factor in continually increasing labor costs. Control of labor costs by increasing worker productivity represents the biggest challenge for management in the hospitality industry today.

The need for better analysis of labor costs by management also indicates the necessity of work analysis and design. In the past, food cost

---

[1]Carnes, R.B., and Brand, H. 1977. Productivity and new technology in eating and drinking places. Monthly Labor Review 100, No. 9, 9-15.

TABLE 1.1
INDEXES OF PRODUCTIVITY IN FOOD SERVICE ESTABLISHEMENTS 1958–76

Year	Output per Hour*	Year	Output per Hour
1958	91.3	1968	101.9
1959	90.3	1969	100.1
1960	90.0	1970	103.5
1961	90.8	1971	101.2
1962	91.8	1972	104.4
1963	93.8	1973	106.0
1964	93.1	1974	102.8
1965	96.0	1975	105.0
1966	98.0	1976	103.2
1967	100.0		

*(1967 = 100)

was a good criterion of effective management for the food service aspects of the hospitality industry. This probably is no longer true. Frequently we find that labor is "built-in" for many products such as the processed foods but still wind up as a food or material cost. A better analysis of cost is made when the labor can be broken down into direct versus indirect labor used to provide the various products and services of the hospitality field. A work analysis and design program will eventually lead to work measurement which then will give the best indication of labor expenditures and consequently labor cost.

TABLE 1.2
INDICATORS OF THE NEED FOR WORK ANALYSIS AND DESIGN

1. Guests waiting to check in or check out, or to be admitted
2. Excessive overtime wages
3. Excessive employee turnover
4. Fluctuations in rooms and food sales
5. Customer and employee complaints
6. Reduced profits
7. Bottlenecks in food production
8. Wasted materials
9. Peaks and valleys in work loads
10. Excessive china and glass breakage
11. Lack of information when needed
12. Employees not using their highest skills
13. Poor utilization of equipment
14. Delays in service (see Fig. 1.1)
15. Unnecessary movement of materials
16. Excessive employee travel
17. Frequent accidents
18. Low employee morale
19. Inefficient use of space
20. Excessive paperwork
21. Poor forecasting of labor needs
22. Difficulty in meeting production schedules
23. Poor employer-employee relations
24. Poor quality food
25. Poor working conditions (see Fig. 1.2)
26. Excessive absenteeism

There are many other factors that indicate the importance and necessity of a work analysis and design program for the hotel, restaurant and institutional field. Following are some of the specific indicators pointing out this need.

FIG. 1.1. CUSTOMERS WAITING FOR SERVICE INDICATE THAT ROOM FOR IMPROVEMENT IN THE WORK SYSTEM EXISTS

WORK ANALYSIS AND DESIGN OBJECTIVES

Work analysis and design refers to a program aimed at analyzing and improving all the factors involved in accomplishing work. The general objectives of a work analysis and design program are to provide services and products with the least amount of time, effort and money. This indicates that some of the techniques and tools of Industrial Engineering have to be used to analyze the entire operation of the hotel, restaurant or institution. Some of the standard engineering techniques that could be used for analysis include flow diagrams, process charts, operation analysis techniques and the use of motion pictures. Other analytical tools that may be used include engineering economics, cost analysis, work sampling and mathematical programming.

FIG. 1.2. THE LOW OVERHEAD IN THIS STORAGE AREA MAKES EVEN
INVENTORYING A DIFFICULT TASK

It should be understood that a work analysis and design program is not
limited to a particular type of job or task or a particular group of people.
The work analysis and design program should involve analysis of all
levels of personnel including supervisors, department heads and managers as well as the hourly paid employees.

Satisfactory results can be obtained only if there is a true understanding of the objectives and goals of the work analysis and design
program. The right attitude and approach on the part of both management and labor are prerequisites to increased productivity. The re-

sults are not necessarily satisfying if a narrow or limited approach to a work analysis and design program is taken. In some instances a short-sighted approach to work analysis and design has left the wrong impression on employees and consequently has given them a reason to object to such programs.

A basic understanding of the philosophies of a work analysis and design program is the first step in assuring its success. This should include a knowledge of the benefits to be expected and the problems that may arise. The benefits that could be expected from such a program are broken down into three general areas. The first area is in the general improvement of the entire operation. If a true understanding of the program is shared both by management and labor, then the results should be better employer-employee relationships. This should minimize problems of labor turnover and excessive absenteeism. The work analysis and design program should provide better and faster service and a higher quality product to the customers. This is accomplished primarily through a reduction in the waste of materials, time and labor.

The second area involves benefits to management. Of particular interest to management should be the fact that a good work analysis and design program usually improves the morale of the employees. In fact, they have been proven to be better than most "suggestion systems" that have been tried. It has been found that the training of the employees is simplified and more meaningful when work analysis and design is accomplished on their tasks. Another benefit for management would be the easier planning and scheduling of work loads for various departments in the hotel, restaurant or institution.

The third area would be of particular interest to the employees. Work analysis and design programs have shown time and time again that any task can be done easier and quicker and with less human effort. Minimizing the human effort required to do a task as shown in Fig. 1.3 is one of the prime objectives of a work analysis and design program. Also of benefit to the employee would be the fact that better working conditions, Fig. 1.4, tools and equipment, Fig. 1.5, and workplaces, Fig. 1.6, usually result wherever a work methods program is initiated.

The success of a work analysis and design program also requires an understanding of the conflicts that may arise between management and labor. The importance of participation by all staff members should not be underestimated. Many programs have failed because of this lack of mutual understanding behind what the program is trying to accomplish. Many management people blame failure of a work analyis and design program to the employee's inherent resistance to change. In reality, the resentment of criticism is probably the cause of failures of these pro-

FIG. 1.3. THE EASY WAY OF MOVING MILK CANS

grams rather than the so-called resistance to change. Perhaps this resistance to change is caused by the fact that the changes are proposed by
management. Another factor that may enter the picture is fear of the
unknown effect that a work methods program will have on the employee.
Many employees will probably have the feeling that the only result of the
program would be to eliminate their particular job.

It is therefore very important that the aims of the work analysis and
design program be set forth early and understood fully by all parties
concerned. When the only objective of the program is to produce more
work by the hourly paid employees, it becomes a gimmick or device
prescribed by management for the worker. In such a situation the methods used are designed specifically for this purpose and frequently cause
the problems of resistance to change and fear on the employees' part.
Frequently a work analysis and design program is thought of only as a
way to find short cuts, gadgets or perhaps lead to mechanization. Under
this philosophy the importance of participation by all involved is ne-
glected.

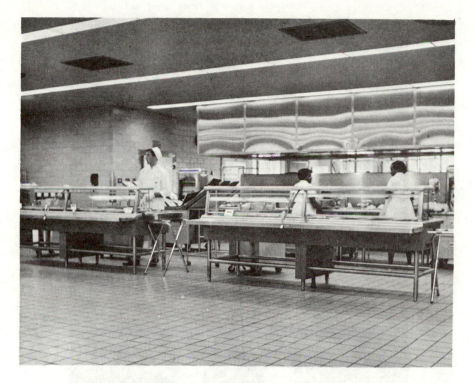

FIG. 1.4. A MODERN WELL DESIGNED WORK AREA LEADS TO BETTER
EMPLOYEE MORALE AND PRODUCTIVITY

BASIC AREAS OF WORK ANALYSIS AND DESIGN

Many areas of knowledge are used in work analysis and design. The
definitions and descriptions of some of these areas will clarify their use
and show the interrelationships that exist among them.

Human Engineering

Human Engineering is the technique of using knowledge about the
human body and it limitations for the design of tasks, equipment, tools,
work spaces and work environment to provide for the maximum effectiveness of the human body. It is literally "designing for human
beings." The concepts of Human Engineering are used to develop well-
lighted working areas as shown in Fig. 1.7. Properly designed tools such
as the pie marker shown in Fig. 1.8, are also developed by using Human
Engineering techniques.

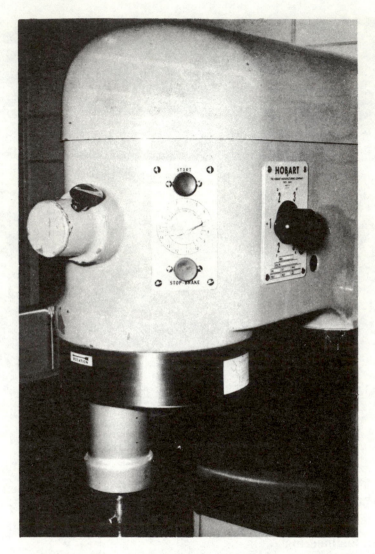

FIG. 1.5. EQUIPMENT WITH PROPERLY DESIGNED CONTROLS AND DISPLAYS
ADD TO EMPLOYEE PERFORMANCE

Methods Engineering

Methods engineering analyzes each operation of a given task in order to eliminate unnecessary elements and to find the best method of performing the necessary elements. Methods engineering is basically the applications of analytical techniques to the development of improved methods of doing work. Figure 1.9 shows an improved method of adding juice to fruit cups.

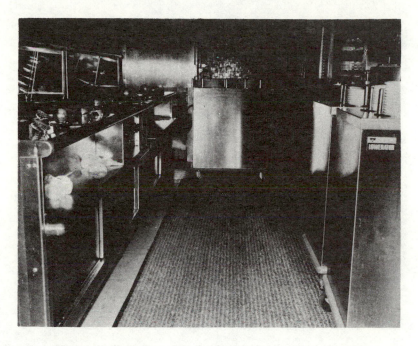

FIG. 1.6. THIS CARPETED WORK AREA REDUCES EMPLOYEE FATIGUE AND
KEEPS NOISE TO A MINIMUM

Motion Study

This analyzes movements of the members of the human body including the hands, eyes and feet for the purpose of eliminating wasted motions and establishing a better sequence and coordination of movements. Micromotion study is a refined phase of motion study that utilizes motion pictures for analyzing movements in great detail. The never ending task of trimming lettuce shown in Fig. 1.10, can be analyzed by motion or micromotion study.

Time Study

A time study determines the actual elapsed time for performing a task or the elements of a task by an accurate timing device. Time study usually includes adjusting measured times based on performance rating and other factors to obtain a standard time. The standard time represents the time that should be required to perform a task by a worker following a standard method and working at a standard pace.

FIG. 1.7. A MODERN WELL-LIGHTED WORK AREA HELPS EMPLOYEES ACHIEVE
MAXIMUM PRODUCTIVITY

FIG. 1.8. PROPERLY DESIGNED TOOLS SAVE TIME AND
EFFORT IN MARKING PIES

FIG. 1.9. THE FAST, EASY METHOD OF ADDING JUICE TO FRUIT CUPS

Work Design

This is a systematic analysis of existing or contemplated work systems to find or formulate the most effective way to meet the objectives of work. Work design utilizes all areas of knowledge regarding work as they are needed. Work design is based on the philosophy of creating the ideal system of men, machines and materials to provide the desired products and services.

Work Measurement

This procedure measures the effort required for the output of work. Time study and predetermined motion times are examples of the techniques of work measurement. Productivity indices and ratios are also work measurement concepts indicating the amount of work required to accomplish a given output.

Work Sampling

This statistical procedure determines and measures the elements of a task or job. The analysis is based on random samples of the task or job.

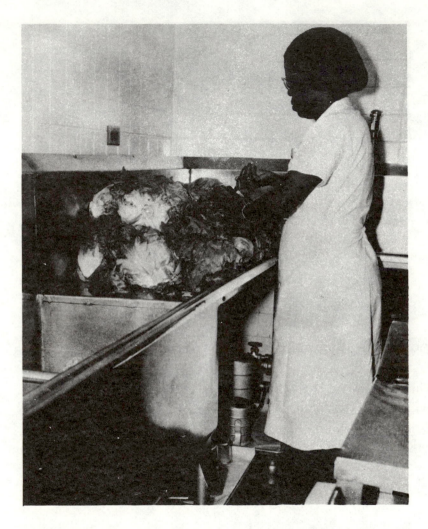

FIG. 1.10. TRIMMING LETTUCE INVOLVES MANY COMPLEX HAND MOVE-
MENTS THAT CAN BE ANALYZED BY MOTION STUDY

This procedure is simply the use of statistical sampling techniques
applied to work systems.

Work Simplification

Work simplification is a systematic analysis of the factors that affect
work in order to save effort, time or money. It is a broad concept that

involves utilizing many of the procedures discussed above for simplifying existing work.

TABLE 1.3
SOME PROBLEM SITUATIONS THAT COULD BE IMPROVED
BY WORK ANALYSIS AND DESIGN

Processing hotel or motel reservations
Check-in and check-out procedures, admitting
Design and layout of front office areas for smooth customer flow
Front office record keeping
Simplification of front office forms
Mail handling procedures
Handling incoming telephone calls
Billing and cashiering
Method of handling credit accounts
Communications between front office and housekeeping
Transporting patients
Processing requests for maintenance work
Method of making beds
Transporting food to rooms
Distribution of linens
Flow of work in laundry areas
Transporting chairs, tables, cots and other furniture
Banquet set-up
Collection of wastes
Preparing banquet meals
Layout and design of rooms
Layout and design of kitchen areas
Keeping medical records
Assigning maids or nurses to rooms
Handling employee records
Requisitioning procedure
Method of doing clerical operations
Communications between cooks and waitresses
Flow of food through food preparation areas
Method of inventorying food and supplies
Elimination of hazards
Storage of perishable items

One or more of the above mentioned areas of work analysis and design may be used to solve or improve many problems frequently encountered in the Hotel, Restaurant and Institutional field. A partial list of some of these common problems are given in Table 1.3.

Many successful work analysis and design programs have been carried out in hotels, restaurants and institutions to solve some of these perplexing problems facing management today. The results of these programs are presented in the later chapters of this text.[1]

---

[1]See especially Chapters 8, 9, and 11.

Philosophies of Work Analysis and Design

HISTORY AND DEVELOPMENT

The philosophies of work analysis and design have changed over the years as more and more knowledge regarding work systems has accumulated. The early philosophies were based primarily on the concept that work systems exist and that improvements have to be made in these systems. These early philosophies placed the emphasis on the analysis of existing work. The analysis of existing work consequently led to the development of principles and laws that relate to work systems, such as the principles of motion economy.

The recent philosophies of work analysis and design are based on using the results of past studies for the creation and development of ideal future work systems. The modern philosophy of work analysis and design emphasizes the *design* portion of the program.

A brief description of the development of these philosophies is important to fully appreciate the work analysis and design concepts. The earliest attempt to apply scientific methods to the analysis of work is attributed to Fredrick W. Taylor. In the early 1880's, Taylor studied work with the aid of a stopwatch in an attempt to improve the skills of workers. These early attempts to analyze and improve work were referred to as scientific management by Taylor. Taylor's philosophy was to divide the work of a man into simple elementary movements in order to determine the unnecessary movements and discard them. The next step in Taylor's approach was to determine how several skilled workmen accomplished the necessary movements required to do the job, and based on the timing of these movements, to select the quickest and best method of making these movements. Determinations were also made for the amount of time that should be allowed for delays, interruptions, accidents and for rest to off-set physical fatigue. Taylor's work placed a great deal of emphasis on the materials, equipment and tools used in accomplishing the tasks. The work of Taylor was the beginning of that portion of work analysis referred to as time study.

The concepts of motion and micromotion study were developed by Frank Gilbreth and his wife Lillian. Frank Gilbreth's observations that people accomplished the same tasks using their own peculiar methods led to his investigations to find the one best way of performing a task. He placed primary emphasis on the study of motion trying to determine which motions were the easiest and least fatiguing. The earlier studies by Gilbreth were aided by the use of pictures, however the greatest of Gilbreth's contributions did not come until he adapted the motion picture camera in his analysis techniques. The early work of Gilbreth is referred to as motion study. The technique of micromotion study using motion pictures is attributed to both Mr. and Mrs. Gilbreth.

In the 1930's, Allen H. Moganson developed the concept that motion and time study should be conducted with the participation of the workers. This concept was commonly referred to as work simplification. Moganson's concepts emphasized the fact that human beings have a natural desire to participate in the study of their particular job.

The years following these early developments were filled with applications of these techniques to existing work. This period produced a large increase in the productivity of workers, primarily in the manufacturing industries. The continued emphasis to study work led to more refined and sophisticated techniques. And as the work improvement programs progressed, the nature of the tasks began to change. Workers were trained to do tasks in specific ways, the tasks became more and more standardized and more specialization was introduced. This period was also characterized by studies that were carried out under the assumption that work was merely a mechanical thing and human dignity and individual enterprise were not important.

During the 1950's, changes in the philosophies of work analysis were noted. More emphasis was placed on analyzing the human factor. Studies aimed at determining why people work, their needs and desires, and their responses to various physical and mental environments were begun.

The philosophies of work analysis and design were changed to include the mental aspects of the worker as well as the physical aspects of accomplishing the work. This does not mean that the early pioneers of work analysis and design ignored the mental activities. In fact the early philosophies of Taylor and the Gilbreths were based on the enhancement of human dignity, but unfortunately these philosophies were not always maintained in many work improvement programs. As more knowledge regarding the physiological, social and egoistic characteristics of people became available, the philosophies of work analysis and design took on a systems approach. The systems approach of incorporating all the factors effecting work, including human behavior, is the basic philosophy of work analysis and design today.

The modern concept of work analysis and design assumes that work can be encountered in two states or conditions—existing work systems, or nonexistent work systems. The primary emphasis placed on analyzing existing work is to find improved methods and procedures. The analysis of nonexisting work stresses the development of an ideal system. Nonexistent work includes all tasks not yet performed in any way but anticipated because of a change in the products or services involved. For example, the anticipation of installing a data processing system in a hotel or hospital represents an area of nonexisting work for the particular hotel or hospital. The location for placing the data processing equipment, the type of personnel required and the type of tasks or jobs that will be done in the system should be anaylzed by a work analysis and design program so the system is as technologically ideal as possible. This idea of designing nonexisting work reduces to a minimum the amount of improvement needed after the system is functioning.

EXISTING WORK SYSTEMS

The study of existing work is essential for achieving increased productivity. The primary objective of studying existing work systems is to identify and eliminate unnecessary work, and to arrange the necessary work in the best possible order. The basic philosophy used to accomplish this objective is to break down the work into elements that can be individually analyzed. The procedure involved in the breakdown includes the observation of the job or task, recording the basic elements and then subjecting each element to a critical measure of necessity. As the knowledge and application of work analysis developed, it was found that the individual elements could be placed into a limited number of categories. The gross procedures of accomplishing work were broken down into operations, delays, storages, inspections and movements. Finer procedures of analyzing work were usually based on subdivisions of these gross elements. For example, the gross operations were further broken down into basic categories of hand motions, such as reaching, obtaining and placing. Basic hand motions in turn were broken down into fundamental elements or therbligs.[1]

After the work is broken down into the desired size elements, each element is questioned regarding its necessity and importance for the completion of the task. The standard procedure is to ask the following questions:

What is the purpose or function of the element?

Why is the element necessary?

---

[1]The Gilbreths coined the word therblig (Gilbreth spelled backwards) to identify the fundamental hand motions.

When should the element be done?
Where should the element be done?
How should the element be done?
Who should do the element?

The analysis, questioning and manipulation of the work elements resulted in the concept of "developing a better method." Developing a better method consists of four basic steps: (1) elimination; (2) combination; (3) rearrangement; and (4) simplification.

Elimination removes the unproductive elements of the task making it possible to be done with less physical effort and in a shorter time. The gross elements frequently eliminated from tasks are the delays and movements. Occasionally, operations, inspections and storages can be eliminated if the quality of the work is not affected. The elimination step is used in the finer analysis of work to remove wasted motions of workers. Of the four concepts of developing a better method, the elimination step obviously results in the greatest savings of time and manpower. The elimination of unnecessary work should be considered as a continuing process rather than a "one shot" technique.

When the elimination of unproductive elements has been accomplished, the combination step is applied. Combination in one sense, is a form of elimination since combining two or more elements into one reduces the total number of elements. Each element of the task can be compared with others to see if a combination is feasible. Operations, inspections and movements can frequently be combined without affecting the end result of the task.

The next step in developing a better method is to rearrange the remaining productive elements into the best possible sequence. Rearranging the sequence of elements is also related to the elimination step because moving an element to an earlier or later part of the sequence may eliminate a delay, movement or storage element. The primary purpose of rearrangement is to provide a smooth flow of activities. Rearrangement is also used to balance the elements of a task between the workers' hands. The rearrangement of elements has to conform to any precedence requirements that exist for the task.

Simplification is the last step to be done in arriving at a better method. Simplification refers to reducing the skills necessary for performing each element. The objective of this step is to find the way each element can be done easily and repetitively with the least amount of human effort. The principles of motion economy are used to guide the simplification process. The reduction of skills sets the stage for mechanization and automation of tasks. It is relatively easy to mechanize and automate tasks composed of lower skilled elements. Highly skilled elements are difficult and expensive to reproduce by machines and controls.

The analysis and design of existing work systems in hotels, restaurants and institutions can result in a substantial increase of productivity. It has been estimated that the level of productivity in the food service industry is approximately 45%. The reason for this low productivity is attributed to the preponderance of nonproductive activities, high turn-over rate and the instantaneous demand characteristics of this industry. Increasing this low level of productivity presents an interesting and challenging problem for work analysts.

CONTEMPLATED OR FUTURE WORK SYSTEMS

The analysis and design of contemplated or future work systems is just as important, if not more so, than existing work. The objective in analyzing and designing future work is to create a system that consists of the minimum number of components required to accomplish the desired function of the work. In theory, a properly designed future work system should eliminate the necessity for improvement after the system becomes existent. The development of future work systems should be based on the optimum use of human and physical resources.

Analyzing and designing future work systems is highly desirable since it eliminates many of the human relations problems that are encountered when developing improved methods for existing work systems. The problems of resistance to change, employee fear of job loss and lack of employee participation are minimized.

The first and most important step in analysis and design of future work is to identify the work system. Contemplated or future work systems are usually brought about when changes in the materials, products, equipment or services are anticipated. The food service operation that plans to use "boil in the bag" foods is in reality thinking about a future work system. The anticipated changeover to a computerized reservation and registration system also represents future work. The planning of expanded or new facilities involves the design of future work to the greatest extent.

Each new facility that is installed, such as shown in Fig. 2.1, creates a new and different work system. Once the future work system is properly identified, the analysis and design process is similar to that used for existing work. Obviously the development of future work systems would not involve observation and recording of existing procedures but the remaining steps in the process are the same. Since the human and physical limitations of existing work systems are not present, the design of future work can approach the development of the ideal work system. Various types of models describing the ideal work system can be used as guides in developing future work systems.

FIG. 2.1. INSTALLATION OF A WELL–PLANNED FACILITY FOR A FUTURE WORK SYSTEM

Extensive use of the fundamental laws or principles developed through the study of existing work systems are called for in designing future work. The principles of motion economy, flow and materials handling are examples of areas of knowledge that can be used. Recent development of statistical, mathematical and other analytical techniques can also aid the development of desired future work systems. The analysis and design of future work systems challenges the creative abilities of analysts to the fullest extent.

MANAGEMENT PHILOSOPHY

The role of management in the work analysis and design program is critical to the success of the program. Management must stimulate and maintain the proper attitude among the organization as well as provide the means of implementing the work analysis and design program. This indicates that management must understand, support and practice the basic philosophies of work analysis and design. The mere demanding of increased productivity from employees is not sufficient and frequently this approach results in reduced morale and other employee problems.

Implementing and maintaining a work analysis and design program within an organization is not always easy. Management must be aware of the problems that may be encountered and be prepared to meet them by proper organization and policies.

The most successful work analysis and design program are those that are developed within the structure of the organization. The use of outside

FIG. 2.2.   THE SELECTION OF NEW EQUIPMENT BEST SUITED TO THE WORK SYSTEM IS AN IMPORTANT PART OF A WORK ANALYSIS AND DESIGN DEPARTMENT

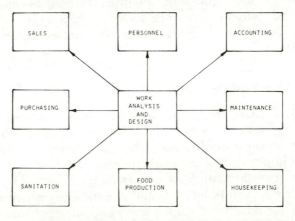

FIG. 2.3.   SCHEMATIC RELATIONSHIP BETWEEN THE WORK ANALYSIS AND DESIGN DEPARTMENT AND OTHER DEPARTMENTS

consultants to carry out the details of the program is not always desirable. The usual reaction by employees to outside consultants is negative; frequently creating the feeling that an "efficiency expert" has been brought in to make them work harder. Another problem with outside help is that it frequently results in a "one shot" approach to the problem and not the continuing approach necessary to attain the goals of the program. Probably the best use of consultants is to have them set up the basics of the program and train the required personnel to carry out the program. The most desirable situation is to place the responsibility of the program within the organization; preferrably to a separate department. The work analysis and design function has historically been the responsibility of the industrial engineering department in the manufacturing industries and has worked very successfully.

Since the work analysis and design program affects all aspects of the organization, it should report to someone with broad organizational authority, such as the general manager or the administrator. An ideal situation for the larger hotels, restaurants and institutions would be to have a separate work analysis and design department headed by a manager. The functions of such a department would be easy to define and justify. The department would be responsible for conducting the various studies required to analyze and design work. This would include the setting of standards. It would also act in an advisory capacity regarding the relayout and redesign of areas and the planning of new or expanded facilities. The work analysis and design department would also evaluate new equipment such as the broiler shown in Fig. 2.2, from the standpoint of ease of operation. The department would have the responsibility of preparing adequate training manuals and training needs that are based on their studies and on the principles of time and motion economy. The staff may also be responsible for estimating labor needs, scheduling labor and possibly determining the labor costs involved in the operation of other specific departments within the organization. Thus the work analysis and design department would be a service function of the entire organization. Figure 2.3 schematically shows the relationship between the work analysis and design department and other departments.

The work analysis and design staff should be composed of well qualified individuals. In addition to basic knowledge of analysis and design of work, the individuals should be versed in basic management principles, psychology, analytical techniques and human behavior. The staff should be able to discuss problems of sales, market analysis, food production, personnel work, maintenance and housekeeping with the various department heads and personel involved. The ability to work with and educate supervisors and workers is desirable so acceptability and confidence in the work analysis and design program can be achieved.

A suggested job description for a work analysis and design department manager is listed below.

JOB DESCRIPTION—WORK ANALYSIS AND DESIGN MANAGER

Basic function: To analyze and design work systems making optimum use of human and physical resources in order to help meet the objectives of the organization.
Responsibilities:
1. Utilize the techniques and philosophies of work analysis and design to increase the productivity of the employees.
2. Develop methods and procedures as required to improve the quality of products and services to guests and customers.
3. Develop and recommend policies for introducing and carrrying out the work analysis and design program.
4. Advise management of the work systems that should be studied or designed.
5. Direct and coordinate the department staff to obtain measurable improvements.
6. Develop and maintain standards of performance.
7. Conduct education programs for employees.
8. Assist in preparing information for union negotiations.
9. Assist in the planning of remodeling and expansion projects.
10. Plan and design efficient information flow systems.
11. Investigate new systems and procedures for possible adaption.
12. Prepare estimates of costs for making changes in work systems.
13. Develop plans for future work analysis and design projects.
14. Assist in preparation of training programs and training aides.
15. Develop and maintain a productive environment.
16. Assist in budget and cost analysis.

MANAGEMENT POLICIES

General management policies regarding the work analysis and design program can do much to create the proper attitude among the employees. These policies must show a concern for the individuals involved and provide an opportunity for employee self-improvement. A program aimed at only increasing the output of workers will meet resistance and fail.

One area of concern to workers is their job security. Most work analysis and design programs result in the elimination of jobs that have a low skill level. Fortunately, there is a high enough turnover rate in most hotels, restaurants and institutions that this problem can be minimized. When union demands of job security are involved, employees can be guaranteed work in other areas if their jobs are eliminated. Another solution is to wait until a period of expansion when more or new jobs are created. Displaced workers are the responsibility of both labor and management and cooperative efforts will give the best results. Increasing productivity benefits both labor and management and this fact should be reflected by the policies governing the work analysis and design program.

Overcoming the so called "resistance to change" has been emphasized by many individuals. The employee attitude of resisting change has been described as an inherent quality of all people. In reality, the "resistance to change" has been brought about by poorly managed work analysis and design programs. The following procedures will minimize the problem of "resistance to change."

1. Maintain a friendly, personal relationship between the work analyst and the employee.

2. Make limited use of outside consultants in dealing with employees. Consultants are best used in nonemployee contact areas.

3. Explain the employee's part in the program thoroughly.

4. Plan to share the benefits of changes with the employee.

5. Plan changes with the help of the employee.

6. Properly prepare the employee for change by providing as much information about the change as possible. Lack of knowledge frequently leads to imaginary problems in addition to the real ones.

7. Encourage full participation of supervisors in helping employees accept change.

8. Make changes during slack periods to avoid confusion.

9. Publicize the benefits of completed changes that are of interest to employees; e.g., better working conditions, easier work methods and improved equipment.

Another responsibility of management is to create and maintain interest in the work analysis and design program. This type of program must be continuous if the employees are to become interested and participate. The surest way to create and maintain interest is to constantly keep the employee aware of the program. Signs, bulletins and publicity in newsletters as well as person to person communications should constantly refer to the program. Employees and supervisors need continuous reassurances of the objectives of the program. Staff meetings and conferences can also be used to promote the work analysis and design program.

Management's responsibility in a work analysis and design program should be clearly understood. Work analysis and design should be considered by management as a tool, and should be carefully used in order to realize the expected benefits.

Management should be aware that a work analysis and design program is not a sure cure for all the ills encountered in employee productivity. In fact, many of the grievances presently existing in manufacturing industries deal specifically with time standards that have been brought about as a result of a work analysis and design program.

It should also be understood that a work improvement program may not always result in a reduction of payroll cost. In fact, if labor productivity is increased by the use of work analysis and design programs, then management should be prepared to pay for it through increased wages. There will be problems arising with unions that will have to be considered. In many instances it would be possible to invite the union representative in the beginning stages of the work analysis and design program. If the local union is still working on the philosophy that they are trying to get better wages and better working conditions for their members, then they should have very little to complain about regarding such programs. The drawbacks encountered should not outweigh obvious benefits and advantages of the program.

Another factor to be considered is the cost of a good work analysis and design program. This is hard to determine in terms of dollars and cents because of the broad scope of the program. Probably the biggest cost involved is the training or hiring of work methods analysts. Many hospitals have found it a good investment to hire Industrial Engineers to carry on the work analysis and design program. Then, of course, the time involved in training personnel in new methods and procedures is indeed important and costly. The return on the investment in such a program is even harder to determine. If the return shows up as increased productivity per employee, this can be easily determined; however, it is pretty difficult to measure the improved employee morale or the better and faster service to customers that may also result from such a program.

Other industries have shown that increased employee productivity and increased profits go hand in hand. They have also shown that increased productivity can not be accomplished overnight or even in a few months. It can only be accomplished by the cooperative efforts of management and labor in a continuing program.

The hotel, restaurant and institutional industry is at a stage where it can capitalize on the benefits of a work analysis and design program. Undertaking such a program will indeed be challenging and rewarding.

Work Analysis and Design Procedures

STEPS

Work analysis and design consists of a systematic procedure of applying the basic philosophies to actual situations. The procedure may be characterized by the following steps.

1. Identification and description of the work system.
2. Determination of factors affecting the work system.
3. Collection and analysis of data.
4. Formulation of alternative work systems.
5. Selection of feasible work system.
6. Testing the work system.
7. Installation of the work system.
8. Establishment of performance criteria for the work system.

This is a general breakdown of the work analysis and design procedure. Depending on the situation, certain steps may be combined or in a few instances eliminated. Parts of the procedure may have to be repeated to attain the objectives of the study. For example, it may be found that additional data are needed during the "formulation" or "selection" steps of the procedure. In this situation the procedure backs up to the "collection of data" step, and then resumes again. The analysis and design procedure applied to future or proposed work may call for several iterations of the steps outlined. A description of each of the steps will be presented to illustrate the general procedure.

IDENTIFICATION AND DESCRIPTION OF THE WORK SYSTEM

The analysis and design of work may be applied to two different situations: the improvement of existing work systems and the design of future or new work systems. The most important and frequently the most difficult step in the procedure is to describe adequately and identify the work system to be studied.

The identification and description step is composed of three parts.
1. Selecting the work system to be studied.
2. Determining the function of the work system.
3. Stating the objectives of the study in light of the function.

If the work system selected is extremely large or complex, it may be desirable to break it down into components for study. When this is the case, the three parts of the identification and description step are completed for each component of the work system.

All work systems (both present and future) should be eligible for selection for study. The ultimate goal of a work analysis and design program is to study all work systems. Practical approaches to this goal indicate that the systems that may show the greatest benefit should be studied first. This approach gives the needed impetus and drive for the entire program. The work systems may be ranked in order of importance based on the expected benefits or advantages.

Many sources of information can be used in identifying the work systems to study. Some of these sources of information for existing work systems include:

Complaints

Few people complain from habit. Most complaints are indications that something is wrong with the work system. Employees may complain about heat, fatigue, poor supervision, too much work, noise or rush periods. Customers may have complaints regarding the quality of food or service, long check-in and check-out times, poor sanitation, lack of attention or slow service. Each complaint should serve as a clue to possible improvements in the work system. Determining the cause of the complaint may sometimes lead to a quick solution of the problem.

Budgets and Cost Accounting Records

Budgets can be studied to determine where the most money is being spent. High labor costs are especially indicative of a particular work system needing improvement. Food and beverage cost records may indicate unnecessary waste of materials. Replacement costs for china, glassware and equipment can also be pinpointed by the records.

Productivity Indices

Records of the number of rooms cleaned per maid, number of guests served per waitress or the portions of food prepared per kitchen employee are measures of productivity that can be analyzed for trends. If the levels of productivity are not constantly increasing, the work systems can be improved.

Environmental Conditions

Many physical and nonphysical conditions affect the performance of workers. Slippery floors, poor lighting, poor ventilation and lack of proper equipment are examples of physical conditions affecting performance. Nonphysical conditions that affect worker performance include poor training, poor communications or low employee morale. Any of these factors can justify studies to improve the conditions.

Work Systems Not Previously Studied

Many work systems may appear to be functioning smoothly, however this is not an indication that it does not need improvement. Work systems that involve higher level personnel such as supervisors, department heads and managers may be subjected to work analysis and design. The problems of scheduling, controlling and planning are just as subject to study as the physical tasks performed by hourly workers.

Preliminary Studies

The use of gross study techniques such as work distribution or sampling frequently point out areas needing immediate attention. These techniques are especially suited to nonrepetitive activities. Process analysis of products and individuals may also be used to determine specific areas to be studied in greater detail.

Discussion Groups

When other sources of information can not be easily interpreted or making a preliminary study is not feasible, the work system to be selected for analysis can be decided by a discussion group. The discussion group should be composed of individuals who are well acquainted with the overall functioning of the organization. The discussion groups may be formed according to primary functions such as food service, guest and patient relations, sales or control.

Contemplation of Future Work System

The fact that a future work system is being contemplated is justification enough to conduct work analysis and design on the system.

Future work systems are always studied from one standpoint or another. The cost of equipment, space needed, structural alterations and interruptions of service are frequently considered prior to installing the new system. The work analysis and design of the new work system will indicate other areas such as: number and skill of workers needed; best procedures and methods for the tasks involved; type and extent of training program; best flow of materials; location and design of workplaces; best product design; need for specialized equipment and tools; and measures of performance. The importance of studying contemplated or future work systems must be constantly emphasized in the program.

The second part of the identification and description step of work analysis and design is to determine the function of the work system or the components of the work system if it has been subdivided. The function describes what is achieved or obtained by the work system or work system components. For example, the function of the food production work system is to provide meals for guests or patients. The function should specify precisely the purpose of the work system or component. Typical examples of work systems and their functions are shown in Table 3.1.

TABLE 3.1
TYPICAL FUNCTIONS OF WORK SYSTEMS

Work System	Function
Dishwashing	Provide clean tableware
Accounting	Provide records of control
Personnel department	Provide qualified personnel
Housekeeping	Maintain physical facilities
Check-out procedure	Determine guest liabilities
Sales and marketing effort	Provide customers
Receiving activities	Determine quality and quantity of incoming materials
Work analysis and design	Increase productivity

The reason for indicating the function of the work system or work system component is to justify the existence of that system or component. The simple fact that a work system exists or is being contemplated does not justify its existence. The criteria for the existence of work systems should be whether they are providing the required functions for accomplishing the objectives of the organization. Function determination provides the first place where unnecessary work can be identified and eliminated.

The selection of the work system and the determination of functions lead to the statement of the objectives for the study. The broad objective of all work analysis and design studies remains the same: to increase productivity. More specific goals as reducing cost, eliminating delays, shortening times or finding easier methods are related to the specific system selected. The statement of specific goals should be accompanied by appropriate measures of improvement or comparison between systems.

FACTORS AFFECTING THE WORK SYSTEM

The purpose of determining the factors affecting the selected work system is to indicate what type of data will be needed for the improvement or design. In the same sense that the work system had to be identified before it could be studied, the factors affecting work have to be identified before their effects can be determined.

The basic factors affecting work systems are: raw materials or ingredients; process or procedures; methods; design of workplace, tools and equipment; product design; physical environment; and nonphysical environment. Many of these factors are interrelated and affect each other as well as the work system. For example, product design and raw materials affect the process; and the design of the workplace affects the methods.

The nature and form of the raw materials or ingredients will dictate the amount of effort required to change them into the desired final products. The various types and length of storages, the type and amount of handling and the speed of production are affected by the raw materials or ingredients. The variation in raw materials can be illustrated by the many ways food ingredients can be obtained. Food ingredients may be obtained fresh, canned, dried, raw frozen, cooked frozen, freeze dried, preprocessed or partially processed. The different forms of food ingredients may require additional, fewer or different production steps.

The process or procedure identifies the sequence of operations or activities needed to accomplish the work. The number and complexity of operations and inspections and the frequency of movements affect the ease and speed of completing the work. Unnecessary delays in the process may cause bottlenecks and result in poor service to the customer.

The way workers use their hands, eyes or other body members in doing a job is referred to as the method. Methods affect the speed of performing operations or inspections. The number, speed and complexity of body member motions determines the performance and skill of workers. Awkward motions result in fatigue which in turn may cause errors or accidents to happen. Methods also play an important part in the final appearance of the product. This is especially important in the food service aspects. Methods of work usually form the basis for training programs and can influence the creation of good attitudes among employees.

The design of workplaces, tools, and equipment is important from the standpoint of their relation to processes and methods. Proper location of workplaces can reduce movements and improve the sequence of operations resulting in improved efficiency. The location of workplaces in relation to storage areas, service areas or equipment determines the flow of materials and workers. Back tracking flow or crossing of flow can hamper the activities of individuals and add unnecessary costs to the work system. Providing adequate tools and equipment simplifies and speeds the completion of work. The use of materials handling equipment in reducing human effort and increasing productivity has been proven by many industries.

The final product design primarily determines the type of processes and type of equipment or machines needed. Complicated product designs call for complicated and expensive processes. As the product design becomes simpler, output from a given work system should increase. Product design can also affect major policy changes affecting entire work systems. For example, the decision to buy completely processed foods instead of doing the processing may eliminate a large portion of the production work system. The decision to have laundry sent out instead of operating a laundry within the operation eliminates the entire laundry work system. Product design is more important in the manufacturing industries where the number and variety of products are much greater than in the hospitality industry.

The physical environment of work systems consists of temperature, relative humidity, ventilation, lighting, sound, color and noise. Each of these factors can have a detrimental effect on the performance of individuals and some even have an effect on the product quality. Poor physical conditions may cause fatigue, errors, sloppy work and accidents which are reflected in the output of the work system.

The nonphysical environment consists of the feelings of the workers, the social conditions and human response to certain situations. The attitude and morale of employees can not be as easily measured as the other factors, but their importance should not be underestimated. A worker's feelings toward his job, the supervisor and other workers affects not only his own performance but the image of the entire organization as well.

All of the above mentioned factors affect work to a greater or lesser extent. Part of the purpose of work analysis and design is to identify and correct those factors that have a detrimental effect on the productivity of the work system. The design of future work should be based on the latest knowledge of these factors and their effects. Many of these factors are described in greater detail in later chapters.

COLLECTION AND ANALYSIS OF DATA

The collection of data about the work system is simplified if the first two steps of the analysis and design procedure are carefully and completely accomplished. The important data required pertains to the functions identified in the first step and to the factors described in the second step. As a work system is broken down into elements, each element is analyzed from the standpoint of the function involved and the factors that affect the element.

Three methods of gathering data are generally used for existing work systems. The most common method of data gathering is direct visual observation by the analyst. The observer must be capable of seeing all the pertinent activities to be recorded. Complete knowledge of the job being studied and even participation in the activities will help an observer develop an analytical eye. Direct visual observation requires only a sheet of paper or a form on which to record the activities observed. Sometimes combining visual observations with discussion will result in more valuable data. Direct observation is best suited to gross analysis techniques such as process charting, activity analysis and work sampling.

The second method of gathering data is to use motion pictures. The motion pictures are used to record the activities and then the analyst uses the motion pictures for recording the data. The use of motion pictures results in an accurate and permanent record of the activities. The work of the analyst is simplified because the film can be viewed several times or projected at slower speeds if needed. Considerable care is used in taking the motion pictures so all pertinent activities are recorded on the film. Since motion picture equipment and film are costly, this method of gathering data is limited in its use. Motion pictures are used for complex activities and motions that are difficult to observe visually. The motion pictures used in gathering data can also be used to sell new methods or can help in the training of individuals in new methods.

Discussion is the third method used to gather data. The discussion may be between the analyst and one worker, or several individuals depending on the work system being studied. The discussion method is not as accurate as the direct visual or motion picture methods and should be used accordingly. Discussion is best suited when analyzing activities that are lengthy and easily recognized. Data for function analysis or paperwork analysis is frequently gathered by discussion. The discussion method may also bring documents or past records regarding the work system into the analysis. Production records, material requests, purchase orders and sales bookings can be brought into the discussion and may provide valuable information. Past records are invaluable sources of data for analyzing variations in demands for products and services.

The discussion method is more personal than other methods and can be used to develop worker participation in the work analysis and design program.

Gathering data for future work systems is primarily accomplished through discussion, past records and simulation of the proposed system. Much of the data obtained from existing work systems can also be adapted to the design of future work. The information gathered in the earlier steps of the work analysis and design procedure also act as data for the design of future systems. Identifying the functions and anticipating the influence of factors on the proposed system will guide the development of the system. When existing sources do not provide adequate data, a model simulating the proposed system can be constructed and analyzed.

FORMULATION OF ALTERNATIVES

A single solution to work analysis and design problems does not usually exist. The complexity and interactions of work systems are such that they can not be easily quantified and predicted. The effects of the many factors affecting work systems may need further study and evaluation. As new systems are developed, using more sophisticated equipment and techniques, additional factors emerge and have to be studied. The unknown reactions and responses of men to new work systems also prohibit finding the one best solution. Thus, the practical approach to solving work analysis and design problems involves formulating a number of alternative solutions. Then a feasible solution can be selected from the alternatives.

The formulation of alternative work systems for improvement or design situations should be guided by fundamental principles. The principles of motion economy, flow, materials handling and layout design should be used in the formulation step.

The procedure for formulating alternative work systems should be based on creating ideal systems. The goal of creating an ideal system is to have no work at all. This is theoretically impossible, but using this concept should result in systems that approach the ideal. Present day systems that approach the ideal are characterized by a high degree of mechanization and automation. Such systems also have a minimum of human labor.

A good starting point in formulating alternatives is to eliminate the need for the function of the work system. If the function can be eliminated, the best solution of eliminating the work system has been

attained. Eliminating an entire work system does not occur very frequently. However, many parts or components of the work system may
be eliminated by questioning the necessity of the functions they perform. Once the necessity of a function has been established, the materials required and the products resulting from the work system are
the next items to consider. The least amount of effort is required when
the number of materials used and the specifications of the final product
are at a minimum. These two factors will determine to a large extent
the components required in the work system. The processing, methods,
machines, equipment and the skill of workers are dependent upon these
two factors. It should not be assumed that the formulation of alternatives is a set procedure. The statements regarding the materials and
products are used as a convenient starting point. As the system is
developed, it is frequently desirable to change the materials or product
design for the benefit of other components. In some instances, several
changes may have to be made in the starting assumptions before a
desirable system is developed.

The next area of concern is the process or the sequence of steps
required to change the raw materials into the desired product. If a
product is not involved, the process of rendering the service is considered. The processes of rendering services are frequently found in the
hotel, restaurant and institutional field. The minimum work required
to complete the process exists when the number of steps in the process
is a minimum and each of the steps are as simple as possible. Any
materials handling in the process should be kept at a minimum and
should be as mechanized as possible. Storage periods required to maintain the quality of materials or products should also be minimized. If
the process requires workers to go from workplace to workplace, the
total distance traveled should be held to a minimum. Maximum use of
machines or equipment to accomplish the process should be made.

When the process of the work system has been developed, the method
of performing each step in the process is developed next. During this
procedure, it may again be necessary to change some parts of the
partially developed work system. The most productive methods result
when the motions of worker's body members are minimized and kept in
a simultaneous, smooth and symmetrical pattern. Body member motions are dependent upon the layout of the workplace and it is best to
develop the method and the workplace at the same time. The principles
of motion economy (presented in Chapter 4) may help develop both the
method and workplace. Maximum utilization of hand tools and equipment should be incorporated in the method.

The final area of formulation of alternatives involves creating a
productive environment for the work system. The physical environment

as characterized by atmospheric conditions, lighting, noise etc., should be specified for the entire work system. The desired physical conditions for each material, product, process and method as well as for the workers should be determined. Certain processes may require less effort and work if done at higher or lower temperatures. Materials and products, especially foods, have to be protected from detrimental temperatures, moisture or odors. The knowledge required to provide the desired physical environment for the work system is beyond the scope of this book, however the most important factors affecting work performance are summarized in Chapter 5.

Creating the nonphysical or social environment for the work system is a more difficult problem. Development of the nonphysical environment includes consideration of fatigue, boredom, motivation and morale. Providing periods of rest, utilizing worker skill, good training programs and developing suitable crew tasks can help provide the proper conditions. Human tasks should be developed so the worker feels that he is contributing something worthwhile to the work system. If possible, the worker should be consulted regarding the changes or new tasks that he will be encountering.

The formulation of alternatives demands creative and imaginative abilities. The many areas of knowledge involved would favor a group approach to make sure all the factors and interrelationships of the work system are considered and evaluated. The composition of such a group might include people trained as work analysts, engineers, psychologists and social scientists.

If a group approach is not feasible, the individual responsible for formulating the alternatives should use as many resources from the related fields of knowledge as possible.

SELECTION OF A FEASIBLE SOLUTION

The creation of several alternative work systems leads to the need to select one of these alternatives. The objective of selection is to find the best and most feasible work system for accomplishing the desired function.

The primary factor in evaluating several systems for selection is cost. Costs can be considered in separate categories of installation costs, operating costs and indirect costs. Total installation costs include many items: new equipment; labor for installation; interest charges; insurance; taxes; time lost during installation; design of special features; and training materials and time. All these costs should be determined or estimated for all the alternative work systems under consideration.

Operating costs include such items as direct labor costs, fringe benefits, charges for utilities, material costs, replacement charges and maintenance costs. The specific items to be included in comparing operating costs depend on the situation. The design of future work systems would probably call for including all the items for the comparison. On the other hand, alternatives of existing work systems would not necessarily have to include all the items. Items such as utility costs or maintenance charges for example, may not vary between the existing work system and the suggested alternatives.

A comparison of overhead and other indirect costs are desirable when the alternatives are to involve using expanded or new facilities. The presence of considerable automatic equipment in the alternatives also calls for an indirect cost comparison because of the depreciation factor.

The summary of the cost comparisons can be shown by the format indicated in Fig. 3.1.

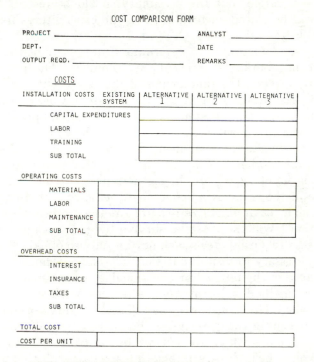

FIG. 3.1. COST COMPARISON FORM FOR EVALUATING ALTERNATIVE
WORK SYSTEMS

Another factor considered when evaluating alternatives for selection is safety. The suggested alternatives should be scrutinized for possible hazards for either the workers or the materials and products in the work system. The matter of safety is especially important in the design of future work since new hazards may have been created in the formulation step. A safety check list similiar to one shown in Chapter 6 can be used to systematically evaluate the alternatives.

Other factors that can be used to evaluate alternatives include: expected productivity levels, psychological effects on workers, difficulty of controlling quality and the ease of supervision and management. The choice of evaluation criteria should relate to the function of the work system.

TESTING THE PROPOSED WORK SYSTEM

The formulation and selection of a proposed work system does not guarantee that the system will be workable in actual situations. It is not the intent of the work analysis and design procedure to arrive at an unworkable situation, but the possibility should be tested. More emphasis should be placed on testing when the expenditures for the new system are large.

The purpose of testing is to determine if any parts of the proposed system are not workable, efficient and complete. The procedure for testing is to question the functioning of the equipment, methods, processes and tasks designated in the work system. Questions to be answered during the testing step include: Will the equipment function properly without frequent breakdowns? Does the equipment need constant adjustment? Is the equipment designed within the physical limitations of the workers? Will the entire system stop if one piece of equipment is out of order? Are the methods designated easy for workers to do? Are methods involving equipment designed so both the worker and the equipment are highly efficient? Are the processes completed at the right time? Will the material survive the processes and methods? Are any tasks requiring crews making the full use of skills?

It is not necessary to test all parts of the system. Emphasis should be placed on testing the untried or questionable components.

The easiest method of testing completely new work systems is to use physical models. The models may be full scale or small scale depending on the component of the work system being tested. A full scale model of a workplace or a piece of equipment can be constructed to test a complicated method to be used by workers. In many cases, existing workplaces or equipment can be modified for testing purposes. A mockup of a sandwich assembly workplace will determine whether the suggested methods of assembling sandwiches are feasible.

Small scale models may be used to test larger components of work systems. Scale models of workplaces, equipment and storage areas can be arranged in a proposed layout of the work system to check flow of materials or worker traffic. A scaled layout of a work system on a planning board such as shown in Fig. 3.2 may also be used.

Another method of testing would be to simulate the proposed work system. The models described above are a simple type of simulation. Another form of simulation involves "acting out" a proposed method of activity. In this case an individual goes through the various proposed motions without using the actual materials or equipment. This method can be combined with the physical models to make a more realistic test.

More sophisticated simulations using mathematical or statistical techniques can be used if sufficient information regarding the proposed work system is available.

Testing new types of equipment or machines may possibly be done by a loaning or leasing arrangement with the manufacturer. If this is impossible, seeking information regarding the performance of the equipment from the other users or the manufacturers will suffice.

Testing the proposed work system should be done whenever it is possible. A little extra time spent in testing may save costly installations of unworkable systems.

FIG. 3.2. SCALED WORK SYSTEM LAYOUT TO CHECK FLOW OF
MATERIALS AND TRAFFIC PATTERNS

INSTALLATION OF PROPOSED WORK SYSTEM

The installation of the proposed work system consists of planning the installation, making the actual installation and training the workers to use the new system.

The installation should be planned so there is minimum interference with operating work systems. When the proposed system is an improvement of an existing system, two methods can be planned. The first method involves making the installation in steps so the system will continue to operate during the installation. The steps are planned so that installation or major changes of equipment and machines occur during a nonworking shift or during slack periods of working shifts. Installations in or near public areas should be planned for minimum inconvenience of guests.

The second method requires stopping the operation for the period of time required to make the installation. Although this method stops production or services rendered, it is more economical than the installation-by-steps procedure. Major installations should be planned for the slack season or a slack period if possible. One problem encountered in stopping the operation of the system is the handling of the employees involved. One suggestion is to temporarily reassign the employees to another system. Another alternative is to arrange for the employees to take their vacations during the installation period.

The installation of a future work system is usually in a new or expanded area and many of the problems encountered with changeovers in existing systems are not present.

The actual installation should be supervised and checked by the analyst or designer. This is to assure that the desired relationship between workplaces, storages and equipment are provided. It would also assure that the design of special workplaces, storage locations of materials and tools and the desired environment are attained.

The last part of the installation procedure is to train the workers to operate the system as it was designed. The training program may vary from a ten minute orientation session to a lengthy extensive training period depending on the characteristics of the changes made in the work system. Simple changes in the process or equipment require only a few words of instruction, while changes in methods and motions require longer training periods to allow the employee to learn. Regardless of the length of time required for training, special emphasis is needed to assure that the proposed system will function as designed.

The training program should be aided by using the information gathered during the work analysis and design procedure. Motion pictures, analysis charts or flow diagrams are good visual aids for training purposes. Written procedures of the improved methods should be prepared and used in the training so misunderstandings of how to do a task are minimized. The written procedure should include information about the tools, materials and equipment needed for the operation and a diagram of the workplace showing the desired layout. The procedure to be followed should be indicated in the proper sequence. Standard written procedures for assembling sandwiches are shown in Fig. 3.3. Figure 3.4 shows a written standard method for sweeping.

Periodic check-ups after completion of the initial training program should be made to see that the suggested procedure is being followed. Individuals have a knack of reverting to old and known methods and this tendency should be controlled. These check-ups are best done by supervisors, which again points out the importance of having the supervisors participate in the analysis and design program.

DETERMINING PERFORMANCE OF THE NEW SYSTEM

The performance of the work system should be measured after it is completely installed and running smoothly. Measuring the performance is necessary to gauge the success of the new system. For improvement programs, the performance between the old and the new systems can be compared to see if the expected increase in productivity or effectiveness has been achieved. For future work, the performance is used as the starting point for measuring future improvements to the system. The performance of the new system is also an indication of how successfully the work analysis and design program was carried out.

The performance of work systems can be expressed in many ways. Usual measures of work performance are expressed as ratios of times to units, or units to times. Minutes per customer is a frequently used measure of services. The performance of checking in or checking out guests can be expressed by this ratio. Time per output unit is also used to describe production processes. Minutes per meal, hours per room and seconds per form are examples of production performance. The inverse relationship of units to time can also be used. Illustrations of this type of performance criteria include customers per minute, meals per hour, square feet per hour and dishes per hour.

Other performance criteria can be expressed as percentage or ratios of nontime units. The percentage of machine or equipment utilization and percent idle time exemplify the percentage concept. Examples of the ratio of nontime units are dollars per guest, rooms per maid, meals per employee and patients per nurse.

Most measurements of performance are expressed as a range of values because of the inherent variability of work system outputs. This variability is extremely pronounced in the work systems encountered in hotels, restaurants and institutions. When a single value of performance is given, it usually refers to the average.

Performance criteria can be measured and established in several different ways. Time study is probably the most frequently used technique when the criteria of performance involve time units. Sampling studies are also used to gather the same type of information as time study.

Accounting and cost control records can also be used to measure performance criteria. This technique is primarily used when the performance criteria do not involve time units. For example, the meals produced per employee for a given work period can be obtained by this method.

The performance of the new work system should be continually checked to safeguard the investment of the work analysis and design program.

JOB: PRODUCTION METHOD FOR 24 SANDWICHES
(1 Operator)

What To Do	How To Do It
1. Place 16 matching slices of bread on board.	1. Use both hands. 2. Pick up 4 slices of bread with each hand or pick up 8 slices in both hands. 3. Place slices of bread in 4 orderly rows of 4 each.
2. Spread softened butter or margarine on all bread slices.	1. Use right hand. 2. Use spatula to spread butter. 3. Spread butter evenly to edges of bread by using one stroke of spatula away from you and another stroke towards you. 4. Another method is to spread butter from right to left, completely covering bread slice in one motion.
3. Place filling on buttered bread.	1. Use right hand. 2. Place scoop or portion of sandwich filling on vertical center rows of bread. Transfer sliced cheese, tomatoes, or meat with fork. 3. *If filling is placed in the center of bread slice,* use one stroke of a spatula away from you and one stroke towards you to spread filling evenly to edges of bread. 4. *If filling is placed in upper right hand corner of bread slice,* press filling lightly with tip of spatula and spread it to upper left corner of bread, then complete an *"S" motion* with blade of spatula spreading the filling as you go. (A left-handed person would reverse this procedure by dipping the filling onto the upper left corner of the bread slice.)
4. Close sandwiches.	1. Use both hands. 2. For each sandwich: Turn 2 corresponding bread slices from outside rows over the filling on center rows, matching edges of bread.

JOB: PRODUCTION METHOD FOR 24 SANDWICHES (*Continued*)

What To Do	How To Do It
5. Place 8 more slices of bread on top of completed sandwiches.	1. Use both hands. 2. Place a bread slice on top of each sandwich in center of board.
6. Place 16 more slices of bread at side of center sandwiches.	1. Use both hands. 2. Drop off 2 slices of bread at a time on both sides of completed sandwiches.
7. Spread softened butter or margarine on 16 top bread slices.	1. Repeat step 2.
8. Place filling on buttered bread.	1. Repeat step 3.
9. Place 2 bread slices on top of filling.	1. Use both hands. 2. For each sandwich: Turn 2 matching bread slices from outside row over filling on center rows, matching edges of bread.
10. Repeat steps 2, 3, and 9, except place only 1 slice of bread on top the third time.	1. Use both hands. 2. Completed sandwiches are stacked three high.
11. Cut sandwiches. (*This method could employ 2 operators, a sandwich maker and a sandwich wrapper. If the wrapper does the cutting, introduce second operator at Step 11.*)	1. Use both hands. 2. Steady each stack of sandwiches, placing thumb and forefinger of left hand over knife point. 3. Draw knife from upper left hand corner diagonally through center stacks to lower right, cutting through all three sandwiches at one time. 4. Use a sharp knife held in right hand, in a straight downward motion, when cutting each sandwich stack.
12. Transfer sandwiches.	1. Use both hands. 2. Slide board with sandwiches to wrapping area. Wrap each cut sandwich before proceeding to make more sandwiches. 3. Stack wrapped sandwiches in wire baskets, on bun pans or trays; allow some space for air circulation between each row for quick chilling. 4. Label sandwich containers with variety they contain.
13. Refrigerate sandwiches.	1. Use both hands. 2. Place filled sandwich containers in refrigerator on shelves or a movable rack during the entire holding period. 3. Maximum refrigerated storage time should never be more than 24 hr at 40° F or lower.
14. Continue entire procedure until desired number of sandwiches have been completed.	

FIG. 3.3.   STANDARD WRITTEN PROCEDURE FOR ASSEMBLING 24 SANDWICHES

Reprinted with permission from *Modern Sandwich Methods,* American Institute of Baking, Chicago.

Breakdown No.   TITLE: SWEEPING A FLOOR
Equipment Needed: Supplies Needed:
   1 ea. Janitor's Push Broom   NONE
   1 ea. Floor Brush—16 in.
   1 ea. Pick-Up Pan w/Handle
   1 ea. Putty Knife
   1 ea. Trash Container

WHAT TO DO	HOW TO DO IT
1. Sweep corners and under fixed objects	1. Using 16-in. floor brush, sweep soil and trash from corners and under fixed objects into open where it can be reached with push broom.
2. Sweep floor	2. a. Sweep a small section at a time, using push broom.
NOTE:	Size of area to sweep at one time depends on amount of soil and/or trash.
	Sweep until accumulation of trash and/or soil = capacity of pick-up pan.
	b. Push soil and trash forward with broom head, bristles on floor.
CAUTION:	End each stroke of broom with COMPLETE STOP, bristles on floor. Lift head gently.
AVOID:	Ending stroke vigorously and/or with an upward sweep of head, bristles off floor–that raises dust.
NOTE:	Pick up directly and deposit in trash container trash objects too large to be swept into pick-up pan readily.
	c. Remove gum or other foreign substances sticking to swept floor area with wet putty knife.
	d. Pick up soil and trash from swept area in pick-up pan.
	e. Deposit contents of pick-up pan in trash container.
	f. Move movable objects when needed to sweep under them.
	g. Move up trash container and tools to forward edge of swept section.
	h. Repeat Step 2.a for next area, and repeat for each succeeding area until entire floor is swept.
3. Return equipment	3. a. Return broom, floor brush, pick-up pan and putty knife to location directed by supervisor.
	(1) Hang brush and broom so that bristles are free from pressing against any surface.
	b. Dump contents of trash container (plus container, if disposable) where directed by supervisor.
	c. Return nondisposable trash container to location designated by supervisor.

FIG. 3.4.   STANDARD WRITTEN PROCEDURE FOR SWEEPING A FLOOR

Source: John Welch, A Task Unit Concept for On the Job Training in Food Service, Manual 66, Univ. Missouri Ext. Div.

Principles of Work Analysis and Design

SUMMARY OF PRINCIPLES

The principles of work analysis and design have been developed from many different fields of knowledge. Although many of the principles have been implied in the earlier chapters, and others will be elaborated upon in the remaining chapters, a brief summary of these principles will clarify many questions regarding the work analysis and design procedure. The principles will also provide the basis for the "formulation of alternatives" step described in the work analysis and design procedure.

The principles will be presented in five categories.

Principles of Work Analysis and Design
Principles of System Design
Principles of Layout
Principles of Materials Handling
Principles of Motion Economy

It is needless to state that all the areas affecting work are not represented by these principles, nor are the principles presented entirely complete. An attempt has been made to present those principles that have the greatest direct effect on work and serve as the basis of work analysis and design.

PRINCIPLES OF WORK ANALYSIS

The principles of work analysis reflect the philosophies and procedures used to study work systems. These philosophies are summarized in Table 4.1.

TABLE 4.1
PRINCIPLES OF WORK ANALYSIS AND DESIGN

1. All work systems should be subjected to study for the purpose of finding improvements.
2. Work systems should be studied by using a systematic procedure. The procedure involves the following steps:
   a. Identification and description of the work system.

TABLE 4.1 *(Continued)*

b. Determination of factors that affect the work system.
c. Collection and analysis of data.
d. Formulation of alternative work systems.
e. Selection of feasible work system.
f. Testing the work system.
g. Installation of the work system.
h. Establishment of performance criteria for the work system.
3. All factors affecting the performance of the work system should be investigated. The factors are categorized as follows:
a. Raw materials.
b. Process.
c. Methods.
d. Workplaces, tools and equipment.
e. Product design.
f. Physical environment.
g. Nonphysical environment.
4. The work system should be broken down into identifiable parts to see if any part can be eliminated, combined, rearranged or simplified.
5. Improvements should be based on the principles of systems design, layout, materials handling and motion economy.

PRINCIPLES OF SYSTEMS DESIGN

The principles of systems design are used to develop the basic framework of the work system. An attempt to envision the total system is made before worrying about the details of the work system components. In reality, the development of the components may require a change in the original concept of the total system. The principles of systems design should guide the formulation of the ideal work system by indicating the approach and concepts that should be used. Table 4.2 summarizes the principles of systems design.

TABLE 4.2
PRINCIPLES OF SYSTEMS DESIGN

1. The work system should provide products and services at the lowest possible cost and with the least effort.
2. The system should be as automatic as possible. This may be accomplished by maximum use of equipment with automatic controls.
3. The communication and paperwork required for the system should be minimized.
4. Similar activities within the system should be placed together if possible. For example, all vegetable cleaning should be confined to one area of the kitchen.
5. Activities that are performed in sequence should be placed close to each other.
6. Any activity that does not contribute more than it costs should be eliminated.
7. Control functions should recover the loss of at least the amount they cost.
8. Functions of the work system that service other functions should be placed close to each other.
9. The system should be as flexible as possible.
10. The system should be designed on the basis of complete analysis of the factors involved.
11. The system should utilize the skills of the personnel to their fullest extent.
12. The system should provide for the fallabilities of the personnel involved.
13. The system should incorporate the latest ideas and techniques of accomplishing work.

PRINCIPLES OF LAYOUT

The analysis and design of a work system is the first step to achieving a good layout of physical facilities. It is difficult to discuss layouts without making reference to the work system to be carried on in the area under consideration. Conversely, it is difficult to discuss work systems without referring to the layout. When the analysis and design of work involves building new facilities, the layout of these facilities should be based on the details of the proposed work system.

An existing layout will place some limitations on the work system or work systems if more than one is involved. This is the situation frequently encountered in the analysis and design of existing work. Since the improvement of existing work systems is so closely associated with the layout, valuable information can be obtained by reviewing the characteristics of good layout. Table 4.3 reviews some of the basic principles of layout that are related to the work system.

TABLE 4.3
PRINCIPLES OF LAYOUT

A. Materials or products
  1. The products should be designed for ease of production.
  2. The raw material used should require the minimum number of processing steps.
  3. The size, shape and packaging of materials should be suitable to the processes to be performed.
  4. The layout should protect the materials and products from detrimental factors such as moisture, dust, vibration and temperature changes.
  5. Provide a flexible layout to handle changes in the products or materials.
  6. The layout should provide for in-process storage of materials.
  7. Materials storage areas should facilitate taking inventory.
  8. Provide facilities for storing waste and scrap materials.

B. Machines and Equipment
  1. The equipment provided in the layout should be united to the required processes.
  2. Maximum use of the equipment should be planned.
  3. The layout should provide the required utilities to equipment and machines as economically as possible.
  4. The layout should provide for easy operation of the equipment.
  5. Storage space should be provided for hand tools and equipment.
  6. Provide for flexible use of equipment.
  7. The layout should facilitate movement of mobile equipment.
  8. Sufficient access space for equipment maintenance should be provided.
  9. Proper venting or exhausting of equipment should be provided. Figure 4.1 shows billowing clouds of moisture and heat that should be quickly exhausted from the work area.
  10. The layout should protect the equipment from damage.

C. Workers
  1. The layout should safeguard the workers by eliminating hazards.
  2. Adequate light should be provided.
  3. Dust, fumes and other undesirable factors should be guarded against.
  4. The layout should be free of distracting activities.
  5. The layout should provide a productive physical environment.
  6. The design of workplaces should correspond to the height of the workers.
  7. The layout should provide adequate working space. Figure 4.2 shows a well planned working space for baking tasks.
  8. Man-machine layouts should be based on efficient utilization of both.

TABLE 4.3 (Continued)

9. Color coding should be used to facilitate identification of tools, equipment or hazards.
10. The layout should anticipate crew activities and provide space for them.
11. The layout should provide adequate space for customer or patient activities.

D. Movement
1. The layout should provide for easy movement of materials and workers.
2. Provide for smooth flow into and out of workplaces.
3. The layout should prevent backtracking.
4. Cross traffic should be minimized.
5. Delays in the movement of materials should be minimized.
6. The layout should provide adequate space for movement of guests or patients.
7. Materials should be delivered to workers to minimize walking.

FIG. 4.1. HEAT AND MOISTURE PRODUCING EQUIPMENT SUCH AS THIS POT WASHING SINK SHOULD HAVE PROVISIONS FOR VENTING OR EXHAUSTING

TABLE 4.3 *(Continued)*

8. Movements should be over the shortest possible distance.
9. The arrangement of spaces should minimize movements.
10. Provide gravity movements whenever possible.
11. The layout should provide safe movement of materials, workers and equipment involved in crew activities.
12. Bypassing should be minimized by proper arrangement of equipment.

E. Building Features
1. Proper heights and clearances should be provided.
2. Plan sufficient door widths.
3. The layout should provide efficient aisles.
4. Interior walls should not impede movement.
5. Provide door locations to facilitate entry and exit.

FIG. 4.2.   ADEQUATE WORKING SPACE MAKES WORK EASIER IN THIS BAKE SHOP

TABLE 4.3 *(Continued)*

6. Column spacing and locations should not interfere with movements or operations.
7. Receiving facilities should be located close to storage areas.
8. Building materials should facilitate cleaning and maintenance.

F. Service Factors
1. Lounges should be provided for guests and employees.
2. Space for inspection, weighing or control should be provided.
3. The layout should provide for efficient housekeeping.
4. Space for lockers, drinking fountains and washrooms should be provided.
5. Provide space for repair and service equipment.
6. The layout should facilitate movement of special equipment to guests or patients.
7. Adequate utilities should be provided for equipment and machines.
8. Special needs of products or equipment such as water or steam should be provided at the point of use. Figure 4.3 shows an arrangement that provides water when required for a steam jacketed kettle.

G. Waiting Factors
1. The layout should provide efficient storage for materials.
2. The quality of products in-waiting should be safeguarded.
3. Waiting of customers should be anticipated and provided for.
4. Delays in material flow should be minimized.
5. The layout should provide for temporary delays of materials between processes when required.

FIG. 4.3. PROVIDING WATER AT THE POINT OF USE
REDUCES EXCESS WORKER TRAVEL

PRINCIPLES OF MATERIALS HANDLING

Materials handling refers to the movement and storage of materials and products as they proceed through the work system. Of all the activities associated with materials and products, materials handling often accounts for a greater portion of labor costs than any of the other activities such as operations or inspections. Materials handling does not add appreciable value to the product and therefore is considered as an undesirable activity. The primary objective of materials handling is to eliminate the movements and storages of materials and products. Movements and storages that can not be eliminated should be done as easily and economically as possible.

Materials handling in hotels, restaurants and institutions primarily involves such items as food, beverages, dishes, luggage, linen, empty bottles and trash, garbage, silverware, mobile equipment, pots and pans, paperwork, banquet tables, drugs and cleaning supplies. These materials are frequently moved from one location to another by hand or by trucks or carts pushed by employees.

The amount of materials handling involved in a given work system is dependent upon the location and arrangement of storage areas, workplaces and equipment. Therefore the first prerequisite to a good materials handling system is a good layout. Conversely, a good layout is characterized by a minimum amount of materials handling. After the layout has been determined, materials handling can be improved to some extent by good planning and using the principles of materials handling. The principles of materials handling are summarized in Table 4.4.

TABLE 4.4
PRINCIPLES OF MATERIALS HANDLING

1. All material movements and storages should be minimized.
2. Materials should not be moved by workers unless absolutely necessary. Figure 4.4 shows a conveyor system for moving soiled dishes.
3. Materials that have to be put down should be prepositioned to eliminate the need to rehandle them.
4. Materials should be stored as close to the point of first use as possible.
5. Movements of materials should be over the shortest and straightest routes.
6. Materials should be handled in bulk when they must be intermittently stored.
7. Inspections should take place in the line of flow to avoid lateral movements of the materials.
8. Mechanical aids should be used when men must lift more than 50 lbs (22.7 kg) or when women lift more than 25 lbs (11.3 kg).
9. Use gravity to aid the flow of materials.
10. Mechanized conveyors should be used when materials follow a fixed route repetitively.
11. Materials should be moved from one workplace to another without intermediate setdown when possible.
12. Provisions should be made to move scrap or trash at the point of creation.
13. Leveling devices should be used to keep materials at convenient work heights.

FIG. 4.4. SOILED DISHES ARE MOVED FROM DINING
AREA TO DISHWASHING AREA BY A MECHANICAL
CONVEYOR

TABLE 4.4 *(Continued)*

14. Well-designed containers and tote pans should be used to facilitate picking up and carrying.
15. Containers should be interlocking so greater loads can be moved with safety.
16. Frequently moved machines, equipment or furniture should be provided with wheels.
17. Use specialized (pneumatic, hydraulic, etc.) materials handling systems whenever applicable. Figure 4.5 shows a belt conveyor for moving soiled dishes along the dish table.
18. Packaging materials should be conducive to easy handling.
19. Consideration should be given to moving workers or machines to the material especially when large quantities are involved.
20. Consideration should be given to changing the design of the product to improve its materials handling characteristics.

PRINCIPLES OF MOTION ECONOMY

The principles of motion economy were developed from the early work of the Gilbreths. Additional studies of motion were conducted to supplement the work of the Gilbreths until a fairly complete set of principles were derived. The principles of motion economy are used in

FIG. 4.5. DISHES ARE MOVED ALONG THIS SOILED DISH TABLE BY A BELT
CONVEYOR

the development of work methods, the workplace and the tools and
equipment needed to complete an operation.

The studies of the motions of the human body members indicate there
are five characteristics of easy movement: simultaneous movements;
symmetrical movements; natural movements; rhythmical movements;
and habitual movements.

Simultaneous Movements

Movements of the hands that begin and end at the same time are
easier than movements where one hand requires a longer or shorter
time to complete the motion. Simultaneous movements are best accomplished when both hands are doing identical work. If each hand is
doing different work, the tendency is to have the right hand (for a
right-handed person) work faster and thus violate the concept of simultaneous movements. The work of each hand should be planned so
they take the same amount of time to complete. If this is difficult to do,
individuals can be trained to balance the time required for each hand to
do the different tasks.

Symmetrical Movements

Movements of the hands are easiest if they are symmetrical about the center line of the body. Symmetry indicates that the right hand moves to the right of the center line, while the left hand moves to the left of the center line. Movements that cause both hands to move to the right or left of the center line at the same time are not symmetrical. Movements directly forward from the body should start with both hands at the body and move forward at the same time and return at the same time. The difficulty of performing nonsymmetrical motions can be shown by attempting to draw simultaneously a square with one hand while the other hand draws a circle. Examples of nonsymmetrical movements are shown in Fig. 4.6. Symmetrical movements are easiest when the hands move in the same plane.

Combining symmetry with simultaneous movements creates a time balance and sense of equilibrium for the entire body. When a choice between symmetry and simultaneity has to be made, it is more important to maintain simultaneity of movements.

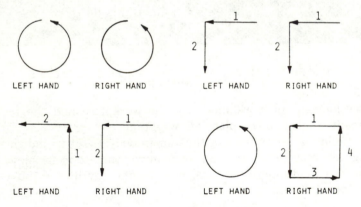

FIG. 4.6. EXAMPLES OF NONSYMMETRICAL HAND MOVEMENTS

Natural Movements

Movements that correspond to the physical structure of the body are easiest. For example, the movement of the extended arm will result in an arc. This indicates that curved movements are more natural than straight movements of the arm. The same is true for movements of the forearm pivoted at the elbow or the movements of the hands and fingers.

Natural movements are also the fastest to make. Movements along an arc are faster than movements along a rectangular pattern. The movements along the rectangular pattern involve acceleration, deceleration and a change in direction which accounts for the longer time.

Consideration should also be given to the natural shape and position of the hand and fingers. It is much easier to grasp an object suspended with the long dimension in a vertical plane compared to suspension with the long dimension in a horizontal plane. The exertion of force is also associated with the shape and position of the body members. The greatest force that fingers can achieve are when the movement of the fingers is toward the palm. The arms exert the greatest force when the bicep muscle is used.

The various types of natural movements are classified according to the muscle system involved. These classes of movement are:

Class 1. Finger movements.

Class 2. Finger and wrist movements.

Class 3. Finger, wrist and forearm movements.

Class 4. Finger, wrist, forearm and upper arm movements.

Class 5. Finger, wrist, forearm, upper arm and shoulder movements.

The first class movements (finger movements) require the least amount of time and effort to perform and are also the weakest type of movement. Fifth class movements are the least efficient, but can exert the greatest force. The design of methods should consider the speed and force limitations of the various classes of motion. Levers and controls for example, should be designed so the amount of force required to turn or move them matches the appropriate classification of motion.

Rhythmical Movements

The simultaneous, symmetrical and natural movements are descriptive of parts of the total motion pattern needed to accomplish a task. A total motion pattern that creates a rhythm when repeated frequently is the easiest to perform. Rhythm indicates that the last part of the cycle should flow smoothly into the first part of the next cycle. Rhythm can be improved by minimizing the changes of direction involved in the motion pattern.

Habitual Movements

The creation of rhythmic patterns of simultaneous, symmetrical and natural movements leads to the development of habitual movements. Habitual movements indicate that the cycle of movements are made in exactly the same way each time the cycle is repeated. Habitual movements become automatic after a period of time and much fatigue and strain can be eliminated.

The principles of motion economy are devoted to accomplishing the five basic characteristics of easy movements. The principles may be divided into three groups: (A) pertaining to the use of the human body, (B) pertaining to the design and layout of the workplace and (C) pertaining to the design of tools and equipment. The basic principles according to the breakdown are given in Table 4.5.

FIG. 4.7. LENGTH OF HAND MOVEMENTS CAN BE MINIMIZED BY PROPER ARRANGEMENT OF WORK

TABLE 4.5
PRINCIPLES OF MOTION ECONOMY

A. Use of the human body
   1. The number of motions required to complete a task should be minimized.
   2. The length of necessary motions should be minimized. Figure 4.7 shows a worker using short motions to accomplish the required task.
   3. Both hands should be used for work and should begin and end their activities simultaneously. Simultaneous movements for unloading a dishwasher are shown in Fig. 4.8.
   4. Motions of hands and arms should be in symmetrical and opposite directions.
   5. Both hands should not be idle at the same time except for rest.
   6. Motions should be confined to the lowest possible classifications needed to perform the task satisfactorily.
   7. Smooth curved motions should be developed in preference to straight-line or angular motions.
   8. Motion patterns should be developed for rhythmic and habitual performance.
   9. The motions should be arranged to take advantage of momentum.
  10. The number of eye fixations required for the task should be minimized.
  11. Intermittent use of the different classifications of movements should be provided to combat fatigue.

FIG. 4.8. USING SIMULTANEOUS HAND MOTIONS TO UNLOAD DISHES FROM THE DISHWASHER

TABLE 4.5 *(Continued)*

B. Design and layout of the workplace
  1. Materials, tools and controls should be located within the normal working area. The workplace shown in Fig. 4.9 causes the worker's hands to reach beyond the normal working area.
  2. Materials and tools should have a fixed location.
  3. Work requiring the use of eyes should be done within the normal field of vision.
  4. Tools and materials should be prepositioned to facilitate picking up.
  5. Gravity feed bins or containers should be used to deliver incoming materials close to the point of use.
  6. Gravity should be used to deliver outgoing materials.
  7. The height of the working surface should be designed to allow either a standing or sitting position. Special equipment such as the stand shown in Fig. 4.10 will give the proper working height to equipment.
  8. The environment of the workplace should be conducive to productive motions.

C. Design of tools and equipment
  1. Tools, hand equipment and controls should be designed for easy grasp. The poorly placed valve pictured in Fig. 4.11 makes it hard to grasp and turn.
  2. Two or more tools should be combined if possible.
  3. Jigs, fixtures or foot operated devices should be used to relieve the work of the hands. Figure 4.12 shows a foot operated hand sink.
  4. Equipment should be designed so the inherent capabilities of the body members are fully utilized.
  5. Levers and controls should be designed to make maximum contact with the body member.

FIG. 4.9.   POOR DESIGN OF THIS SOILED DISH TABLE CAUSES THE HANDS
TO BE OUT OF THE NORMAL WORK AREA

FIG. 4.10.   CORRECT WORKING HEIGHTS OF EQUIPMENT CAN BE
OBTAINED WITH SPECIAL STANDS

FIG. 4.11.   THE PLACEMENT OF THESE CONTROL VALVES MAKES THEM VERY DIFFICULT TO GRASP AND USE

FIG. 4.12.   HAND SINK EQUIPPED WITH FOOT OPERATED LEVERS

The principles of motion economy that pertain to the human body are specifically aimed at reducing the physical effort or energy required to perform work. Some of these principles are self explanatory or were discussed earlier. Additional discussion should clarify and point out the importance of the principles.

The use of both hands to do work seems to be a logical principle leading to increased productivity. However, studies have shown that working with both hands instead of one hand at a time results in less fatigue even though the same amount of work may have been accomplished. Greater effort is required when one hand is working under load while the other hand is idle because the body tries to put itself in balance. Obviously the time required to do the work with both hands is about 50% shorter. Thus using both hands to accomplish work is not only productive but also less fatiguing.

Momentum of body members is developed when the body members are put into motion. Since effort is required to start and stop the motion, the developed momentum should be put to effective use. This is done by using continuous instead of stop and start movements and by beginning or ending activities while the body members are in motion.

Many tasks require close coordination between the movements of the hands and the eyes. When the work requires the concentrated use of the eyes, it should be arranged so the number of eye movements are minimized.

Highly repetitive tasks using short movements are conducive to monotony and fatigue. Some of the monotony and fatigue can be alleviated by using occasional longer movements during the task. Care should be taken not to carry this mixing of short and long movements too far since it may result in extra effort. Exact ratios of the various types of movements are not available and judgement has to be used. The individual differences among workers will also have an effect on this problem. A motion pattern that feels comfortable for one worker may feel awkward for others.

The principles related to the design of the workplace and tools and equipment are primarily indicating situations that lead to easy body member motions. Locating tools within the normal working area forces the motions of the hands to stay in the area. Placing objects in fixed positions leads to the development of habitual motions and using gravity flow minimizes the total number of motions required.

5

Human Engineering

INTRODUCTION

Human Engineering is the application of principles, philosophies and scientific research to the design of machines and equipment, work areas, work methods and the working environment for human beings. Human Engineering draws from many fields of study including acoustics, anthropology, illumination engineering, physics, psychology, thermodynamics and time and motion study. Each field contributes knowledge that is useful in understanding the effects of external factors on the mental and physical capabilities of man.

The general objective of Human Engineering is to increase the effectiveness of man or a man-machine combination in accomplishing a given task or job. Specifically, Human Engineering attempts to create a system of work methods, work environment and work aids (tools, equipment, controls, instruments, etc.) so that man may accomplish his task or job with speed and accuracy. It is also concerned with the safety and comfort of the worker, therefore creating a working situation that is not only productive but desirable as far as the worker is concerned.

The use of Human Engineering in the hotel, restaurant and institutional field involves two phases. The first phase consists of identifying and understanding the various factors that affect man's work. The second phase is concerned with the methods, techniques and recommendations commonly used to create the proper work situation. This two-phased approach will be used to present the material on Human Engineering.

ENVIRONMENT

One of the more important aspects of Human Engineering is concerned with environmental conditions and their effect on worker performance. Environmental conditions encompass such areas as temperature, relative humidity, air circulation, illumination, color and noise. Most of these areas have been investigated scientifically and their effects on performance are well-known. In some instances, certain environmental conditions reduce productivity directly. In other cases, the environmental effect may be indirect, such as decreasing employee morale which in turn may result in decreased production.

TEMPERATURE, RELATIVE HUMIDITY AND AIR MOVEMENT

A person's sense of thermodynamic comfort depends primarily on the combination of air temperature, relative humidity (RH) and air movement to which he is exposed. A fourth factor, the temperature of walls, ceilings, floors or objects in the room is also important if it varies greatly from the air temperature.

The feeling of comfort that exists with an air and surrounding temperature of 70°F (21.1°C), a relative humidity of 50% and no air movement, may change to a feeling of warmth if the relative humidity is increased to 100%; or it may change to a feeling of coldness if the air movement is increased to 15mph (24.1 km/hr). Another change in the feeling of comfort can be brought about by altering the temperature of the surroundings. A person will feel cold in a room whose wall, ceiling and floor temperatures are 40°F (4.4°C) even though the air temperature is 70°F (21.1°C). And conversely, a person will feel warm in a 70°F (21.1°C) air temperature room if the temperature of his surroundings is 120°F (48.9°C). These changes are caused by the radiation heat transfer between the human body and its surroundings.

Temperature, relative humidity and air movement can be combined into various indices that precisely describe certain environmental conditions. One of these indices is referred to as the effective temperature. The effective temperature is the combination of air temperature and relative humidity. The temperature of the surroundings is assumed to be the same as the air temperature and no air movement is involved.

For example, the combination of 75°F (23.9°C) air temperature and 100% RH gives an effective temperature of 75°F (23.9°C). Another combination that results in an effective temperature of 75° (23.9°C) is 89°F (31.7°C) air temperature and 10% RH. Both of the above combinations of air temperature and relative humidities result in the same sensation of thermodynamic comfort.

Generally speaking, for any given air temperature, the effective temperature increases with an increase in the relative humidity. For example, at 70°F (21.1°C) air temperature increases from 10% to 100% RH result in increases in the effective temperature from 63.3° to 70°F (17.2° to 21.1°C).

Figure 5.1 shows the relationship between air temperature, relative humidity and effective temperature.

For most people, effective temperatures that range from 69° to 73°F (20.6° to 22.8°C) are the most comfortable in the summer, while effective temperatures in the range from 65° to 70°F (18.3° to 21.1°C) are the most comfortable in the winter. Variations of the effective temperatures from the comfort zones described above lead to sensations of warmth, coldness, dampness or dryness.

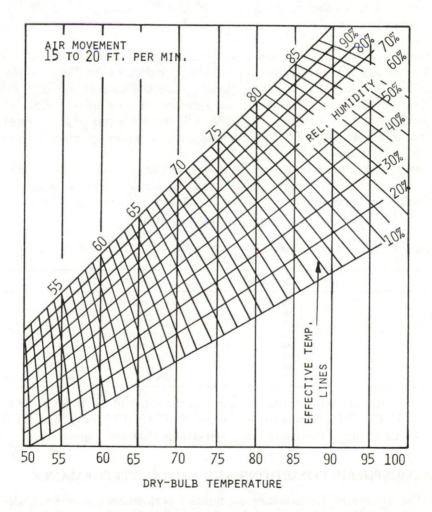

FIG. 5.1. RELATIONSHIP BETWEEN AIR TEMPERATURE, RELATIVE HUMIDITY AND EFFECTIVE TEMPERATURE

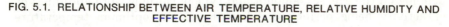

Reprinted by permission from *ASHRAE Guide and Data Book.*

A better indicator of the feeling of comfort as related to environment is a combination of three factors: namely air temperature, relative humidity and air movement. These factors are combined into a comfort index. The comfort index differs from the effective temperature because variations in air movement can be considered. The comfort index is determined to be the degree of warmth or coolness felt by individuals at a certain air temperature in still saturated air. For example, all combinations of air temperatures, relative humidities and air movements have a comfort index of 70°F (21.1°C) when they produce a thermodynamic sensation similar to that when a person is exposed to still saturated air at 70°F (21.1°C).

It can be shown that changes can be made in one of the factors of the comfort index and still maintain a desirable comfort level. For example, with no air movement, comfort exists with air temperature at 75°F (23.9°C) and 70% RH. The air temperature can rise to 80°F (26.7°C) with the relative humidity still at 70% if the air is caused to move at approximately 2 mph (3.22 km/hr), because the subject would still be in the comfort zone.

Another indicator of a person's thermodynamic comfort is skin temperature. The relationship between mean skin temperature and sensations of thermodynamic comfort are shown in Table 5.1.

TABLE 5.1

RELATIONSHIPS BETWEEN SKIN TEMPERATURE AND THERMODYNAMIC SENSATIONS*

Skin Temperature °F	Sensation
84	Very cold
86	Cold
88	Cool
90	Comfortably cool
92	Comfortable
94	Warm
96	Hot
98	Very hot

The optimum skin temperatures are in the range of 91° to 93°F (32.8° to 33.9°C). Skin temperatures below 88°F (31.1°C) or above 94°F (34.4°C) result in thermodynamic sensations that are unpleasant.

ATMOSPHERIC CONDITIONS AND HUMAN PERFORMANCE

The effects of temperature on human performance may vary, depending on the age, sex, amount and type of clothing worn and the type of activity being performed. There is no one optimum temperature that can be recommended for all situations.

*See metric conversion chart in Appendix.

Generally speaking, people over forty years of age prefer slightly higher temperatures than younger people. Women also prefer higher temperatures than men in similar situations. A person doing physical work can be comfortable in a cool environment while a person doing sedentary work in the same environment will feel cold.

Apart from these individual differences, the general effects of temperature and relative humidity on human performance have been investigated. A study of telegraph operators receiving Morse code under different effective temperatures is reported by Mackworth (1946). The study determined the average number of mistakes that the operators made under different temperatures and relative humidities. The results of the study are shown in Fig. 5.2.

When the effective temperatures were maintained in the range from 80° to 92°F (26.7° to 33.3°C), the average number of mistakes was fairly

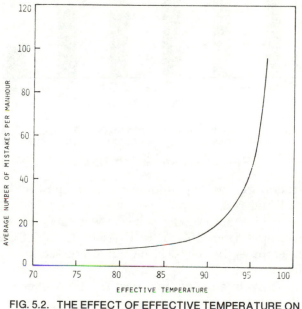

FIG. 5.2.   THE EFFECT OF EFFECTIVE TEMPERATURE ON
THE AVERAGE NUMBER OF MISTAKES PER MAN HOUR
FOR TELEGRAPH OPERATORS RECEIVING MORSE CODE

Reprinted with permission from E. J. McCormick,
Human Factor Engineering, McGraw-Hill Book Co.,
New York. (After Mackworth)

constant and at an acceptable level. However, at effective temperatures above 92°F (33.3°C), the average number of mistakes increased rather rapidly with the increasing temperatures.

The effect of temperature extremes on physical performance are also known to be detrimental. Figure 5.3 shows the relationship between the

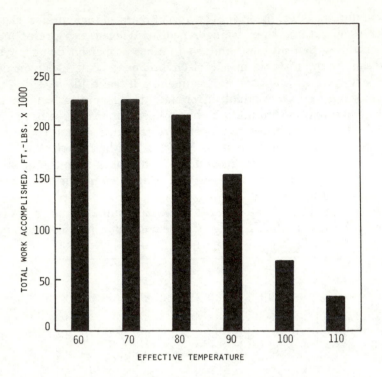

FIG. 5.3.   THE EFFECT OF EFFECTIVE TEMPERATURE ON TOTAL
WORK ACCOMPLISHED IN A WEIGHT LIFTING TASK

From data drived from *ASHRAE Guide.*

effective temperature and the total work accomplished by subjects
doing a weight-lifting task.

The physical performance of the subjects was fairly constant at effective temperatures from 60° to 75°F (15.6° to 23.9°C). At higher
effective temperatures, the physical output decreased at a rapid rate
with increasing temperatures.

The general effects of effective temperatures on worker performance
are given in Table 5.2.

Controlling Atmospheric Conditions

Realizing the importance of the proper atmospheric conditions
on worker output, every means that can be used to provide optimum
conditions should be used. Regulating the air temperature is fairly easy
with a good heating or air-conditioning system. Controlling the relative
humidity, air movement and temperatures of the surroundings are more
difficult.

TABLE 5.2

**EFFECTS OF EFFECTIVE TEMPERATURE ON WELL–BEING
AND PERFORMANCE OF HUMANS***

Effective Temperature F°	Effects
Below 55	Physical stiffness of extremities, increased accidents.
55-65	Discomfort, morale problems, period of adjustment needed.
65-73	Optimum working conditions.
73-80	Discomfort, morale problems, labor turnover.
80-90	Reduced physical and mental output, increased errors and accidents.
90-100	Marked reduction in work capacity, circulatory strain.
100-110	Tolerable for very short periods of times.

Problems of low humidity, which are most frequent during the winter, are best solved by installation of humidifying equipment in conjunction with the heating system. High humidity is more difficult to control and several approaches may have to be used.

One of the most economical methods of alleviating high humidities (and high temperatures) is by ventilation. Ventilation requirements are generally stated as providing a certain cubic feet (meters) of fresh air per minute per square foot (meter) of floor space. For example, in an average workroom which does not contain any pieces of high temperature equipment, or moisture producing equipment (steamers, steam kettles, dishwashers, etc.) an average ventilation rate of one cfm per square foot (0.305 cubic meters per minute per square meter) of floor space would be sufficient. If the workroom does contain many heat producing or moisture producing pieces of equipment, 4 to 5 cfm of fresh air per square foot (0.113 to 0.142 cubic meters per minute per square meter) of floor space should be provided.

For extreme conditions of high temperatures and high relative humidity, the only feasible solution appears to be the use of air conditioning equipment. Although air conditioning is expensive, it can be expected to increase worker productivity from 5 to 15%.

In addition to controlling the temperature, relative humidity and air movement, it is also important to insulate sources of heat and moisture that are present in the work area. Taking the commercial kitchen as an example, steam jacketed kettles, fry kettles, bain maries, etc., can be insulated and shielded or vented so the amount of heat and moisture emitted into the work area is minimized.

ILLUMINATION

Another factor of the working environment that affects efficiency and performance is the illumination of the working areas. Insufficient

*See metric conversion chart in Appendix.

lighting as shown in Fig. 5.4 not only causes errors and accidents but may also be harmful to a person's eyes. Good lighting can easily increase work output from 10 to 20% depending on the improvement in the level and quality of the illumination.

In order to provide proper illumination, it is necessary to know the type of task that is to be done, the speed and accuracy with which it must be performed and the length of time the task is to be performed.

Tasks that require a person to see fine detail such as reading instructions, checking quality or doing bookwork need a high level of illumination. Tasks that do not involve fine detail can be satisfactorily done at lower levels of illumination. If speed and accuracy are desired in a particular task, and the persons involved are expected to do these tasks for long periods of time, the highest level of illumination should be provided.

FIG. 5.4.   POORLY LIT WORK AREAS ARE NOT CONDUCIVE TO GOOD WORKER PERFORMANCE

It is very difficult to specify exact levels of illumination for all the various tasks that may be encountered in the Hotel, Restaurant and Institutional field. The current general recommendations for the minimum footcandles of illumination required for satisfactory vision are given in Table 5.3.

TABLE 5.3

RECOMMENDED LEVELS OF ILLUMINATION FOR HOTELS, RESTAURANTS AND INSTITUTIONS[1]

	Recommended Foot-candle Levels
Hospitals	
Anesthetizing and preparation room	30
Autopsy and morgue	
Autopsy room	100
Autopsy table	1000
Museum	50
Morgue, general	20
Central sterile supply	
General, work room	30
Work tables	50
Glove room	50
Syringe room	150
Needle sharpening	150
Storage areas	30
Issuing sterile supplies	50
Corridor	
General in nursing areas—daytime	20
General in nursing areas—night (rest period)	3
Operating, delivery, recovery, and laboratory suites and service areas	30
Cystoscopic room	
General	100
Cystoscopic table	2500
Dental suite	
Operatory, general	70
Instrument cabinet	150
Dental entrance to oral cavity	1000
Prosthetic laboratory bench	100
Recovery room, general	5
Recovery room, local for observation	70
Electromyographic suite	
General	30
Local for insertion of needle electrodes	1000
Encephalographic suite	
Work room, general	30
Work room, desk or table	100
Examining room	30
Preparation rooms, general	30
Preparation rooms, local	50
Storage, records, charts	30
Emergency operating room	
General	100
Local	2000
EKG, BMR, and specimen room	
General	30
Specimen table	50
EKG machine	50
Examination and treatment room	
General	50
Examining table	100
Exits, at floor	5

[1]IES Lighting Handbook, Fourth Edition. Illuminating Engineering Society, New York.

TABLE 5.3 *(Continued)*

	Recommended Foot-candle Levels
Eye, ear, nose, and throat suite	
Darkroom, (variable)	0-10
Eye examination and treatment	50
Ear, nose, throat room	50
Flower room	10
Formula room	
Bottle washing	30
Preparation and filling	50
Fracture room	
General	50
Fracture table	200
Splint closet	50
Plaster sink	50
Intensive care nursing areas	
General	30
Local	100
Laboratories	
General	50
Close work areas	100
Linens (see Laundries)	
Sorting soiled linen	30
Central (clean) linen room	30
Sewing room, general	30
Sewing room, work area	100
Linen closet	10
Lobby (or entrance foyer)	
During day	50
During night	20
Locker rooms	20
Medical records room	100
Nurses station	
General—day	70
General—night	30
Desk for records and charting	70
Table for doctors making or viewing records	70
Medicine counter	100
Nurses gown room	
General	30
Mirror for grooming	50
Nurseries, infant	
General	30
Examining, local at bassinet	100
Examining and treatment table	100
Nurses station and work space (see Nurses station)	
Obstetrical suite	
Labor room, general	20
Labor room, local	100
Scrub-up areas	30
Delivery room, general	100
Substerilizing room	30
Delivery table	2500
Clean-up room	30
Recovery room, general	30
Recovery room, local	100
Patients' rooms (private and wards)	
General	10
Reading	30
Observation (by nurse)	2

TABLE 5.3 *(Continued)*

	Recommended Foot-candle Levels
Night light, at floor (variable)	0.5-1.5
Examining light	100
Toilets	30
Pediatric nursing unit	
General, crib room	20
General, bedroom	10
Reading	30
Playroom	30
Treatment room, general	50
Treatment room, local	100
Pharmacy	
Compounding and dispensing	100
Manufacturing	50
Parenteral solution room	50
Active storage	30
Alcohol vault	10
Radioisotope facilities	
Radiochemical laboratory, general	30
Uptake or scanning room	20
Examining table	50
Retiring room	
General	10
Local for reading	30
Solarium	
General	20
Local for reading	30
Stairways	20
Surgical suite	
Instrument and sterile supply room	30
Clean-up room, instrument	100
Scrub-up area	30
Operating room, general	100
Operating table	2500
Recovery room, general	30
Recovery room, local	100
Anesthesia storage	20
Substerilizing room	30
Therapy, physical	
General	20
Exercise room	30
Treatment cubicles, local	30
Whirlpool	20
Lip reading	150
Therapy, occupational	
Work area, general	30
Work tables or benches, ordinary	50
Work tables or benches, fine work	100
Toilets	30
Utility room	
General	20
Work counter	50
Waiting rooms, or areas	
General	20
Local for reading	30
X-ray suite	
Radiographic, general	10
Fluoroscopic, general (variable)	0-10
Deep and superficial therapy	10

TABLE 5.3 *(Continued)*

	Recommended Foot-candle Levels
Control room	10
Film viewing room	30
Darkroom	10
Light room	30
Filing room, developed films	30
Storage, undeveloped films	10
Dressing rooms	10
Hotels	
Bathrooms	
Mirror	30
General	10
Bedrooms	
Reading (books, magazines, newspapers)	30
Inkwriting	30
Make-up	30
General	10
Corridors, elevators, and stairs	20
Entrance foyer	30
Front office	50
Linen room	
Sewing	100
General	20
Lobby	
General lighting	10
Reading and working areas	30
Marquee	
Dark surroundings	30
Bright surroundings	50
Laundries	
Washing	30
Machine and press finishing, sorting	70
Flat work ironing, weighing, listing, marking	50
Fine hand ironing	100
Library	
Reading room	
Study and notes	70
Ordinary reading	30
Stacks	30
Book repair and binding	50
Cataloging	70
Card files	70
Check-in and check-out desks	70
Locker rooms	20
Nursing homes	
Corridors and interior ramps	20
Stairways other than exits	30
Exit stairways and landings, on floor	5
Doorways	10
Administrative and lobby areas	
Day	50
Night	20
Chapel or quiet area	
General	5
Local for reading	30
Physical therapy	20
Occupational therapy	30
Work table, coarse work	100
Work table, fine work	200

TABLE 5.3 (Continued)

	Recommended Foot-candle Levels
Recreation area	50
Dining area	30
Patient care unit (or room), general	10
Patient care room, reading	30
Nurse's station, general	
Day	50
Night	20
Nurse's desk, for charts and records	70
Nurse's medicine cabinet	100
Utility room, general	20
Utility room, work counter	50
Pharmacy area, general	30
Pharmacy, compounding, and dispensing area	100
Janitor's closet	15
Toilet and bathing facilities	30
Barber and beautician areas	50
Restaurants, lunch rooms, cafeterias	
Dining areas	
Intimate type	
Light environment	10
Subdued environment	3
Leisure type	
Light environment	30
Subdued environment	15
Quick service type	
Bright surroundings	100
Normal surroundings	50
Cashier	50
For cleaning	20
Food displays—twice the general levels but not under	50
Kitchen, commercial	
Inspection, checking, preparation and pricing	70
Other areas	30
Schools	
Auditoriums	
Assembly only	30
Study halls	70
Classrooms	
Regular work	70
Chalkboards	150
Drafting rooms	100
Laboratories	
General work	70
Close work	150
Lecture rooms	
General work	70
Special exhibits	150
Manual arts	100
Sewing rooms	150
Sightsaving classes	150
Corridors and stairs	20
Gymnasiums	
General exercising	30
Exhibition games	50

Other factors that should be considered in the design of the lighting system besides the level of illumination include: the uniform lighting of the object; a brightness contrast between the object and the background; and the quality and color of the light source.

A good lighting system provides uniform illumination over all the work areas and working surfaces without shadows or light and dark areas. The use of numerous low wattage light sources provides more uniform illumination than a few high wattage light sources. Well designed luminaires are also important in providing even distribution of light. The luminaires should be designed so that light is provided at a wide angle (preferably 45° from the horizontal axis of the luminaire) to illuminate vertical and horizontal surfaces equally.

In order for an object to be quickly and easily seen, it must have a certain amount of contrast in relation to its surrounding. Best results are obtained with a contrast ratio of 3 to 1 with the object being the brighter. Care must be taken not to have too great a contrast ratio. A contrast ratio greater than 10 to 1 is very hard on a person's eyes and quickly leads to eye strain and fatigue. Contrast ratios are easily changed by using different colors or surfaces for surrounding areas.

The quality and color spectrum of the light source is important from the standpoint of color perception. Most light sources contain a variety of wavelengths of the color spectrum. Depending on the surface upon which the light falls, certain wavelengths are absorbed while others are reflected. The wavelengths that are reflected give us the perception of color. For example, if a surface absorbs all wavelengths of the color spectrum except blue, then the surface would appear blue. If the light source did not contain the blue wavelengths, then the surface would not reflect any of the wavelengths and would appear black. Thus the perception of color is dependent on the characteristics of the surface and the nature of the color wavelengths emitted from the light source.

Color perception can therefore be varied by using different surface characteristics or by using different light sources. Changing the light source usually gives the best results in controlling the color appearance of objects.

Since a variety of light sources are available, knowledge of their effects on color perception is important for proper lighting design. For example, the cold form of fluorescent lighting makes human skin appear pale, and makes most foods look unappetizing. Incandescent lamps or the warm fluorescent lamps enhance the red colors making people appear healthier looking and foods more appetizing. Table 5.4 gives the effects of various light sources on color changes.

TABLE 5.4
APPEARANCE OF SOME PAINTED COLOR SURFACES UNDER FLUORESCENT AND INCANDESCENT–FILAMENT LAMPS

Color names were first assigned to the samples as they appeared under the fluorescent daylight lamp since this light most closely simulates natural daylight. The other color names, reading from left to right, for each color and tint are related as much as possible to those in the first left-hand column. The fact that color changes take place with tungsten-filament lamps as well as with the white and soft-white fluorescent lamps is illustrated.

Fluorescent Daylight	Incandescent (60-Watt Filament)	Fluorescent White	Fluorescent Soft White
(C) Grayed greenish yellow	Golden yellow (free from greenishness)	Grayed yellow (slightly green)	Yellowish buff
(T) Ivory (bluish)	Deep ivory	Ivory (yellowish)	Ivory (pinkish)
(C) Medium blue	Very grayed purplish blue	Slightly purplish blue	Light purplish blue
(T) Pale blue	White[1]	Pale bluish gray	Pale bluish purple
(C) Medium brown (coolest)	Medium brown (slightly orange)	Medium brown (slightly warmer)	Medium brown (slightly pink)
(T) Very pale pink	Pale reddish buff	Pale pinkish buff	Grayed purplish pink
(C) Deep purple (bluish)	Deep purple (reddish brown)	Deep purple (less bluish)	Deep purple (reddish)
(T) Pale bluish purple	Pale yellowish red	Grayed reddish purple	Medium reddish purple
(C) Medium green-blue	Medium blue-green	Grayed medium blue	Grayed medium blue (slightly purplish)
(T) Very pale blue	White[1]	Pale bluish gray	Very pale purplish white
(C) Very grayed dark green	Grayed yellow-green	Grayed green (slightly yellowish)	Grayed green (slightly brownish)
(T) Very pale green-blue	Medium ivory	Pale buff	Very pale purplish gray
(C) Deep rose	Medium red	Grayed medium red	Medium rose
(T) Light pink (slightly purplish)	Yellow-red (very pale)	Light pink (warmer)	Light pink (redder)

(C) Full color.
(T) Tint of color.
[1]In each case, four samples of the same color were viewed under the four light sources at the same time. These two colors marked white only appeared so by comparison with the other three samples. By turning off the other three lamps and viewing these samples alone, the bluish quality of both returns. Surrounding these samples with a white surface will also cause the bluish appearance to return.

In addition to providing the recommended level and quality of illumination, consideration should also be given to other problems that may exist in the lighting system. One of these areas is glare which can cause eye fatigue and decrease the ability of an individual to see. Glare may be present in two forms. Direct glare resulting from a light source where the light falls directly into the observer's eyes, or indirect glare where the brightness comes from objects that reflect the light into the observer's eyes.

There are very simple precautions or remedies that can reduce the problems of glare. In the case of direct glare, one obvious solution would be to reduce the brightness of the light source. This may be accomplished by using low wattage bulbs instead of high wattage bulbs. The use of the lower wattage bulbs may reduce the level of illumination below recommendations and additional bulbs may have to be provided. If it is impossible to reduce the level of brightness of the glare source, another alternative would be to increase the brightness surrounding the glare source. This would have the same effect as reducing the glare source itself.

Any direct glare that is emitted from a luminaire should be eliminated or shielded. Brightness from the light source is objectionable to most people if it exists in an area within 30° above the line of sight. Therefore, shielding should extend to a point 30° below the horizontal.

Several methods can be used to reduce indirect glare. Some of the problem may be alleviated if a good level of illumination is provided around the reflecting surface. This may be accomplished by using diffuse or indirect lighting systems. Frequently the position of the light source can be changed and consequently the reflected glare would be eliminated. Surfaces producing the glare could be changed to a material that would diffuse or absorb rather than reflect the light. One of the most frequently encountered sources of indirect glare in the hospitality field is the extensive use of highly polished stainless steel equipment and surfaces. Equipment theoretically should not reflect more than 30 to 50% of the light falling on it.

Indirect glare may also come from the walls, ceilings and floors of work rooms. Proper selection of paints or surfacing material will quickly eliminate this problem. Generally acceptable levels of reflectance for work areas are as follows:

Ceilings	80-85%
Upper Walls	50-60%
Lower Walls	30-40%
Floors	20-30%

Table 5.5 gives the reflectance values for paints and may be used to develop a color scheme for workrooms or work areas.

COLOR

As indicated earlier, color and illumination are closely related. However, certain aspects of color deserve separate attention because of their interesting effect on human beings. Colors, used alone or in combination, can create conditions that can reduce fatigue, improve morale and even increase productivity. Good color planning can also reduce accidents.

TABLE 5.5

REFLECTANCE VALUES OF PAINTS[1]

Color	Reflectance (%)
White	85
White eggshell	82
Light cream	75
Light gray	75
Light yellow	75
Light buff	70
Lemon yellow	66
Ivory	63
Light green	62
Cream	57
Medium gray	55
Buff	55
Medium green	52
Ceiling blue	49
Apple green	44
Tan	42
Yellow	39
Medium blue	35
Dark gray	30
Orange	18
Dark red	13
Dark blue	8
Dark green	7
Dark brown	4

[1]Percentages may vary depending on type and make of paint.

The use of color to achieve certain physical and mental effects are very complex. However, it is possible to achieve the desired conditions with some basic knowledge of the functions of color.

Color and illumination combine to give us the perception of contrast. Contrast is desirable from the standpoint of reducing eye fatigue and making objects easy to see. When objects and their surroundings are the same color or the same shade a person is forced to look harder to separate the object from its surroundings. The use of a single color, or color monotony as it is known, is one of the primary reasons why such areas have high accident rates and low employee morale.

Desirable contrasts can be achieved by one of the following methods: 1) using a light color with a darker version of the same color; 2) using a warm color in combination with a cool color such as ivory and medium blue; or 3) using a color with its complementary color, for example, peach and gray blue or pale pink and light green.

Too much contrast is just as hard on the eyes as not enough contrast. For this reason, the contrast between walls and the equipment or other objects in the work area should be kept at a moderate level.

In addition to contrast, certain colors have been found to be more fatiguing to the eyes. The so-called warm colors such as the reds and oranges tend to tire the eyes the fastest. The cooler colors such as the blues and greens are found to be much easier on the eyes. Colors that are somewhat grayed as compared to a pure white or a pure green are also easier on the eyes.

Color can also play an important part in the emotional reactions and feelings of people. For example, a feeling of warmth can be created by using the colors red, orange or yellow. When a feeling of coolness is desired, the blues, greens or violets should be used.

A feeling of spaciousness can be created by using the whites and light blues, while a sense of confinement is created by the darker colors.

Colors can also suggest action or lack of movement. Brilliant colors such as red, orange or yellow seem to advance and are used to draw attention to signs or danger areas. Light, cool colors appear to recede and are frequently used as a method of hiding undesirable objects such as overhead ductwork or piping.

Objects can be made to appear larger than they actually are by using yellow or white colors.

Dark colors create a sensation of heaviness as compared to light colors.

Some individuals associate certain colors with mood. Some may be stimulated or excited by the warm colors and subdued by the cool colors. Other color associations include: blue, green—tranquil or calm; yellow—cheerful; black—powerful or strong; red, orange—hostile or defiant; and purple—dignified. Table 5.6 summarizes some of the common functional uses of color.

TABLE 5.6

FUNCTIONAL USES AND ASSOCIATIONS OF COLOR

Sensation Desired or Association	Best Colors to Use
Attention getting	red, orange, yellow
Warmth	orange, red
Coolness	blue, green, violet
Spaciousness	white, light blue
Closeness	dk. brown, dk. green, dk. blue
Heaviness	black, dark brown
Lightness	white, ivory, cream
Largeness	yellow, white, red
Smallness	black, dark brown
Action or movement	red, orange, yellow
Idleness	white, light blue, light gray
Distress	orange, red, black
Comfort	blue, green, yellow
Contrast	use complementary or warm-cool color combinations.

The value of color should not be underestimated. A survey conducted by Mill and Factory Magazine (Anon. 1963) of 500 manufacturing plants showed the following results. Upon the introduction of the use of color, the percentages of affirmative replies to the relation of color on the following areas were noted:

Improved housekeeping	84%
Greater safety	80%
Improved visibility	75%
Improved worker morale	72%
Better company image	67%
Improved worker conditions	61%
Greater productivity	28%

NOISE

Many investigations have been made into the effects of noise on worker efficiency, however not too many comparative results have been reported. Loud noise (80 to 90 decibels) is undesirable because it leads to distractions, errors and accidents thus reducing worker performance. Other studies indicate that most people can adjust to moderate noise levels (50 to 60 decibels) without any decrease in productivity. Persons exposed to continuous, very high levels of noise may suffer temporary or permanent hearing loss. Although many conflicting and inconclusive results have been found regarding the effect of noise, they all point to the need for reducing high noise levels as much as possible.

Probably the most important factor of noise is its annoyance to people. The most annoying noises are those that are high-pitched and intermittent, such as the screeching of metal to metal contact or the banging of a metal object on a hard surface. The distracting effect of the noise may bear no relationship at all to its loudness. For example, a door banging or a dish dropping may be very distracting although the actual noise level may be very low. Any noise which is relatively loud compared to background noise can also distract an employee from his work.

Working in an absolute silence may be just as bad as working in a noisy environment. In fact most individuals work better at physical tasks when there is a moderate level of noise present. This moderate level of noise evidently leads to a feeling of activity.

Generally acceptable noise levels for various situations are given in Table 5.7.

TABLE 5.7

ACCEPTABLE NOISE LEVELS

Type of Space	Sound Level (Decibels)
Hospitals, conference rooms	30-35
Hotels, motels	35-40
Offices	40-45
Restaurants	45-50

NOISE CONTROL

The best way to control unwanted noise is to reduce it at its source. If the source of the noise is machinery or mechanical equipment, much can be done to reduce it to an acceptable level. Proper maintenance, repair and lubrication can do wonders in quieting a noisy compressor or motor. Noise producing equipment should be mounted on rubber or springs and not directly to hard surfaces that act as sounding boards.

Another technique used to control noise is isolation of the source. This is accomplished by constructing enclosures around equipment or areas so the noise is confined and not allowed to be transmitted to other areas. Enclosures constructed of common building materials such as wood, plywood or plasterboard can reduce noise levels by 20 or 30 decibels.

When complete isolation is not possible because of required air circulation or for maintenance or inspection reasons, baffles of sound absorbing material can be placed above or partially around the equipment. This solution is not as good as isolation but will reduce the general noise level in the area.

A common noise control technique that is used when many noise producing sources are present is to place acoustical materials on the ceiling, walls and floors. Acoustical materials absorb a portion of the sound hitting them therefore reducing the amount that is bounced back into the space. The selection, design and placement of acoustical materials is best left in the hands of the acoustical engineer.

MUSIC

The use of music to stimulate or create certain moods in people has been employed for many years. However, the greatest strides in scientifically providing music for certain effects have been made during the last 20 years. Properly programmed music has been proven to be a good morale booster which results in increased employee production. There are even indications that music decreases lateness of employees.

The benefits of music are the greatest when persons are engaged in physical tasks. The music has to be patterned to fit the efficiency curve of employees. Most people are highly efficient 2 to 2½ hours after they start work. Then their performance drops off and continues at a lower level for a period of time. There usually is some increase in performance as the meal period is approached. This same pattern usually exists after the meal period with the performance hitting lower levels than before the meal period.

Thus the music provided should be moderate and cheerful during high efficiency periods and more pronounced with increased tempo and rhythm during low efficiency periods. Mild and restful music should be provided during the meal period.

WORKPLACE DESIGN

Workplaces and working areas should be designed so they are compatible with the anthropometric dimensions and physical limitations of the people who will be using them. Workplace design can affect the attitude of a person to his work as well as affect the method of work he uses. Well designed workplaces usually result in good work methods, while poorly designed workplaces led to unproductive work methods.

A well designed workplace allows the worker to stand or sit at will. This is accomplished by designing the workplace for a standing position and providing a raised seat so the working level does not change. The raised seat will also call for a foot rest.

If seating can be provided for the worker, the design of the seat should be according to the dimensions of the individuals. Proper seat design reduces fatigue and increases productivity.

The basic characteristics of good seating are detrmined by: (1) the height; (2) the length, width and slope of the seat; and (3) the design of the backrest.

Seat height should be somewhat less than the distance from the underside of the knee to the heel. Some allowance is made for the curve of the thigh, usually one or two inches (25.4 or 50.8 mm). A good seat height (from footrest to seat) for men is 17 in. (432 mm) while the seat height for women should be 15 in. (381 mm).

The seat length should be from 12 to 14 in. (305 to 356 mm) and the width should not be less than 13 in (330 mm). Too long a seat would cut into the back of the legs of small persons, while too narrow a seat would be uncomfortable for people with wide pelvises. The seat itself should slope back at an angle of 3 to 5° so the body does not tend to slide off.

Backrests are of two main types: (1) giving a continuous support to the back, or (2) giving support to the small of the back. Since there is a wide variability in the slope and position of the small of the back, narrow back rests should be adjustable for height. Narrow backrests should also pivot horizontally so they may adjust themselves to individual differences of people. Fixed backrests are not desirable since they cut into the backs of those people who do not fit perfectly into the seat.

The worktable or work surface height is dependent on the task to be performed. For simple, light manual tasks, the optimum work surface height should be 2 to 3 in. (50.8 to 76.2 mm) below the elbow of the operator. Work surface heights that vary from this recommendation will impair the performance of the individual or lead to fatigue.

If the work is of a heavy nature, the best work surface height is where the operator's wrist bends. Work surface heights varying between just below the elbow to the wrist can be used for intermediate or moderately heavy work tasks.

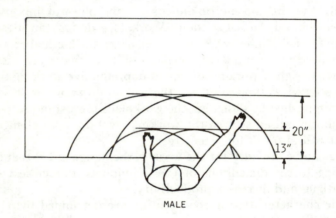

MALE

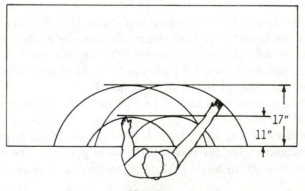

FEMALE

FIG. 5.5.   NORMAL AND MAXIMUM HORIZONTAL WORK
AREAS FOR MALES AND FEMALES

The best working width and depth of a work surface is illustrated by the normal and maximum working areas. The normal work area for the right hand is found by pivoting the hand at the elbow and scribing an arc on the working surface. The individual should be in normal working position at the work surface. The same procedure is used for determining the normal work area for the left hand. The area where the two arcs overlap is the normal work area for two-handed tasks.

Maximum working areas are found by scribing arcs with the hand extended from the shoulder. The area formed by the overlapping arcs of the left hand and right hand constitutes the maximum zone for two-handed work. Figure 5.5 shows the normal and maximum horizontal work areas for males and females.

Highly repetitive tasks should always be performed in the normal work areas if possible. Occasional movements of the hands into the maximum work areas are permissible but should be kept to a minimum. Movements that have to go beyond the maximum work areas are undesirable because they necessitate bending the body.

The area under the work surface should provide sufficient leg room. If seating is provided, a minimum of 25 in. (635 mm) of clearance under the work surface should be allowed for positioning the legs. The distance from the top of the seat to the bottom of the work surface should be at least seven inches (77.8 mm). For standing positions at an enclosed work table, a 4 by 4 in. (102 by 102 mm) kick room is necessary.

If shelves are used in the work area, they should be located in such a manner that their contents can be easily seen and reached. Shelving should not be higher than 76 in. (1930 mm) from the floor for women and 82 in. (2083 mm) from the floor for men. If shelving is placed over a table or counter, the dimensions of shelf placement shown in Fig. 5.6 should be used. The width of the shelving will depend upon the contents to be stored.

Materials, tools, or small equipment frequently used at a work area should be stored or placed between 26 in. (660 mm) and 52 in. (1321 mm) from the floor. Objects most frequently used by the left hand should be stored on the left side of the work area, and those used by the right hand should be placed on the right side.

The normal direction of the flow of work across the work surface or work area is from left to right.

EQUIPMENT DESIGN

Proper equipment design is important if a worker is to use the equipment easily and comfortably. Good equipment design also enables a worker to accomplish given tasks in the shortest time.

The most important aspects of equipment design deal with the details of conveying information to the operator (referred to as displays), the controls for adjusting the equipment, and the physical limitations of the human body.

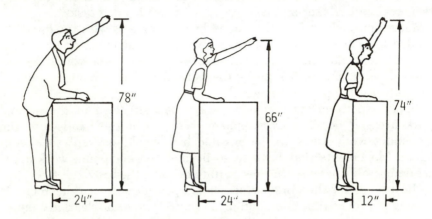

FIG. 5.6. MAXIMUM REACH OF WORKERS OVER OBSTRUCTIONS FOR SHELF PLACEMENT

DISPLAYS

Displays should be designed so that optimum operator efficiency is present regardless of the type of activity required. There are three types of activity usually associated with the display-man system: watching, which occurs when the operator is waiting for something to happen; warning, when the operator is aware that something in the equipment is not functioning properly; and action, when the operator takes steps to correct the condition by using a control. These three activities may be illustrated by a fry cook using a deep fat fryer which is equipped with an indicating thermometer and a temperature control. When frying, the cook will (or should) watch the indicating thermometer periodically. If the temperature of the fat drops below the desirable range, the thermometer will be the warning display and indicates to the cook that he should increase the temperature by adjusting the temperature control.

The displays on equipment should preferably be located to the top left of center and not more than 10° above or 45° below the line of vision of the operator. Figure 5.7 shows good placement of controls and displays on the equipment. The shape and design of the dial, markings and the pointer have a direct bearing on the accurate reading of the indicated measurements. This was reported by Sleight (1948) in a study comparing the readability of 5 dial styles: vertical, horizontal, semicircular, round and open-window. All the dials were comparable in size of gradations, distance between gradations and the size and form the numerals. The study was conducted with 60 males viewing each of 17 different dial settings for 0.12 sec.

FIG. 5.7. PROPER PLACEMENT OF CONTROLS AND DISPLAYS MAKE EQUIPMENT EASY TO USE

The results of the study showed that the fewest errors, (0.5%), were made with the open-window type dial. Figure 5.8 shows a scale with the open-window type dial. The vertical dial resulted in the largest (35.5%) errors. Results of the complete study are shown in Fig. 5.9.

FIG. 5.8. OPEN-WINDOW TYPE OF DIAL REDUCES ERRORS

The legibility of dials is also dependent on the make-up of the individual numerals. The best ratio of the stroke width of the numeral compared to the stroke length should be ⅙ to ⅛. The total width to height ratio of the numerals should be ⅔. Numerals should be large enough to be easily read at the expected distance the observer is away from the dial. For a reading distance of 28 in. (711 mm), the height of the letters should be 9/64 in. (3.57 mm).

Placement of the numerals on the dial face is important from the standpoint of fast and accurate legibility. For dials that have a fixed scale and a moving pointer, the numerals should be oriented vertically and not radially.

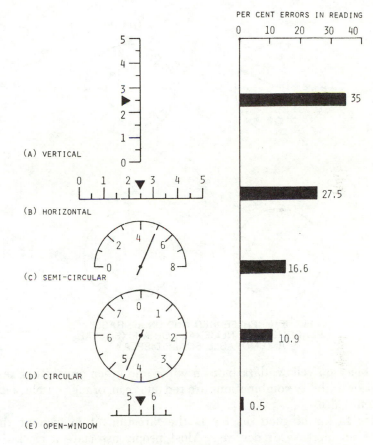

FIG. 5.9. PER CENT ERRORS IN READING FIVE DIFFERENT DIALS

(Adapted from Sleight) Reprinted with permission from E. J.
McCormick, *Human Factor Engineering.* McGraw-Hill Book Co.,
New York.

The pointer should not obscure any of the numerals, and the index or starting point of the scale is preferably in the 12 o'clock position.

When the dial has a fixed pointer and a movable scale, the numerals should be oriented radially on the dial face. With the pointer at the 12 o'clock position, the numerals will be oriented vertically at the reading position. Numeral placement on fixed dials and fixed pointer-movable scales is shown in Fig. 5.10.

The numerals should also be oriented vertically in the open-window type dial. At least 2 or 3 figures should appear in the window at the same time.

The best legibility of dials is accomplished by using black numerals on a white background. Other combinations rated to have good legibility

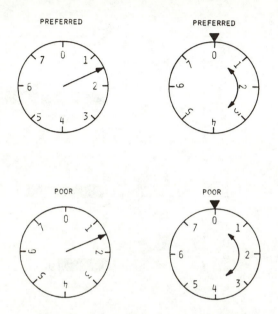

FIG. 5.10.   PREFERRED AND UNDESIRABLE
PLACEMENT OF NUMERALS ON A FIXED DIAL
AND MOVABLE SCALE DISPLAY

include black on yellow, dark blue on white and green on white. Examples of poor legibility combinations are red on green, orange on black and orange on white.

Another factor of good display is the direction of movement that indicates an increase or decrease. Most people associate a clockwise, upward or left to right movement with an increasing action. Dials should therefore be designed with this association in mind. Figure 5.11 shows the desirable direction of movement for different types of dials.

CONTROLS

All controls should be placed within the normal reaching areas of the operator. This means the controls should be placed from 33 in. (838 mm) to 56 in. (1422 mm) above the floor, and within 16 in. (406 mm) on either side of the center line of the operator. Figures 5.12, 5.13 and 5.14

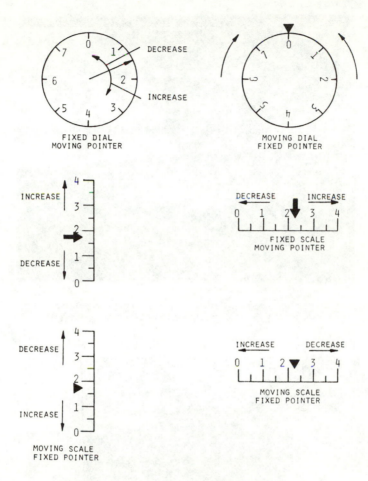

FIG. 5.11. PREFERRED DIRECTION OF MOVEMENT FOR DIALS

show poor location of controls making it difficult for workers to use them.

Emphasis should also be placed on the control-display relationship. This is the relationship, for example, between a valve and its related display such as a pressure gauge. The direction of movement of the control should be comparable to the direction of the movement of the display. If the valve is turned clockwise to increase pressure, then the gauge should also move clockwise to indicate increased pressure.

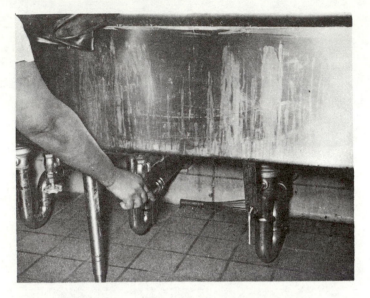

FIG. 5.12.   THE VERTICAL ORIENTATION AND LOW PLACEMENT
OF THESE STEAM VALVES MAKE THEM DIFFICULT TO USE

FIG. 5.13.   REACHING FOR THE POORLY PLACED STEAM VALVE FOR THIS
KETTLE MAY CAUSE A BURN

FIG. 5.14. THIS CONTROL IS AT A GOOD HEIGHT BUT TOO FAR BEHIND THE
KETTLE FOR EASY OPERATION

All controls on a given piece of equipment, regardless of whether they
are associated with a display or not, should produce the same effect
from the same type of movement. If one valve is turned clockwise to
increase, then all other valves on the equipment turned in the clockwise
direction should also result in an increase.

PHYSICAL LIMITATIONS OF THE HUMAN BODY

The design of work and equipment should always be within the limitations of body dimensions, body structure and movements. Table 5.8 presents the average body dimensions for males and females that can be used to check the proper design of equipment. Dimensions in Table 5.8 correspond to the sketches in Fig. 5.15.

TABLE 5.8

BODY DIMENSIONS FOR THE DESIGN OF EQUIPMENT [1,2]

	Male In.		Female In.
a. Height	69		65
b. Eye level	65		61
c. Elbow height	42		40
d. Maximum height of controls	56		52
e. Minimum height of controls	35		33
f. Maximum distance of controls from center			
line of body	18		14
g. Body width	19		17
h. Maximum span at working level	60		52
i. Normal span at working level	48		43
j. Elbow height above seat	9		9
k. Seat length	16		15
l. Seat width		14-20	
m. Depth of seat below work surface		7-9	
n. Buttock to knee	24		22
o. Minimum leg room (back of seat to			
tip of toe)	34		32
p. Back of seat to front edge of bench		12-15	
q. Seat height	17		15
r. When operator is seated at high bench,			
depth of footrest below seat	17		15
s. Maximum forward reach from front			
edge of bench	20		17
t. Normal forward reach from front			
edge of bench	13		11
u. Minimum distance of display from eye	18		18

[1]Source: Murrell, K.F.H., 1957. Data on Human Performance for Engineering Designers. Engineering *184*, No. 4771, 194-198.
[2]See Fig. 5.15.

It must be noted that the dimensions in Table 5.8 are averages and may not represent the best criteria for design in certain cases. For example, placing a control at a distance that an average man can reach may not be convenient for people who have less than the average arm reach. Since averages generally correspond to the point where 50% of the people have lesser dimensions and 50% have greater dimensions, using such a dimension for placement of controls may be inconvenient for approximately one-half of the population.

A better design criteria for maximum or minimum situations would be to use a dimension that would fit a larger portion of the population.For example, if the placement of the control is to meet the needs of 95% of the population, the distance to the control should not be greater than

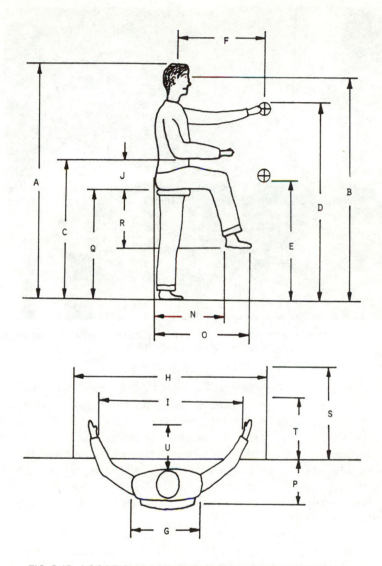

FIG. 5.15. LOCATION OF DIMENSIONS SPECIFIED IN TABLE 5.8

the arm reach of 5% of the population. Figure 5.16 shows the placement of electrical outlets that are beyond the normal reach of the worker when the heated carts are in position.

Body Structure and Movement

Human tasks should be designed so the limitations of body structure and body movements are not violated.

FIG. 5.16. POOR PLACEMENT OF ELECTRICAL OUTLET CAUSES WORKER
TO STRETCH CONSIDERABLY

Limbs are suitable for the application of force while the spine is not. The spine is intended to be used in an almost vertical position and is fairly inefficient when it is flexed or bent. The worker shown in Fig. 5.17 is causing undue strain to his back by reaching over the table. When picking up heavy objects, the knees should be bent and the spine kept erect. Limits of weight to be lifted by people without mechanical aid are 50 lb (22.7 kg) for men and 25 lb (11.3 kg) for women.

The best posture for doing normal tasks, either seated or standing is to have the spine erect.

Certain body movements and actions are easier than others. For example, curved movements rather than angular movements of the hands are faster and produce less fatigue.

Fatigue

Fatigue is dependent on such factors as the type of work, working conditions, total hours worked, the number and type of rest periods and mental attitude of the person. Fatigue in people is very complex to understand because it involves not only physiological changes of the body but is also affected by mental factors.

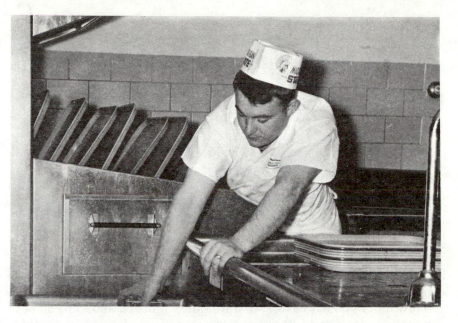

FIG. 5.17. POORLY PLANNED OR DESIGNED TASKS CAN CAUSE BACK STRAIN

The most effective means of combating fatigue are:
1. Simplify the task—30 to 50% of the work done in hotels, restaurants and institutions is unnecessary.
2. Provide adequate input of calories—especially for doing heavy manual tasks.
3. Keep force requirements below maximum limits—provide mechanical aids for lifting, moving, etc.
4. Remove disturbing distractions such as excessive noise and vibration.
5. Provide adequate illumination without glare.
6. Maintain optimum working environment from the standpoint of temperature, relative humidity and air movement.
7. Allow adequate rest periods—especially under adverse working conditions.
8. Guard against boredom primarily through job enlargement.
9. Maintain a desirable working pace throughout the work period.

The importance of human engineering as it affects worker performance is a very broad and detailed field and should not be underestimated. Only a few of the more pertinent factors have been presented here. The reader is encouraged to consult the literature in the field for more detailed information on specific aspects of human engineering.

Design For Safety

INTRODUCTION

Safety or accident prevention programs are usually a separate function in large business and manufacturing organizations. This is also true of extremely large hospitals or hotels. However, many hotels, restaurants and institutions do not have a separate safety function and some do not have any safety or accident prevention programs at all. Evidence of this fact is pointed out by a Bureau of Labor Statistics study (Anon. 1958) that showed an accident frequency rate of 18 disabling injuries per million man hours worked for food service establishments. This rate of accidents is approximately three times the average rate reported by other major industries. The need for a continuing safety program, primarily in the food service aspect of hotels, restaurants and institutions, is apparent.

One solution to the problem of accidents is to make the safety program an integral part of a work analysis and design program. The general objectives and goals of safety programs are similar to the objectives and goals of work analysis and design programs and the two programs could be easily combined. In fact most work analysis and design programs are continually dealing with safety and most safety programs have to deal with equipment and work methods. When separate safety and work analysis and design programs are maintained in an organization, close cooperation between the two programs is a necessity.

Since most accidents occur in the kitchens or other food service areas of hotels, restaurants and institutions, this area will be emphasized in presenting the material on safety as a part of the work analysis and design program.

SAFETY MANAGEMENT

The success of the safety program rests primarily with managerial and supervisory personnel. Managers, assistant managers and supervisors should be responsible for maintaining safe working conditions and for instilling safety in their employees. Supervisors, in cooperation with the work analyst, should establish safe procedures for work, including rules for operating machines in their departments. Procedures should also be set up for handling unexpected stoppages of machines and other occurrences that may lead to an accident. Supervisors as well as employees should always report unsafe acts or unsafe conditions so they may be quickly remedied. Accidents do not happen—they are caused by unsafe acts or unsafe conditions. When these acts or conditions are corrected, the accident will not occur.

All employees should be trained in general safety rules and procedures that apply to their tasks and to the equipment or machines they use. Periodic refresher courses will assure continued safety. The employees are usually the first ones to encounter unsafe conditions and therefore have to form the basic defense against accidents. It is good company policy to issue general safety instructions to all employees. Table 6.1 shows a set of safety instructions for cafeteria operations.

TABLE 6.1
GENERAL SAFETY INSTRUCTIONS FOR CAFETERIA OPERATIONS [1]

PERSONAL SAFETY RULES

1. Be sure you understand and comply with all rules governing conduct and personal protection in your work area.
2. Clean up spilled materials promptly and completely.
3. Do not attempt to lift heavy or bulky equipment beyond your physical capacity. No individual is expected to lift items exceeding 50 lb without the help of fellow workers or the use of lifting equipment.
4. Female employees are not to lift weights in excess of 25 lb.
5. Do not carry sharp objects in your pockets.
6. Always use established aisles and walkways. Do not take shortcuts between machines or through roped-off areas.
7. Running is not permitted in any work area.
8. When walking on intraplant roads, walk on the left and always face the traffic.
9. Workers engaging in horseplay, teasing, or distraction of fellow workers are subject to disciplinary action.
10. Smoking and open flames are prohibited in posted areas.
11. The wearing of hand protection, eye protection, protective clothing and other safety equipment specified by division procedures and safety department recommendations is mandatory.
12. Clothing appropriate for the work being done shall be worn. Loose sleeves, tails, ties, lapels, cuffs, or other loose clothing that can be entangled in moving machinery shall not be worn.
13. Every injury, regardless of its nature or extent, shall be reported to supervision immediately afterwards.

[1] Reprinted with permission from G. J. Wolnez, Accident Prevention in the Plant Kitchen, National Safety News.

TABLE 6.1 *(Continued)*

SAFE WORKING PRACTICES

1. Know and follow the area work procedures at all times.
2. If in doubt concerning the safe way to perform a job, ask your supervisor before proceeding with the task.
3. Take necessary precautions to ensure that tools, equipment and materials present no hazard by location or use.
4. Do not use makeshift ladders.
5. Do not remove, displace, damage, destroy or carry off any safety device, safeguard, notice or warning furnished for use at any plant.
6. Watches, rings, or tags shall not be worn by employees when working around machinery. Symbolic or religious necklaces that are worn in keeping with convictions must be provided with a weak link to prevent strangulation if accidentally entangled in moving machinery.
7. Do not use or handle liquid or solid materials marked with red "target" unless you understand the safe handling procedures for such materials.
8. It is mandatory to observe all safety rules and regulations in all plant areas.

RULES FOR USE OF EQUIPMENT

1. Moving, rearranging and repair of machines and equipment shall be performed by authorized personnel only.
2. Do not alter or attempt to repair any article of safety equipment without authorization from your immediate supervisor.
3. Do not substitute tools, equipment or methods without authorization from your supervisor.
4. Do not use defective equipment; report it to your supervisor immediately.
5. Do not operate machines or equipment that you have not been authorized to operate.
6. Never operate machines or equipment provided with guards unless such guards are in place and operational.
7. Do not use equipment subject to periodic inspection or testing, unless it has been tested or inspected for the current period.
8. Keep table drawers and cabinet and locker doors closed when not in use.
9. No equipment or machine shall be operated when it is red-tagged as dangerous.
10. No unauthorized person shall make electrical or mechanical repairs to equipment.
11. Portable ladders must be well secured, in good condition and in a level position.
12. Each employee is responsible for knowing the operation and location of fire extinguishers in his work area.
13. It is prohibited to use drinking cups, cans or glass jars to hold any industrial chemical or solvent.
14. Misplaced equipment creates a hazard. Each employee is responsible for seeing that each piece of equipment is in its proper place.
15. Carts and other movable pieces of equipment are not to be loaded to the extent of obscuring the vision of the operator.
16. Storage: Proper equipment is provided (step ladders, etc.) and will be used when loading or unloading stored items at or above head level.
17. Ice boxes and floors will be kept clear, clean and nonslippery at all times.
18. Knives are to be properly stored when not being used for the purpose intended.
19. Rest rooms must be kept clean and uncluttered at all times. Each employee is responsible for placing his used clothing in the container or locker provided.
20. Areas barricaded for the purpose of steam cleaning, repairs, etc., must be observed at all times.
21. The area around the meat saw is to be "chained" when the saw is being operated.
22. Carts are to be pushed, and the cart operator must face or look in the direction of travel.
23. When frying or handling hot pans in or out of the oven, protective clothing (arm covering) shall be worn at all times.
24. Pots, pans and similar utensils must never be placed on racks or stored above eye level. Store all same-size pans together.
25. When operating machinery (cutters, grinders, etc.) devote your attention to the job and refrain from talking and visiting.

TABLE 6.1 (*Continued*)

SLICING, CUTTING AND CHOPPING MACHINES

1. Before starting any machine, be sure that the guards are in place and the machine is properly set to operate.
2. Clear the immediate area around all equipment required for the cutting, slicing or chopping operation.
3. Never place your fingers in the cutting chute; always use the plungers provided.
4. If the machine jams, shut off the power immediately and use a wooden push stick to free the blades of obstructions.
5. Do not clean the cutting or rotating surface of the above machines unless you are positive that the power source has been disconnected.
6. If any of the above machines are not functioning properly, stop operation and notify the supervisor immediately.
7. Pay close attention to your job when operating the above machines—a moment of distraction could result in an accident.
8. Always return the slicing-machine table to the zero position when you have finished using the machine; this will prevent injury during clean-up of the machine.
9. When using chopping or slicing attachments on the mixing machine, be sure that the attachment is firmly fixed in the operating position and the guard is in place.
10. Never leave a machine running without attention. Shut off the power even if you must leave for only a moment.

MEAT SAWS

1. Before starting machine, make sure that the guards are in place and the machine is properly set to operate.
2. The floor area immediately around a machine must be clean and uncluttered.
3. Close off the work area with the chains provided.
4. Adjust all guards to proper height and distance for the specified cutting operation to be performed.
5. Feed the meat into the blade with the pusher provided. Do not place your fingers in the immediate vicinity of the blade.

CUTLERY

1. When not in use, knives or other sharp instruments should be stored in the racks provided.
2. Always select the correct knife for the job.
3. Pay close attention to the job whenever you are handling sharp knives. Distractions cause accidents.
4. Before using a knife, inspect it for defects; the handle must be dry and free from splinters and burrs and the blade should be properly sharpened.
5. Special metal-mesh gloves should be worn during boning and cutting operations.
6. Butcher's steels, used for sharpening knives, should be operated by keeping the blade edge of the knife away from the body.
7. Only authorized and properly trained persons will be permitted to sharpen knives.

DISHWASHING EQUIPMENT

1. Floors around dishwasher should be mopped frequently to prevent slips and falls.
2. Only authorized workers shall make adjustments on automatic equipment.
3. If a machine jams, shut off the power and the hot water immediately. Serious scalds can result from reaching into the washing area.
4. Handle trays with care and do not overload machine.
5. When moving carts, trays, or utensils, consider your fellow workers in the area. Rush periods and close quarters call for job concentration in order to prevent accidents.

STEAM-CLEANING OPERATIONS

1. Do not leave the steam-cleaning nozzle unattended.
2. Clear the immediate area of all personnel during steam-cleaning operations.
3. Do not spray electrical connection with steam, unless you are sure it is completely waterproofed.

TABLE 6.1 (*Continued*)

4. Aprons, eye protection, rubber gloves and boots will be worn during all steam-cleaning operations.
5. To prevent tripping, return the steam hose to the storage rack when the operation is completed.

STEAM EQUIPMENT

1. Operate all steam equipment within the limits recommended by the manufacturer.
2. Steam kettles should be drained of water before the steam valves are open.
3. Always open the steam valves slowly.
4. Report steam leaks or other mechanical problems to your supervisor immediately.
5. Never fill steam kettles to a point where splashing will occur and injure workers.
6. Do not stir the contents of a steam kettle when off balance; use the small step provided or get help from a fellow worker.

GARBAGE DISPOSERS

1. Do not, under any conditions, reach into the grinding chamber. If the machine is jammed, stop it immediately and report the problem to supervisor.
2. Electric garbage disposers operate safely and efficiently only when sufficient water is used. Valve must be set so the water swirls around the cone.
3. Do not stuff or pack waste into the opening.
4. Do not operate when the guard is removed.
5. Do not allow glass, metal, crockery or plastics to enter the grinder. If this occurs, stop the grinder immediately and notify supervisor.
6. Do not attempt to repair any garbage grinders in the facility.
7. Wear eye protection and hand protection when operating the garbage can steam cleaner.

SAFE WORKING ENVIRONMENT

Safety programs are best initiated by a thorough inspection for unsafe conditions. It is usually beneficial to enlist the aid of experts at this starting point to make sure the program will get off to a good start. Fire department personnel, insurance agents and safety engineers should be consulted for this initial inspection. All potential accident causes determined by the inspection should be eliminated or at least fully explained to the employees involved. Employees may hesitate to cooperate on safety programs unless management has taken the initial steps to eliminate hazards.

Cause and Prevention of Accidents

The most frequent types of accidents in the food service area, their causes and the recommended remedies to provide a safer work environment are summarized below.

1. **Falling.**— Falling may be caused by slippery floors, highly polished floors, steep stairways such as shown in Fig. 6.1, or by the obstructions

left in aisleways (Fig. 6.2). Areas that are constantly wet or greasy should be equipped with nonskid flooring. Figure 6.3 shows one type of abrasive floor covering that can be installed on existing tile floors. Slatted wood floors may be used in areas where oil or grease spillage occurs frequently. Carpeting is also a possibility. All stairways should conform to specified tread and riser dimensions and should be equipped with sturdy hand rails. All work and traffic areas should be kept clean. Suitable storage areas should be provided for equipment and supplies and employees must be required to put items in their designated storage places as soon as they are through using them.

FIG. 6.1. STEEP STAIRWAYS AND ANGLED STEPS MAY LEAD TO ACCIDENTS

2. **Bumping.**—Bumping is frequently encountered in areas where there is not ample clearance overhead or between objects. Narrow aisleways, low hanging shelves, protruding levers or square corners on tables or equipment lead to bumps. Congested areas may also cause workers to bump into one another and consequently lead to an accident. All sharp corners and protrusions should be eliminated or at least rounded, or shielded. Color coding may be helpful in drawing the employee's attention to protruding objects.

FIG. 6.2.   OBSTRUCTIONS IN AISLEWAYS ARE ONE OF THE PRIMARY CAUSES
OF ACCIDENTS IN KITCHENS

3. **Snagging.**—Exposed gears, belts and other moving parts of machines and equipment can snag clothing, hand held objects or even the hands. All moving parts should be completely enclosed to prevent employees from coming in contact with them. Guards should be kept in place and correctly adjusted. Interlocks that stop the machines when guards are removed should be installed where feasible. Special guards should be provided where it is possible for the hands to come close to moving parts. The garbage disposal shown in Fig. 6.4 is large enough to allow entry of the hand. A guard over the opening as pictured in Fig. 6.5 allows food but not the hand to come in contact with the blade.

4. **Cutting.**—The improper use of equipment, hand tools and poor guarding of moving edges are the causes of cutting. Many of the machines used in food service operations do not have sufficient guarding of cutting edges. In such cases, additional guarding should be installed and kept in place. Figure 6.6 shows a typical food chopper where it is possible to feed the hand directly into the blade if the employee is not careful. Figure 6.7 shows the installation of two metal plates that would keep the fingers away from the blade. It is easy for the fingers to contact the cutting blade when feeding vegetables into the vegetable cutting ma-

chine shown on Fig. 6.8. Figure 6.9 shows the installation of metal guards that increase the distance from the fingers to the blades making contact extremely difficult. Metal plates attached to the bun slicing machine shown in Fig. 6.10 keep the fingers an additional 8 in. (203 mm) away from the blade.

FIG. 6.3. NONSKID FLOORING WILL MINIMIZE SLIPPING IN THIS PREPARATION AREA

5. **Burning.**—Hot grease, steam, hot water or hot pipes cause most of the burns in food service operations. Proper training in the use of fryers, kettles and steamers is essential in preventing burns. All steam and hot water lines should be placed where they present no hazard. If this is not

possible, the lines should be fully insulated so employees cannot be burned by making contact with them. Figure 6.11 shows the insulated shielding of a steam line for a table-mounted kettle. The shield shown in Fig. 6.12, protects employees from burns to the legs. The steam garbage can cleaner in Fig. 6.13, is equipped with a metal guard over the foot controls to prevent accidental operation of the pedals which could expose employees to live steam.

Courtesy of Aerojet-General Corp.

FIG. 6.4. THE OPENING OF THIS GARBAGE DISPOSER IS LARGE ENOUGH TO PERMIT ENTRY OF THE HAND

Courtesy of Aerojet-General Corp.

FIG. 6.5. METAL GUARD OVER GARBAGE DISPOSAL KEEPS THE HANDS AWAY FROM THE OPENING

Courtesy of Aerojet-General Corp.

FIG. 6.6. IT IS POSSIBLE TO FEED THE HAND DIRECTLY INTO THE
BLADE OF THIS FOOD CHOPPER

Courtesy of Aerojet-General Corp.

FIG. 6.7. THE TWO METAL PLATES INSTALLED ON THE CHOPPER
KEEP THE HANDS AN ADDITIONAL 8 IN. AWAY FROM THE BLADE

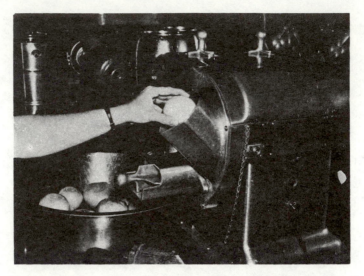

Courtesy of Aerojet–General Corp.

FIG. 6.8. IT IS EASY FOR THE FINGERS TO CONTACT THE BLADE
WHEN FEEDING VEGETABLES INTO THIS VEGETABLE CUTTING
MACHINE

Courtesy of Aerojet–General Corp.

FIG. 6.9. INSTALLATION OF GUARDS ON THE VEGETABLE CUTTING
MACHINE INCREASES THE DISTANCE FROM THE FINGERS TO THE
BLADES

Courtesy of Aerojet–General Corp.

FIG. 6.10. THE TWO METAL PLATES INSTALLED ON THIS BUN
SLICING MACHINE KEEP THE FINGERS AN ADDITIONAL 8 IN. AWAY
FROM THE BLADE WHEN FEEDING BUNS

FIG. 6.11. THE STEAM LINE FOR TABLE MOUNTED STEAM KETTLES
SHOULD BE INSULATED TO PREVENT BURNS

FIG. 6.12. THIS LOW LEVEL SHIELD PROTECTS THE
WORKERS' LEGS FROM BURNS

6. **Electrical Shock.**—Most electrical shocks are caused by improper grounding of equipment and machines and by frayed wires or deteriorated electrical insulation on wires. All electrical equipment should be properly installed in accordance with electrical safety codes. Only equipment that bears Factory Mutual approval or are listed by Underwriters Laboratories should be used. Periodic inspections should be made to assure the safety of electrical equipment. Built-in ground wires with three-prong plugs should be used for portable equipment. Grounding outlets as shown in Fig. 6.14 should be provided where such equipment is frequently used. Heavy duty water-proof wiring should be used.

7. **Pinching or Mashing.**—The exposed moving parts of equipment, heavy portable equipment that is moved about the kitchen, and falling lids may result in pinched or mashed fingers and feet. The heavy lids of steam kettles can be counterbalanced as shown in Fig. 6.15 to keep them from falling on the fingers.

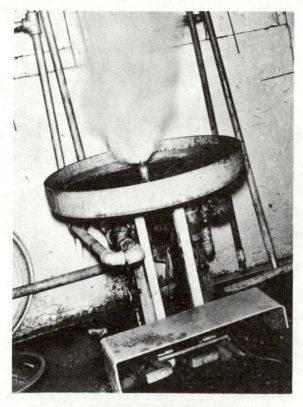

Courtesy of Aerojet-General Corp.

FIG. 6.13. METAL GUARDS OVER FOOT CONTROLS
PREVENT ACCIDENTAL STEPPING ON THE PEDAL AND
EXPOSING WORKER TO LIVE STEAM

8. **Dropping.**—Dropping is primarily caused by sweaty or greasy hands or by stiffness of fingers resulting from exposure to the cold. Employees should be trained to keep their hands dry. Frequently carried objects such as tote pans should be equipped with adequate handles. The wearing of gloves by employees is recommended when the hands contact hot or cold objects for a long period of time.

9. **Falling Objects.**—Improperly placed objects on shelves, falling equipment and hand tools or tipping of equipment result in many injuries. Suitable storage facilities for supplies, tools, and minor equipment should be provided to prevent falling of these items. Tables that support

equipment should be sturdily built and be large enough to keep the weight of the equipment from tipping them over. Portable equipment carts should have casters that lock to prevent movement when the equipment is in use.

FIG. 6.14. GROUNDING OUTLETS SHOULD BE PROVIDED FOR PORTABLE
ELECTRICAL EQUIPMENT

10. **Physical Strain.**—Physical strain is caused by lifting heavy objects, by using improper lifting methods, or by working in awkward positions. Mechanical lifting aids should be used for heavy objects. Using portable carts will minimize the strain caused by carrying heavy objects. Tables and work areas should be of proper dimensions so workers do not have to stretch or bend extensively.

After the hazards have been eliminated, periodic inspections are necessary to maintain continually the safety attitude in the organization. Such inspections are easily made with a safety check list as shown in Table 6.2. The inspections can be used to prepare monthly safety reports and can form the basis for a safety awards program. Cash awards to employees with good safety records can reduce accident losses to a minimum.

Courtesy of Aerojet-General Corp.

FIG. 6.15. THE COUNTERBALANCE ON THIS STEAM KETTLE LID PREVENTS
THE LID FROM FALLING ACCIDENTALLY ON EMPLOYEES' HANDS OR FINGERS

TABLE 6.2

FOOD SERVICE SAFETY CHECK LIST [1]

Location_____ Date checked _____
                                          By_____

Cuts

1. Are knives and other cutting tools stored
   in racks with blades protected?   Yes___   No___   Comments___
2. Are tools of the correct size used for the
   work to be done?   Yes___   No___   Comments___
3. Is a board used for cutting, dicing and
   mincing?   Yes___   No___   Comments___
4. When a knife is used, is the cut always
   made downward and never toward the
   hand?   Yes___   No___   Comments___
5. Are sharp tools collected on a tray and
   washed separately?   Yes___   No___   Comments___
6. Are sharp tools ever left in the dishwater? Yes___   No___   Comments___
7. Are all broken dishes, defective utensils
   and opened tin cans promptly discarded?   Yes___   No___   Comments___
8. Are the knives kept sharp?   Yes___   No___   Comments___

[1]Reprinted with permission from G.T. Wolnez, Accident Prevention in the Plant Kitchen, National Safety News.

TABLE 6.2 (Continued)

Burns

1. Are there enough potholders or asbestos gloves for all to use?	Yes___	No___	Comments___
2. Are potholders dry and in good repair?	Yes___	No___	Comments___
3. Are potholders always used to handle hot utensils?	Yes___	No___	Comments___
4. Are asbestos gloves used on hot utensils?	Yes___	No___	Comments___
5. Are the handles tight on all pots and lids?	Yes___	No___	Comments___
6. Is a puller or proper tool used to reach in the oven to bring pans to the front of the oven before removing?	Yes___	No___	Comments___
7. Are careful instructions given to new employees for the use of steamers, hot serving tables and trunnion kettles?	Yes___	No___	Comments___
8. Is care given to prevent spattering, splashing or boiling over of food?	Yes___	No___	Comments___
9. Is food stirred with a long-handled spoon or paddle?	Yes___	No___	Comments___
10. Are fat fires prevented by not filling fat containers too full?	Yes___	No___	Comments___
11. Are fat fires treated by placing a cover over fire?	Yes___	No___	Comments___
12. Are steam tables, ovens and stoves allowed to cool before cleaning?	Yes___	No___	Comments___
13. Are pans properly loaded to prevent tipping and splashing hot grease?	Yes___	No___	Comments___

Miscellaneous Accidents

1. Are floors in good repair?	Yes___	No___	Comments___
2. Are floors clean and dry to avoid slipping?	Yes___	No___	Comments___
3. Are traffic lanes straight and "In" and "Out" doors marked to avoid collisions?	Yes___	No___	Comments___
4. Are all traffic lanes, exits and entrances clear?	Yes___	No___	Comments___
5. Are electric connections made with dry hands?	Yes___	No___	Comments___
6. Are the pilot lights burning and all burners checked before lighting gas?	Yes___	No___	Comments___
7. Are trays loaded and carried carefully?	Yes___	No___	Comments___
8. Are trays ever tilted or overcrowded when they are loaded?	Yes___	No___	Comments___
9. Are closet doors kept closed?	Yes___	No___	Comments___
10. Are floor mats placed where needed to prevent slipping?	Yes___	No___	Comments___
11. Are floor mats placed so that workers will not trip on them when they are being cleaned?	Yes___	No___	Comments___
12. Is there a place to stack cases of food so workers will not trip on them?	Yes___	No___	Comments___
13. Is there a place to stack crates of produce until they can be put away?	Yes___	No___	Comments___
14. Do all cupboard doors slide or have suitable catches so that the doors will stay closed?	Yes___	No___	Comments___
15. Are all electric cords located so they are not a hazard for the free movement of personnel during the preparation and service of food?	Yes___	No___	Comments___
16. Are all electric outlets where water cannot be splashed or spilled on them?	Yes___	No___	Comments___
17. Are greasy rags stored in a covered metal container?	Yes___	No___	Comments___

TABLE 6.2 (*Continued*)

18. Are matches stored in a covered metal container?	Yes___	No___	Comments___
19. Are all handles on equipment located or protected so they cannot catch on clothing?	Yes___	No___	Comments___
20. Are work spaces adequately lighted?	Yes___	No___	Comments___
21. Does every staff member know the location of shut-offs for water, electricity, gas and steam that supply the kitchen, in case of water leak or fire?	Yes___	No___	Comments___
22. Are directions posted on the machine for the operation of all motor-driven equipment?	Yes___	No___	Comments___
23. Are the stands of the machine equipment sturdy so that they will not tip over?	Yes___	No___	Comments___
24. Is fixed equipment securely bolted to the floor or to the table or on a stand?	Yes___	No___	Comments___
25. Is all motor-driven equipment grounded and always shut off, and operation permitted to stop, before adjustments are made or food is removed?	Yes___	No___	Comments___
26. Does any gas equipment need adjusting?	Yes___	No___	Comments___
27. Are pilot lights on all gas equipment operating properly and tested periodically?	Yes___	No___	Comments___
28. Do all can openers cut clean?	Yes___	No___	Comments___
29. Is a step ladder or step stool available in order to reach high shelves safely?	Yes___	No___	Comments___
30. Is the step ladder or step stool available in good repair?	Yes___	No___	Comments___
31. Are there adequate first-aid supplies?	Yes___	No___	Comments___
32. Are injured people sent to the nurse?	Yes___	No___	Comments___
33. Is there a carbon dioxide (CO_2)fire extinguisher in the kitchen?	Yes___	No___	Comments___
34. Is the fire extinguisher easily accessible but not near the range or oven?	Yes___	No___	Comments___
35. Does the staff have drills on how to operate the fire extinguisher?	Yes___	No___	Comments___

Safe Clothing

1. Does everyone wear medium or low-heeled well-fitting shoes with soles that do not slip easily?	Yes___	No___	Comments___
2. Do people wear noncombustible aprons that do not have long ties or loose pockets?	Yes___	No___	Comments___
3. Do all staff members avoid wearing loose pins or earrings that may fall into food?	Yes___	No___	Comments___
4. Do all employees avoid wearing bracelets that may catch on equipment handles?	Yes___	No___	Comments___

7

Function and Activity Analysis

INTRODUCTION

A systematic and desirable approach to work analysis is to first obtain information about the entire work system and then to proceed with the analysis of the components of the work system. The general picture of a work system may be obtained from the organizational structure as presented in the organization chart. The organization chart relates the responsibilities and accountabilities of the individuals and work groups in the organization. The largest identifiable components of a work system are the functions performed by each member or work group in the organization. These functions can then be subdivided into activities or tasks which represent the next identifiable components of the work system. The men, materials, machines and processes involved in the activity or task represent the final component of the work system.

FUNCTION ANALYSIS

Thus the analysis of work systems should begin with an investigation of the general functions of the work system. The identification and allocation of functions to the various work groups of an organization is referred to as function analysis. Function analysis is usually accomplished with the aid of the organization chart. Each member or work group shown on the organization chart is analyzed to determine the primary functions performed. The objective of function analysis is to determine the necessary functions and to find the best relationship among these necessary functions required to attain the goals of the organization.

The most important part of function analysis is the proper identification of the functions. Functions and activities are sometimes considered to be the same thing, however for purposes of analysis, a differentiation between them should be made. The function should be indicative of describing *what* is occuring while the activities show *how* the function is accomplished. The function can be thought of as the results of many related activities. Illustrations of functions in a food service organization might include purchasing, food preprocessing, food production, food service, providing clean dishes, menu planning, supervision, sanitation, maintenance and cost control to name a few. Each of these functions can be associated with the group of activities that have to be done to accomplish the function. For example, the activities involved in purchasing include writing specifications, checking prices, determining quantities, etc. The function of food production is associated with such activities as food storage, raw food preparation, reading recipes, cooking, portioning, clean up, etc.

The identification of the functions of a member or work group of the organization can be easily accomplished by using a function analysis form. A sample function analysis form for analyzing divisions or departments is shown in Fig. 7.1. These forms are usually completed with

FUNCTION ANALYSIS FORM

Department or Division	Personnel	Analyst E.A.K.
Supervisor		Date

Function: To provide and maintain qualified, well trained personnel for all operating positions in the organization.

Primary Function Components:

Employment	Wage administration
Dismissal	Employee records
Training	Safety
Union relations	Working conditions

Raw Materials and Equipment Needed for the Function:
   Ordinary stenographic equipment and supplies

Units of Output:

Remarks:

FIG. 7.1. TYPICAL FUNCTION ANALYSIS FORM FOR A PERSONNEL DEPARTMENT

the cooperation of the supervisors of the departments or work groups. It is important to note that certain functions identified in one organization may not appear in other organizations because of different company philosophies or objectives. For example, a restaurant using a set menu will not have a menu planning function. Some organizations may have a work analysis and design function while others may not. In some cases a primary function in one organization may appear as a secondary function in another organization.

The usual procedure that is followed in function analysis is to complete the function analysis forms for each member or work group of the organization. Then each of the identified primary functions are questioned as to their necessity in achieving the organization's goals and objectives. The check list shown in Table 7.1 may be used to analyze the functions and their allocations to individuals or work groups.

TABLE 7.1
CHECK LIST FOR FUNCTION ANALYSIS

1. Are all the necessary functions of the organization allocated? Frequently, some of the most important functions of an organization are not allocated to any person or group. Omission of such functions as quality control, cost analysis, methods improvement and market development indicate that an improvement in the organizational structure could be expected.

2. Are any unnecessary functions allocated? As stated earlier, one of the objectives of work analysis is to eliminate unnecessary work and this also applies to functions. Any functions that do not add value to the products or services provided by the organization should be carefully scrutinized to determine whether they are absolutely necessary or not.

3. Are any functions duplicated needlessly? Duplication of functions results in duplication of effort and man power.

4. Are similar functions grouped together? The function of processing consists of similar activities regardless of the materials being processed. Thus the food processing functions should be grouped together.

5. Are dependent functions close together? Dishwashing and food service, food purchasing and food receiving, and payroll and budget control are examples of dependent functions and should be closely associated.

6. Are functions which are performed in sequence placed close together? Sequential functions such as menu planning and food purchasing or food preparation and food processing should be placed together both organizationally and physically.

7. Are functions which act as controls or checks on other activities placed in groups which are independent of the activities? Food cost control, for example, should be assigned to a group not directly involved with food purchasing and production. Having the chef determine food costs is not advisable, however the chef should be constantly informed of food costs. Similarly, the control of beverage cost should not be assigned to bartenders but to another independent member or group.

8. Are the functions allocated so they are accomplished at the lowest possible cost? The allocation of housekeeping or record keeping functions to nurses when they can be accomplished just as satisfactorily by other members are costly.

9. Are the functions allocated so they minimize the amount of communication? Occasionally, the re-allocation of functions among the organizational groups will reduce the need for communication between the groups. Communication should be kept to the minimum required to accomplish the function because it does not add value to products or services.

10. Are the functions allocated so the amount of paperwork involved is kept to a minimum? A re-allocation of functions may possibly result in reduced paperwork required for control and information.

FUNCTION CHARTS

Function charts are used to graphically display the allocations of functions to each member or work group in the organization. The function chart is similar to the format of an organization chart, and in many instances an existing organization chart can be used. Constructing the function chart merely involves indicating the functions performed under the appropriate member or work group of the organization. In most cases the functions may be taken directly from the function analysis forms. A simple function chart for a restaurant is shown in Fig. 7.2. The function chart is helpful in determining if all the necessary functions of the organization have been allocated to a member or work group as well as determining the relationships of the functions.

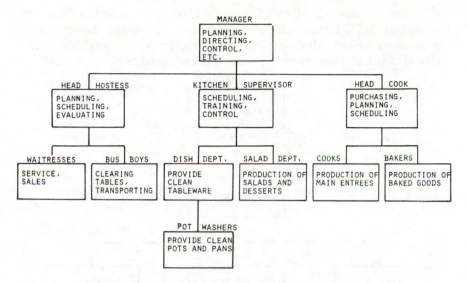

FIG. 7.2.   FUNCTION CHART FOR A FOOD SERVICE OPERATION

Function Flow Chart

A function flow chart may be constructed to show various relationships between the primary functions of the organization and the flow of materials or other objects. A chart showing the flow of materials between functions is illustrated in Fig. 7.3. The chart is easily made by connecting the boxes identifying the functions with lines and arrows which represent the direction of flow. The function flow chart of materials is frequently used as a guide to planning layouts. Function flow charts may also be used to show the flow of paperwork or communications required to accomplish the functions involved.

Job Descriptions

Function analysis is an ideal way to gather information needed to develop job descriptions. Job descriptions should include information about the functions and activities of the job, as well as the equipment and materials that are used to accomplish the functions. A job description for the owner-manager of a food service establishment is shown in Fig. 7.4.

Activity Analysis

Activity analysis enables a further breakdown of the functions performed by a department or work group to be accomplished. The activity analysis is made after, or in some cases in conjunction with, the function analysis. In one sense, function analysis can be thought of as the analysis of the whole organization, while activity analysis is the analysis of the member or work group of the organization.

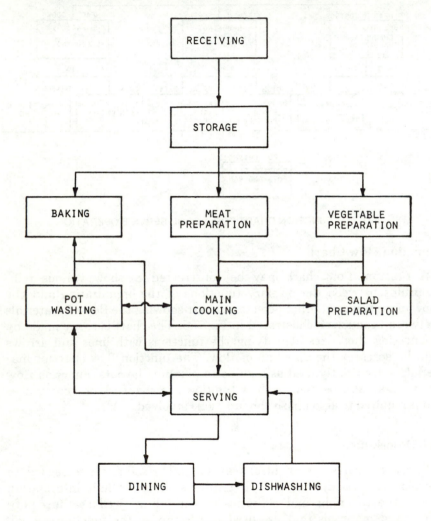

FIG. 7.3. FUNCTION FLOW CHART FOR A FOOD SERVICE OPERATION

Activity analysis involves describing the activities that are performed by individuals or a work group and the time it takes to perform them. Some of the information and results obtained through activity analysis include:

1. Determination of the activities that take the most time.

2. Identification of the individuals who are working on the activities and the time they take to perform them.
3. Pinpointing unnecessary or duplicated activities.
4. Indication of whether or not skills are used properly.
5. Indication of whether or not the total work is evenly distributed among the group.
6. Identification of individuals doing too many unrelated tasks.
7. Pinpointing areas where other analysis techniques may be profitably used.
8. Pinpointing areas where training or supervision should be improved.

The activity analysis is made by observing and chronologically recording the activities of the individuals. The starting times and indications of the work output for each activity are also recorded. The amount of time spent on each activity is found by subtraction. The data for activity analysis is recorded on a form as shown in Fig. 7.5.

The data for the activity analysis can be obtained in several different ways. The most accurate method is to use an observer who watches and records the activities of the individual or group being analyzed. This method is costly because an activity analysis usually covers a period of many days. This length of study has to be used so a representative picture of the activities is obtained. If large groups of individuals are being studied, more than one observer may have to be used.

The continuous observation method has some limitations in this type of study. One problem occurs when the duration of each activity is very short and it becomes difficult to observe and record all the activities accurately. Another problem is that long periods of observation are very fatiguing and may lead to errors by the observer. The individual being observed may become irritated when the observation is carried out continuously over a period of several days.

Another method of gathering data for the activity analysis is to have the worker record what he does. This method is desirable when the worker has to move around a great deal in accomplishing his activities. Although the difficulties encountered by using outside observers are eliminated, an additional burden is placed on the worker, therefore this method should be used when the full cooperation of the workers can be obtained. The idea of letting workers analyze their own activities frequently leads to an interest and appreciation of work analysis and design on the part of the worker.

A preprinted form may be used to simplify the worker's recording of his activities that would occur during the day and the worker only has to check the time involved. Figure 7.6 shows a form that may be used by a food service supervisor for self analysis of activities.

JOB DESCRIPTION FOR OWNER-MANAGER

JOB DESCRIPTION NO. 1   TITLE: Owner-Manager

DATE ISSUED: _____   APPROVED BY: _____

I. MANAGERIAL FUNCTIONS

A. *Planning*—Determines the objectives of the enterprise. Plans the organization and direction through supervision, control and coordination of the human resources of the enterprise to accomplish the objectives. Plans for enterprise representation to create a favorable "corporate image" to employees, customers, purveyors, and the public-at-large. Establishes standards of performance in all categories of operations, and measures of deviations therefrom for purpose of evaluation. Plans and promulgates policies, rules and directives to implement the accomplishment of the enterprise objectives.

B. *Organizing*—Analyzes the operation into component task units. Assembles related task units into jobs and formalizes the job with a job description. Draws a job specification from each job description. Provides facilities and designates personnel to train all employees in their respective positions to the standards required by the establishment. Schedules time of employees for the maximum utilization of manpower.

C. *Directing*—Directs the activities of the personnel to meet the standards of the enterprise by:

1. *Supervising*—Determines the effective span of control in each category of work. Assigns jobs to work units (under leaders), and work units to departments (under supervisors). Assigns leaders to work units and supervisors to departments. Supervises to see whether personnel employed meet job specifications and whether individuals are trained to meet the standards of the enterprise for their respective positions. Subrogates responsibility for the performance of assigned tasks to individual employees and the supervision to see whether tasks are performed to the standards of the enterprise to leaders and supervisors. Supervises work of leaders and supervisors to see whether they meet their assigned responsibilities.

2. *Controlling*—Delegates to leaders and supervisors the authority to see that tasks assigned to personnel under their respective direction are performed to meet the standards of the establishment. Controls directly the employment, training, and performance of employees through the supervisory level. Controls other employees at all lower levels strictly through the "chain of command."

3. *Coordinating*—Coordinates the activities of subordinate work units and/or departments. Supervises to see whether and controls to see that leaders and/or supervisors similarly coordinate the work of individuals within their work units and/or departments.

D. *Representing*—Presents and represents the "corporate image" or personality of the establishment to employees, customers, purveyors and the public-at-large.

E. *Evaluating*—Continuously compares the performance of operations and personnel with preselected enterprise standards, measuring deviations from the standards with preselected scales. Analyzes deviations. Takes corrective action indicated by analyses when performance falls below standards, and action to raise standards when superior performance indicates the practicability of so doing.

The results obtained by having a worker record his activities can not always be considered completely accurate. It is unlikely that the worker would record all the delays or rest periods that occur during the day. However, the data can provide information regarding the productive activities performed by the worker and an approximation of the time spent on each activity.

JOB DESCRIPTION FOR OWNER-MANAGER (*Continued*)

II. OPERATIONAL FUNCTIONS

A. *Personnel*—Plans, promulgates, disseminates, supervises, and controls personnel policies with respect to the selection, training, interrelationships, discipline and compensation (including fringe benefits) of all employees. Establishes promotion and merit pay increase policy and administers same. Hires and controls employment tenure of employees through supervisory level, and consults with Assistant Manager on all matters of employee discipline and tenure through leader level. Delegates authority to supervisors and leaders and subrogates responsibility to all levels. Provides channels of communication both upward and downward throughout the organization, including effective means of hearing and acting upon both grievances and suggestions. Establishes facilities for terminal interviews and for a study of the results obtained from them as a step in reducing employee turnover and increasing organization morale.

B. *Financial*—Plans, directs, supervises and controls the financial affairs of the enterprise. Requires the keeping of adequate records to provide information needed for management decisions in financial matters. Retains complete responsibility for the use and flow of working capital. Determines cash withdrawals from and investments by the establishment. Sets menu prices.

C. *Materials*—Plans menus. Forecasts needs for materials used by workers; foodstuffs, supplies, and replacements. Supervises and controls purchasing, delivery, receipt, storage, inventory, processing and service of materials to insure that the right amount of the right material is at the right place at the right time to insure the smooth flow of production and service. May delegate authority and subrogate responsibility for purchasing, receiving, storage, processing and service, but retains the responsibility for the maintenance of establishment standards and the economical utilization of all materials.

D. *Machines*—Conducts a continuing search for machines which will automatize operations economically while maintaining establishment standards in quality production. Makes decisions on whether machines are labor *saving* or labor *aiding*. Conducts a continuing survey for work simplification and layout efficiency improvement. Provides a plan and policy for adequate and systematic equipment maintenance, repair, and replacement.

E. *Methods*—Provides for the uniform excellence of products by the perfection, standardization and production control of recipes and product appearance. Standardizes and controls portion sizes. Supervises whether standards are met and controls that they are met. Sets and supervises policies and standards for sanitation, service, menu substitutions, and the handling of customer complaints. Conducts a continuing study of methods of improving products, service, sanitation, atmosphere, and customer and community relations.

Courtesy of John Welch

**FIG. 7.4. JOB DESCRIPTION FOR OWNER-MANAGER OF A FOOD
SERVICE OPERATION**

Sampling procedures (discussed in Chapter 8) can also be used to gather the data for activity analysis. This method is probably the most frequently used technique today. The sampling study gives a more accurate picture when the activity pattern varies from day to day. This is due to the fact that the sampling is done over a longer period of time. One drawback to the sampling procedure is that the activities must be

ACTIVITY ANALYSIS DATA SHEET

Department _____ Individual _____
Job _____ Description _____
Method of Observation _____ Date _____

Time	Activity Description	Performance Units

FIG. 7.5. FORM USED FOR ACTIVITY ANALYSIS

clearly defined in advance and in some instances this may be difficult.

The use of time-lapse photography (motion pictures taken at a rate of one frame per second) for activity analysis is limited to situations where the workers remain in a small area. This is a convenient but somewhat expensive procedure for data gathering, especially if only one worker is analyzed. This technique is more suitable when a large number of workers are involved in a limited area and the analysis would require more than 1 or 2 visual observers to gather data.

ACTIVITY ANALYSIS FORM

Food Service Supervisor _____ Date _____

Activity	Time						
	7:00	7:10	7:20	7:30	7:40	7:50	8:00
	(Above Time Intervals Extended as Needed for Analysis)						

Organizing
Supervising
Controlling
Personnel training
Financial planning
Menu planning
Purchasing
Sanitation
Food preparation
Employee relations
Scheduling
Personal
Miscellaneous

FIG. 7.6. PREPRINTED FORM FOR SELF ANALYSIS OF ACTIVITIES

Activity Charts

The results of the activity analysis may be presented in the form of activity charts. Activity charts include a breakdown of the activities and the percentage of time required for each activity. A typical activity chart from a study of waitress activities is shown in Fig. 7.7. Figure 7.8 shows the activity chart for the waitresses after new procedures and schedules were installed.

Work Distribution Charts

The work distribution chart is used to display the results of work groups when more detailed information is desired. The work distribution chart shows the relationships between the activities, the work-

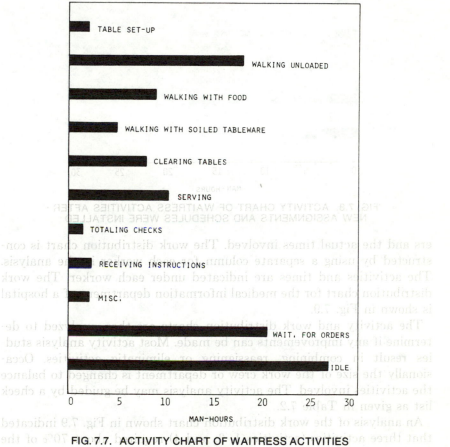

FIG. 7.7. ACTIVITY CHART OF WAITRESS ACTIVITIES BEFORE STUDY

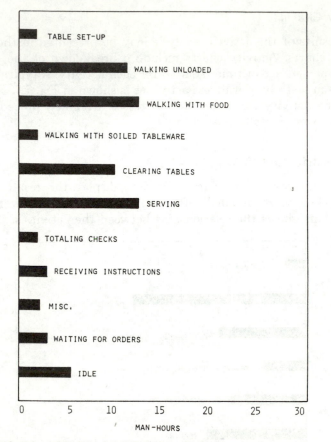

FIG. 7.8. ACTIVITY CHART OF WAITRESS ACTIVITIES AFTER
NEW ASSIGNMENTS AND SCHEDULES WERE INSTALLED

ers and the actual times involved. The work distribution chart is constructed by using a separate column for each worker in the analysis. The activities and times are indicated under each worker. The work distribution chart for the medical information department of a hospital is shown in Fig. 7.9.

The activity and work distribution charts are then analyzed to determine if any improvements can be made. Most activity analysis studies result in combining, reassigning or eliminatig activities. Occasionally the size of the work crew or department is changed to balance the activities involved. The activity analysis may be guided by a check list as given in Table 7.2.

An analysis of the work distribution chart shown in Fig. 7.9 indicated that three activities (activities 1, 3, and 4) required about 70% of the total man hours of the department. Activity 1 (preparing reports) required the most time and was an area where a continuous back log of work occurred. The activity of writing receipts for checks by the junior secretary was unnecessary and could be eliminated. The handling of nonmedical information could be done by another department and was also eliminated from the activities of the junior secretary.

The activity of abstracting lengthy reports required skilled personnel while the preparation of Blue Cross and other reports could be done by less skilled individuals. These activities were reassigned according to the skill required. Related activities were identified and combined.

The handling of incoming telephone calls and keeping departmental records appeared to be spread too thin. These activities were assigned to one individual.

The resultant proposed work distribution chart for the department is shown in Fig. 7.10.

Activity Relationship Charts

Relationship charts are used to show the importance of the closeness of activities. The relationship chart is made by listing all the activities that are involved in a work system and expressing the closeness relationship between all combinations of activities. An activity relationship chart is shown in Fig. 7.11. The desired degree of closeness between the activities is expressed on a relative basis. A letter designation is frequently used for this purpose as follows: (A) absolutely necessary; (B) especially important; (C) important; (D) not important; (X) undesirable.

In addition to indicating the desired closeness it is sometimes desirable to show the reason for closeness. The reasons may be expressed by a number code as: (1) flow; (2) efficient use of personnel; (3) efficient use of equipment; (4) environmental factors (noise, odor, etc.); and (5) efficient use of utilities.

TABLE 7.2 CHECK LIST FOR ACTIVITY ANALYSIS

1. Are the activities appropriate for the function?
2. Can any activities be eliminated or combined?
3. Can similar activities be done in sequence?
4. Are any activities taking too much time to complete?
5. Are the proper skills being used for each activity?
6. Can any activities be reassigned to other workers to balance the work load?
7. Can the activities be done at a different place?
8. Would a different sequence eliminate or facilitate any of the activities?
9. Can any of the activities be aided by the use of equipment?
10. Would better training of the worker simplify the activity?
11. Would increasing or decreasing the number of workers increase the effectiveness of any activities?
12. Can unproductive activities be reduced by changing the arrangement of workplaces and equipment?

(Present)

WORK DISTRIBUTION CHART

DEPARTMENT Medical Information

SECTIONS Input and Reply Sections

CHARTED BY DATE R. T. Rollins 10/24/61

No.	Activity	Hrs per week	R. T. Rollins — Department Head	M. M. Davis — Reply Section Supervisor	A. P. Daly — Senior Secretary	A. Henry — Senior Clerk #1	F. H. Gates — Senior Clerk #2	M. A. Nowell — Junior-Secretary	M. Willard — Clerk Typist #1	J. G. Burns — Clerk Typist #2
1.	Preparing long reports of hospitalization and treatment	98	Abstracts complicated and lengthy reports from medical records — 12	Abstracts complicated and lengthy reports — 13	Abstracts lengthy reports — 9; Takes dictation and types dictation — 14			Takes dictation and types dictation — 15	Types reports — 20	Types reports — 15
2.	Preparing brief reports and summaries	38		Prepares replies to Social Security inquiries — 10; Prepares autopsy letters to next-of-kin — 3; Prepares disability forms replies — 8	Prepares replies for Blue Cross, Red Cross, and other agencies — 6			Prepares replies for Red Cross, etc. — 4; Prepares disability forms replies — 7		
3.	Receiving requests for medical information	48				Reviews incoming mail — 12; Receives telephone requests — 3	Interviews walk-ins — 17; Receives telephone requests — 10	Prepares receipts for checks received — 2	Receives telephone requests — 2	Receives telephone requests — 2

7. Can the activities be done at a different place?

Work Distribution Chart — Medical Information Department (Existing Situation)

No.	Activity	Total hrs/wk	Component tasks (hrs)
4.	Processing requests for medical information	48	Controls processing of medical information requests 13; Handles checks and cash received 3; Requisitions charts 2; Handles delayed reply notices 3; Requisitions charts 4; Handles requests from out-patients re charges paid for clinic visits 4; Locates charts 3; Photocopies summaries 10
5.	Handling inquiries and complaints	7	Handles telephoned complaints 7; 3
6.	Supervision	18	Supervises activity of others 8; Handles personnel matters 2; Spotchecks work of department 4; Answers workers' questions
7.	Miscellaneous	23	Conferences, meetings 4; Maintains departmental records 2; Filing 1; Meetings 4; Maintains statistical records 2; Maintains statistical records 2; Maintains statistical records 2; Messenger duties 1½; Orders and controls department supplies 1½; Filing 8; Types correspondence 10
	Total hours per week	**280**	35	35	35	35	35	35	35	35

FIG. 7.9). WORK DISTRIBUTION CHART FOR MEDICAL INFORMATION DEPARTMENT–EXISTING SITUATION

Reprinted with permission from A.C. Bennett, *Methods Improvement in Hospitals*, J.B. Lippincott Co., Philadelphia.

(Proposed)

WORK DISTRIBUTION CHART

DEPARTMENT
Medical Information

SECTIONS
Input and Reply Sections

CHARTED BY R. T. Rollins   DATE 11/6/61

No.	Activity	Hrs per week	NAME R. T. Rollins POSITION Department Head — Tasks	Hrs per week	NAME M. M. Davis POSITION Reply Section Supervisor — Tasks	Hrs per week	NAME A. Henry POSITION Input Section Supervisor — Tasks	Hrs per week	NAME A. P. Daly POSITION Senior Secretary — Tasks	Hrs per week	NAME F. H. Gates POSITION Senior Clerk — Tasks	Hrs per week	NAME M. A. Nowell POSITION Junior Secretary — Tasks	Hrs per week	NAME M. Willard POSITION Clerk Typist #1 — Tasks	Hrs per week	NAME J. G. Burns POSITION Clerk Typist #2 — Tasks	Hrs per week
1.	Preparing long reports of hospitalization and treatment	103	Abstract complicated and lengthy reports from medical records	17	Abstract complicated and lengthy reports	17			Abstract lengthy reports; Type reports	5; 20			Type reports	20	Type reports	20	Type reports	4
2.	Preparing brief reports and summaries	38			Prepare replies to Social Security inquiries; Prepare autopsy letters to next-of-kin	10; 3			Prepare replies for Blue Cross, Red Cross and other agencies	10			Prepare disability forms replies	15				
3.	Receiving requests for medical information	46					Review incoming mail	12			Interview walk-ins; Receive incoming telephone requests	17; 17						

Work Distribution Chart — Medical Information Department

No.	Activity	Hours	Task breakdown	Hours
4.	Processing requests for medical information	48	Control processing of medical information requests	13
			Handle checks and cash received	3
			Handle delay reply notices	3
			Photocopy summaries	10
			Type correspondence	10
			Requisition and locate charts	9
5.	Handling inquiries and complaints	3	Handle telephoned complaints	3
6.	Supervision	19	Supervise activity of others	4
			Supervise activity of others	4
			Answer workers' questions	4
			Spotcheck work of department	4
			Handle personnel matters	3
7.	Miscellaneous	23	Conferences, meetings	4
			Meetings	4
			Meetings	1
			Supervise maintenance of departmental records	1
			Filing	2
			Messenger duties	1½
			Order and control department supplies	1½
			Assist in maintaining departmental records	2
			Assist in maintaining departmental records	1½
			Filing	4
			Filing	8
			Filing	1½
	Total hours per week	**280**		35 / 35 / 35 / 35 / 35 / 35 / 35 / 35

FIG. 7.10. PROPOSED WORK DISTRIBUTION CHART FOR THE MEDICAL INFORMATION DEPARTMENT

Reprinted with permission from A.C. Bennett, *Methods Improvement in Hospitals*, J.B. Lippincott Co., Philadelphia.

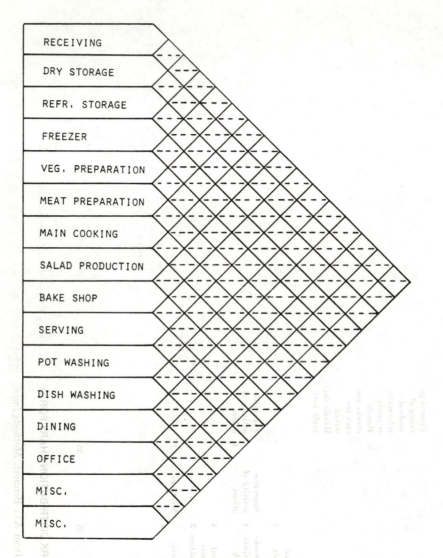

FIG. 7.11. AN ACTIVITY RELATIONSHIP CHART FOR A FOOD SERVICE OPERATION

Sampling Studies

INTRODUCTION

Sampling is a statistical technique for estimating the occurrence of two or more types of activities. It is based on the statistical inference that the characteristics of the total can be estimated by observing the characteristics of a sample taken from the total. For example, assume that the percentage of time a piece of equipment was in use compared to the idle time has to be determined. There are two methods that may be used for this determination. The first method involves making a continuous time study, indicating the times the equipment was in use and when it was idle. The second method would be to make a number of random instantaneous observations, recording whether the equipment was in use or not. These random observations would constitute the samples. The calculated percentage of the idle or working time from the random samples is used as the estimate of the true situation.

The sampling technique can also be used to determine the percentage of more than two activities. In the above example, other factors that could have been estimated, besides the working or idle time, might have been adjustment time, breakdown time, maintenance time and warm-up time of the equipment.

The procedure of sampling applied to a work situation is commonly referred to as work sampling. This commonly used terminology does not indicate all the possible uses of statistical sampling and is therefore somewhat misleading. Sampling studies may be used in any area where measurable quantities such as time, distance, numbers, etc., are available. Thus, sampling can be used to estimate the number of people waiting in line to check in or check out of a hotel, or the number of people and time involved waiting for elevators on various floors of a hotel.

ADVANTAGES AND DISADVANTAGES OF SAMPLING STUDIES

Sampling studies of a problem or situation may be more advantageous

131

than a continuous type of study for the following reasons:

1. A single observer can make a sampling study of several activities or occurrences. The normal procedure in the continuous study is to have one observer per activity being studied.
2. The sampling procedure is more economical, primarily because fewer man hours of observation are required.
3. Since the sampling study is carried out over a longer period of time, there is less chance that day-to-day variations will affect the results.
4. Individuals being observed in the study will behave more normally if randomly timed simultaneous observations rather than continuous observations are made.
5. Special training for making the sample observations is not required. Most supervisors can be quickly trained to be data gatherers for the sampling study.
6. Sampling studies do not require stopwatches or other special equipment.

There are some situations where sampling studies are not the best method to use. Some of these situations are:

1. When detailed information or a very fine breakdown of elements is required, it is best to use a continuous study.
2. When a single activity is being observed, the sampling study is not too economical.
3. Sampling studies should not be used if individuals have difficulty understanding the statistical nature of the procedure.
4. Changes in methods or patterns of activities may not be indicated by the sampling study.

In general, sampling is a much coarser technique than continuous study and should be used accordingly. Fortunately, many of the activities encountered in the hotel, restaurant and institutional field, because of their nonroutine or nonrepetitive nature, are best studied by the sampling technique.

Sampling is based on some fundamental concepts of statistics. Probability, randomness and the normal distribution should be understood to fully appreciate the value of statistical sampling.

PROBABILITY

The laws of probability are related to expected occurrences. For example, if a coin were tossed, the expected occurrence that it would be heads is 50%. In the process of tossing a coin, it is feasible that heads may come up 2 or 3 times in a row. If the coin were tossed only six times, it is highly unlikely that half of the time it would be heads and half the time it would be tails. However, if the coin were tossed 1,000 times, the outcome would be much closer to the 50% heads and 50% tails expected. Hence, the larger number of tosses gives a more accurate result. The same is true for sampling. If few samples are taken, the results may not be very accurate. As the number of samples increases, the accuracy of the sampling study increases.

RANDOMNESS

Randomness refers to a characteristic of the sample. If the sample is not chosen at random, it may not represent the population from which it was drawn. Randomness is achieved when each sample of a given population has an equal chance to be chosen. Samples that are chosen because of personal preference to certain characteristics are said to be biased samples.

The best procedure to follow for obtaining random samples is to use a table of random numbers. A random number table is completely free of bias. A table of five digit random numbers is given in Table 8.1.

The table of random numbers can be used to select random samples for any type of sampling study. This is done by numbering the total population and relating these numbers to the table. If 50 samples were to be taken from a population of 500 people to get an estimate of their average height, each of the 500 people would be assigned a separate number. The 50 individuals to be used as the sample would be the ones whose assigned numbers corresponded to the first 50 numbers read from the random number table. The table of random numbers can be read in any orderly manner, such as left to right, top to bottom or diagonally.

A table of random times can be derived from a table of random numbers. This is done by relating times to numbers. Table 8.2 shows random times that were obtained in this manner.

The table of random times is used in the following way. Assume that 15 random observations are to be made of an activity during an eight-hour work period. The total time population for the eight-hour period includes the times between 8:00 A.M. to 12:00 Noon, and 1:00 P.M. to 5:00 P.M., assuming a one hour lunch period is not to be included in the population. From the table of random times, the first 15 times that correspond to the total time population are used. These random times as selected from Table 8.2 (read vertically—top to bottom) are shown on page 143.

TABLE 8.1
TABLE OF RANDOM DIGITS[1]

10097	32533	76520	13586	34673	54876	80959	09117	39292	74945
37542	04805	64894	74296	24805	24037	20636	10402	00822	91665
08422	68953	19645	09303	23209	02560	15953	34764	35080	33606
99019	02529	09376	70715	38311	31165	88676	74397	04436	27659
12807	99970	80157	36147	64032	36653	98951	16877	12171	76833
66065	74717	34072	76850	36697	36170	65813	39885	11199	29170
31060	10805	45571	82406	35303	42614	86799	07439	23403	09732
85269	77602	02051	65692	68665	74818	73053	85247	18623	88579
63573	32135	05325	47048	90553	57548	28468	28709	83491	25624
73796	45753	03529	64778	35808	34282	60935	20344	35273	88435
98520	17767	14905	68607	22109	40558	60970	93433	50500	73998
11805	05431	39808	27732	50725	68248	29405	24201	52775	67851
83452	99634	06288	98083	13746	70078	18475	40610	68711	77817
88685	40200	86507	58401	36766	67951	90364	76493	29609	11062
99594	67348	87517	64969	91826	08928	93785	61368	23478	34113
65481	17674	17468	50950	58047	76974	73039	57186	40218	16544
80124	35635	17727	08015	45318	22374	21115	78253	14385	53763
74350	99817	77402	77214	43236	00210	45521	64237	96286	02655
69916	26803	66252	29148	36936	87203	76621	13990	94400	56418
09893	20505	14225	68514	46427	56788	96297	78822	54382	14598
91499	14523	68479	27686	46162	83554	94750	89923	37089	20048
80336	94598	26940	36858	70297	34135	53140	33340	42050	82341
44104	81949	85157	47954	32979	26575	57600	40881	22222	06413
12550	73742	11100	02040	12860	74697	96644	89439	28707	25815
63606	49329	16505	34484	40219	52563	43651	77082	07207	31790
61196	90446	26457	47774	51924	33729	65394	59593	42582	60527
15474	45266	95270	79953	59367	83848	82396	10118	33211	59466
94557	28573	67897	54387	54622	44431	91190	42592	92927	45973
42481	16213	97344	08721	16868	48767	03071	12059	25701	46670
23523	78317	73208	89837	68935	91416	26252	29663	05522	82562
04493	52494	75246	33824	45862	51025	61962	79335	65337	12472
00549	97654	64051	88159	96119	63896	54692	82391	23287	29529
35963	15307	26898	09354	33351	35462	77974	50024	90103	39333
59808	08391	45427	26842	83609	49700	13021	24892	78565	20106
46058	85236	01390	92286	77281	44077	93910	83647	70617	42941
32179	00597	87379	25241	05567	07007	86743	17157	85394	11838
69234	61406	20117	45204	15956	60000	18743	92423	97118	96338
19565	41430	01758	75379	40419	21585	66674	36806	84962	85207
45155	14938	19476	07246	43667	94543	59047	90033	20826	69541
94864	31994	36168	10851	34888	81553	01540	35456	05014	51176
98086	24826	45240	28404	44999	08896	39094	73407	35441	31880
33185	16232	41941	50949	89435	48581	88695	41994	37548	73043
80951	00406	96382	70774	20151	23387	25016	25298	94624	61171
79752	49140	71961	28296	69861	02591	74852	20539	00387	59579
18633	32537	98145	06571	31010	24674	05455	61427	77938	91936
74029	43902	77557	32270	97790	17119	52527	58021	80814	51748
54178	45611	80993	37143	05335	12969	56127	19255	36040	90324
11664	49883	52079	84827	59381	71539	09973	33440	88461	23356
48324	77928	31249	64710	02295	36870	32307	57546	15020	09994
69074	94138	87637	91976	35584	04401	10518	21615	01848	76938

TABLE 8.1 (continued)

09188	20097	32825	39527	04220	86304	83389	87374	64278	58044
90045	85497	51981	50654	94938	81997	91870	76150	68476	64659
73189	50207	47677	26269	62290	64464	27124	67018	41361	82760
75768	76490	20971	87749	90429	12272	95375	05871	93823	43178
54016	44056	66281	31003	00682	27398	20714	53295	07706	17813
08358	69910	78542	42785	13661	58873	04618	97553	31223	08420
28306	03264	81333	10591	40510	07893	32604	60475	94119	01840
53840	86233	81594	13628	51215	90290	28466	68795	77762	20791
91757	53741	61613	62269	50263	90212	55781	76514	83483	47055
89415	92694	00397	58391	12607	17646	48949	72306	94541	37408
77513	03820	86864	29901	68414	82774	51908	13980	72893	55507
19502	37174	69979	20288	55210	29773	74287	75251	65344	67415
21818	59313	93278	81757	05686	73156	07082	85046	31853	38452
51474	66499	68107	23621	94049	91345	42836	09191	08007	45449
99559	68331	62535	24170	69777	12830	74819	78142	43860	72834
33713	48007	93584	72869	51926	64721	58303	29822	93174	93972
85274	86893	11303	22970	28834	34137	73515	90400	71148	43643
84133	89640	44035	52166	73852	70091	61222	60561	62327	18423
56732	16234	17395	96131	10123	91622	85496	57560	81604	18880
65138	56806	87648	85261	34313	65861	45875	21069	85644	47277
38001	02176	81719	11711	71602	92937	74219	64049	65584	49698
37402	96397	01304	77586	56271	10086	47324	62605	40030	37438
97125	40348	87083	31417	21815	39250	75237	62047	15501	29578
21826	41134	47143	34072	64638	85902	49139	06441	03856	54552
73135	42742	95719	09035	85794	74296	08789	88156	64691	19202
07638	77929	03061	18072	96207	44156	23821	99538	04713	66994
60528	83441	07954	19814	59175	20695	05533	52139	61212	06455
83596	35655	06958	92983	05128	09719	77433	53783	92301	50498
10850	62746	99599	10507	13499	06319	53075	71839	06410	19362
39820	98952	43622	63147	64421	80814	43800	09351	31024	73167
59580	06478	75569	78800	88835	54486	23768	06156	04111	08408
38508	07341	23793	48763	90822	97022	17719	04207	95954	49953
30692	70668	94688	16127	56196	80091	82067	63400	05462	69200
65443	95659	18288	27437	49632	24041	08337	65676	96299	90836
27267	50264	13192	72294	07477	44606	17985	48911	97341	30358
91307	06991	19072	24210	36699	53728	28825	35793	28976	66252
68434	94688	84473	13622	62126	98408	12843	82590	09815	93146
48908	15877	54745	24591	35700	04754	83824	52692	54130	55160
06913	45197	42672	78601	11883	09528	63011	98901	14974	40344
10455	16019	14210	33712	91342	37821	88325	80851	43667	70883
12883	97343	65027	61184	04285	01392	17974	15077	90712	26769
21778	30976	38807	36961	31649	42096	63281	02023	08816	47449
19523	59515	65122	59659	86283	68258	69572	13798	16435	91529
67245	52670	35583	16563	79246	86686	76463	34222	26655	90802
60584	47377	07500	37992	45134	26529	26760	83637	41326	44344
53853	41377	36066	94850	58838	73859	49364	73331	96240	43642
24637	38736	74384	89342	52623	07992	12369	18601	03742	83873
83080	12451	38992	22815	07759	51777	97377	27585	51972	37867
16444	24334	36151	99073	27493	70939	85130	32552	54846	54759
60790	18157	57178	65762	11161	78576	45819	52979	65130	04860

TABLE 8.1 (*Continued*)

03991	10461	93716	16894	66083	24653	84609	58232	88618	19161
38555	95554	32886	59780	08355	60860	29735	47762	71299	23853
17546	73704	92052	46215	55121	29281	59076	07936	27954	58909
32643	52861	95819	06831	00911	98936	76355	93779	80863	00514
69572	68777	39510	35905	14060	40619	29549	69616	33564	60780
24122	66591	27699	06494	14845	46672	61958	77100	90899	75754
61196	30231	92962	61773	41839	55382	17267	70943	78038	70267
30532	21704	10274	12202	39685	23309	10061	68829	55986	66485
03788	97599	75867	20717	74416	53166	35208	33374	87539	08823
48228	63379	85783	47619	53152	67433	35663	52972	16818	60311
60365	94653	35075	33949	42614	29297	01918	28316	98953	73231
83799	42402	56623	34442	34994	41374	70071	14736	09958	18065
32960	07405	36409	83232	99385	41600	11133	07586	15917	06253
19322	53845	57620	52606	66497	68646	78138	66559	19640	99413
11220	94747	07399	37408	48509	23929	27482	45476	85244	35159
31751	57260	68980	05339	15470	48355	88651	22596	03152	19121
88492	99382	14454	04504	20094	98977	74843	93413	22109	78508
30934	47744	07481	83828	73788	06533	28597	20405	94205	20380
22888	48893	27499	98748	60530	45128	74022	84617	82037	10268
78212	16993	35902	91386	44372	15486	65741	14014	87481	37220
41849	84547	46850	52326	34677	58300	74910	64345	19325	81549
46352	33049	69248	93460	45305	07521	61318	31855	14413	70951
11087	96294	14013	31792	59747	67277	76503	34513	39663	77544
52701	08337	56303	87315	16520	69676	11654	99893	02181	68161
57275	36898	81304	48585	68652	27376	92852	55866	88448	03584
20857	73156	70284	24326	79375	95220	01159	63267	10622	48391
15633	84924	90415	93614	33521	26665	55823	47641	86225	31704
92694	48297	39904	02115	59589	49067	66821	41575	49767	04037
77613	19019	88152	00080	20554	91409	96277	48257	50816	97616
38688	32486	45134	63545	59404	72059	43947	51680	43852	59693
25163	01889	70014	15021	41290	67312	71857	15957	68971	11403
65251	07629	37239	33295	05870	01119	92784	26340	18477	65622
36815	43625	18637	37509	82444	99005	04921	73701	14707	93997
64397	11692	05327	82162	20247	81759	45197	25332	83745	22567
04515	25624	95096	67946	48460	85558	15191	18782	16930	33361
83761	60873	43253	84145	60833	25983	01291	41349	20368	07126
14387	06345	80854	09279	43529	06318	38384	74761	41196	37480
51321	92246	80088	77074	88722	56736	66164	49431	66919	31678
72472	00008	80890	18002	94813	31900	54155	83436	35352	54131
05466	55306	93128	18464	74457	90561	72848	11834	79982	68416
39528	72484	82474	25593	48545	35247	18619	13674	18611	19241
81616	18711	53342	44276	75122	11724	74627	73707	58319	15997
07586	16120	82641	22820	92904	13141	32392	19763	61199	67940
90767	04235	13574	17200	69902	63742	78464	22501	18627	90872
40188	28193	29593	88627	94972	11598	62095	36787	00441	58997
34414	82157	86887	55087	19152	00023	12302	80783	32624	68691
63439	75363	44989	16822	36024	00867	76378	41605	65961	73488
67049	09070	93399	45547	94458	74284	05041	49807	20288	34060
79495	04146	52162	90286	54158	34243	46978	35482	59362	95938
91704	30552	04737	21031	75051	93029	47665	64382	99782	93478

TABLE 8.1 (*Continued*)

94015	46874	32444	48277	59820	96163	64654	25843	41145	42820
74108	88222	88570	74015	25704	91035	01755	14750	48968	38603
62880	87873	95160	59221	22304	90314	72877	17334	39283	04149
11748	12102	80580	41867	17710	59621	06554	07850	73950	79552
17944	05600	60478	03343	25852	58905	57216	39618	49856	99326
66067	42792	95043	52680	46780	56487	09971	59481	37006	22186
54244	91030	45547	70818	59849	96169	61459	21647	87417	17198
30945	57589	31732	57260	47670	07654	46376	25366	94746	49580
69170	37403	86995	90307	94304	71803	26825	05511	12459	91314
08345	88975	35841	85771	08105	59987	87112	21476	14713	71181
27767	43584	85301	88977	29490	69714	73035	41207	74699	09310
13025	14338	54066	15243	47724	66733	47431	43905	31048	56699
80217	36292	98525	24335	24432	24896	43277	58874	11466	16082
10875	62004	90391	61105	57411	06368	53856	30743	08670	84741
54127	57326	26629	19087	24472	88779	30540	27886	61732	75454
60311	42824	37301	42678	45990	43242	17374	52003	70707	70214
49739	71484	92003	98086	76668	73209	59202	11973	02902	33250
78626	51594	16453	94614	39014	97066	83012	09832	25571	77628
66692	13986	99837	00582	81232	44987	09504	96412	90193	79568
44071	28091	07362	97703	76447	42537	98524	97831	65704	09514
41468	85149	49554	17994	14924	39650	95294	00556	70481	06905
94559	37559	49678	53119	70312	05682	66986	34099	74474	20740
41615	70360	64114	58660	90850	64618	80620	51790	11436	38072
50273	93113	41794	86861	24781	89683	55411	85667	77535	99892
41396	80504	90670	08289	40902	05069	95083	06783	28102	57816
25807	24260	71529	78920	72682	07385	90726	57166	98884	08583
06170	97965	88302	98041	21443	41808	68984	83620	89747	98882
60808	54444	74412	81105	01176	28838	36421	16489	18059	51061
80940	44893	10408	36222	80582	71944	92638	40333	67054	16067
19516	90120	46759	71643	13177	55292	21036	82808	77501	97427
49386	54480	23604	23554	21785	41101	91178	10174	29420	90438
06312	88940	15995	69321	47458	64809	98189	81851	29651	84215
60942	00307	11897	92674	40405	68032	96717	54244	10701	41393
92329	98932	78284	46347	71209	92061	39448	93136	25722	08564
77936	63574	31384	51924	85561	29671	58137	17820	22751	36518
38101	77756	11657	13897	95889	57067	47648	13885	70669	93406
39641	69457	91339	22502	92613	89719	11947	56203	19324	20504
84054	40455	99396	63680	67667	60631	69181	96845	38525	11600
47468	03577	57649	63266	24700	71594	14004	23153	69249	05747
43321	31370	28977	23896	76479	68562	62342	07589	08899	05985
64281	61826	18555	64937	13173	33365	78851	16499	87064	13075
66847	70495	32350	02985	86716	38746	26313	77463	55387	72681
72461	33230	21529	53424	92581	02262	78438	66276	18396	73538
21032	91050	13058	16218	12470	56500	15292	76139	59526	52113
95362	67011	06651	16136	01016	00857	55018	56374	35824	71704
49712	97380	10404	55452	34030	60726	75211	10271	36633	68424
58275	61764	97586	54716	50259	46345	87195	46092	26787	60939
89514	11788	68224	23417	73959	76145	30342	40277	11049	72049
15472	50669	48139	36732	46874	37088	73465	09819	58869	35220
12120	86124	51247	44302	60883	52109	21437	36786	49226	77837

TABLE 8.1 (*Continued*)

19612	78430	11661	94770	77603	65669	**86868**	12665	30012	75989
39141	77400	28000	64238	73258	71794	31340	26256	66453	37016
64756	80457	08747	12836	03469	50678	03274	43423	66677	82556
92901	51878	56441	22998	29718	38447	06453	25311	07565	53771
03551	90070	09483	94050	45938	18135	36908	43321	11073	51803
98884	66209	06830	53656	14663	56346	71430	04909	19818	05707
27369	86882	53473	07541	53633	70863	03748	12822	19360	49088
59066	75974	63335	20483	43514	37481	58278	26967	49325	43951
91647	93783	64169	49022	98588	09495	49829	59068	38831	04838
83605	92419	39542	07772	71568	75673	35185	89759	44901	74291
24895	88530	70774	35439	46758	70472	70207	92675	91623	61275
35720	26556	95596	20094	73750	85788	34264	01703	46833	65248
14141	53410	38649	06343	57256	61342	72709	75318	90379	37562
27416	75670	92176	72535	93119	56077	06886	18244	92344	31374
82071	07429	81007	47749	40744	56974	23336	88821	53841	10536
21445	82793	24831	93241	14199	76268	70883	68002	03829	17443
72513	76400	52225	92348	62308	98481	29744	33165	33141	61020
71479	45027	76160	57411	13780	13632	52308	77762	88874	33697
83210	51466	09088	50395	26743	05306	21706	70001	99439	80767
68749	95148	94897	78636	96750	09024	94538	91143	96693	61886
05184	75763	47075	88158	05313	53439	14908	08830	60096	21551
13651	62546	96892	25240	47511	58483	87342	78818	07855	39269
00566	21220	00292	24069	25072	29519	52548	54091	21282	21296
50958	17695	58072	68990	60329	95955	71586	63417	35947	67807
57621	64547	46850	37981	38527	09037	64756	03324	04986	83666
09282	25844	79139	78435	35428	43561	69799	63314	12991	93516
23394	94206	93432	37836	94919	26846	02555	74410	94915	48199
05280	37470	93622	04345	15092	19510	18094	16613	78234	50001
95491	97976	38306	32192	82639	54624	72434	92606	23191	74693
78521	00104	18248	75583	90326	50785	54034	66251	35774	14692
96345	44579	85932	44053	75704	20840	86583	83944	52456	73766
77963	31151	32364	91691	47357	40338	23435	24065	08458	95366
07520	11294	23238	01748	41690	67328	54814	37777	10057	42332
38423	02309	70703	85736	46148	14258	29236	12152	05088	65825
02463	65533	21199	60555	33928	01817	07396	89215	30722	22102
15880	92261	17292	88190	61781	48898	92525	21283	88581	60098
71926	00819	59144	00224	30570	90194	18329	06999	26857	19238
64425	28108	16554	16016	00042	83229	10333	36168	65617	94834
79782	23924	49440	30432	81077	31543	95216	64865	13658	51081
35337	74538	44553	64672	90960	41849	93865	44608	93176	34851
05249	29329	19715	94082	14738	86667	43708	66354	93692	25527
56463	99380	38793	85774	19056	13939	46062	27647	66146	63210
96296	33121	54196	34108	75814	85986	71171	15102	28992	63165
98380	36269	60014	07201	62448	46385	42175	88350	46182	49126
52567	64350	16315	53969	80395	81114	54358	64578	47269	15747
78498	90830	25955	99236	43286	91064	99969	95144	64424	77377
49553	24241	08150	89535	08703	91041	77323	81079	45127	93686
32151	07075	83155	10252	73100	88618	23891	87418	45417	20268
11314	50363	26860	27799	49416	83534	19187	08059	76677	02110
12364	71210	87052	50241	90785	97889	81399	58130	64439	05614

TABLE 8.1 (*Continued*)

59467 58309	87834 57213	37510 33689	01259 62486	56320 46265
73452 17619	56421 40725	23439 41701	93223 41682	45026 47505
27635 56293	91700 04391	67317 89604	73020 69853	61517 51207
86040 02596	01655 09918	45161 00222	54577 74821	47335 08582
52403 94255	26351 46527	68224 90183	85057 72310	34963 83462
49465 46581	61499 04844	94626 02963	41482 83879	44942 63915
94365 92560	12363 30246	02086 75036	88620 91088	67691 67762
34261 08769	91830 23313	18256 28850	37639 92748	57791 71328
37110 66538	39318 15626	44324 82827	08782 65960	58167 01305
83950 45424	72453 19444	68219 64733	94088 62006	89985 36936
61630 97966	76537 46467	30942 07479	67971 14558	22458 35148
01929 17165	12037 74558	16250 71750	55546 29693	94984 37782
41659 39098	23982 29899	71594 77979	54477 13764	17315 72893
32031 39608	75992 73445	01317 50525	87313 45191	30214 19769
90043 93478	58044 06949	31176 88370	50274 83987	45316 38551
79418 14322	91065 07841	36130 86602	10659 40859	00964 71577
85447 61079	96910 72906	07361 84338	34114 52096	66715 51091
86219 81115	49625 48799	89485 24855	13684 68433	70595 70102
71712 88559	92476 32903	68009 58417	87962 11787	16644 72964
29776 63075	13270 84758	49560 10317	28778 23006	31036 84906
81488 17340	74154 42801	27917 89792	62604 62234	13124 76471
51667 37589	87147 24743	48023 06325	79794 35889	13255 04925
99004 70322	60832 76636	56907 56534	72615 46288	36788 93196
68656 66492	35933 52293	47953 95495	95304 50009	83464 28608
38074 74083	09337 07965	65047 36871	59015 21769	30398 44855
01020 80680	59328 08712	48190 45332	27284 31287	66011 09376
86379 74508	33579 77114	92955 23085	92824 03054	25242 16322
48498 09938	44420 13484	52319 58875	02012 88591	52500 95795
41800 95363	54142 17482	32705 60564	12505 40954	46174 64130
63026 96712	79883 39225	52653 69549	36693 59822	22684 31661
88298 15489	16030 42480	15372 38781	71995 77438	91161 10192
07839 62735	99218 25624	02547 27445	69187 55749	32322 15504
73298 51108	48717 92926	75705 89787	96114 99902	37749 96305
12829 70474	00838 50385	91711 80370	56504 56857	80906 09018
76569 61072	48568 36491	22587 44363	39592 61546	90181 37348
41665 41339	62106 44203	06732 76111	79840 67999	32231 76869
58652 49983	01669 27464	79553 52855	25988 18087	38052 17529
13607 00657	76173 43357	77334 24140	53860 02906	89863 44651
55715 26203	65933 51087	98234 40625	45545 63563	89148 82581
04110 66683	99001 09796	47349 65003	66524 81970	71262 14479
31300 08681	58068 44115	40064 77879	23965 69019	73985 19453
26225 97543	37044 07494	85778 35345	61115 92498	49737 64599
07158 82763	25072 38478	57782 75291	62155 52056	04786 11585
71251 25572	79771 93328	66927 54069	58752 26624	50463 77361
29991 96526	02820 91659	12818 96356	49499 01507	40223 09171
83642 21057	02677 09367	38097 16100	19355 06120	15378 56559
69167 30235	06767 66323	78294 14916	19124 88044	16673 66102
86018 29406	75415 22038	27056 26906	25867 14751	92380 30434
44114 06026	79553 55091	95385 41212	37882 46864	54717 97038
53805 64150	70915 63127	63695 41288	38192 72437	75075 18570

TABLE 8.2
TABLE OF RANDOM TIMES

2:18	8:45	3:41	3:12	5:59	8:50	7:14	7:05	11:44
9:36	12:56	1:11	6:30	6:35	7:05	1:28	12:09	12:26
7:22	1:09	12:51	8:18	1:01	4:18	2:10	11:01	2:31
7:28	6:52	11:19	8:21	12:19	8:35	9:42	2:40	8:06
9:57	5:04	8:02	1:41	12:01	10:12	4:41	5:49	9:04
12:50	12:06	10:12	7:53	5:20	11:54	6:21	9:30	1:06
8:08	7:48	8:27	2:28	8:03	7:42	3:30	7:25	4:32
7:53	4:36	3:32	7:36	8:55	8:24	9:40	6:37	6:35
10:42	5:57	5:23	5:01	7:37	3:47	8:05	1:22	12:08
6:12	11:05	3:53	2:54	2:30	12:20	6:15	10:30	7:39
11:40	8:37	1:12	10:27	11:58	8:31	8:49	1:11	8:41
11:16	7:25	7:31	4:25	3:40	9:45	7:13	6:02	8:13
8:18	4:21	3:08	12:09	10:29	3:58	5:53	6:27	2:57
11:19	9:52	6:53	4:26	7:59	11:25	1:29	1:14	12:30
10:07	5:31	10:48	5:37	11:06	7:35	4:07	12:41	3:20
10:47	6:16	11:15	7:42	6:16	1:17	8:30	3:16	7:45
10:31	5:41	7:43	9:34	10:30	11:50	2:48	9:00	6:37
4:38	9:05	10:14	4:05	1:22	4:01	2:20	5:57	3:41
1:21	12:50	4:06	6:23	7:26	2:07	9:59	12:41	7:55
1:26	1:58	7:08	1:17	1:41	3:04	8:37	5:31	11:00
2:52	8:08	1:12	11:36	8:21	7:30	1:59	12:53	8:11
12:37	10:25	5:47	10:22	10:04	3:46	10:10	11:09	10:30
10:52	6:32	7:12	9:30	4:24	6:11	11:41	11:22	5:00
6:06	3:59	12:35	1:45	3:47	11:20	4:01	12:58	5:33
7:53	8:14	3:40	1:28	2:04	10:28	2:35	4:14	3:40
6:16	2:22	3:59	11:12	1:43	8:31	6:48	1:47	10:43
11:08	7:57	12:01	1:03	1:51	2:50	11:36	10:02	9:09
8:10	11:20	8:45	12:40	5:51	1:01	8:07	9:07	2:09
7:56	8:13	10:46	11:21	10:32	6:04	10:22	6:22	7:51
4:59	12:53	7:30	2:16	9:31	6:34	5:36	12:13	10:58
3:28	4:37	2:09	3:50	1:51	5:23	5:31	1:51	7:37
2:42	3:17	6:33	1:08	9:40	9:42	11:01	12:04	1:48
1:17	8:06	5:24	7:39	1:35	11:52	6:08	8:33	6:57
6:26	6:45	3:26	10:52	1:07	11:04	8:56	8:30	2:40
11:06	8:32	6:52	5:56	11:07	10:00	11:04	3:06	5:23
4:03	2:25	8:28	10:19	4:30	3:35	10:56	4:20	2:18

TABLE 8.2 (Continued)

2:12	8:30	5:48	7:18	1:22	10:19	6:33	5:54	12:50
9:42	11:33	10:26	6:16	9:54	10:37	3:32	1:05	8:10
1:45	4:03	7:58	12:37	11:06	9:38	7:50	1:55	1:09
10:34	1:19	5:48	12:32	1:07	1:52	3:20	3:46	12:18
3:17	2:11	12:08	12:59	1:42	9:51	11:12	5:14	11:41
1:37	1:41	1:15	3:05	8:20	5:18	7:34	3:09	5:13
3:16	7:06	4:19	9:48	8:51	10:52	12:35	5:59	4:49
1:52	7:00	7:00	8:07	4:11	1:33	4:07	5:11	11:38
6:49	6:32	5:09	9:38	3:42	9:59	11:47	2:05	9:27
7:29	7:33	5:47	12:42	4:27	7:24	3:58	8:35	10:25
6:10	4:11	8:18	5:54	7:11	5:04	3:14	3:30	6:20
1:28	2:25	12:13	2:48	2:45	4:46	9:09	3:23	10:27
11:01	5:12	7:26	7:21	4:25	3:52	10:41	12:25	3:21
5:31	2:31	4:08	9:51	9:14	9:46	7:05	7:07	7:01
1:42	9:06	7:25	8:56	12:21	1:23	8:18	7:47	11:07
3:05	12:34	8:27	1:55	2:33	9:39	4:31	3:08	6:33
5:28	12:27	6:50	7:10	12:36	8:20	8:31	10:08	4:20
8:10	3:48	1:25	5:25	10:26	8:26	1:13	7:11	10:52
4:01	11:15	9:46	8:06	3:29	6:49	2:38	3:45	7:46
5:11	4:49	10:32	6:18	10:01	8:10	7:58	10:43	8:22
6:17	12:03	2:29	1:57	2:14	8:47	11:53	6:20	10:45
4:18	9:34	9:08	4:38	4:14	4:27	12:51	1:17	11:56
9:45	10:52	12:08	11:40	10:30	10:32	11:26	8:25	9:18
6:21	11:49	10:00	11:23	4:24	11:39	12:30	10:17	7:41
1:01	5:26	9:37	3:07	11:20	7:34	5:12	4:08	5:58
12:54	5:40	6:31	3:29	3:31	2:05	6:44	5:52	2:33
9:06	8:12	11:54	4:15	2:31	10:35	7:09	8:28	9:53
10:04	10:20	12:20	1:42	11:14	5:54	2:44	3:35	12:31
11:27	7:36	5:17	5:44	12:08	5:18	4:19	3:18	6:49
8:47	6:21	12:34	7:47	9:08	12:32	3:55	11:17	7:07
4:13	4:44	1:54	2:59	11:02	11:32	3:05	12:01	3:36
2:40	2:17	8:36	12:39	7:08	3:01	9:47	7:27	2:50
5:23	11:56	10:15	1:18	8:22	10:31	10:19	5:47	8:37
1:23	5:01	3:27	7:32	2:55	1:11	3:17	12:12	2:57
3:12	3:40	12:06	7:49	3:55	7:37	10:58	5:50	6:39
5:40	11:57	12:40	11:25	11:01	8:05	1:04	1:57	8:34
4:39	12:43	5:11	5:59	11:08	5:16	10:09	7:07	7:44
4:11	5:20	3:05	8:03	1:54	8:35	12:48	12:17	7:14
6:29	4:40	4:04	5:25	5:20	4:09	11:46	4:53	11:03

TABLE 8.2 (Continued)

9:24	3:08	9:11	7:06	1:22	12:37	4:16	3:56	4:45
7:40	12:43	6:17	1:54	7:47	5:06	11:31	8:12	8:20
8:29	7:27	12:39	4:09	10:55	8:35	11:19	7:30	11:50
3:52	5:47	8:59	1:46	1:57	2:13	8:59	1:15	11:32
2:02	9:01	1:34	8:50	2:05	5:46	8:07	10:43	12:31
10:00	8:32	7:53	6:59	12:55	9:36	8:20	1:24	7:04
1:04	9:30	3:06	10:44	8:02	4:39	1:12	8:37	1:38
5:09	5:37	12:35	5:41	2:06	4:48	8:55	5:29	7:51
12:10	8:25	8:28	12:22	6:38	1:06	2:52	5:20	11:40
4:25	2:11	11:49	1:05	7:39	10:40	8:13	11:14	1:46
8:54	3:35	11:30	5:08	5:21	10:38	8:30	8:42	8:21
6:59	10:59	12:15	10:31	12:44	8:32	2:22	9:18	10:39
7:33	4:19	8:19	6:15	8:01	3:35	6:55	11:11	2:02
2:19	3:15	1:36	12:54	7:11	1:03	4:40	4:41	1:47
2:27	8:57	9:41	6:07	3:00	2:21	7:39	12:05	4:25
3:29	11:55	12:00	2:39	1:03	12:24	12:18	11:38	2:47
12:53	7:11	3:20	1:07	6:09	10:37	1:18	8:02	8:52
12:11	1:30	10:34	11:31	1:28	12:01	11:29	5:12	8:03
10:08	7:13	6:33	2:00	8:26	4:21	10:20	7:35	7:14
10:05	9:48	8:14	1:02	11:16	11:47	10:53	7:59	4:35
1:20	5:23	8:48	9:58	9:44	6:31	9:38	4:53	4:58
3:56	7:15	6:49	11:58	4:29	1:00	12:51	10:29	12:26
4:44	4:48	5:15	11:08	5:11	4:19	9:05	12:55	9:57
3:26	3:51	4:18	4:25	9:31	5:44	1:35	6:59	3:25
1:41	6:52	3:48	6:34	8:52	10:17	10:57	9:41	11:42

2:18	11:19
9:36	10:07
9:57	10:47
8:08	10:31
10:42	4:38
11:40	4:21
11:16	1:26
8:18	

Note that the times from the table that are not in the prescribed total time population are discarded. Once the random times are selected they may be oriented chronologically as shown below:

8:08	11:16
8:18	11:19
9:36	11:40
9:57	1:26
10:07	2:18
10:31	4:21
10:42	4:38
10:47	

Thus the 15 observations for the sampling study are made according to this time schedule.

Normal Distribution

The normal curve describes a frequency distribution that represents the probability of certain chance occurrences. A normal curve is shown in Fig. 8.1.

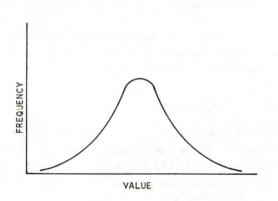

FIG. 8.1. THE NORMAL DISTRIBUTION CURVE

A perfect normal curve has the characteristic of being symmetrical about the center. The value at the center is referred to as the mean since it represents the greatest frequency of occurrence. There is also a relationship in the normal curve between the areas under the curve and the distances measured to either side of the mean. Figure 8.2 shows three of the area-to-distance relationships for a normal curve. The distances on either side of the mean value are referred to as standard deviations.

In the upper illustration of Fig. 8.2, the shaded area represents 68.27% of the total area under the curve. Its corresponding distance is referred to as one standard deviation (1 S.D.) on either side of the mean. The middle illustration shows the area under the curve corresponding to two standard deviations. This area will be 95.45% of the total area under the curve. The lower illustration shows the area under the curve to be 99.73% at three standard deviations.

The relations between the areas under the curve and the standard deviations are used to determine the validity of sampling studies. The validity of the study is expressed as the confidence level.

Confidence Level

The confidence level of a sampling study expresses the percentage of times that the random samples represent the facts. A confidence level of 95% indicates that the probability of the samples representing the true facts is 95%. In other words, there is a 5% chance that the samples will not represent the true facts. The confidence level of 95% (actually 95.45% rounded off to 95%) corresponds to the area under the normal curve at 2 standard deviations. One standard deviation results in a confidence level of approximately 68%. This indicates that the sampling study will represent the facts 68% of the time, and that 32% of the time it would not.

The confidence level has to determined before the sampling is begun since the total number of samples is dependent on it. For most studies, a confidence level of 95% is usually chosen.

Accuracy of Sampling Study

Another statistical characteristic of sampling studies is the accuracy. Accuracy describes the allowable tolerance limits of the study within the desired confidence level. The accuracy is a direct function of the number of samples taken. The greater the number of samples, the greater the accuracy of the study.

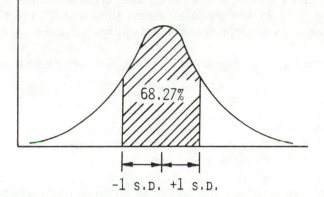

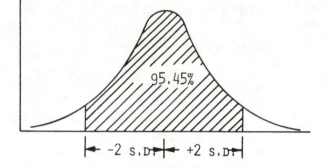

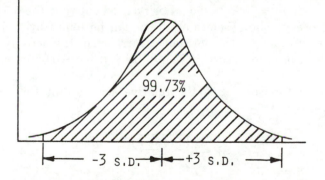

FIG. 8.2. AREA–DISTANCE RELATIONSHIPS OF THE
NORMAL DISTRIBUTION CURVE

Accuracy and confidence level are stated together. Thus a 5% accuracy with 95% confidence level means that 95% of the time the results of the study will represent the facts with a tolerance of ±5%.

The formula for calculating accuracy at the 95% confidence level is:

$$SP = 2 \sqrt{\frac{P(1-P)}{N}}$$

where   S = Relative accuracy expressed as a decimal
P = Percent occurrence of an activity expressed as a decimal
N = Total number of samples

Example.—Assume that the measured occurrence of an activity by sampling is 40% as determined by taking 2,000 samples. Therefore: P=0.40 and N=2000

Substituting into the equation:

$$S(0.40) = 2 \sqrt{\frac{(0.40)(1-0.40)}{2000}}$$

$$S(0.40) = 2 \sqrt{0.00012}$$

$$S = 2 \frac{(\pm 0.01095)}{0.40}$$

$$S = \pm 0.055 \text{ or } \pm 5.5\%$$

Therefore it can be stated that 95% of the time, the measured activity will be accurate to ±5.5%. It should be pointed out that the 5.5% is the relative accuracy. The absolute accuracy can be found by multiplying the relative accuracy by the per cent occurrence of the activity. In this example the absolute accuracy would be 0.40 × ±0.055=±0.022 or ±2.2%.

The formula for calculating the relative accuracy at the 68% confidence level is:

$$SP = \sqrt{\frac{P(1-P)}{N}}$$

Using the same assumptions as in the previous example, that is P=0.40 and N=2000, the calculation would be:

$$S(0.40) = \sqrt{\frac{(0.40)(1 - 0.40)}{2000}}$$

$$S(0.40) = \sqrt{0.00012}$$

$$S = \frac{\pm 0.01095}{0.40}$$

$$S = \pm 0.027 \text{ or } \pm 2.7\%$$

Therefore it can be stated that 68% of the time, the measured activity will represent the facts within a relative accuracy of ±2.7%.

PROCEDURE FOR CONDUCTING SAMPLING STUDIES

The procedure for a sampling study can be divided into ten basic steps:
1. Define the problem and state objectives of study.
2. Determine the limits of the study, confidence level and accuracy.
3. Make preliminary percentage estimates of activities that are to be studied.
4. Determine total number of samples to be taken.
5. Select the samples or determine the random observation times if needed.
6. Design the data sheet.
7. Taking the samples or observations.
8. Summarizing the data.
9. Checking the accuracy of the study.
10. Evaluating the results of the study.

Defining the Problem

Considerable thought should be given to describing in detail the problem or problems to be studied. A little extra time spent in this first step usually leads to a well designed and efficient sampling study.

The problem at hand may be very simple such as determining the productivity of a baker, or it may be complex such as determining the usage of several pieces of kitchen equipment.

Setting Limits of the Study

Once the problem has been defined, the statistical limits such as confidence level and accuracy should be decided. It should be remembered that both the confidence level and the accuracy affect the total number of samples that will be involved.

A general guide can be given for selecting the proper confidence level for certain types of studies. If the purpose of the study is to spot trouble areas; to get a preliminary idea of an activity occurrence; or to obtain a general picture of utilization; a confidence level of 68% is satisfactory. Such studies are usually conducted in the accuracy range of ±3% to ±10%. The number of samples in this situation would not be too large.

If the purpose of the study is to get an accurate estimate of an activity occurrence, or perhaps to get more specific and detailed information on utilization or delays, then a confidence level of 95% should be used. A great majority of the sampling studies are carried out at the 95% confidence level. Accuracy ranges for such studies are between ±1% and ±5%.

There would be very few studies encountered in the hotel and restaurant field that would demand a confidence level higher than 95% or an accuracy better than ±1%. Studies requiring extreme confidence or accuracy are best studied by other techniques.

Making Preliminary Estimates of Expected Activities

A preliminary estimate of the percentage of each of the activities to be studied must be made prior to determining the total number of samples to be used. This estimate is best obtained by taking a preliminary 100 to 200 random samples of the activities and determining the percentages involved. These preliminary samples should not be discarded but used in the total number of samples. In other words, some sampling has to be done before the actual total number of samples can be determined.

Determining the Required Number of Samples

The total number of samples required for a study depends on the estimated percentage of the activity to be studied, the confidence level and the accuracy. The same equations that were used to determine the accuracy are rearranged and used to calculate the number of samples required.

The equation for determining the number of samples for the 95% confidence level is:

$$N = 4\,\frac{(1 - P)}{S^2 P}$$

where   N = Number of samples
P = Per cent occurrence of the activity expressed as a decimal
S = Relative accuracy expressed as a decimal

Example.—Assume the estimated percentage of the activity to be measured is 30% and the desired accuracy is ±4% at the 95% confidence level.

Substituting into the equation:

$$N = 4 \ \frac{(1 - 0.30)}{(0.04)^2(0.30)}$$

$$N = 4 \ \frac{(0.70)}{(.0016)(0.30)}$$

$$N = 5{,}833 \text{ samples}$$

The equation for determining the number of samples at the 68% confidence level is:

$$N = \frac{(1 - P)}{S^2 P}$$

Example.—Again assume that the estimated percentage of the activity is 30% and the desired accuracy is ±4%, but at the 68% confidence level.

$$N = \frac{(1 - 0.30)}{(0.04)^2(0.30)}$$

$$N = \frac{(0.70)}{(.0016)(0.30)}$$

$$N = 1{,}458 \text{ samples}$$

The above examples also point out that four times as many samples are needed for the 95% confidence level compared to the 68% confidence level.

Since a majority of sampling studies are carried out at the 95% confidence level, Table 8.3, which gives the number of samples, has been provided to eliminate the computations at this level.

Selecting Samples and Determining the Random Observation Times

Some sampling studies require merely a given number of samples to be taken from a large population and do not involve time directly. For example, assume the objective of a study is to determine the average height of workers for purposes of designing work surfaces. The sample is composed of individuals selected at random and the only observation

TABLE 8.3

TABLE FOR DETERMINING THE NUMBER OF OBSERVATIONS FOR A GIVEN DEGREE OF ACCURACY AND VALUE OF p, 95% CONFIDENCE LEVEL

Per Cent of Total Time Occupied by Activity or Delay p	Degree of Accuracy									
	±1	±2	±3	±4	±5	±6	±7	±8	±9	±10
1	3,960,000	990,000	440,000	247,500	158,400	110,000	80,800	61,900	48,000	39,600
2	1,960,000	490,000	217,800	122,500	78,400	54,400	40,000	30,600	24,200	19,600
3	1,293,300	323,300	143,700	80,800	51,700	35,900	26,400	20,200	16,000	12,900
4	960,000	240,000	106,700	60,000	38,400	26,700	19,600	15,000	11,900	9,600
5	760,000	190,000	84,400	47,500	30,400	21,100	15,500	11,900	9,390	7,600
6	626,700	156,700	69,600	39,100	25,100	17,400	12,800	9,790	7,790	6,270
7	531,400	132,900	59,000	33,200	21,300	14,800	10,800	8,300	6,560	5,310
8	460,000	115,000	51,100	28,800	18,400	12,800	9,380	7,190	5,680	4,600
9	404,400	101,100	44,900	25,300	16,200	11,200	8,250	6,320	5,000	4,040
10	260,000	90,000	40,000	22,500	14,400	10,000	7,310	5,630	4,450	3,600
11	323,600	80,900	36,000	20,200	12,900	8,990	6,600	5,060	4,000	3,240
12	293,300	73,300	32,600	18,300	11,700	8,150	5,980	4,580	3,620	2,930
13	267,700	66,900	29,700	16,700	10,700	7,440	5,460	4,180	3,310	2,680
14	245,700	61,400	27,300	15,400	9,830	6,830	5,010	3,840	3,040	2,460
15	226,700	56,700	25,200	14,200	9,070	6,300	4,620	3,540	2,800	2,270
16	210,000	52,500	23,300	13,100	8,400	5,830	4,280	3,280	2,590	2,100
17	195,300	48,800	21,700	12,200	7,810	5,420	3,980	3,050	2,410	1,950
18	182,200	45,600	20,200	11,400	7,290	5,060	3,720	2,850	2,250	1,820
19	170,500	42,600	18,900	10,700	6,820	4,740	3,480	2,660	2,110	1,710
20	160,000	40,000	17,800	10,000	6,400	4,440	3,260	2,500	1,980	1,600
21	150,500	37,600	16,700	9,400	6,020	4,180	3,070	2,350	1,860	1,510
22	141,800	35,500	15,800	8,860	5,670	3,940	2,890	2,220	1,750	1,420
23	133,900	33,500	14,900	8,370	5,360	3,720	2,730	2,090	1,650	1,340
24	126,700	31,700	14,100	7,920	5,070	3,520	2,580	1,980	1,560	1,270
25	120,000	30,000	13,300	7,500	4,800	3,330	2,450	1,880	1,480	1,200
26	113,800	28,500	12,600	7,120	4,550	3,160	2,320	1,780	1,410	1,140
27	108,100	27,000	12,000	6,760	4,330	3,000	2,210	1,690	1,340	1,080
28	102,900	25,700	11,400	6,430	4,110	2,860	2,100	1,610	1,270	1,030
29	97,900	24,500	10,900	6,120	3,920	2,720	2,000	1,530	1,210	980
30	93,300	23,300	10,400	5,830	3,730	2,590	1,900	1,460	1,150	935
31	89,000	22,300	9,890	5,570	3,560	2,470	1,820	1,390	1,100	890
32	85,000	21,300	9,440	5,310	3,400	2,360	1,730	1,330	1,050	850
33	81,200	20,300	9,000	5,080	3,250	2,260	1,660	1,270	1,000	810
34	77,600	19,400	8,630	4,850	3,110	2,160	1,580	1,210	960	775
35	74,300	18,600	8,250	4,640	2,970	2,060	1,520	1,160	915	745
36	71,100	17,800	7,900	4,440	2,840	1,980	1,450	1,110	880	710
37	68,100	17,000	7,570	4,260	2,720	1,890	1,400	1,060	840	680
38	65,300	16,300	7,250	4,080	2,610	1,810	1,330	1,020	805	655
39	62,600	15,600	6,950	3,910	2,500	1,740	1,280	986	775	625
40	60,000	15,000	6,670	3,750	2,400	1,670	1,220	940	740	600
41	57,600	14,400	6,400	3,600	2,300	1,600	1,170	900	710	575
42	55,200	13,800	6,140	3,450	2,210	1,530	1,130	865	680	550
43	53,000	13,300	5,890	3,310	2,120	1,470	1,080	830	655	530
44	50,900	12,700	5,660	3,180	2,040	1,410	1,010	795	630	510
45	48,900	12,200	5,430	3,060	1,960	1,360	1,000	765	605	490

46	47,000	11,700	5,220	2,940	1,880	1,300	960	735	580	470
47	45,100	11,300	5,010	2,820	1,800	1,250	920	705	555	450
48	43,300	10,800	4,810	2,710	1,730	1,200	885	675	535	435
49	41,600	10,400	4,630	2,600	1,670	1,160	850	650	515	415
50	40,000	10,000	4,440	2,500	1,600	1,110	815	625	495	400
51	38,430	9,610	4,270	2,400	1,540	1,070	785	600	475	385
52	36,020	9,230	4,100	2,310	1,480	1,030	755	575	455	370
53	35,470	8,870	3,940	2,220	1,420	985	725	555	435	355
54	34,070	8,520	3,790	2,130	1,360	945	695	530	420	340
55	32,730	8,180	3,640	2,050	1,310	910	670	510	405	325
56	31,430	7,860	3,490	1,960	1,260	870	640	490	390	315
57	30,180	7,550	3,350	1,890	1,210	840	615	470	375	300
58	28,970	7,240	3,220	1,810	1,160	805	590	450	360	290
59	27,800	6,950	3,090	1,740	1,110	770	565	435	345	280
60	26,670	6,670	2,960	1,670	1,070	740	545	415	330	265
61	25,570	6,390	2,840	1,600	1,020	710	520	400	315	255
62	24,520	6,130	2,720	1,530	980	680	500	385	305	245
63	23,490	5,870	2,610	1,470	940	650	480	365	290	235
64	22,500	5,630	2,500	1,410	900	625	460	350	275	225
65	21,540	5,390	2,390	1,350	860	600	440	335	265	215
66	20,610	5,150	2,200	1,290	825	570	420	320	255	205
67	19,700	4,925	2,190	1,230	790	545	400	305	245	195
68	18,820	4,705	2,090	1,180	750	520	385	295	230	190
69	17,970	4,490	2,000	1,120	720	500	365	280	220	180
70	17,140	4,285	1,900	1,070	685	475	350	265	210	170
71	16,340	4,085	1,815	1,020	655	455	335	255	200	165
72	15,560	3,890	1,730	970	620	430	315	245	190	155
73	14,790	3,700	1,640	925	590	410	300	230	180	145
74	14,050	3,510	1,560	880	560	390	285	220	175	140
75	13,330	3,330	1,480	835	535	370	270	210	165	135
76	12,630	3,160	1,400	790	505	350	255	195	155	125
77	11,950	2,990	1,330	745	480	330	245	185	145	120
78	11,280	2,820	1,253	705	450	315	230	175	140	110
79	10,630	2,660	1,180	665	425	295	215	165	130	105
80	10,000	2,500	1,110	625	400	275	205	155	125	100
81	9,380	2,345	1,040	585	375	260	190	145	115	94
82	8,780	2,195	975	550	350	245	180	135	110	88
83	8,190	2,050	910	510	325	225	165	130	100	82
84	7,620	1,905	845	475	305	210	155	120	94	76
85	7,060	1,765	785	440	280	195	145	110	87	71
86	6,510	1,630	725	405	260	180	130	100	80	65
87	5,980	1,495	665	375	240	165	120	93	74	60
88	5,450	1,300	605	340	220	150	110	85	67	55
89	4,940	1,235	550	310	200	135	100	77	61	49
90	4,440	1,110	495	280	175	125	90	69	55	44
91	3,960	990	440	250	160	110	80	62	49	40
92	3,480	870	385	220	140	96	70	54	43	35
93	3,010	750	335	190	120	83	61	47	37	30
94	2,550	640	285	160	100	71	52	40	31	26
95	2,110	525	234	130	85	59	43	33	26	21
96	1,670	420	185	105	67	46	34	26	21	17
97	1,240	310	140	78	50	34	25	19	15	12
98	815	205	91	51	33	23	17	13	10	8
99	405	100	45	25	16	11	8	6	5	4

¹Reprinted with permission from Ralph M. Barnes, Motion and Time Study, 4th Edition, John Wiley & Sons, New York

required would be to measure their height which obviously could be done at any time.

However, if the study demands instantaneous random observations of an activity, such as occurs when determining the percentage of productive versus idle time of individuals, the times for the observations should be obtained from Table 8.2. The procedure for selecting random observation times was discussed earlier in this chapter.

The total number of random time observations will affect the study span. The study span is defined as the total length of time over which observations are to be made. If a large number of observations are to be made, the study span may involve a period of days or even weeks. When significant daily variations in the activity to be observed are present, it is best to stretch the study span over a longer period of time.

When the length of the study span has been decided, the number of daily observations may be calculated by dividing the study span (in days) into the total required number of observations. Then the random observation times for each day during the entire span can be found. The observation times for each day should be different as determined from the table of random times.

Design of Data Sheet

The data sheet for a sampling study should be designed so that adequate space is provided for the following:
1. Preliminary information—date, study title, observer
2. Breakdown of elements
3. Totals
4. Computations
5. Notes

Figure 8.3 shows a simple but adequate data sheet for a sampling study of the productivity of a baker.

Taking the Random Observations

Random time observations of an activity should be made instantaneously at the designated time. If a random time observation is to be made at 8:08, it should be made *precisely* at 8:08 or else discarded. An observation made before or after the designated time may introduce bias into the results.

Individuals can be quickly trained to make the instantaneous observations of an activity. However, one thing to guard against is the matter of expectation. This is present when an observer records the activity that is expected to occur just after making the instantaneous observation. For example, an observer may see an individual standing at a worktable at the observation time (a delay element), but record the activity as a work element because the worker started to work within a few seconds after the observation. It is usually a good idea to have observers watch typical activities that will be sampled prior to the study so they may become familiar with them.

PRODUCTIVITY STUDY OF HEAD BAKER

Date _____ 12-11-65 _____   Observer _____ E.A.K. _____

Observation Times	Productive			Nonproductive	
	"Make Ready"	"Do"	"Clean Up"	"Idle"	Absent
8:08				√	
8:18	√				
9:36		√			
9:57		√			
10:07					√
10:31		√			
10:42	√				
10:47				√	
11:16		√			
11:19			√		
11:40		√			
1:26				√	
2:18		√			
4:21			√		
4:38			√		
Totals	2	6	3	3	1

Total Observations = 15
Total Productive Observations = 11
Total Nonproductive Observations = 4
Productive Ratio = $\frac{11}{15}$ = 0.733 or 73.3%

Nonproductive Ratio = $\frac{4}{15}$ = 0.267 or 26.7%

FIG. 8.3. TYPICAL DATA SHEET FOR SAMPLING STUDY OF HEAD BAKER

Summarizing the Data

Essential information that should be summarized after each day's study include the total number of observations, the total number of each element in the various activity categories and subtotals of main category activities. These summaries are used to determine the percentage of each of the measured elements, as well as the percentage of the main activities. Examples of these calculations are shown on the data sheet in Fig. 8.3.

TABLE 8.4

TABLE FOR DETERMINING THE DEGREE OF ACCURACY FOR A GIVEN NUMBER OF OBSERVATIONS AND VALUE OF p, 95% CONFIDENCE LEVEL [1]

Number of Observations

Per Cent of Total Time Occupied by Activity or Delay, p	10,000	9000	8000	7000	6000	5000	4000	3000	2000	1000	900	800	700	600	500
1	±19.9	±21.0	±22.3	±23.8	±25.7	±28.1	±31.5	±36.3	±44.5	±62.9	±66.3	±70.4	±75.2	±81.3	±89.0
2	14.0	14.8	15.7	16.7	18.1	19.8	22.1	25.6	31.3	44.3	46.7	49.5	52.9	57.2	62.6
3	11.4	12.0	12.7	13.6	14.7	16.1	18.0	20.7	25.4	35.9	37.9	40.2	43.0	46.5	50.8
4	9.8	10.3	11.0	11.7	12.7	13.9	15.5	17.9	21.9	31.0	32.7	34.6	37.0	40.0	43.8
5	8.7	9.2	9.8	10.4	11.3	12.3	13.8	15.9	19.5	27.6	29.1	30.8	33.0	35.6	39.0
6	7.9	8.3	8.9	9.5	10.2	11.2	12.5	14.5	17.7	25.0	26.4	28.0	29.9	32.3	35.4
7	7.3	7.7	8.2	8.7	9.4	10.3	11.5	13.3	16.3	23.1	24.3	25.8	27.6	29.8	32.6
8	6.8	7.2	7.6	8.1	8.8	9.6	10.7	12.4	15.2	21.5	22.6	24.0	25.6	27.7	30.3
9	6.4	6.7	7.1	7.6	8.2	9.0	10.1	11.6	14.2	20.1	21.2	22.5	24.0	26.0	28.4
10	6.0	6.3	6.7	7.2	7.6	8.5	9.5	11.0	13.4	19.0	20.0	21.2	22.7	24.5	26.8
11	5.7	6.0	6.4	6.8	7.3	8.1	9.0	10.4	12.7	18.0	19.0	20.1	21.5	23.2	25.4
12	5.4	5.7	6.1	6.5	7.0	7.7	8.6	9.9	12.1	17.1	18.1	19.2	20.5	22.1	24.2
13	5.2	5.5	5.8	6.2	6.7	7.3	8.2	9.5	11.6	16.4	17.3	18.3	19.6	21.1	23.1
14	5.0	5.2	5.5	5.9	6.4	7.0	7.8	9.1	11.1	15.7	16.5	17.5	18.7	20.2	22.2
15	4.8	5.0	5.3	5.7	6.2	6.7	7.5	8.7	10.6	15.1	15.9	16.8	18.0	19.4	21.3
16	4.6	4.8	5.1	5.5	5.9	6.5	7.3	8.4	10.3	14.5	15.3	16.2	17.3	18.7	20.5
17	4.4	4.7	4.9	5.3	5.7	6.3	7.0	8.1	9.9	14.0	14.7	15.6	16.7	18.0	19.8
18	4.3	4.5	4.8	5.1	5.5	6.0	6.8	7.8	9.5	13.5	14.2	15.1	16.1	17.4	19.1
19	4.1	4.4	4.6	4.9	5.3	5.8	6.5	7.5	9.2	13.1	13.8	14.6	15.6	16.9	18.5
20	4.0	4.2	4.5	4.8	5.2	5.7	6.3	7.3	8.9	12.7	13.3	14.1	15.1	16.3	17.9
21	3.9	4.1	4.3	4.6	5.0	5.5	6.1	7.1	8.7	12.3	12.9	13.7	14.6	15.8	17.4
22	3.8	4.0	4.2	4.5	4.9	5.3	6.0	6.9	8.4	11.9	12.6	13.3	14.2	15.4	16.8
23	3.7	3.9	4.1	4.4	4.7	5.2	5.8	6.7	8.2	11.6	12.2	12.9	13.8	14.9	16.4
24	3.6	3.8	4.0	4.3	4.6	5.0	5.6	6.5	8.0	11.3	11.9	12.6	13.5	14.5	15.9
25	3.5	3.7	3.9	4.1	4.5	4.9	5.5	6.3	7.8	11.0	11.6	12.3	13.1	14.1	15.5
26	3.4	3.6	3.8	4.0	4.4	4.8	5.3	6.2	7.5	10.7	11.2	11.9	12.8	13.8	15.1
27	3.3	3.5	3.7	3.9	4.2	4.7	5.2	6.0	7.4	10.4	11.0	11.6	12.4	13.4	14.7
28	3.2	3.4	3.6	3.8	4.1	4.5	5.1	5.9	7.2	10.1	10.7	11.3	12.1	13.1	14.4
29	3.1	3.3	3.5	3.7	4.0	4.4	5.0	5.7	7.0	9.9	10.4	11.1	11.8	12.8	14.0
30	3.05	3.2	3.4	3.65	3.9	4.3	4.8	5.6	6.8	9.7	10.2	10.8	11.6	12.5	13.7
31	3.00	3.1	3.3	3.60	3.85	4.2	4.7	5.5	6.7	9.4	9.9	10.6	11.3	12.2	13.4
32	2.90	3.05	3.25	3.50	3.75	4.1	4.6	5.3	6.5	9.2	9.7	10.3	11.0	11.9	13.0
33	2.85	3.00	3.20	3.40	3.70	4.0	4.5	5.2	6.4	9.0	9.5	10.1	10.8	11.6	12.7
34	2.80	2.90	3.10	3.30	3.60	3.9	4.4	5.1	6.2	8.8	9.3	9.9	10.5	11.4	12.5
35	2.70	2.85	3.05	3.25	3.50	3.85	4.3	5.0	6.1	8.6	9.1	9.6	10.3	11.1	12.2
36	2.65	2.80	3.00	3.20	3.45	3.8	4.2	4.9	6.0	8.4	8.9	9.4	10.1	10.9	11.9
37	2.60	2.75	2.90	3.10	3.35	3.7	4.1	4.8	5.8	8.3	8.7	9.2	9.9	10.7	11.7
38	2.55	2.70	2.85	3.05	3.30	3.6	4.0	4.7	5.7	8.1	8.6	9.0	9.7	10.4	11.4
39	2.50	2.65	2.80	3.00	3.25	3.55	3.95	4.6	5.6	7.9	8.3	8.8	9.5	10.2	11.2
40	2.45	2.60	2.75	2.90	3.15	3.45	3.85	4.5	5.5	7.8	8.2	8.7	9.3	10.0	11.0
41	2.40	2.55	2.70	2.85	3.10	3.40	3.80	4.4	5.4	7.6	8.0	8.5	9.1	9.8	10.7
42	2.35	2.50	2.65	2.80	3.05	3.30	3.70	4.3	5.3	7.4	7.8	8.3	8.9	9.6	10.5
43	2.30	2.45	2.60	2.75	2.95	3.25	3.65	4.2	5.2	7.3	7.7	8.1	8.7	9.4	10.3
44	2.25	2.40	2.50	2.70	2.90	3.20	3.55	4.1	5.0	7.1	7.5	8.0	8.5	9.2	10.1
45	2.20	2.35	2.45	2.65	2.85	3.15	3.50	4.05	4.95	7.0	7.4	7.8	8.4	9.0	9.9

	±2.15	±2.30	±2.40	±2.60	±2.80	±3.05	±3.40	±3.95	±4.85	±6.9	±7.2	±7.7	±8.2	±8.8	±9.7
46	2.15	2.30	2.40	2.60	2.80	3.05	3.40	3.95	4.85	6.9	7.2	7.7	8.2	8.8	9.7
47	2.10	2.25	2.35	2.55	2.75	3.00	3.35	3.85	4.75	6.7	7.1	7.5	8.0	8.7	9.5
48	2.10	2.20	2.30	2.50	2.70	2.95	3.30	3.80	4.65	6.6	6.9	7.4	7.9	8.5	9.3
49	2.05	2.15	2.30	2.45	2.65	2.90	3.20	3.70	4.55	6.5	6.8	7.2	7.7	8.4	9.1
50	2.00	2.10	2.25	2.40	2.60	2.85	3.15	3.65	4.45	6.3	6.7	7.1	7.6	8.2	8.9
51	1.96	2.06	2.19	2.34	2.53	2.77	3.10	3.58	4.38	6.20	6.53	6.93	7.41	8.00	8.76
52	1.92	2.02	2.15	2.29	2.48	2.71	3.04	3.51	4.29	6.07	6.40	6.79	7.26	7.84	8.59
53	1.88	1.98	2.10	2.25	2.43	2.66	2.97	3.43	4.20	5.95	6.27	6.65	7.11	7.68	8.41
54	1.84	1.94	2.05	2.20	2.38	2.60	2.91	3.36	4.11	5.82	6.13	6.51	6.95	7.51	8.23
55	1.81	1.91	2.02	2.16	2.34	2.56	2.86	3.30	4.05	5.72	6.03	6.40	6.84	7.39	8.09
56	1.77	1.87	1.98	2.12	2.29	2.50	2.80	3.23	3.96	5.60	5.90	6.26	6.69	7.23	7.92
57	1.73	1.82	1.93	2.07	2.23	2.45	2.74	3.16	3.87	5.47	5.77	6.12	6.54	7.06	7.74
58	1.70	1.79	1.90	2.03	2.19	2.40	2.69	3.10	3.80	5.38	5.67	6.01	6.43	6.94	7.60
59	1.66	1.75	1.86	1.98	2.14	2.35	2.62	3.03	3.71	5.25	5.53	5.87	6.27	6.78	7.42
60	1.63	1.72	1.82	1.95	2.10	2.30	2.58	2.98	3.64	5.15	5.43	5.76	6.16	6.65	7.29
61	1.59	1.68	1.78	1.90	2.05	2.25	2.51	2.90	3.56	5.03	5.30	5.62	6.01	6.49	7.11
62	1.57	1.65	1.76	1.88	2.01	2.22	2.48	2.87	3.51	4.96	5.23	5.55	5.93	6.41	7.01
63	1.53	1.61	1.71	1.83	1.98	2.16	2.42	2.79	3.42	4.84	5.10	5.41	5.78	6.25	6.84
64	1.50	1.58	1.68	1.79	1.94	2.12	2.37	2.74	3.35	4.74	5.00	5.30	5.67	6.12	6.71
65	1.47	1.55	1.64	1.76	1.90	2.08	2.32	2.68	3.29	4.65	4.90	5.20	5.56	6.00	6.57
66	1.44	1.52	1.61	1.72	1.86	2.04	2.28	2.63	3.22	4.55	4.80	5.09	5.44	5.88	6.44
67	1.40	1.48	1.57	1.67	1.81	1.98	2.21	2.56	3.13	4.43	4.67	4.95	5.29	5.72	6.26
68	1.37	1.44	1.53	1.64	1.77	1.94	2.17	2.50	3.06	4.33	4.57	4.84	5.18	5.59	6.13
69	1.34	1.41	1.50	1.60	1.73	1.89	2.12	2.45	3.00	4.24	4.47	4.74	5.06	5.47	5.99
70	1.31	1.38	1.46	1.57	1.69	1.85	2.07	2.39	2.93	4.14	4.37	4.63	4.95	5.35	5.86
71	1.28	1.35	1.43	1.53	1.65	1.81	2.02	2.34	2.86	4.05	4.27	4.53	4.85	5.26	5.72
72	1.24	1.31	1.39	1.48	1.60	1.75	1.96	2.26	2.77	3.92	4.13	4.38	4.69	5.06	5.55
73	1.21	1.28	1.35	1.45	1.56	1.71	1.91	2.21	2.71	3.83	4.03	4.28	4.57	4.94	5.41
74	1.18	1.24	1.32	1.41	1.52	1.67	1.87	2.15	2.64	3.73	3.93	4.17	4.46	4.82	5.28
75	1.15	1.21	1.29	1.37	1.48	1.63	1.82	2.10	2.57	3.64	3.83	4.07	4.35	4.69	5.14
76	1.12	1.18	1.25	1.34	1.45	1.58	1.77	2.04	2.50	3.54	3.73	3.96	4.23	4.57	5.01
77	1.09	1.15	1.22	1.30	1.41	1.54	1.72	1.99	2.44	3.45	3.63	3.85	4.12	4.45	4.87
78	1.06	1.12	1.19	1.27	1.37	1.50	1.68	1.94	2.37	3.35	3.53	3.75	4.01	4.33	4.74
79	1.03	1.09	1.15	1.23	1.33	1.46	1.63	1.88	2.30	3.26	3.43	3.64	3.89	4.21	4.61
80	1.00	1.05	1.12	1.20	1.29	1.41	1.58	1.83	2.24	3.16	3.33	3.54	3.78	4.08	4.47
81	0.97	1.02	1.08	1.16	1.25	1.37	1.53	1.77	2.17	3.07	3.23	3.43	3.67	3.96	4.34
82	0.94	0.99	1.05	1.12	1.21	1.33	1.49	1.72	2.10	2.97	3.13	3.32	3.55	3.84	4.20
83	0.90	0.95	1.01	1.08	1.16	1.27	1.42	1.64	2.01	2.85	3.00	3.18	3.40	3.67	4.02
84	0.87	0.92	0.97	1.04	1.12	1.23	1.38	1.59	1.95	2.75	2.90	3.08	3.29	3.55	3.89
85	0.84	0.89	0.94	1.00	1.08	1.19	1.33	1.53	1.88	2.66	2.80	2.97	3.17	3.43	3.76
86	0.81	0.85	0.91	0.97	1.05	1.15	1.28	1.48	1.81	2.56	2.70	2.86	3.06	3.31	3.76
87	0.77	0.81	0.86	0.92	0.99	1.09	1.22	1.41	1.72	2.43	2.57	2.72	2.91	3.14	3.44
88	0.74	0.78	0.83	0.88	0.96	1.05	1.17	1.35	1.65	2.34	2.47	2.62	2.80	3.02	3.31
89	0.70	0.74	0.78	0.84	0.90	0.99	1.10	1.28	1.57	2.21	2.33	2.47	2.65	2.86	3.13
90	0.67	0.71	0.75	0.80	0.86	0.95	1.06	1.22	1.50	2.12	2.23	2.37	2.53	2.74	3.00
91	0.63	0.66	0.70	0.75	0.81	0.89	1.00	1.15	1.41	1.99	2.10	2.22	2.38	2.57	2.82
92	0.59	0.62	0.66	0.71	0.76	0.83	0.93	1.08	1.32	1.87	1.97	2.09	2.23	2.41	2.64
93	0.55	0.58	0.61	0.66	0.71	0.78	0.87	1.00	1.23	1.74	1.83	1.94	2.08	2.25	2.46
94	0.50	0.53	0.56	0.60	0.65	0.71	0.79	0.91	1.12	1.58	1.67	1.77	1.89	2.04	2.24
95	0.46	0.48	0.51	0.55	0.59	0.65	0.73	0.84	1.03	1.45	1.53	1.63	1.74	1.88	2.05
96	0.41	0.43	0.46	0.49	0.53	0.58	0.65	0.75	0.92	1.30	1.37	1.45	1.55	1.67	1.83
97	0.35	0.37	0.39	0.42	0.45	0.49	0.55	0.64	0.83	1.10	1.17	1.24	1.32	1.43	1.57
98	0.28	0.30	0.31	0.33	0.36	0.40	0.44	0.51	0.63	0.88	0.93	0.99	1.06	1.14	1.25
99	0.20	0.21	0.23	0.24	0.26	0.28	0.32	0.37	0.45	0.63	0.67	0.71	0.79	0.82	0.89

Checking the Accuracy of the Study

After the sampling is completed, a calculation of the accuracy is made to determine if it is within the previously stated accuracy range. The accuracy is calculated by using the formula presented earlier in the discussion of accuracy.

Example.—Assume that the final results of a productivity study at 95% confidence level and ±5% accuracy showed the following:

Total productive observations	3500
Total nonproductive observations	1500
Total observations	5000

Then the percentage of idle time is:

$$P = 1500 \div 5000 = 0.30$$

Substituting P = 0.30 and N = 5000 into the equation

$$SP = 2\sqrt{\frac{P(1-P)}{N}}$$

$$S(0.30) = 2\sqrt{\frac{0.30(1-0.30)}{5000}}$$

$$S(0.30) = 2\sqrt{0.000042}$$

$$S = 2\frac{(\pm 0.0065)}{0.30}$$

$$S = \pm 0.043 \text{ or } \pm 4.3\%$$

Since the relative accuracy of ±4.3% is below the required ±5% accuracy, the number of observations used for the study was sufficient.

In this problem, it can be stated that the percentage of idle time determined represented the facts with 95% confidence. The relative accuracy of ±4.3% means that the results were correct within the ±4.3% of 30% (±4.3% × 30% = ±1.3%), or the true value was between 28.7% and 31.3%.

If the calculation of the relative accuracy had been greater than the required ±5% accuracy, this would have indicated that not enough observations were made, and additional sampling would be needed. In this situation, a second calculation of the number of observations required would be made using an estimated percentage of 30% idle time.

The relative accuracy of sampling studies can also be determined from Table 8.4.

Evaluating the Results

When the sampling study has been completed, the results should be used with the following understandings. First, the results are an estimate of the actual facts and should be stated as such. The estimate fortunately is probably the best and most reliable that can be obtained without resorting to finer study techniques. Either the relative or absolute accuracy of the estimate should be computed and presented with the results.

Secondly, the results of the sampling study are subject to the probability of misrepresenting the facts. At the 95% confidence level, the chance of misrepresentation is 5%. This should not be considered as a drawback because a 95% chance of being right in many situations is highly acceptable.

Selected Examples of Sampling Studies

To help illustrate the method and uses of sampling studies in the hotel, restaurant and institutional field, selected studies recently reported in the literature will be presented.

One of the earliest uses of sampling in the hospital field was reported by Torgersen (1959). The objective of the study was to determine the activities performed by registered nurses and the percentage of time spent in these activities. The study was conducted at the 600 bed Ohio State University Hospital and therefore involved some teaching and research as part of its function.

The normally expected work activities of the nurses were categorized into ten separate categories. Special emphasis was placed on separating the professional activities from the nonprofessional. Professional activities included such areas as giving medicine, bandaging, preparing medications, keeping patients' records, scheduling of patients and teaching. Nonprofessional activities were considered those that could be done by other supporting personnel such as nurses aides, orderlies, student nurses or housekeeping personnel. Examples of activities considered to be nonprofessional include taking temperatures, feeding, making beds, obtaining bed linen and housekeeping.

The results of the sampling study are summarized in Table 8.5.

The study showed that almost 20% of the nurses' work load consisted

TABLE 8.5

RESULTS OF SAMPLING STUDY OF REGISTERED NURSES' ACTIVITIES

Category of Work	Number of Observations	Occurrence %
1. Professional contact with patient (administering medications and/or treatments)	141	8.7
2. Nonprofessional contact with patient (i.e., feeding, obtaining material, making bed)	217	13.5
3. Professional preparation—related to category 1 (preparing medication, obtaining bandages, etc.)	192	11.9
4. Nonprofessional preparation—related to category 2 (obtaining thermometer, foods, linen, etc.)	67	4.2
5. Travel time not included in categories 3 and 4	48	3.0
6. Professional communication about the patient (includes keeping patients' records)	629	39.1
7. Professional personnel work (staff meetings, training periods)	125	7.8
8. Nonprofessional housekeeping (light cleaning)	16	1.0
9. Professional teaching	33	2.0
10. Personal and idle time (includes meals and breaks)	142	8.8
Totals	1610	100%

of nonprofessional tasks or tasks that could be performed by other personnel.

The other significant finding was that 39.1% of the nurses' time was spent in communications or information exchange about the patient. From the standpoint of work analysis, this area seemed to hold the most promise for improvement.

The information provided by the sampling study can enable the hospital to make changes that would improve the nurses' efficiency and result in better patient care.

A similar sampling study of nurses' activities was conducted at Johns Hopkins Hospital (1961). In this study the activities were separated into productive and nonproductive categories. The productive activities were broken down into the following subcategories:

1. Direct patient care: any activity requiring contact between patient and nurse.

2. Indirect patient care: activities in preparation or completion of patient care.

3. Paperwork: activities concerned with writing or reading of records or forms.

4. Communication: activities involving oral communications with other personnel.

5. Other: escorting patients, doing necessary errands, cleaning up, travel, etc.

The nonproductive activities included the normal personal time required for meals and rest periods and all other activities not defined previously as productive.

Table 8.6 presents the results obtained from the study at Johns Hopkins Hospital. The study indicated that the largest portion (26.4%) of the nurses' time was spent in direct patient care. The most revealing part of the study was that 25.4% of the nurses' time was spent in nonproductive activities.

A study investigating the activities of the dietary staff was conducted at University Hospital at the University of Iowa by Marteney and Ohlson (1964). The dietary staff was composed of 19 professional personnel, 5 food service supervisors, 12 clerks and 5 nutrition interns. Observations of the dietary staff were made in office areas as well as production areas.

TABLE 8.6

RESULTS OF SAMPLING STUDY OF NURSES AT JOHNS HOPKINS HOSPITAL

		Number of Observations	Occurrence %
A. Productive:			
	1. Direct patient care	1206	26.4
	2. Indirect patient care	794	17.4
	3. Paperwork	526	11.5
	4. Communication	627	13.7
	5. Other	259	5.7
B. Nonproductive		1164	25.4
	Totals	4576	100

The activities were categorized into 11 groups as follows:

1. Patient factors: visiting and instructing patients, writing diets, calculating intakes, working with medical staff.

2. Supervision: food preparation, food service, inspection of food and kitchens.

3. Assisting in food preparation.

4. Menu planning.

5. Teaching.

6. Purchasing, receiving and inspection.

7. Employee matters: payroll, hiring, dismissal.

8. Administration: planning, directing, control.

9. Sanitation, housekeeping and maintenance.

10. Personal time: meals, rest periods, idleness.

11. Miscellaneous: public relations, research, conferences.

The study was conducted over a six week period and involved a total of 662 observations. A summary of the observations and per cent activity determinations is shown in Table 8.7.

TABLE 8.7

PERCENTAGE TIME DISTRIBUTION OF ACTIVITIES OF A DIETARY STAFF

Activity	Number of Observations	Occurrence %
Patient factor	252	38
Supervision	81	12
Food preparation	22	3
Menu planning	48	7
Teaching	16	3
Purchasing, receiving, inspecting	15	2
Employee matters	25	4
Administration	16	3
Sanitation, housekeeping, maintenance	15	2
Personal	150	23
Miscellaneous	22	3
Totals	662	100%

The approximate time distribution of the four classifications of the dietary staff among the activity categories is shown in Table 8.8.

TABLE 8.8

PER CENT TIME DISTRIBUTION OF DIETARY STAFF FOR EACH ACTIVITY CATEGORY

Activity Category	Percentage of Time			
	Professional Personnel	Food Service Supervisors	Clerks	Nutrition Interns
Patient factors	32	32	53	30
Supervision	15	20	2	20
Food preparation	1	13	..	10
Menu planning	6	2	12	5
Teaching	5	..	1	..
Purchasing	1	1	5	1
Employee matters	5	5	2	3
Administration	4	..	2	..
Sanitation	3	3	2	..
Personal	25	24	17	27
Miscellaneous	3	..	4	4

This particular study gave a composite picture of the interrelationship between activities and individuals when different individuals were involved in the same type of activity.

A sampling study of the activities of three food service managers was conducted in a cafeteria operation at Cornell University by Sanford and Cutlar (1964). The three food service managers used for observation were identified as:

Manager A: Cafeteria Manager

Manager B: Assistant Cafeteria Manager and Student Personnel Supervisor

Manager C: Assistant Cafeteria Manager and Food Production Supervisor.

The sampling was accomplished over an eight-week period during which an average of 900 meals per day was served. Approximately 1,000 observations were made on each of the three managers. A confidence level of 95% and an accuracy range of ±3% were chosen for the study.

Expected activities were derived from the job descriptions of the three managers. The activities were grouped into six main categories. Three of these categories were broken down into more definite activities. The breakdown of activities and the results of the study are shown in Table 8.9.

The information from this sampling study could be used to improve control procedures, improve personnel utilization, or even act as a guide for selecting managerial personnel.

TABLE 8.9

TIME DISTRIBUTION FOR THREE FOOD SERVICE MANAGERS IN A CAFETERIA OPERATION

Activity	% Occurrence of Activity		
	Manager A	Manager B	Manager C
1. Planning and organizing	17.4	8.3	7.6
Menu and production	14.5	1.4	7.3
Scheduling	2.3	5.7	—
Policy and procedure	0.6	1.2	0.3
2. Directing and controlling	37.0	20.3	51.8
Production and service	16.7	13.1	41.2
Procurement and inventory	15.5	0.1	7.5
Equipment maintenance	0.8	0.3	0.8
Personnel management	4.0	6.8	2.3
3. Evaluation and conferences	2.9	1.9	1.3
4. Direct labor	14.4	47.4	21.4
5. Personal time	22.7	15.4	14.4
Meals	12.6	6.1	10.6
Changing uniforms	1.8	1.0	2.7
Other	8.3	8.3	1.1
6. Miscellaneous	5.7	6.8	3.5

An analysis of the direct labor spent in various food service activities of two Veterans Administration hospitals was made by the sampling

procedure (Schell and Korstad, 1964). The same methods and procedures for conducting the study were used at each hospital. Both
hospitals were of comparable size. A total of 3,536 observations were
taken at the hospitals.

The breakdown of activities and the resulting percentage of time for
each activity are shown in Table 8.10. The activities included in the
"others" category were delivery of food to patients, paperwork, supervision, on-the-job training, etc. It should be noted that the primary
objective of this study was to determine the importance of various
activities in the food service operation, and not the productivity of the
workers.

TABLE 8.10

PER CENT TIME DISTRIBUTION OF VARIOUS ACTIVITIES IN TWO
HOSPITAL FOOD SERVICE OPERATIONS

	% Occurrence	
Activity	Hospital A	Hospital B
Preparation	15.3	15.6
Distribution	12.1	14.7
Service	30.5	24.8
Dishwashing	16.0	20.1
Cleaning	7.5	10.0
Others	18.6	14.8

There were some basic differences between the two hospitals that
may account for the discrepancies in the per cent occurrence of certain
activities. For example, all dishwashing was done in one area in Hospital A, while Hospital B had six separate dishwashing areas. Hospital A
also had a longer serving period which may partially account for the
higher service activity.

9

Product Process Analysis

INTRODUCTION

Product process analysis basically involves determining the procedure used to work on or modify products and materials. A complete product process analysis would include the following.

1. Identification of the products or materials to be studied.
2. Description of the products or materials: size, shape, packaging, etc.
3. Location of workplaces and storage areas involved in the process.
4. Breakdown of the process or procedure into basic categories of:
   a. operations
   b. movements
   c. delays
   d. storages
   e. inspections
5. Chronological sequence of the steps in the process.
6. Identification of the equipment or machines used.
7. Determination of distances products or materials are moved.
8. Determination of time for each phase of the process.
9. Determination of quantity of products or materials involved.
10. Description of product flow.

The information gathered from product process analysis may be used in several ways depending on the objective of the study. One use of such information is to find improvements and simplifications in an existing work system. In this situation the analysis identifies unnecessary delays or movements that may be eliminated, or indicates where operations or inspections may be combined or simplified. It may also indicate the need for new or different types of equipment or machines for the process.

The product analysis may indicate the need for instituting changes in the products or materials. These changes are usually minor, such as using frozen vegetables instead of fresh; precut meats instead of whole-

63

sale cuts; or plastic tableware instead of china. Occasionally, major product changes such as the use of completely preprocessed foods or "boil-in-the-bag" foods are brought about by the analysis. Major product changes are generally characterized by drastic changes in work areas, equipment and operations.

Product analysis is also used in the design and layout of new work areas and facilities. Good design and layout of facilities are based on efficient flow of the products and materials as they proceed through the facility. For example, planning information for kitchens is obtained by product analysis of the recipes to determine food flow, while information for planning laundries is obtained by analysis of linen flow.

PRODUCT PROCESS CHARTS

Product process charts are graphical displays of the procedure used to work on products. These charts provide a systematic means of gathering and showing the data for product analysis. The construction of the chart is based on a breakdown of all steps in the procedure into five basic categories: operation, movement, delay, storage or inspection. Each category is indicated by a geometric symbol. The product process chart symbols and their use are shown in Table 9.1.

TABLE 9.1

SYMBOLS FOR PRODUCT PROCESS CHART

Category	Symbol	Used to Represent
Operation	◯	Expenditure of human or mechanical effort on the product at one workplace.
Movement	○	Change in location of the product from one workplace to another.
Delay	▽	Waiting of the product, for no special reason.
Storage	▽	Storage of the product, primarily for control or quality reasons.
Inspection	☐	Determination of quantity or quality of the product (a specialized operation).

The correct use of the symbols is dependent on the definition and identification of the workplaces used in the process. For charting purposes, the workplace may be conceived as any limited area where work is accomplished. It could be a worktable, a piece of equipment, the combination of a table and one piece of equipment or even a designated area on the floor. Some knowledge of the process being analyzed will help in determining the best definition and location of workplaces to use.

The workplace is the key to the use of the movement symbol. The movement symbol is used only when the product location is changed from one designated workplace to another. Thus minor movements of the product within any designated workplace are not charted as movements in the product process chart. As an illustration, if a six-foot worktable is a designated workplace, movement of the product from the left side to the right side of the table would not be shown by the movement symbol. The movement within the workplace is assumed to be part of the operation performed at the workplace. However, if the worktable is designated as two workplaces, the left half and the right, then a movement of the product from the left side to the right would be shown as a movement in the process chart. The relation between workplace designation and the use of the movement symbol is shown in Fig. 9.1.

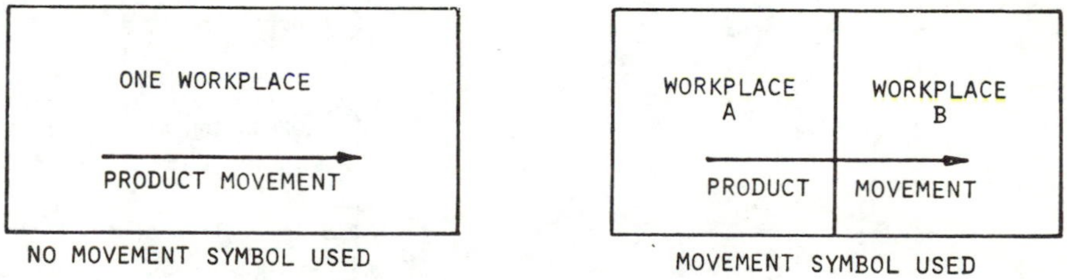

ONE WORKPLACE

PRODUCT MOVEMENT →

NO MOVEMENT SYMBOL USED

WORKPLACE A   WORKPLACE B

PRODUCT | MOVEMENT

MOVEMENT SYMBOL USED

FIG. 9.1. RELATIONSHIP BETWEEN WORKPLACE DESIGNATION AND USE OF THE MOVEMENT SYMBOL

It can be seen that the designation of the workplace can affect the amount of detail present in the product process chart. If many small workplaces are used, the number of movements appearing in the chart will be greater than if fewer, larger workplaces are designated. The three areas shown in Fig. 9.2 can be designated as one workplace and the resultant process chart would be very brief. If the three areas are designated as three workplaces, then the resultant process chart becomes quite detailed.

The designation of the workplaces is dependent on the objective of the study. If the purpose of the study is to analyze the details of the procedure and possibly suggest improvements, then a greater number of smaller workplaces would give the best results. When the purpose of the study is to gather information for design and layout, fewer and larger workplace designations are usually quite satisfactory. The important point is that the designation of the workplaces for any given study should be consistent. A workplace diagram should accompany the product process chart.

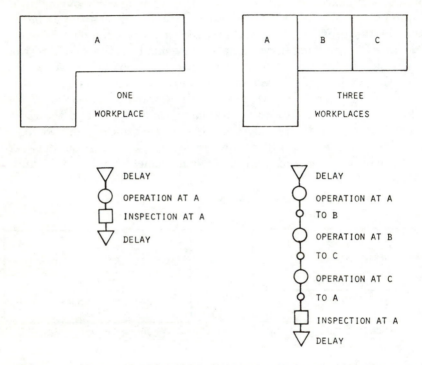

FIG. 9.2. WORKPLACE DESIGNATION AND RESULTANT PRODUCT PROCESS CHART

The operation symbol can also be used to control the amount of detail present in the product process chart. Figure 9.3 shows how an activity at one workplace may appear in the chart depending on the use of the operation symbol.

The amount of detail desired in the product process chart should be determined before the analysis is made.

Constructing the Product Process Chart

Product process charting is relatively easy. Usually the data is gathered by direct observation. The observations represent what is happening to the product and not what the worker or machine is doing. As

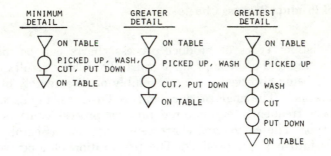

FIG. 9.3. DIFFERENT PRODUCT PROCESS CHARTS RESULTING FROM DIFFERENT USAGE OF THE OPERATION SYMBOL

the observations are made, they are recorded by the appropriate symbol and a brief written description. The symbols are placed vertically in chronological sequence and joined by a straight line. If other information is being observed, such as time or distance, these are also recorded and placed beside the appropriate symbol.

Certain conventions are used to prepare and standardize the more complicated product process charts. These conventions and their meanings are shown in Table 9.2.

TABLE 9.2

CONVENTIONS USED IN PRODUCT PROCESS CHARTING

Convention	Represents
⊕	Combined activity of an operation and an inspection, where the operation is the predominant activity.
⊡	Combined activity of an inspection and an operation where the inspection is the predominant activity.
O→	Material removed from the product, but not charted (i.e., removing packaging materials).
O←	Material added to the product, but not charted (i.e., adding water to product).
⊖⌐	Part of the product being returned to an earlier step in the process.
⊖⌐	Assembly of the product.
⊖⌐	Disassembly of the product.
⌀	A gap in the chart indicating that some steps in the process are missing.
⤳	Crossing of lines when products are not interrelated at this point.
Ⓡ	Repeating a cycle of activities within the chart.

Types of Product Process Charts

Three distinct types of product process charts can be made. The simplest chart is the single product chart. This chart results when one product is being observed and no assembly or disassembly of the product takes place. The single product chart is illustrated in Fig. 9.4.

The most frequently encountered product process chart is the converging type. The converging chart represents the assembly of many materials into a single product. The preparation of food would represent a converging product process chart.

The diverging type of chart represents the disassembly or breakdown of one product into components. The cutting of wholesale meats into the various retail cuts would result in the diverging type of chart.

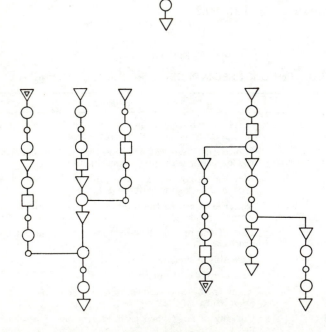

FIG 9.4. FORMAT FOR PRODUCT PROCESS CHARTS OF A
SINGLE PRODUCT, CONVERGING TYPE OF PRODUCT AND
DIVERGING TYPE OF PRODUCT

The converging and diverging types of charts are simply a series of single product charts that are combined to show their interrelationships as illustrated in Fig. 9.4.

Format of the Product Process Chart

Product process charts should be constructed according to a standard

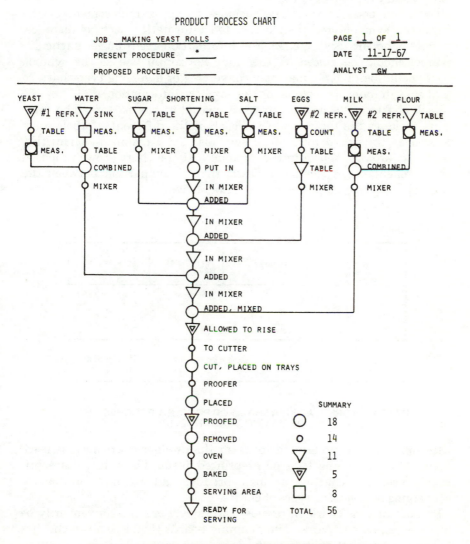

FIG. 9.5. TYPICAL PRODUCT PROCESS CHART FORMAT

format. Use of a standardized format will result in a neat and understandable chart, in addition to containing all the important information. Figure 9.5 shows an acceptable format for a product process chart. The workplace diagram for the chart is shown in Fig. 9.6.

The top part of the chart should give general information regarding the product and process being analyzed. The information should include a brief description of the product, the process, whether the chart is of an existing process or a proposed process, the date, the observer's initials and the number of pages.

The main body of the chart includes the proper placement of the geometric symbols and their associated information such as distance, time, equipment used, etc. All the information regarding a particular symbol should be placed on the same horizontal line as the symbol. Care should be taken in making a converging or diverging type chart, so that enough room is provided for the auxiliary information.

Each chart should have a summary placed at the bottom. The summary includes the total number of each of the different symbols used, as well as the grand total of all symbols. Total distances, quantities, time, etc. are also shown in the summary. If the chart shows proposed improvement of an existing process, then a comparison between the original and proposed processes should be shown.

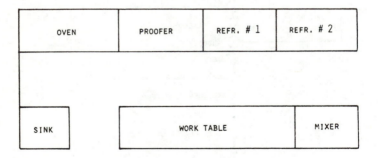

FIG. 9.6.   WORKPLACE DIAGRAM FOR PRODUCT PROCESS CHART
OF MAKING YEAST ROLLS

In some cases, a preprinted form for the product chart may be used. Figure 9.7 shows one type of preprinted form. These forms are primarily used for charting a single product and are not suitable for converging or diverging types of charts.

Product process charts of proposed work systems can conveniently be made on planning boards. The planning boards (Fig. 9.8) allow changes in the process chart to be easily made.

Flow Diagram

A flow diagram may accompany product process charts. The flow diagram shows the flow of the product through the areas where the product is worked on. The flow of the product can be shown by drawing lines on the workplace diagram depicting the movement between workplaces. It is best to make the flow diagram to scale.

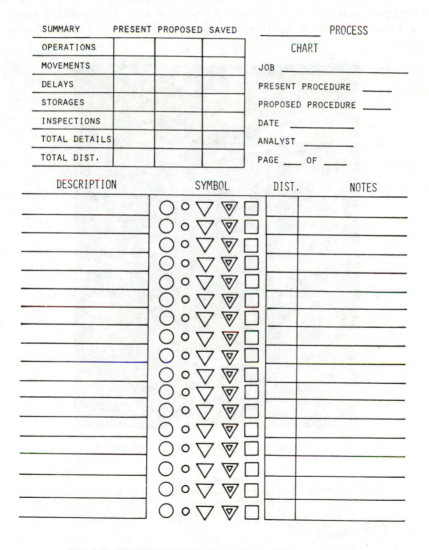

FIG. 9.7.   PREPRINTED FORM FOR PROCESS CHARTING

Analyzing the Product Process Chart

After the product process chart of a procedure is constructed, it is analyzed to see if any improvements in the procedure can be made. The usual procedure in analyzing the charts is to question each component of the process to see if it can be eliminated, combined, rearranged or simplified. A systematic analysis can be made by using a check list similar to the one shown in Table 9.3. After the analysis of the existing procedure is completed, a chart of the proposed method is constructed. The proposed chart may then be used to install the improved procedure.

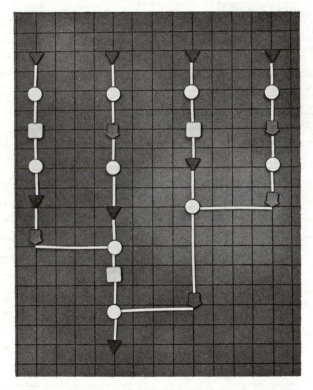

FIG. 9.8.   PROCESS CHARTING ON PLANNING BOARDS

TABLE 9.3
CHECK LIST FOR PRODUCT PROCESS ANALYSIS

Can any step in the processing of the product be eliminated or simplified by:
  1. Obtaining materials in different form
  2. Combining materials
  3. Changing the shape
  4. Using different materials

TABLE 9.3 *(Continued)*

5. Changing packaging
6. Using preprocessed materials
7. Using a different machine or piece of equipment
8. Combining processes
9. Reducing delays
10. Reducing distances product is moved
11. Combining inspections with operations
12. Changing location of storage areas
13. Using different workplace locations
14. Processing with another product
15. Performing an operation at an earlier time
16. Changing the method of processing
17. Processing in transit
18. Changing the location of an operation
19. Reducing back-tracking
20. Reducing the number of inspections

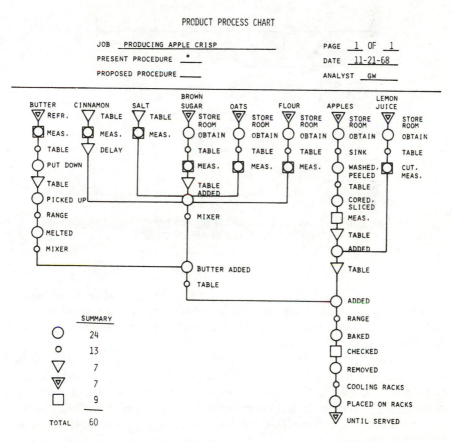

FIG. 9.9. PRODUCT PROCESS CHART OF PRODUCING APPLE CRISP—ORIGINAL
METHOD

Illustrations of Product Process Charts

The following illustrations will help clarify the use of the product process charting technique. Figure 9.9 shows the product process chart of an existing method of producing apple crisp. The workplace diagram for the process is shown in Fig. 9.10. It is important to remember that the product process chart depicts the procedures associated with the materials or ingredients. Thus, movements are shown in the chart whenever the ingredients are moved between any of the identified workplaces.

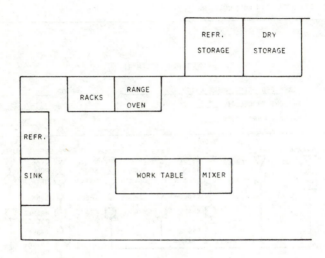

FIG. 9.10.   WORKPLACE DIAGRAM FOR PRODUCT PROCESS
CHART OF PRODUCING APPLE CRISP

The operations and inspections indicate that the ingredients are being worked on at one workplace. All delays and storages are also identified as to location. The summary shows that a total of 60 symbols was used to chart the existing procedure.

The product process chart of the proposed method of producing apple crisp is shown in Fig. 9.11. Improvements in the process were made primarily by changing the locations of stored materials thus eliminating unnecessary movements and operations. A comparison of the summaries of the original and proposed charts shows that nine steps were eliminated from the process.

Figure 9.12 shows the procedure used in washing dinnerware at a university cafeteria. A rack type dishwashing machine is used in this operation. The flow diagram for the dinnerware washing procedure is shown in Fig. 9.13.

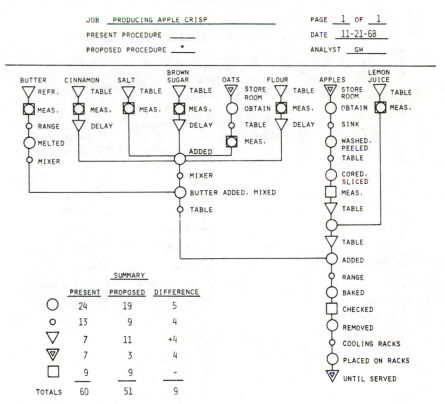

FIG. 9.11. PROPOSED PRODUCT PROCESS CHART OF PRODUCING APPLE CRISP

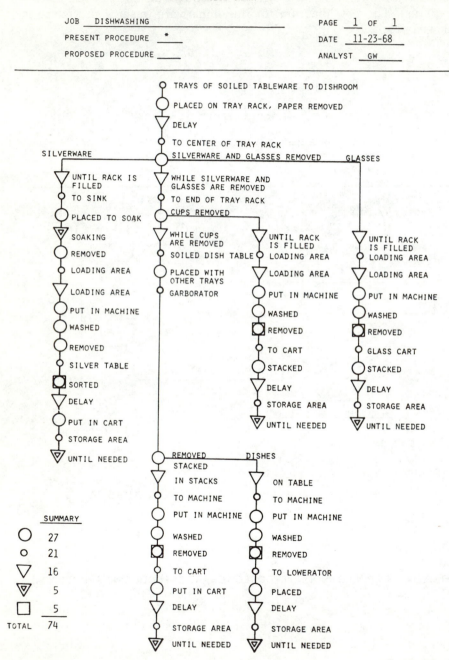

FIG 9.12.   PRODUCT PROCESS CHART OF DISHWASHING PROCEDURES

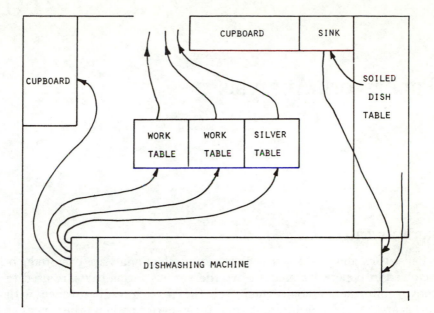

FIG. 9.13.   FLOW DIAGRAM OF DISHWASHING PROCEDURES

Paperwork Analysis

INTRODUCTION

Paperwork analysis is a special case of product analysis. The products involved in paperwork analysis are the various forms that are used to convey information. Since many of the procedures performed with forms are unique and different from those performed on other types of products, slightly different analysis techniques are used in paperwork analysis.

The basic differences between paperwork analysis and product analysis are in the symbols and the formats of the charts used to analyze forms. Three additional symbols representing activities associated only with forms are used in addition to the regular product process analysis symbols. The charts used to analyze paperwork are somewhat time oriented since the origination of some forms may be dependent on other forms used in the procedure. These differences will be further discussed and illustrated later.

The importance of paperwork analysis has generally not been stressed in relation to other work analysis procedures. It should be pointed out that paperwork does not create value, but instead adds costs to the products and services being offered. In recent years, the pressure for additional management information has created a large volume of paperwork. Unfortunately, much of this paperwork has been created without too much thought given to work methods and work design.

Paperwork analysis consists primarily of investigating the flow of forms used to accomplish a certain objective. In this situation the procedure used for working on forms is analyzed in the manner similar to a product analysis. The objective of paperwork analysis is to simplify and improve the procedures used. Paperwork analysis can be applied to the forms used for checking-in procedures at a hotel or admitting procedures at a hospital, purchasing or ordering, hospital records, payroll, processing applicants for employment, etc.

FORM PROCESS CHARTS

The form process chart is used to display graphically the procedure used to work on forms. The form process chart is constructed in essentially the same manner as a product process chart. The geometric symbols used to construct the form process chart are shown in Table 10.1. Many symbols are the same as used for the product process chart.

The origination symbol is used to designate the starting point of a form into the procedure being analyzed. It does not refer to the printing of forms. An example of origination is the filling in of the guest registration form at a hotel. This action starts the flow of the registration form in the front office procedure. Additional originations of forms occur when the desk clerk uses the information from the registration form to complete the information slips and the account folio.

TABLE 10.1

FORM PROCESS CHART SYMBOLS

Name	Symbol	Used to Represent
Origination	⊚	The initial filling out of a form (usually at one workplace). Number at center indicates total number of copies.
Operation	○	Something done to the form, other than origination.
Movement	○	Change in location of the form from one workplace to another.
Delay	▽	Waiting for the form.
Storage	▽	Storage of the form for control or identification purposes (i.e., in a file cabinet.)
Inspection	□	Checking of form for correctness or comparing form with other information.
Information take-off	┼→	Removal of information from form for use on another form or by some person.
Disposal	⊠	Destruction of form.

The information take-off symbol is used when a form is read and the information taken off is used to originate another form or to cause some action by an individual or machine. The use of the guest registration card to originate the account folio is an example of information take-off. A cashier reading the amount to be collected on a restaurant check is also considered an information take-off.

The disposal symbol usually designates physical destruction of the form. It may also be used to indicate the end of the charting of a form. Theailing of a form which will not be returned and charted further can be shown by the disposal symbol.

Activities such as signing, typing, stapling, separating, adding information, totaling columns of figures and filing are represented on the form process chart by the operation symbol.

The extent of detail on the form process chart is controlled by the workplace designations and the use of the operation symbol. The effects of these variables were discussed for the product process chart and similar effects occur in the form process chart.

Constructing the Form Process Chart

Data for constructing the form process chart is gathered by direct observation or by discussion. In some instances both methods are used simultaneously. The discussion method is helpful when the forms are sent to remote areas of a building or even sent outside of the building. The data should always indicate what is happening to the forms.

The placement of the symbols for the form process chart is sometimes

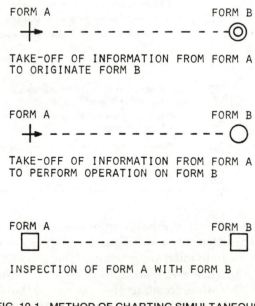

FORM A FORM B

TAKE-OFF OF INFORMATION FROM FORM A
TO ORIGINATE FORM B

FORM A FORM B

TAKE-OFF OF INFORMATION FROM FORM A
TO PERFORM OPERATION ON FORM B

FORM A FORM B

INSPECTION OF FORM A WITH FORM B

FIG. 10.1. METHOD OF CHARTING SIMULTANEOUS
ACTIVITIES ON FORM PROCESS CHARTS

dictated by the time of certain activities. When two forms are involved within the same activity at the same time, the symbols are placed at the same horizontal level on the chart. For example, if one form was being compared to another form for accuracy, the inspection symbols for each form would be placed side by side. It is also recommended that the relationship between the two forms be shown by a dashed line between the symbols. Examples of simultaneous activities and how they are charted on form process charts are shown in Fig. 10.1.

The complexity of the form process chart depends on the number of forms and the number of copies of each form charted. The simplest form process chart results when a single form with no copies is charted. This would correspond to the product process chart of a single product. As more forms or copies are involved, the complexity of the form process chart increases. Since most paperwork procedures involve a number of forms and copies, the placement of the symbols in the process chart must be carefully planned to keep the chart legible.

Format of Form Process Charts

The format of the form process chart is essentially the same as the product process chart. When the flow of paperwork is in a limited area, such as in one department, the form process chart is drawn similar to the product chart. When the paperwork moves between several areas or departments, the areas or departments may be shown on the chart by using vertical columns. Figure 10.2 shows a form process chart involving two separate areas. The subdivision of the chart into areas or departments makes it easier to interpret and analyze.

A basic form process chart is made by using the symbols accompanied by a brief description. Additional information such as distances, times or equipment used may be observed and included in the chart if called for in the objective of the study.

The summary of the chart should show the number of symbols used for the forms charted and the grand total of the symbols for the entire procedure. If distances and times are indicated on the chart, these also should be summarized for each form and for the total chart.

A workplace diagram or a flow diagram should accompany the form process chart.

Check List for Form Process Charts

Improvements in the procedures for working on forms are found by analyzing the form process charts of existing systems. The check list given in Table 10.2 may be used to guide the analysis.

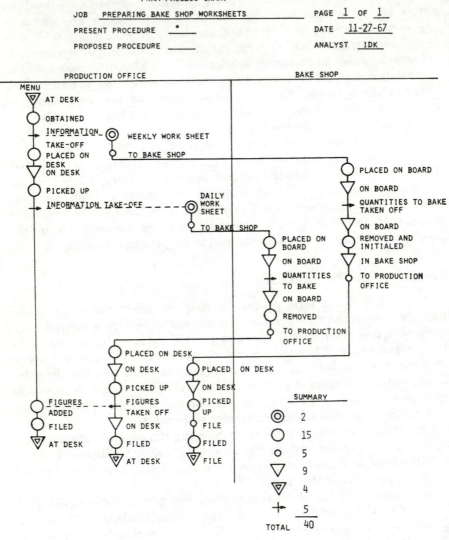

FORM PROCESS CHART

JOB ___PREPARING BAKE SHOP WORKSHEETS___   PAGE _1_ OF _1_

PRESENT PROCEDURE ___*___   DATE _11-27-67_

PROPOSED PROCEDURE _____   ANALYST _IDK_

PRODUCTION OFFICE   BAKE SHOP

MENU
AT DESK
OBTAINED
INFORMATION
TAKE-OFF   WEEKLY WORK SHEET
PLACED ON   TO BAKE SHOP
DESK
ON DESK
                                    PLACED ON BOARD
PICKED UP   ON BOARD
                DAILY   QUANTITIES TO BAKE
INFORMATION TAKE-OFF   WORK   TAKEN OFF
                SHEET
                TO BAKE SHOP   ON BOARD
                                    REMOVED AND
                PLACED ON   INITIALED
                BOARD
                                    IN BAKE SHOP
                ON BOARD   TO PRODUCTION
                QUANTITIES   OFFICE
                TO BAKE
                ON BOARD
                REMOVED
                TO PRODUCTION
                OFFICE
        PLACED ON DESK
            ON DESK   PLACED ON DESK
            PICKED UP   ON DESK
        FIGURES   FIGURES   PICKED   SUMMARY
        ADDED   TAKEN OFF   UP
        FILED   ON DESK   FILE   2
        AT DESK   FILED   FILED   15
                AT DESK   FILE   5
                                        9
                                        4
                                        5
                                TOTAL   40

FIG. 10.2.   FORM PROCESS CHART FOR FLOW OF PAPERWORK BETWEEN TWO
SEPARATE AREAS

Form Process Chart Illustrations

The workplace diagram of an original front office check-in and check-out procedure is shown in Fig. 10.3. The form process chart for the workplace diagram is shown in Fig. 10.4. The form process chart de-

TABLE 10.2

CHECK LIST FOR PAPERWORK ANALYSIS

Can any steps in the processing of paperwork be eliminated or simplified by:
1. Combining forms
2. Changing the design of the form
3. Reducing the number of forms and carbon copies
4. Reducing the operations performed
5. Shortening distances of flow
6. Avoiding duplication of information on forms
7. Using proper spacing for typewritten forms
8. Reducing number of inspections or readings
9. Reducing the number of information take-offs
10. Using standardized size and format of forms
11. Using a uniform filing system
12. Simplifying computational procedures
13. Using machine stamping where feasible
14. Changing to electronic data processing
15. Color coding of forms
16. Using sensitized paper for copies
17. Reducing the amount of copying
18. Changing the order of operations
19. Using mechanical aids for collating
20. Providing adequate lighting
21. Reducing delays in the process
22. Designing the form for efficient reading

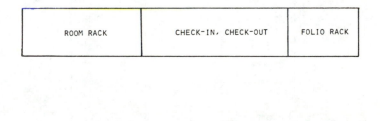

FIG. 10.3. WORKPLACE DIAGRAM FOR CHECK-IN AND CHECK-OUT
PROCEDURES SHOWN IN FIG. 10.4

picts the procedures used to complete the registration card, account folio, and information slips. In this procedure, the registration card is a separate form and is used to complete the account folio and information slips. The three information slips are attached to the folio and are separated after they have been completed.

The improved front office procedure is shown by Fig. 10.5. The improvement included the physical rearrangement of certain work

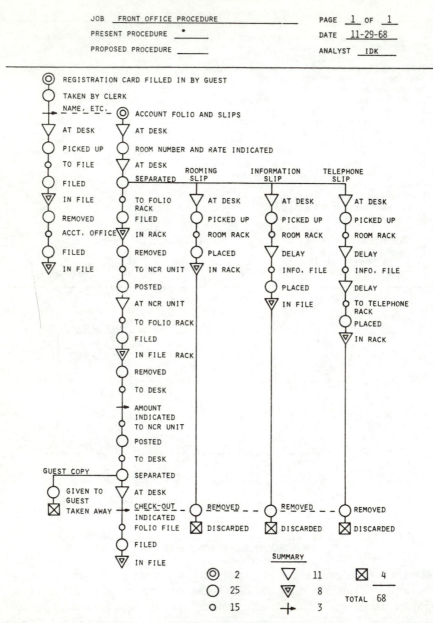

FIG. 10.4. FORM PROCESS CHART FOR CHECK-IN AND CHECK-OUT PROCEDURES
IN A HOTEL

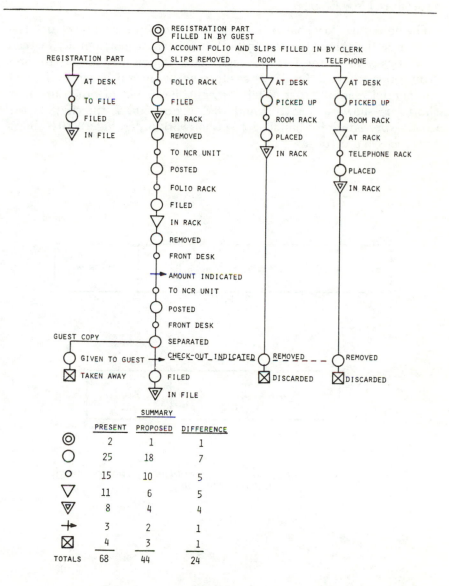

FIG. 10.5. PROPOSED FORM PROCESS CHART OF CHECK-IN AND CHECK-OUT
PROCEDURES

areas as shown in Fig. 10.6. A combined form which has the registration card attached to the bottom was used in the improved procedure instead of separate forms as used in the original procedure.

Procedure Flow Charts

The procedure flow chart is a variation of the form process chart. The procedure flow chart uses symbols that are placed horizontally instead of vertically as in the form process chart. One advantage of the procedure flow chart is that it is easily read because it generally follows the normal reading order of left to right. Examples of procedure flow charts are shown in Fig. 10.7 and 10.8. Figure 10.7 is the chart of the existing procedure for handling a special work order. Figure 10.8 shows the proposed procedure.

CHECK-OUT	FOLIO RACK	NCR 2000	ROOM RACK KEY RACK	CHECK-IN

MAIL RACK	PBX

**FIG. 10.6.   WORKPLACE DIAGRAM FOR PROPOSED PROCEDURES
SHOWN IN FIG. 10.5**

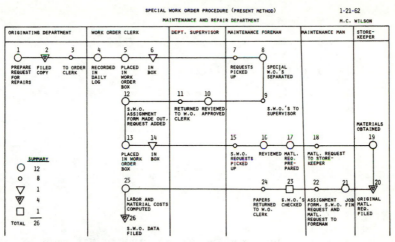

FIG. 10.7. PROCEDURE FLOW CHART FOR MAINTENANCE AND REPAIR DEPARTMENT WORK ORDERS—ORIGINAL METHOD

Reprinted with permission from A. C. Bennett, *Methods Improvement in Hospitals*, J. B. Lippincott Co., Philadelphia.

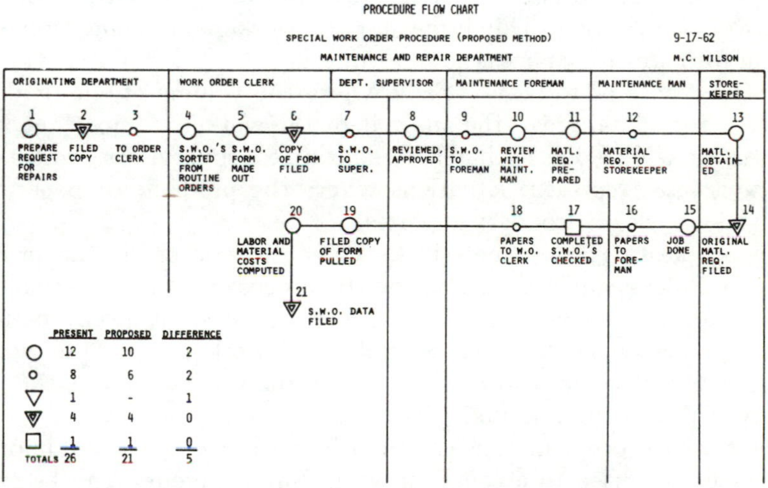

FIG. 10.8. PROPOSED PROCEDURE FLOW CHART FOR MAINTENANCE AND REPAIR DEPARTMENT WORK ORDERS

Reprinted with permission from A. C. Bennett, *Methods Improvement in Hospitals*, J. B. Lippincott Co., Philadelphia.

Worker Process Analysis

INTRODUCTION

The analysis of products and paperwork involves gathering and presenting information regarding these materials. The objective of such analysis is to specifically determine what was happening to the materials, and not who was working on them. Although product and paperwork analysis involves workers to varying degrees, the information gathered does not emphasize what the worker is doing. In general, several different workers are involved in processing given products or paperwork and trying to analyze what the workers are doing from product or form process charts is not meaningful.

In some types of work, especially where the volume of the products involved is not too great, the analysis of the worker is important. The analysis of work done by hotel clerks, nurses, supervisors, waitresses, bus boys, etc., represent situations where the products or paperwork involved may be of secondary importance.

The simplest type of analysis to make on workers is the process analysis. Process analysis determines the procedures that a person uses to accomplish his job or task. The process analysis can only be used when the person moves from workplace to workplace. If the worker does not move between workplaces, other analysis techniques that are presented later should be used.

The worker process analysis is primarily used to simplify and improve the procedures used to accomplish work. Improvements may be made by eliminating or combining steps in the procedure, or possibly by changing the sequence of the operations performed. The rearrangement of workplaces and storage areas may also result in improvements. Worker process analysis frequently points out areas where materials handling equipment or other labor saving devices may be used to reduce worker effort.

Worker process analysis is also useful in planning the procedure to be used for future work. For example, the analysis derived from new food recipes to be produced in a kitchen enables the chef to determine the best procedure to follow in producing the food. These analytical charts are also very helpful in the training of new employees.

WORKER PROCESS CHARTS

The worker process chart is a graphical presentation of the procedure a worker uses to accomplish a task as he or she moves from workplace to workplace. As in the other process charts, the worker's activities are broken down and described by symbols.

Two different sets of symbols are available for making the worker process charts. The geometric symbols are used in the same way described for the other process charts. The use of the geometric symbols results in a regular worker process chart. The other set of symbols is referred to as time symbols and are used to make a worker process *time* chart. The only basic difference between the regular worker process chart and the worker process time chart is in the symbols. The worker process time chart is used when the time of each of the activities performed is to be emphasized. Time charts are frequently used as a visual aid to convey ideas to management or other groups because they are easily interpreted.

The geometric and time symbols for worker process charts are shown in Table 11.1. The geometric symbols for all types of process charts are similar but their meanings are different when used in the different charts.

TABLE 11.1

GEOMETRIC AND TIME SYMBOLS FOR WORKER PROCESS CHARTS

Name	Geometric symbol	Time symbol	Used to represent
Operation	○	■	Worker doing something at one workplace.
Movement	○	▦	Change in location of the worker from one workplace to another.
Delay	▽	▯	Idleness of the worker which is not necessary for completion of the task.
Hold	▽	▱	Maintaining an object in a fixed position.
Inspection	▢	▥	Checking for quantity or quality.
Interval	⬡	◸	Worker activity not related to task or job being performed.

The operation symbol is used to devote such gross activities as mixing, washing, cutting, cleaning, reading, giving instructions, serving, obtaining, assembling, disassembling, etc. The importance of the operation symbol is that it describes what the worker is doing and not how it is done. Some analysts like to separate operations into three subcategories: make ready, do and clean up. This breakdown shows the relation between the nonproductive parts (i.e., the make ready and clean up), and the productive parts (i.e., the do) of the task.

Some analysts prefer the use of two different movement symbols for indicating a change in location by the worker. One symbol is used for movements with a load, and another symbol for movements without a load. This breakdown of the movement symbol is useful if one of the objectives of the analysis is to investigate possible materials handling systems. The normal geometric designation for a movement without load is the small circle as shown in Table 11.1. The geometric designation for movement with a load is the small circle with a horizontal line drawn through it.

The delay symbol is used to represent complete physical and mental inactivity on the part of the worker. Care should be taken in observing an individual for delays because certain mental activities may be going on even though the individual appears to be physically idle. Such mental activities as reading, doing calculations and thinking may be necessary to the completion of a task and are charted as operations, not delays. The worker shown in Fig. 11.1 is checking the temperature gauge on the griddle and this action should be charted as an operation on the worker process chart.

The observer should become thoroughly familiar with the tasks being analyzed so he can make sound judgments of the activities performed by the worker.

The hold symbol should be used whenever a worker is primarily engaged in maintaining an object in a fixed position. An example of the hold activity is represented by a worker holding a pot under a faucet. Many activities are a combination of holding and a doing operation. If such activities are observed, the analyst should determine whether the primary function is holding or an operation. The combined activity of holding a pot with one hand and stirring with the other hand has a primary function of stirring and should be charted as an operation. A combined symbol for hold and operation is not used because the action of holding, even as part of an operation, is undesirable and should be identified separately on the worker process chart.

The only symbols that can be combined to show a dual activity are the operation and inspection symbols. When the primary action of the combined activity is an operation, the large circle with the square

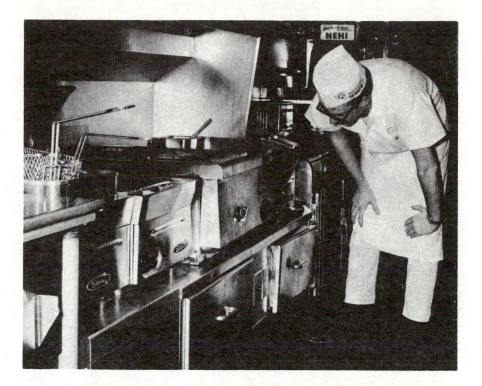

FIG. 11.1. MENTAL ACTIVITIES SUCH AS READING A DIAL OR GAUGE SHOULD BE CHARTED AS AN OPERATION ON WORKER PROCESS CHARTS

inside should be used. However, if the primary action of the combined activity is an inspection, then the circle within the square should be used.

The interval symbol is used to designate productive effort on the part of the worker, but not related to the particular job being charted. As an illustration, assume that the activities of a baker preparing pie dough are to be charted. If during the process the baker stops and checks on cakes in the oven, this activity is shown on the chart by the interval symbol. The interval symbol avoids lengthy charting of activities which have no bearing on the problem studied.

CONSTRUCTING THE WORKER PROCESS CHART

The basic worker process chart consists of three columns: one column for the placement of symbols, one for the description and one for

WORKER PROCESS CHART

JOB __CLEANING BATHROOM__   PAGE _1_ OF _2_

PRESENT PROCEDURE __•__   DATE _3-2-68_

PROPOSED PROCEDURE ____   ANALYST _GW_

DISTANCE   SYMBOL   DESCRIPTION

PICK UP TOWELS FROM RACK, PUT ON FLOOR

3   TO SINK

TURN ON WATER

1   TO TUB

TURN ON WATER

1   TO SINK

PICK UP GLASSES

5   TO CART

PUT DOWN GLASSES, GET CLEAN GLASSES AND CLEANSER

5   TO SINK

PUT DOWN GLASSES, CLEAN SINK

1   TO TUB

CLEAN TUB

6   TO CART

RETURN CLEANSER, OBTAIN WIPING TOWEL

6   TO TUB

WIPE TUB

1   TO SINK

WIPE SINK, OBTAIN WASTE PAPER FROM BASKET

1   TO TOILET

FLUSH TOILET

FIG. 11.2. PART 1—WORKER PROCESS CHART OF ORIGINAL PROCEDURE OF
CLEANING BATHROOM

designation of the distance of movements. Other information such as
the equipment used or the time required for each symbol (this does not
mean using the time symbols but refers to placing the numerical value
of time beside each symbol), are placed in additional columns added to
the chart. Since the worker process chart represents the activities of
one worker, only a single column of symbols is used. The symbols are
placed vertically and in chronological sequence.

The amount of detail present in the chart is dependent on the analyst.
The number of movements appearing in the chart will increase as

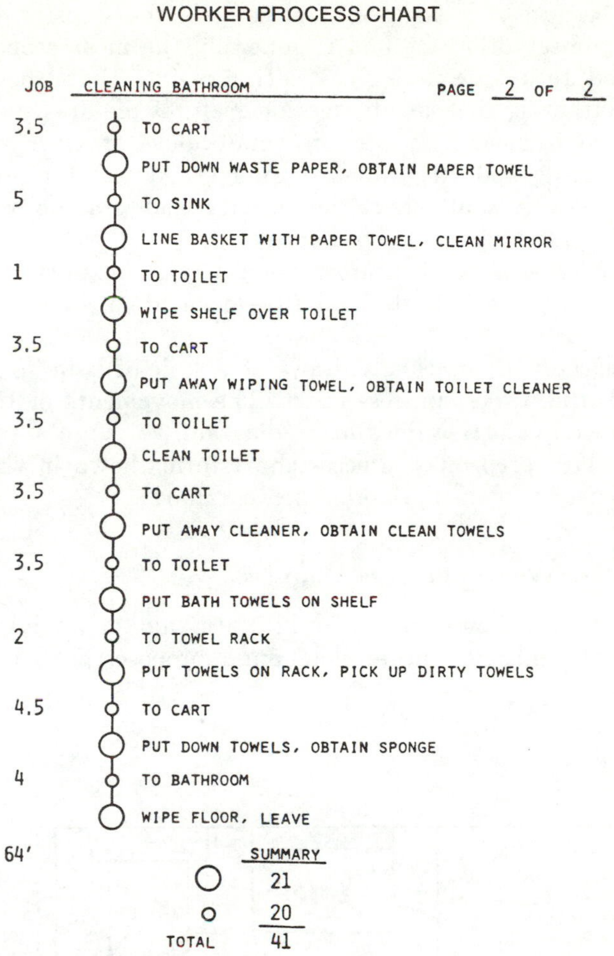

WORKER PROCESS CHART

JOB CLEANING BATHROOM _____   PAGE _2_ OF _2_

3.5	TO CART
	PUT DOWN WASTE PAPER, OBTAIN PAPER TOWEL
5	TO SINK
	LINE BASKET WITH PAPER TOWEL, CLEAN MIRROR
1	TO TOILET
	WIPE SHELF OVER TOILET
3.5	TO CART
	PUT AWAY WIPING TOWEL, OBTAIN TOILET CLEANER
3.5	TO TOILET
	CLEAN TOILET
3.5	TO CART
	PUT AWAY CLEANER, OBTAIN CLEAN TOWELS
3.5	TO TOILET
	PUT BATH TOWELS ON SHELF
2	TO TOWEL RACK
	PUT TOWELS ON RACK, PICK UP DIRTY TOWELS
4.5	TO CART
	PUT DOWN TOWELS, OBTAIN SPONGE
4	TO BATHROOM
	WIPE FLOOR, LEAVE

64'

SUMMARY

◯ 21

○ 20

TOTAL 41

FIG. 11.2. PART II

smaller and smaller workplaces are designated. The normal length of a designated workplace for worker process analysis is six feet (152 mm). Most free standing equipment and machines are designated as separate workplaces. Greater detail can also be obtained by breaking down the work at one workplace into more than one operation symbol. This technique was illustrated with the product process analysis presented in Chapter 9.

The data for the analysis may be gathered by direct observation, discussion or by motion pictures. The discussion method is the least preferred because it is easy to forget some of the steps in an activity. The direct observation method is generally the most economical and widely used technique and gives better results than the discussion method. Gathering the data by motion pictures requires special equipment but is the most accurate if time values of each step in the procedure are desired. Regardless of the method used for gathering the data, the analyst should chart the activity that is actually happening and not what he thinks should be happening.

The same type of general information and a summary as indicated with the other process charts should be included on the worker process chart.

A workplace diagram, usually drawn to a scale of ¼ in. to 1 ft should accompany the worker process chart. The movements of the workers may be shown by the flow lines on the diagram.

The standard preprinted process chart form shown in Chapter 9 is frequently used to make the worker process chart.

Check List for Worker Process Analysis

The check list shown in Table 11.2 will aid in analyzing worker process charts and guide the development of proposed procedures.

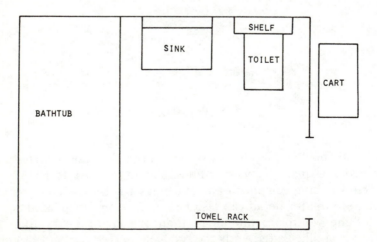

FIG. 11.3. WORKPLACE DIAGRAM FOR BATHROOM CLEANING PROCEDURES

WORKER PROCESS CHART

JOB CLEANING BATHROOM — PAGE 1 OF 1

PRESENT PROCEDURE ____ — DATE 3-2-68

PROPOSED PROCEDURE * — ANALYST GW

DISTANCE	SYMBOL	DESCRIPTION
	○	AT CART, OBTAIN CLEAN TOWELS AND CLEANSER
4.5	o	TO TOWEL RACK
	○	REMOVE DIRTY TOWELS, PLACE CLEAN TOWELS
2	o	TO TOILET SHELF
	○	REMOVE DIRTY TOWELS, PLACE CLEAN TOWELS,
2.5	o	TO TUB
	○	CLEAN TUB
1	o	TO SINK
	○	CLEAN SINK, PICK UP WASTE PAPER AND DIRTY GLASSES
5	o	TO CART
	○	PUT DOWN PAPER AND GLASSES, OBTAIN CLEAN GLASSES, SOAP AND BASKET LINER
5	o	TO SINK
	○	PLACE LINER, GLASSES AND SOAP
2	o	TO TOILET
	○	PICK UP DIRTY TOWELS LEFT ON FLOOR
3.5	o	TO CART
	○	PUT DOWN TOWELS, OBTAIN TOILET CLEANER
3.5	o	TO TOILET
	○	CLEAN TOILET, WIPE FLOOR

SUMMARY

	PRESENT	PROPOSED	DIFFERENCE
○	21	10	11
o	20	9	11
TOTALS	41	19	22
TOTAL DISTANCE	64′	29′	35′

FIG. 11.4. PROPOSED WORKER PROCESS CHART OF BATHROOM CLEANING PROCEDURE

TABLE 11.2

CHECK LIST FOR WORKER PROCESS ANALYSIS

Can any step in the procedure used by individuals be eliminated or simplified by:
1. Combining steps
2. Shortening moves
3. Using new equipment
4. Changing the location of workplaces
5. Changing the location of storage areas
6. Rearranging the order of steps
7. Proper planning
8. Rearranging the equipment
9. Assigning work to someone else

WORKER PROCESS CHART

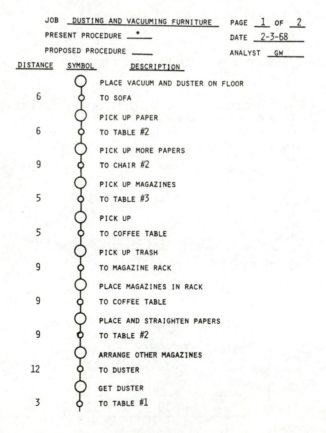

JOB	DUSTING AND VACUUMING FURNITURE	PAGE 1 OF 2
PRESENT PROCEDURE *	DATE 2-3-68
PROPOSED PROCEDURE ___	ANALYST GW

DISTANCE	SYMBOL	DESCRIPTION
	○	PLACE VACUUM AND DUSTER ON FLOOR
6	○	TO SOFA
	○	PICK UP PAPER
6	○	TO TABLE #2
	○	PICK UP MORE PAPERS
9	○	TO CHAIR #2
	○	PICK UP MAGAZINES
5	○	TO TABLE #3
	○	PICK UP
5	○	TO COFFEE TABLE
	○	PICK UP TRASH
9	○	TO MAGAZINE RACK
	○	PLACE MAGAZINES IN RACK
9	○	TO COFFEE TABLE
	○	PLACE AND STRAIGHTEN PAPERS
9	○	TO TABLE #2
	○	ARRANGE OTHER MAGAZINES
12	○	TO DUSTER
	○	GET DUSTER
3	○	TO TABLE #1

FIG. 11.5. PART I—WORKER PROCESS CHART OF ORIGINAL
PROCEDURE OF DUSTING AND VACUUMING FURNITURE

TABLE 11.2 *(Continued)*

10. Obtaining materials in a different form
11. Changing the packaging of the materials
12. Using mechanical aids for transporting materials
13. Redesigning the workplace
14. Combining workplaces
15. Using preprocessed materials
16. Combining inspections
17. Proper training
18. Using better work methods
19. Providing proper environment
20. Changing workplace height
21. Using carts or other equipment as workplaces

WORKER PROCESS CHART

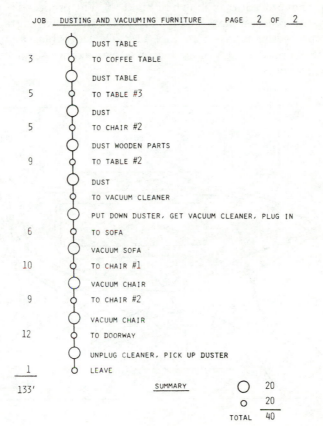

| JOB | DUSTING AND VACUUMING FURNITURE | PAGE | 2 | OF | 2 |

3	DUST TABLE
	TO COFFEE TABLE
5	DUST TABLE
	TO TABLE #3
5	DUST
	TO CHAIR #2
9	DUST WOODEN PARTS
	TO TABLE #2
	DUST
	TO VACUUM CLEANER
6	PUT DOWN DUSTER, GET VACUUM CLEANER, PLUG IN
	TO SOFA
10	VACUUM SOFA
	TO CHAIR #1
9	VACUUM CHAIR
	TO CHAIR #2
12	VACUUM CHAIR
	TO DOORWAY
1	UNPLUG CLEANER, PICK UP DUSTER
	LEAVE

133'

SUMMARY	◯	20
	○	20
	TOTAL	40

FIG. 11.5. PART II

Illustrations of Worker Process Charts

The original procedure followed by a maid cleaning a hotel bathroom is depicted by the process chart shown in Fig. 11.2. A diagram of the bathroom is shown in Fig. 11.3. The process chart shows that the maid walked a total of 64 ft (19.5 m) in completing her tasks. Analysis of the process chart indicated that the maid was making too many unnecessary movements and that considerable improvements in the procedure could be made. The process chart for the proposed method of cleaning the bathroom is shown in Fig. 11.4. By combining operations and eliminating many of the movements, the distance traveled by the maid was reduced to 29 ft (8.84 m).

Figure 11.5 (Part I and Part II) shows the process chart of the original procedure of dusting and vacuum cleaning furniture. The flow diagram for the original procedure is shown in Fig. 11.6. The proposed procedure is shown by the process chart in Fig. 11.7, and the flow diagram for the proposed procedure is given in Fig. 11.8. Considerable savings in the number of operations as well as distance traveled are suggested by the proposed procedure.

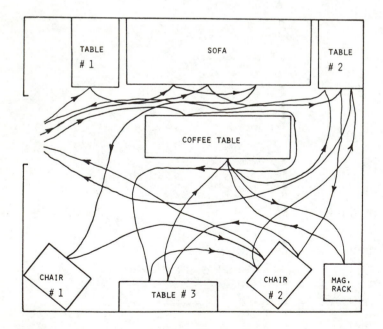

FIG. 11.6. FLOW DIAGRAM OF ORIGINAL PROCEDURE OF DUSTING AND VACUUMING FURNITURE

WORKER PROCESS CHART

JOB __DUSTING AND VACUUMING FURNITURE__   PAGE __1__ OF __1__

PRESENT PROCEDURE _____   DATE __2-3-69__

PROPOSED PROCEDURE __*__   ANALYST __GW__

DISTANCE	SYMBOL	DESCRIPTION
	◯	PLACE VACUUM ON FLOOR AT DOORWAY
3	○	TO TABLE #1
	◯	DUST TABLE
6	○	TO COFFEE TABLE
	◯	PICK UP PAPERS, PUT IN APRON, DUST TABLE
1	○	TO SOFA
	◯	PICK UP PAPERS AND PUT IN APRON
4	○	TO TABLE #2
	◯	PICK UP PAPERS, DUST TABLE
8	○	TO CHAIR #2
	◯	PICK UP PAPERS AND MAGAZINES, DUST CHAIR
5	○	TO TABLE #3
	◯	PICK UP, DUST
8	○	TO MAGAZINE RACK
	◯	PLACE PAPERS AND MAGAZINES IN RACK
6	○	TO VACUUM
	◯	PICK UP VACUUM, PLUG IN
6	○	TO SOFA
	◯	VACUUM SOFA
8	○	TO CHAIR #2
	◯	VACUUM CHAIR #2
9	○	TO CHAIR #1
	◯	VACUUM CHAIR
7	○	TO DOORWAY
	◯	UN-PLUG CLEANER
1	○	LEAVE ROOM

SUMMARY

	PRESENT	PROPOSED	DIFFERENCE
◯	20	13	7
○	20	13	7
TOTALS	40	26	14
TOTAL DISTANCE	133'	72'	61'

FIG. 11.7. PROPOSED WORKER PROCESS CHART OF DUSTING AND VACUUMING PROCEDURES

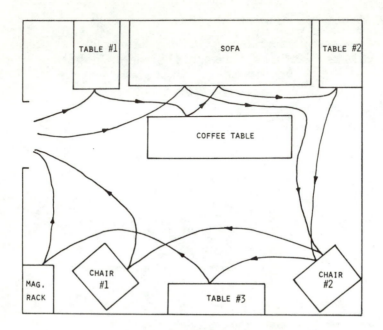

FIG. 11.8. FLOW DIAGRAM OF PROPOSED PROCEDURE OF DUSTING
AND VACUUMING FURNITURE

Constructing the Worker Process Time Chart

Usually the first step in making the process time chart is to make the regular process chart. This is done to identify the activities before obtaining a time value for each activity. This first step could be eliminated if motion pictures are used to gather the data.

After the activity and time data are gathered, the time symbols are placed in a vertical column. The length of each symbol is increased or decreased to correspond to the time involved for each symbol. The symbols are placed without any space between them. Since the length of the time symbol represents the time involved, a time scale is provided on process time charts. The time scale is usually graduated in minutes.

All other information described for the regular worker process chart (distance, description, general information, summary, etc.) are included in the worker process time chart.

The summary for the process time chart gives a breakdown of the times for each symbol and not the number of symbols. Total time and distance for the process are also included in the summary.

Illustration of Worker Process Time Chart

The worker process time chart for an original procedure of preparing Cake a la Mode is shown in Fig. 11.9. The workplace diagram for the process time chart is given by Fig. 11.10.

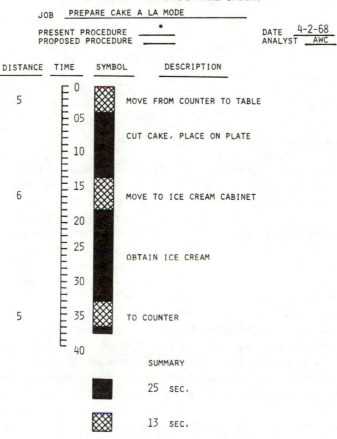

WORKER PROCESS TIME CHART

JOB   PREPARE CAKE A LA MODE

PRESENT PROCEDURE _____ *
PROPOSED PROCEDURE _____

DATE   4-2-68
ANALYST   AWC

DISTANCE	TIME	SYMBOL	DESCRIPTION

5 — MOVE FROM COUNTER TO TABLE

CUT CAKE, PLACE ON PLATE

6 — MOVE TO ICE CREAM CABINET

OBTAIN ICE CREAM

5 — TO COUNTER

SUMMARY

25 SEC.

13 SEC.

FIG. 11.9. WORKER PROCESS TIME CHART OF ORIGINAL PROCEDURE OF PREPARING CAKE A LA MODE

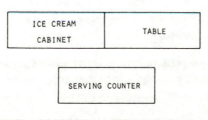

ICE CREAM CABINET	TABLE

SERVING COUNTER

FIG. 11.10. WORKPLACE DIAGRAM FOR PREPARING CAKE A LA MODE PROCEDURE

Designing Work System Layouts

INTRODUCTION

One of the most important factors to consider when improving or designing layouts for work systems is flow. An optimum arrangement of workplaces is achieved when the flow between the various workplaces is minimized. The arrangement of workplaces is relatively easy when the flow is primarily in one direction with very little backtracking or by-passing. However, when considerable backtracking or by-passing are involved in the flow, the arrangement of workplaces to minimize flow becomes difficult. The use of travel charts is a very effective technique to evaluate layouts on the basis of flow.

There are two general concepts regarding the criteria to use for travel charting. The first concept considers the movements of individuals between workplaces as the criteria to evaluate various arrangements. The second concept considers the flow of material between workplaces as the criteria to use for the travel charts. Both concepts are valid criteria to use since the movements of individuals and the flow of materials are usually related. With both concepts, considerable emphasis may be placed on weighing appropriately the desirability of forward movements against the undesirability of backtracking movements.

TRAVEL CHARTING USING MOVEMENTS OF INDIVIDUALS AS CRITERIA

For certain situations, the distance traveled by an employee is a good criterion to use in evaluating alternate arrangements of workplaces and equipment. This is especially true when the weight or volume of materials involved is not too great. The most frequent use of travel charting, when using employee movements as the criteria for evaluation, is to analyze workplaces that are placed in a straight line and where the distance traveled between the workplaces adjacent to one another are equal or can be assumed to be equal. The equipment bank shown in Fig. 12.1 can be easily analyzed by this method of travel charting. The data required for travel charting can be obtained from a worker process analysis.

FIG. 12.1. EQUIPMENT THAT IS TO BE PLACED IN A STRAIGHT LINE CAN BE PLANNED WITH TRAVEL CHARTING TO GET AN EFFICIENT ARRANGEMENT

WORKPLACES PLACED IN A STRAIGHT LINE AT EQUAL INTERVALS

For purposes of illustration, assume that an employee accomplishes certain tasks that require the possible use of four different workplaces. The term workplaces is used to designate work tables, sinks, counters, etc., as well as mechanical equipment. The four workplaces will be designated by the letters A, B, C and D. The tasks involve various sequences of movements between the workplaces by the employee for different product groups as shown in Table 12.1.

For this example it was assumed that each of the product groups is made an equal number of times. In reality, certain product groups may be made more frequently than others, in which case the sequence of movements would be multiplied by a relative frequency factor.

The frequency of movements between the various workplaces can be found by summarizing from the sequence of movements shown in Table 12.1. The frequency of employee movements for the seven product groups is shown in Table 12.2.

TABLE 12.1

SEQUENCE OF MOVEMENTS OF EMPLOYEE BETWEEN WORKPLACES FOR EACH PRODUCT GROUP

Product Group	Sequence of Movements
1	D A B C A C B A
2	C A C B A C A
3	A D A B A
4	D C B D A B C A
5	C A C A D A
6	B C B A
7	D C B

TABLE 12.2

FREQUENCY OF EMPLOYEE MOVEMENTS BETWEEN WORKPLACES

Workplaces		Frequency
From	To	
A	B	3
A	C	4
A	D	2
B	A	4
B	C	3
B	D	1
C	A	6
C	B	5
C	D	0
D	A	4
D	B	0
D	C	2

Constructing the Travel Chart

Construction of the travel chart for the example involves the following steps:

Step 1.—Assume an arrangement using the four workplaces placed in a straight line. (Note that there are 24 possible arrangements for the 4 workplaces.) The arrangement A B C D is assumed for this example.

Step 2.—Using the workplace arrangement shown in step 1, construct a chart consisting of 4 rows and 4 columns as shown on pg. 205.

The same arrangement of workplaces for the column designations must be used for the row designations. The column designations (placed horizontally across the top of the chart) are used to indicate movements "from" the various workplaces. The row designations (placed vertically at the left side of the chart) are used to indicate movements "to" the various workplaces. Since there are no movements

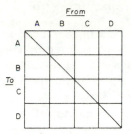

from A to A or from B to B, etc., a diagonal line is drawn through the chart from the upper left hand corner to the lower right hand corner.

Step 3.—The frequency of movements between the various workplaces are placed in the appropriate cells of the chart. For example, the number 3 indicating the frequency of movements from A to B is placed in the cell designated "From A" (1st column) and "To B" (2nd row). In a similar manner, the movements from A to C are placed in the cell designated "From A" (1st column) and "To C" (3rd row). The completed chart is shown below.

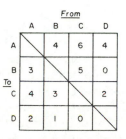

For the particular workplace arrangement shown (A B C D), the travel chart shows the characteristics of the various movements. The cells below the main diagonal show the forward movements. (Forward indicates movements from left to right.) The cells above the main diagonal show the backward movements (right to left). The distance of the cells from the main diagonal indicates the number of workplaces that are by-passed. The cells that are adjacent to the cells of the main diagonal of the chart (both above and below) indicate no by-passing. The cells that are separated from the cells of the main diagonal by one cell indicate that one workplace is by-passed. The cells separated from the main diagonal cells by two cells indicate that two workplaces have been by-passed.

EVALUATING THE EQUIPMENT ARRANGEMENT

Since the distances traveled between the workplaces adjacent to one another are equal, and the by-passing movements are indicated in the travel chart, an index of the total distance traveled can be obtained. This is done by totaling the movements (both forward and backward) according to the number of workplaces by-passed and multiplying the totals by a factor equal to one plus the number of workplaces by-passed. Thus the total movements where no by-passing is involved is multiplied by the factor one. The total movements where one workplace was by-passed is multiplied by the factor two, etc. The grand total of the movements is the index of total distance traveled. The calculation for the example is shown below:

Type of Movement		Total Movements		By-pass Factor	
No by-passing: $3 + 3 + 0 + 4 + 5 + 2$	=	17	×	1	= 17
By-pass 1 workplace: $4 + 1 + 6 + 0$	=	11	×	2	= 22
By-pass 2 workplaces: $2 + 4$	=	6	×	3	= 18
				Index	= 57

The value of the travel chart is that it indicates possible changes in the arrangement of the workplaces that may reduce the index number. For example, it is desirable to get as many of the largest frequencies of movements near the main diagonal of the chart, while the smallest frequencies of movements should be furthest from the diagonal.

Another method of evaluating the workplace arrangement is to emphasize the desirability of forward movements or the undesirability of backtracking. This is done by determining the percentage of the distance moved forward. This percentage is found by dividing the index for forward distances by the index number for the total distance moved. The calculation for the percentage of forward distances moved is shown below:

	Forward Movements	By-pass Factor			Backward Movements	By-pass Factor		
No by-passing	6	×	1	= 6	11	×	1	= 11
By-pass 1 workplace	5	×	2	= 10	6	×	2	= 12
By-pass 2 workplaces	2	×	3	= 6	4	×	3	= 12
		Index		= 22		Index		= 35

$$\% \text{ forward moves} = \frac{22}{22 + 35} = 38.6\%$$

For this method of evaluation, it is desirable to get more numbers below the main diagonal of the travel chart and fewer numbers above it.

IMPROVING THE ARRANGEMENT OF WORKPLACES

Analysis of the travel chart for the first arrangement of workplaces (A B C D) frequently gives an indication of how the arrangement may be improved. For example, the greatest number of movements (6) occurs between A and C. Rearranging the workplaces so that A and C are adjacent will move the 6 closer to the diagonal of the travel chart. Therefore an arrangement such as B A C D may be tried. The travel chart for the workplaces arranged B A C D is shown below:

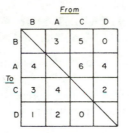

Note that the change from A B to B A changes the numbers in the first 2 rows and the first 2 columns of the travel chart.

The calculation for the various indices for the second travel chart is:

	Forward Movements	By-pass Factor			Backward Movements	By-pass Factor		
No by-passing	8	×	1	= 8	11	×	1	= 11
By-pass 1 workplace	5	×	2	= 10	9	×	2	= 18
By-pass 2 workplaces	1	×	3	= 3	0	×	3	= 0
		Forward index		= 21		Backward index		= 29

Index of total distance = 21 + 29 = 50

$$\% \text{ Forward movement } \frac{21}{21 + 29} = 42.0\%$$

A comparison of the two workplace arrangements shows:

Arrangement	Distance Index	% Forward Movements
A B C D	57	38.6%
B A C D	50	42.0%

Thus the arrangement of B A C D reduced the total distance traveled by 12.3% compared to the arrangement of A B C D, and at the same time increased the percentage of forward movements from 38.6% to 42.0%. Based on the criteria used, the B A C D arrangement of workplaces represents a better layout than the A B C D arrangement.

The use of travel charting for work system layouts where the workplaces are arranged in a single straight line and the distances between the workplaces are equal or can be assumed to be equal is limited in its practical application. A simple modification of the technique of travel charting will allow its use in evaluating workplace arrangements where the distances between the equipment are not equal or cannot be assumed to be equal. This obviously would expand the application of travel charts to more realistic situations.

ARRANGEMENT IN A STRAIGHT LINE WITH DIFFERENT DISTANCES BETWEEN THE WORKPLACES

As an example, assume five different workplaces, designated by letters A, B, C, D and E, are required in the production of certain products. The sequence of movements by employees between the workplaces is shown in Table 12.3 for various product groups.

TABLE 12.3

SEQUENCE OF EMPLOYEE MOVEMENTS BETWEEN WORKPLACES
FOR EACH PRODUCT GROUP

Product Group	Sequence of Movements
1	D A B C A C B A E
2	E C A C B A C A
3	E A D A B A
4	D C B D A B C A
5	E C A C A D A E
6	B C B A
7	D C B E

The frequency of movements between the various combinations of workplaces is summarized from the sequence of movements and is shown in Table 12.4.

TABLE 12.4

FREQUENCY OF EMPLOYEE MOVEMENTS BETWEEN THE FIVE WORKPLACES

Workplaces		
From	To	Frequency
A	B	3
A	C	4
A	D	2

TABLE 12.4 *(Continued)*

A	E	2
B	A	4
B	C	3
B	D	1
B	E	1
C	A	6
C	B	5
C	D	0
C	E	0
D	A	4
D	B	0
D	C	2
D	E	0
E	A	1
E	B	0
E	C	2
E	D	0

For purposes of the example, assume that the workplaces have the following length dimensions.

Workplace	Length Ft
A	4
B	2
C	6
D	2
E	4

Constructing the Travel Chart

Step 1.—Assume an arrangement using the five workplaces placed in a straight line. An arrangement of A B C D E is assumed and shown in Fig. 12.2.

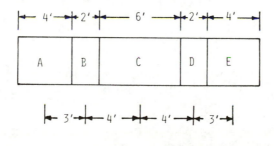

FIG. 12.2. WORKPLACE ARRANGEMENT SHOWING
DISTANCES MOVED

Step 2.—Using the workplace arrangement assumed in step 1, construct a distance chart as shown below. Note that the distances shown in the chart are for the particular workplace arrangement of A B C D E and would not necessarily be the same for other arrangements.

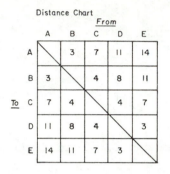

Distance Chart

Step 3.—For the same arrangement, construct a move chart using the frequency of movements given in Table 12.4. The completed move chart is shown below.

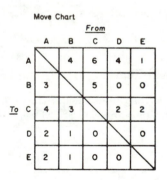

Move Chart

The frequency of movements as shown in the move chart will not change in value but will change position in the chart with different workplace arrangements.

Step 4.—The travel chart is constructed by multiplying each entry on the distance chart by the corresponding entry on the move chart and placing the result in the appropriate cell of the travel chart. The numbers entered on the travel chart indicate the total distances traveled between the various workplaces. The completed travel chart is shown on pg. 211.

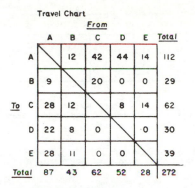

Travel Chart

		From				
	A	B	C	D	E	Total
A		12	42	44	14	112
B	9		20	0	0	29
To C	28	12		8	14	62
D	22	8	0		0	30
E	28	11	0	0		39
Total	87	43	62	52	28	272

Evaluating the Arrangement

Since the entries on the travel chart are actual distances traveled, an absolute measure of evaluating the workplace arrangement is found by totaling all the entries. This is done by subtotaling either the rows or columns and then totaling the subtotals as shown on the chart. The actual distance traveled for this example is 272 ft (82.9 m).

Another measure used to evaluate the arrangement is to determine the percentage of forward distances compared to the total distance traveled. This is done by totaling the distances below the diagonal of the chart (forward moves) and dividing by the total (forward and backward) distance.

Since the entries in the travel chart are the actual distances traveled between the various workplaces, an improved layout is characterized by smaller entries in the travel chart which in turn results in less total distance traveled. Because the entries in the chart are the product of the distance traveled between the workplaces times the frequency of the movements, and since both factors of the product may vary depending on the arrangement assumed, it becomes difficult to rationalize an improvement in the layout. Hence the problem of trying to find layout improvements becomes a matter of trial and error. Of course an optimum layout can be found by trying all possible layouts and determining the distances traveled.

A second workplace arrangement of C A B D E is assumed and is shown in Fig. 12.3.

The distance chart for the workplace arrangement of C A B D E is shown on pg. 212.

Note that the distance chart for the second arrangement is considerably different than the distance chart for the first arrangement.

The move chart for the second workplace arrangement is shown on pg. 212.

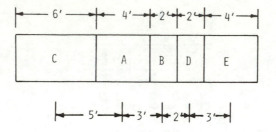

FIG. 12.3.   SECOND WORKPLACE ARRANGE-
MENT SHOWING DISTANCES MOVED

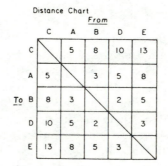

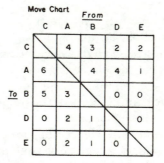

The completed travel chart for the second arrangement is shown on pg. 213.

The total distance traveled in the second arrangement is 242 ft (73.8 m) compared to 272 ft (82.9 m) for the first arrangement. This represents a reduction in distance traveled of 11%.

The use of travel charts to evaluate workplace arrangement, where the distances between adjacent workplaces are not equal, uses an absolute measure of the distance traveled. Although this method of travel

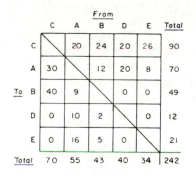

charting is more realistic than when equal distances are assumed between adjacent workplaces, it does not readily show how improvements in layout can be obtained. The method of travel charting using actual distances traveled does however mean that the technique is not limited to straight line arrangements of workplaces, but can be used for any pattern.

TRAVEL CHARTING USING PRODUCT FLOW AS CRITERION

In situations where large quantities of materials are handled between workplaces, such as dishwashing areas, the product movement is a better criterion to use for travel charting. The method of travel charting using product movements is similar to the method described using employee movements. Travel charting with product movements requires information regarding the amounts of materials and the distance that the products are moved between the various workplaces. This information is readily gathered by using the product process or form process charts. The amounts of materials may be indicated by pounds, unit loads or other suitable measurements of quantity.

For problems where the workplaces can be arranged in a straight line, the same procedure of travel charting described with employee movements is used. The only difference is that instead of using the frequency of employee movements, the amount of product flow is used. The amount of product flow should be the total amount moved between the workplaces. For example, if 100 lb (45.4 kg) are moved twice between two workplaces the total amount of 200 lb (90.7 kg) should be indicated in the travel chart. For straight line arrangements, the desirability of flow in one direction can be emphasized by penalizing the backward movements.

The situation where the workplaces can not be arranged in a straight line will be treated here to show the differences in using the travel charting method.

WORKPLACES ARRANGED AT RANDOM

As an illustration, assume that the material flow required to process several products is between six workplaces designated by A, B, C, D, E and F. The workplace may refer to a table, piece of equipment or a storage area. The quantity of materials moved and the sequence of movements are shown in Table 12.5.

TABLE 12.5

QUANTITY OF MATERIALS AND SEQUENCE OF MOVEMENTS FOR EACH PRODUCT GROUP

Product Group	Quantity (lb)	Sequence of Movements
1	100	A B D F
2	300	C A B C E F
3	200	B D F E
4	400	B D A B
5	100	C A C E F
6	200	C B C A B

The total quantity of materials moved between the workplaces is summarized in Table 12.6. The total quantity is determined by summing the quantity of materials moved between each combination of workplaces. For example, the quantity moved from workplace A to workplace B consists of 100 lb (45.4 kg) of product group 1; 300 lb (136 kg) of product group 2; 400 lb (181 kg) of product group 4; and 200 lb (90.7 kg) of product group 6; making a total of 1,000 lb (454 kg). Only those combinations of workplaces that involve material flow are shown.

TABLE 12.6

TOTAL QUANTITY OF MATERIALS MOVED BETWEEN WORKPLACES

Workplace		Quantity of Materials
From	To	Moved (lb)
A	B	1,000
A	C	100
B	C	500
B	D	700
C	A	600
C	B	200
C	E	400
D	A	400
D	F	300
E	F	400
F	E	200

Assuming the workplace arrangement shown in Fig. 12.4, the distance chart showing the distances between workplaces is constructed. It should be noted that the distance chart will remain constant regardless of where the various workplaces are placed. In this case an arbitrary arrangement of workplaces is selected to start the procedure. The distance chart is shown below. Distances are measured from the center of the locations. The distances have been rounded off to the nearest foot to simplify the presentation of the example.

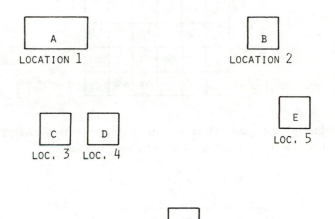

FIG. 12.4. WORKPLACE ARRANGEMENT FOR TRAVEL
CHARTING PROBLEM INVOLVING PRODUCT FLOW

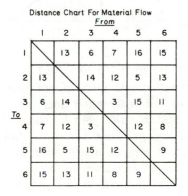

Distance Chart For Material Flow

	From					
	1	2	3	4	5	6
1		13	6	7	16	15
2	13		14	12	5	13
3	6	14		3	15	11
4	7	12	3		12	8
5	16	5	15	12		9
6	15	13	11	8	9	

Next a quantity chart is constructed. The row and column designations on the quantity chart must correspond to the placement of the workplaces in the various locations. The quantity chart is shown below.

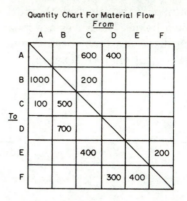

Quantity Chart For Material Flow

To\From	A	B	C	D	E	F
A			600	400		
B	1000		200			
C	100	500				
D		700				
E			400			200
F				300	400	

The product of the quantity times the distance is then computed and arranged into the travel chart as shown below.

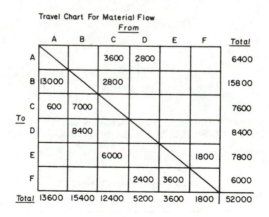

Travel Chart For Material Flow

To\From	A	B	C	D	E	F	Total
A			3600	2800			6400
B	13000		2800				15800
C	600	7000					7600
D		8400					8400
E			6000			1800	7800
F				2400	3600		6000
Total	13600	15400	12400	5200	3600	1800	52000

The total value of 52,000 lb-ft (7192 kg-m) expresses the amount of material flow for the given arrangement of workplaces.

The workplaces should be rearranged and another travel chart constructed to see if the material flow can be reduced. Since the material flow is the product of two variables (distance and quantity), that are not constant for different arrangements, there is no general procedure that can be used to find the optimum solution to the problem quickly. The only guide that can be followed is to try and locate the workplaces involving the greatest quantities of materials close together. The travel chart for a different arrangement of workplaces is shown below. The row or column designations indicate the placement of the workplaces in the six locations. For example, workplace A is at location 4, workplace B is at location 3, etc.

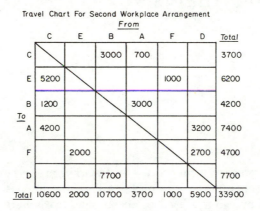

Travel Chart For Second Workplace Arrangement

To \ From	C	E	B	A	F	D	Total
C			3000	700			3700
E	5200				1000		6200
B	1200			3000			4200
A	4200					3200	7400
F		2000				2700	4700
D			7700				7700
Total	10600	2000	10700	3700	1000	5900	33900

The material flow for the second arrangement is 33,900 lb-ft (4688 kg-m) which is 18,100 lb-ft (2504 kg-m) less than the original arrangement. This represents a savings of about 35% and shows that based on material flow, the second layout arrangement is definitely better. Additional arrangements should be tried to see if further improvements can be obtained.

13

Operation Analysis

DEFINITION

The product process, form process and worker process charts described in the earlier chapters are examples of gross analysis techniques. In each case, the procedures used to accomplish work were merely broken down into identifiable parts. The primary purpose of process charting is to identify the undesirable elements of a procedure so they can be eliminated or reduced. Therefore, process charting is a good technique for locating unnecessary operations, excessive travel of personnel, idleness of personnel, inefficient sequences of operations or delays in the flow of materials.

Operation analysis is a finer technique than process charting. An operation analysis investigates the method a person uses to accomplish a given task at one workplace. Method refers to the way a person uses his body members, particularly the hands and arms. Thus, operation analysis is concerned with the motions a person uses in performing an operation. A worker engaged in cleaning vegetables at one workplace as shown in Fig. 13.1 can be studied by operation analysis.

The relation between operation analysis and process charting should now be evident. The activities charted as operations on process charts are further analyzed by operation analysis. In general, process charting primarily identifies *what* is being done, while operation analysis shows how it is done. In reality, operation analysis is a refined process charting technique because it identifies a procedure of work.

As in process charting, the primary objective of operation analysis is to study and improve work. Operation analysis attempts to eliminate all unnecessary motions of a worker and to arrange the remaining necessary motions in the best possible sequence. The principles of motion economy are used as a guide to develop the improved method of work.

218

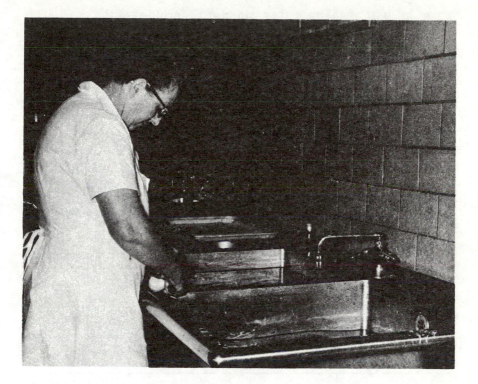

FIG. 13.1.   WORKER ACCOMPLISHING A TASK AT ONE WORKPLACE MAY
BE ANALYZED BY OPERATION CHARTING

Operation analysis can also be used to plan the method of work for new operations. When new tasks are created in an organization, the supervisors can utilize operation analysis techniques to develop the methods to be used and to help train the workers to use the proper methods.

The design of workplaces, especially the location of frequently used materials and hand tools, can also be guided by operation analysis.

OPERATION CHARTS

The operation chart is one of the simpler techniques used to present the method of work performed by an individual at one workplace. The operation chart shows the breakdown of the elements of the work for each body member engaged in a given task. The body members usually involved are the right and left hands. However, if the feet or eyes are an important part of the task they can also be included in the chart. The operation chart shows the sequence of the steps of each body member as well as their relationship to each other while working. Symbols used to represent the various activities of the body members for an operation chart are shown in Table 13.1. The geometric symbols are used to construct a regular operation chart and the time symbols are used to construct an operation *time* chart.

TABLE 13.1

OPERATION CHART SYMBOLS

Name	Geometric symbol	Time symbol	Used to represent
Sub-operation	◯	▮	Body member performing something at one area of a workplace.
Movement	∘	▦	Change in location of the body member from one work area of the workplace to another.
Delay	▽	▯	Idleness of the body member.
Hold	▽	▨	Maintaning an object in a fixed position by the body member.

Although similarity exists between the operation chart symbols and the process chart symbols, they are used to represent different activities for each type of chart. The large circle in an operation chart represents a much smaller subdivision of a task than the large circle does in a process chart. Actions of the hand such as grasping, positioning, placing, folding, using a hand tool, ladling, forming, pressing, etc., are represented on the operation chart by the sub-operation symbol. In general, any action that can not be classified as a movement, delay or hold would be represented by the sub-operation symbol.

The small circle in the operation chart represents a movement of the hands or other body members, while on the worker process chart it represented the movement of the entire body. The movement symbol is used in the operation chart when the body member moves from one designated work area of the workplace to another designated work area. This means that short movements occurring within the designated work area are assumed to be included in the sub-operation symbol. The subdivision of the workplace into smaller areas therefore determines how frequently the movement symbol will appear in the operation chart.

Care should be taken in designating the work areas of the workplace so enough detail will appear in the operation chart. As an analyst becomes more familiar with the operation to be studied, the breakdown of the workplace becomes easier. A general subdivision of the workplace can be accomplished in the following manner. The area directly in front of the operator where both hands are used to accomplish a part of the task should be designated as one work area. The actual dimensions of this work area should be approximately 15 in. (30.5 cm) wide and 12 in. (38.1 cm) deep, and will be referred to as the working area. The areas on either side of the working area should also be designated as separate work areas. The location of frequently used materials, hand tools, equipment and utensils used in the operation are also designated as separate work areas. The typical breakdown of a workplace is shown in Fig. 13.2.

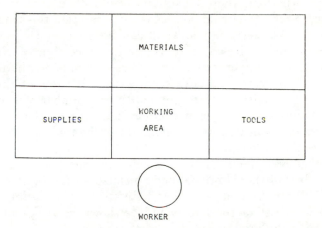

FIG. 13.2. TYPICAL BREAKDOWN OF WORKPLACE INTO
SUBWORK AREAS

Constructing the Operation Chart

The data for the operation chart of an existing operation can be gathered by direct visual observation of the worker. The usual procedure involves observing each hand or body member separately, then combining these separate observations on the chart. It is difficult to observe the motions of both hands and record these activities at the same time. In instances where the activities of the hands are complex and rapid, a number of observations may have to be taken to accurately present the facts. A preferred technique for observing complex and rapid movements is to use motion pictures and construct the operation chart from the pictures.

The operation chart is made by placing the appropriate symbols for the left hand in a single column to the left of the center of the chart and the symbols for the right hand on the right side of the center of the chart. Activities of the hands that occur simultaneously or at about the same time are represented by placing the symbols on the same horizontal line. The description for the left hand activity is placed to the immediate left of the left hand symbol and the description for the right hand activity is placed to the right of the right hand symbol. If distance or time are to be included in the operation chart, additional columns are generally placed between the left hand and right hand symbol columns.

Since the operation chart should show the relationship of activities between the right hand and left hand, an equal number of symbols for each hand should be shown. When an activity of one hand takes a longer time to perform than the activity of the other hand, the symbols for the longer activity should be repeated to maintain the simultaneous time concept. Another method that can be used which reduces the number of symbols drawn is to connect the bottom of the longer symbol with the top of the next different symbol with a straight vertical line. The vertical line then indicates repetition of the symbol for the longer activity to correspond with the number of symbols for the other hand. The number of symbols indicated by the vertical line are counted and indicated in the summary so the total number of symbols for each hand are equal.

When other body members are included in the operation, a column for the symbols of the additional body member should be provided. For example, if the right foot is used to activate a pedal during the operation, the activities of the foot would be shown in a separate column placed on the right hand side of the chart.

The summary of the operation chart shows the number of each symbol used for each body member. In addition, the totals of each type of symbol for the body members are shown, as well as the total number of symbols for the left and right hands. The total number of symbols for the right hand should equal the total number of symbols for the left hand. Distances or times that are shown on the chart are also totaled and shown in the summary. A preprinted form as shown in Fig. 13.3 may be used to construct the operation chart.

Constructing the Operation Time Chart

Data for the operation time chart are best obtained by motion pictures. It is practically impossible for an individual to visually observe all the actions of the hands, read a timing device and record these. activities

OPERATION CHART

OPERATION _____   PAGE ___ OF ___

PRESENT METHOD _____   DATE _____

PROPOSED METHOD _____   ANALYST _____

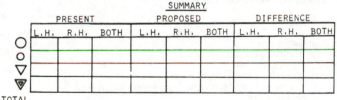

LEFT HAND DESCRIPTION	LEFT HAND SYMBOL	RIGHT HAND SYMBOL	RIGHT HAND DESCRIPTION

SUMMARY

	PRESENT			PROPOSED			DIFFERENCE		
	L.H.	R.H.	BOTH	L.H.	R.H.	BOTH	L.H.	R.H.	BOTH

TOTAL

FIG. 13.3. PREPRINTED FORM FOR OPERATION ANALYSIS

and times accurately. Since the operation time chart is used to emphasize the importance of time in an operation, it should be as accurate as possible.

The format of the operation time chart is similar to the regular operation chart. Individual columns are used for the left hand and right hand time symbols. A description column for each hand is also used. The time scale is usually placed along the left hand edge of the chart. The time symbols are placed in a continuous column with the length of each symbol corresponding to the time of the activity.

Analyzing Operation Charts

The analysis of operations usually results in the greatest improvements in the productivity of individual workers. This is due to the concentrated study that can be made on one worker at one workplace. Such situations enable the analyst to study all the factors involved in accomplishing a task, and to develop improved methods much easier than if several people or several workplaces are involved. Installing new methods is also easier because only one worker is involved.

The analysis of operations may be guided by the check list shown in Table 13.2. The table is subdivided according to the basic factors that affect work.

TABLE 13.2

CHECK LIST FOR OPERATION ANALYSIS

Can the operation or any part of the operation be eliminated, combined, simplified or rearranged by:

I. Materials
  1. Using different raw materials
  2. Changing the packaging
  3. Using standardized materials
  4. Changing the size
  5. Changing the shape
  6. Reducing the weight
  7. Speeding delivery of materials
  8. Using partially preprocessed materials

II. Process or Sequence
  1. Changing order
  2. Changing batch size
  3. Reducing number of steps
  4. Omitting unnecessary steps
  5. Performing two operations at the same time
  6. Changing the processing technique (e.g., steam instead of boil)
  7. Rebalancing the work
  8. Performing operation in another area
  9. Using new equipment
  10. Better training of the operator
  11. Arranging steps in best order

III. Method
  1. Prepositioning parts for easy grasp
  2. Prepositioning tools for easy grasp
  3. Using both hands
  4. Using lowest muscle group possible
  5. Using smooth motions
  6. Reducing hand-eye coordination time
  7. Reducing bending or turning
  8. Performing work in the normal work area
  9. Changing sequence of motions
  10. Reducing delays and holds

TABLE 13.2 *(Continued)*

11. Balancing work between both hands
12. Let feet do part of the work
13. Proper training
14. Shortening distances of movements
15. Reducing abrupt changes in direction
16. Using gravity
17. Picking up more than one part at a time
18. Developing rhythmic movements
19. Using fixtures for holding

IV. Equipment, Workplace, Environment
    1. Changing workplace height
    2. Changing workplace layout
    3. Increasing illumination
    4. Using gravity feed or ejection
    5. Providing seating
    6. Reducing noise and distractions
    7. Changing location of dials and controls
    8. Using better hand tools
    9. Using safer equipment
    10. Changing location of materials stored at workplace
    11. Providing conveyors or chutes
    12. Increasing the speed of machines
    13. Using color coding
    14. Reducing glare

V. Design of Product
    1. Changing requirements of finished product
    2. Changing form or shape
    3. Using preprocessed products
    4. Reducing weight
    5. Reducing the number of parts
    6. Eliminating frills
    7. Using proper spacing and sequence of data forms

OPERATION CHART ILLUSTRATIONS

The original method of preparing a fruit plate is shown by the operation chart given in Fig. 13.4. The fruit plates are prepared by one worker at one workplace. The arrangement of the materials at the workplace is shown in Fig. 13.5. A proposed method of preparing the fruit plate is shown in Fig. 13.6. Part of the improvement in the method resulted by the rearrangement of the materials at the workplace. These proposed material locations at the workplace are shown in Fig. 13.7. The improved method shows better balance as far as using both hands are concerned. Balancing of the work between the hands reduces the number of delays and holds to a minimum.

The operation chart in Fig. 13.8 shows the original method of breading veal cutlets. The workplace for the original method is shown in Fig. 13.9. Although this is a fairly simple operation, it can be improved as shown by the proposed operation chart given in Fig. 13.10. The improved method included the construction of a chute that allows the

OPERATION CHART

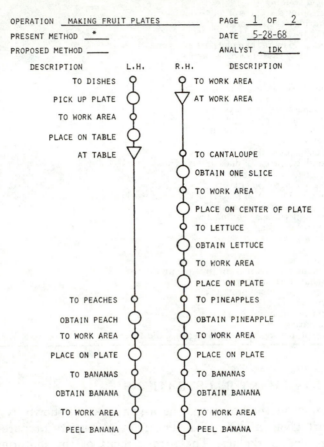

OPERATION ___MAKING FRUIT PLATES___   PAGE __1__ OF __2__
PRESENT METHOD __*__   DATE __5-28-68__
PROPOSED METHOD ____   ANALYST __IDK__

DESCRIPTION	L.H.	R.H.	DESCRIPTION
TO DISHES			TO WORK AREA
PICK UP PLATE			AT WORK AREA
TO WORK AREA			
PLACE ON TABLE			
AT TABLE			TO CANTALOUPE
			OBTAIN ONE SLICE
			TO WORK AREA
			PLACE ON CENTER OF PLATE
			TO LETTUCE
			OBTAIN LETTUCE
			TO WORK AREA
			PLACE ON PLATE
TO PEACHES			TO PINEAPPLES
OBTAIN PEACH			OBTAIN PINEAPPLE
TO WORK AREA			TO WORK AREA
PLACE ON PLATE			PLACE ON PLATE
TO BANANAS			TO BANANAS
OBTAIN BANANA			OBTAIN BANANA
TO WORK AREA			TO WORK AREA
PEEL BANANA			PEEL BANANA

FIG. 13.4. PART I—OPERATION CHART OF ORIGINAL METHOD OF
PREPARING FRUIT PLATES

meat to fall directly into the flour pan from the tenderizer. This allows
both hands to feed the meat into the tenderizer. In the original method
one hand was used to receive the meat from the tenderizer and put it
into the flour pan.

OPERATION CHART

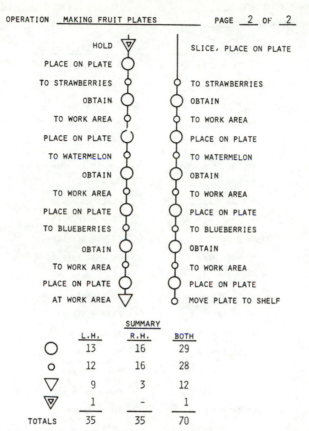

OPERATION MAKING FRUIT PLATES   PAGE 2 OF 2

HOLD	▽		SLICE, PLACE ON PLATE
PLACE ON PLATE	○		
TO STRAWBERRIES	○	○	TO STRAWBERRIES
OBTAIN	○	○	OBTAIN
TO WORK AREA	○	○	TO WORK AREA
PLACE ON PLATE	○	○	PLACE ON PLATE
TO WATERMELON	○	○	TO WATERMELON
OBTAIN	○	○	OBTAIN
TO WORK AREA	○	○	TO WORK AREA
PLACE ON PLATE	○	○	PLACE ON PLATE
TO BLUEBERRIES	○	○	TO BLUEBERRIES
OBTAIN	○	○	OBTAIN
TO WORK AREA	○	○	TO WORK AREA
PLACE ON PLATE	○	○	PLACE ON PLATE
AT WORK AREA	▽	○	MOVE PLATE TO SHELF

SUMMARY

	L.H.	R.H.	BOTH
○	13	16	29
○	12	16	28
▽	9	3	12
▽	1	-	1
TOTALS	35	35	70

FIG. 13.4. PART II

SHELF					
CANT-ALOUPE	PEACHES	LETTUCE	WATER-MELON	PINE-APPLES	BLUE-BERRIES
PLATES		WORK AREA		STRAWBERRIES	
				BANANAS	

FIG. 13.5. WORKPLACE ARRANGEMENT FOR ORIGINAL METHOD
OF PREPARING FRUIT PLATES

OPERATION CHART

DESCRIPTION	L.H.	R.H.	DESCRIPTION
TO DISHES	○	○	TO CANTALOUPE
OBTAIN PLATE	◯	◯	OBTAIN CANTALOUPE
TO WORK AREA	○	○	TO WORK AREA
PLACE ON TABLE	◯	◯	PLACE ON PLATE
TO PEACHES	○	○	TO LETTUCE
OBTAIN PEACH	◯	◯	OBTAIN LETTUCE
TO WORK AREA	○	○	TO WORK AREA
PLACE ON PLATE	◯	◯	PLACE ON PLATE
TO PINEAPPLES	○	○	TO BLUEBERRIES
OBTAIN PINEAPPLE	◯	◯	OBTAIN BLUEBERRIES
TO WORK AREA	○	○	TO WORK AREA
PLACE ON PLATE	◯	◯	PLACE ON PLATE
TO BANANAS	○	○	TO BANANAS
OBTAIN BANANA	◯	◯	OBTAIN BANANA
TO WORK AREA	○	○	TO WORK AREA
PEEL BANANA	◯	◯	PEEL BANANA
HOLD	▽		SLICE BANANA
PLACE ON PLATE	◯		PLACE ON PLATE
TO STRAWBERRIES	○	○	TO STRAWBERRIES
OBTAIN	◯	◯	OBTAIN
TO WORK AREA	○	○	TO WORK AREA
PLACE ON PLATE	◯	◯	PLACE ON PLATE, PICK UP PLATE
TO WATERMELON	○	○	TO WATERMELON
OBTAIN, PLACE ON PLATE	◯	▽	HOLD PLATE
IDLE	▽	○	TO SHELF

SUMMARY

	PRESENT			PROPOSED			DIFFERENCE		
	L.H.	R.H.	BOTH	L.H.	R.H.	BOTH	L.H.	R.H.	BOTH
◯	13	16	29	12	12	24	1	4	5
○	12	16	28	11	12	23	1	4	5
▽	9	3	12	1	-	1	8	3	11
▽	1	-	1	1	1	2	-	1	1
TOTALS	35	35	70	25	25	50	10	10	20

FIG. 13.6. OPERATION CHART OF PROPOSED METHOD OF PREPARING FRUIT PLATES

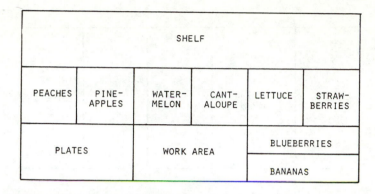

SHELF					
PEACHES	PINE-APPLES	WATER-MELON	CANT-ALOUPE	LETTUCE	STRAW-BERRIES
PLATES		WORK AREA		BLUEBERRIES	
				BANANAS	

FIG. 13.7. PROPOSED ARRANGEMENT OF WORKPLACE FOR PREPARING FRUIT PLATES

OPERATION CHART

OPERATION BREADING CUTLETS   PAGE 1 OF 1
PRESENT METHOD *   DATE 5-3- 68
PROPOSED METHOD ———   ANALYST GW

DESCRIPTION	L.H.	R.H	DESCRIPTION
AT SIDE	▽	○	TO RAW CUTLETS
		◯	OBTAIN CUTLET
TO TENDERIZER	○	○	TO TENDERIZER
AT TENDERIZER	▽	◯	FEED INTO TENDERIZER
TAKE CUTLET	◯	▽	AT TENDERIZER
FLOUR CUTLET	◯	◯	FLOUR CUTLET
TO EGG WASH	○	○	TO EGG WASH
DIP CUTLET IN WASH	◯	◯	DIP CUTLET IN WASH
TO BREADING	○	○	TO BREADING
BREAD CUTLET	◯	◯	BREAD CUTLET
TO PAN	○	▽	DELAY
PLACE IN PAN	◯		

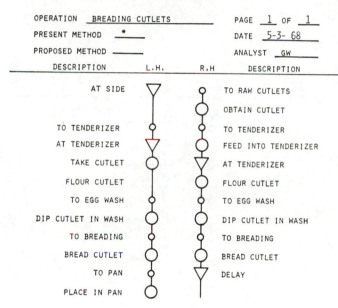

	SUMMARY		
	L.H.	R.H.	BOTH HANDS
◯	5	5	10
○	4	4	8
▽	3	3	6
TOTAL	12	12	24

FIG 13.8. OPERATION CHART OF ORIGINAL METHOD OF BREADING VEAL CUTLETS

RAW CUTLETS	TENDERIZER FLOUR	EGG WASH	BREADING	FINISHED CUTLETS

FIG. 13.9. WORKPLACE ARRANGEMENT FOR ORIGINAL METHOD OF BREADING VEAL CUTLETS

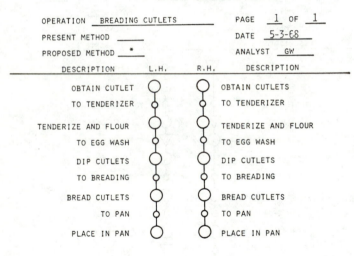

OPERATION CHART

OPERATION __BREADING CUTLETS__   PAGE __1__ OF __1__

PRESENT METHOD _____   DATE __5-3-68__

PROPOSED METHOD __*__   ANALYST __GW__

DESCRIPTION	L.H.	R.H.	DESCRIPTION
OBTAIN CUTLET			OBTAIN CUTLETS
TO TENDERIZER			TO TENDERIZER
TENDERIZE AND FLOUR			TENDERIZE AND FLOUR
TO EGG WASH			TO EGG WASH
DIP CUTLETS			DIP CUTLETS
TO BREADING			TO BREADING
BREAD CUTLETS			BREAD CUTLETS
TO PAN			TO PAN
PLACE IN PAN			PLACE IN PAN

SUMMARY

	PRESENT			PROPOSED			DIFFERENCE		
	L.H.	R.H.	BOTH	L.H.	R.H.	BOTH	L.H.	R.H.	BOTH
○	5	5	10	5	5	10	-	-	-
ο	4	4	8	4	4	8	-	-	-
▽	3	3	6	-	-	-	3	3	6
TOTAL	12	12	24	9	9	18	3	3	6

FIG 13.10. PROPOSED OPERATION CHART OF BREADING VEAL CUTLETS

Multi-activity Analysis

DEFINITION

Multi-activity refers to a situation where one worker works coordinately with one or more other workers and/or one or more machines to accomplish a task. A necessary characteristic of multi-activities is the presence of a time controlling element. The time controlling element could be either a worker or a machine that affects the activity of other workers or machines involved in the task. To illustrate, consider a dishwashing crew of two workers operating a dishwashing machine. The worker who loads the dishwashing machine is the time controlling element for the worker unloading the machine because the unloader cannot perform his or her part of the task until the loader completes his or her part first. The dishwashing machine could also act as the time controlling element. This occurs when the dishwashing machine cannot handle as many dishes as the loader can feed, therefore causing the loader to stop. The unloader may also act as the time control for both the loader and the machine. When the unloader cannot unload fast enough, the dishwashing machine will stop which in turn causes the loader to stop.

The following criteria should be used to determine when a worker is a part of a multi-activity. If the worker in question can perform his or her assigned task without changing his or her method of work and without the presence of the other members of the activity, he or she should not be considered a part of the multi-activity. In other words, the worker who accomplishes a task independent of others can be analyzed individually. The purpose of identifying multi-activities is to analyze the interactions of the workers and machines involved.

Multi-activities are subdivided into five types depending on the number of workers and machines involved. The subdivision is as follows:

1. *Worker and machine* activities involve only one worker and one

machine working coordinately to accomplish a task. The term machine refers to any mechanical device activated and controlled by the worker. Typical worker and machine activities are represented by a person working with a calculator, a cash register, a food mixer, an X-ray machine, a floor polisher, a glasswasher or a slicer.

2. *Worker and multi-machine* activities involve one worker and two or more machines working coordinately. A cook using several pieces of equipment in a short-order kitchen or a person running several data processing machines are examples of this type of activity.

3. *Multi-worker* activities involve two or more workers working coordinately. Machines are not used in this type of activity. Banquet setup crews and maintenance crews are usually involved in multi-worker activities.

4. *Multi-worker and machine* activities involve two or more workers working coordinately with one machine. Examples of this type of multi-activity are dishwashing and mangling crews.

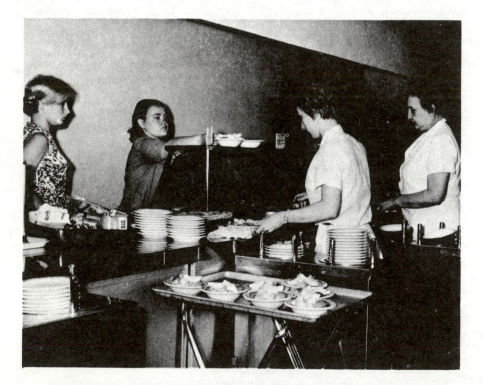

FIG. 14.1.   CAFETERIA LINE REPRESENTS MULTI–ACTIVITY
BETWEEN SERVERS AND CUSTOMERS

5. *Multi-worker and multi-machine* activities involve two or more workers working with two or more machines. The food production staff in institutional kitchens or catering kitchens are frequently involved in multi-worker and multi-machine activities. A typical cafeteria serving line as shown in Fig. 14.1 is also an example of a multi-worker and multi-machine activity.

One objective of analyzing multi-activities is to improve the effectiveness of the workers and/or machines used for accomplishing a task. This is done primarily by eliminating unnecessary delays occurring in the system. A change in the individual work assignments of each member of the multi-activity frequently results in better balance and increases the efficiency of the crew. Multi-activity analysis is also used to determine where more detailed analysis techniques can be applied to improve the work.

In planning work, the multi-activity analysis will aid in determining the number of machines a crew of workers should operate. This type of analysis is also useful in determining the optimum crew size to use.

MULTI-ACTIVITY CHARTS

The multi-activity charts are used to systematically and graphically display the procedures used by the workers and machines working coordinately on a task. Each of the five types of multi-activities can be analyzed by the process charting or operation charting technique. Multi-activity charts are basically the combination of individual charts of workers and machines in such a manner that the interrelationships of the activities are clearly shown. This means that the charts have to show the simultaneity of actions involved in the task. The types of multi-activity charts to use for various situations are shown in Table 14.1.

The symbols used for the regular multi-activity charts are either the geometric worker process chart symbols or the geometric operation chart symbols. Multi-activity time charts use either the process time symbols or the operation time symbols. Only two symbols are used in charting a machine. In the multi-activity process charts, the operation symbol is used when the machine is operating and the delay symbol is used when the machine is not operating. In the multi-activity operation charts, the suboperation and delay symbols respectively are used to indicate whether the machine is operating or not.

Constructing the Multi-activity Process Charts

The procedure for constructing a multi-activity process chart is sim-

TABLE 14.1

CHARTS USED TO ANALYZE MULTI–ACTIVITIES

Multi-activity	*Type of Chart*
1. One worker moving from workplace to workplace where one workplace is a machine.	Worker machine process or process time chart.
2. One worker working at one location with a machine.	Worker machine operation or operation time chart.
3. One worker moving from workplace to workplace where two or more of the workplaces are machines.	Worker multi-machine process or process time chart.
4. One worker working at one location with two or more machines.	Worker multi-machine operation or operation time chart.
5. Two or more workers moving from workplace to workplace where machines are not involved.	Multi-worker process or process time chart.
6. Two or more workers at one workplace where machines are not involved.	Multi-worker operation or operation time chart.
7. Two or more workers moving from workplace to workplace where one workplace is a machine.	Multi-worker machine process or process time chart.
8. Two or more workers at one workplace where the workplace is a machine.	Multi-worker machine operation or operation time chart.
9. Two or more workers moving from workplace to workplace where two or more of the workplaces are machines.	Multi-worker multi-machine process or process time chart.
10. Two or more workers at one workplace where the workplace contains two or more machines.	Multi-worker multi-machine operation or operation time chart.

ilar to that described for the regular worker process chart. The data may be gathered by direct visual observations or by taking motion pictures. The use of motion pictures may be limited if the workers involved in the multi-activity are separated by long distances.

The number of columns to use for the multi-activity process chart depends on the number of workers and machines involved in the activity. Two columns should be provided for each worker charted; one column is for the placement of the symbols and the other column for the description. A separate column should be provided for each machine to be charted. Thus a process chart for a worker and machine activity would consist basically of three columns. The basic process chart analyzing the multi-activity of 2 workers and 3 machines would consist of 7 columns. If other information such as distance is desired, the additional columns have to be provided.

The symbols for each worker and machine are placed in the vertical columns in sequential order. Activities occurring at the same time are shown on the chart by placing the symbols on the same horizontal lines.

The summary of the charts should show the breakdown and the total number of symbols used for each worker and machine.

A diagram showing the location of the various workplaces should be included with the multi-activity process charts. Flow diagrams can also be made. The flow of the different operators can be shown by using different colors for the flow lines.

Constructing the Multi-activity Operation Charts

The multi-activity operation charts are basically combinations of separate operation charts and include columns for the machines when they are a part of the activity. Four columns are required for each worker analyzed. The four columns are used for (1) the symbols for the left hand; (2) the description of the left hand; (3) the symbols for the right hand; and (4) the description of the right hand. A separate additional column is provided for each machine involved in the multi-activity. Thus a basic multi-worker and multi-machine operation chart of 2 workers and 2 machines will have 10 columns. The symbols are placed to show the interrelations between the activities of the workers and machines. The same guides described for making operation charts can be applied to the construction of multi-activity operation charts.

The summary of a multi-activity operation chart should include: (1) the total number of each type of symbol for each hand of each worker charted; (2) the total number of each type of symbol for both hands of each worker charted; (3) the total number of all symbols for each hand of each worker; and (4) the total number of each symbol for each machine.

A workplace diagram showing the breakdown into work areas should be included with the chart.

Check List for Multi-activity Analysis

A check list for analyzing multi-activities is shown in Table 14.2. Since multi-activities can be studied by either process charting or operation charting techniques, the check lists for process charts and operation charts given in the earlier chapters may also be helpful in developing improvements.

TABLE 14.2

CHECK LIST FOR MULTI-ACTIVITY ANALYSIS

Can any steps in a multi-activity procedure be eliminated or simplified by:

1. Using a different size crew
2. Using a different machine
3. Balancing work among individuals
4. Changing order of steps
5. Combining operations
6. Reducing delays
7. Assigning work to other crews
8. Rearranging workplaces and storage areas
9. Balancing worker-machine times
10. Increasing speed or capacity of machines
11. Changing batch size
12. Changing a crew member
13. Better training of crew
14. Rescheduling of tasks
15. Changing the raw materials used
16. Changing the design of the product
17. Working on more than one item
18. Changing location of controls
19. Using automatic timing devices
20. Using automatic feed
21. Using conveyors
22. Reducing duplication of inspections
23. Making use of gravity or inertia
24. Changing the number of machines used

Illustrations of Multi-activity Analysis

The multi-worker process chart shown in Fig. 14.2 depicts the procedures of a drive-in counter worker waiting on a customer. Charting the customer is desirable because it gives an indication of the serving time required per person. The customer is the controlling factor because the worker's activities can not begin until the customer places his or her order. The workplace and flow diagram for the original chart are shown in Fig. 14.3.

The proposed procedures for the multi-worker activity are shown in Fig. 14.4. Since all items are already prepared, the time required for putting together an order is very short and the worker frequently has to wait for the customer to get out his money. In the proposed procedure, the customer is told the cost of the order immediately after ordering so he or she may get his or her money ready while the worker is bagging the order. The flow diagram for the proposed procedures is shown in Fig. 14.5.

A worker machine operation chart for a cashiering operation is shown in Fig. 14.6. An operation analysis is called for because the cashier performs his or her task at one workplace. The workplace and location of the cash register are shown in Fig. 14.7.

MULTI WORKER PROCESS CHART

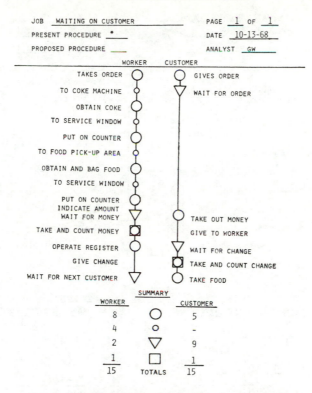

JOB **WAITING ON CUSTOMER** PAGE **1** OF **1**

PRESENT PROCEDURE ***** DATE **10-13-68**

PROPOSED PROCEDURE ____ ANALYST **GW**

	WORKER	CUSTOMER	
TAKES ORDER	○	○	GIVES ORDER
TO COKE MACHINE	○	▽	WAIT FOR ORDER
OBTAIN COKE	○		
TO SERVICE WINDOW	○		
PUT ON COUNTER	○		
TO FOOD PICK-UP AREA	○		
OBTAIN AND BAG FOOD	○		
TO SERVICE WINDOW	○		
PUT ON COUNTER INDICATE AMOUNT WAIT FOR MONEY	▽	○	TAKE OUT MONEY
TAKE AND COUNT MONEY	◻		GIVE TO WORKER
OPERATE REGISTER	○	▽	WAIT FOR CHANGE
GIVE CHANGE		◻	TAKE AND COUNT CHANGE
WAIT FOR NEXT CUSTOMER	▽	○	TAKE FOOD

SUMMARY

WORKER		CUSTOMER
8	○	5
4	○	-
2	▽	9
1	◻	1
15	TOTALS	15

FIG. 14.2. MULTI-WORKER PROCESS CHART OF ORIGINAL PROCEDURE FOR PREPARING ORDER OF TWO HAMBURGERS AND COKE

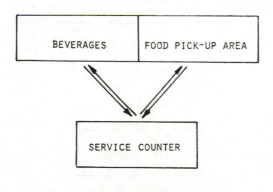

FIG. 14.3. FLOW DIAGRAM OF ORIGINAL PROCEDURE FOR PREPARING ORDER

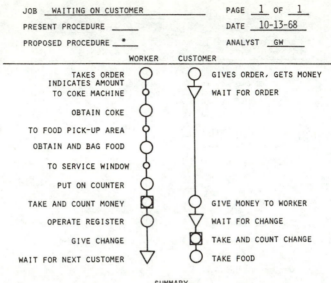

FIG. 14.4. PROPOSED MULTI-WORKER PROCESS CHART OF PROCEDURE
FOR PREPARING ORDER OF TWO HAMBURGERS AND COKE

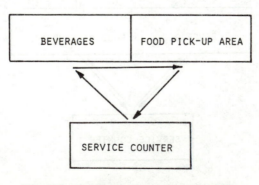

FIG. 14.5. FLOW DIAGRAM OF PROPOSED
PROCEDURE OF PREPARING ORDER

WORKER MACHINE OPERATION CHART

OPERATION __CASHIERING__   PAGE __1__ OF __1__

PRESENT METHOD __*__   DATE __10-24-68__

PROPOSED METHOD _____   ANALYST __GW__

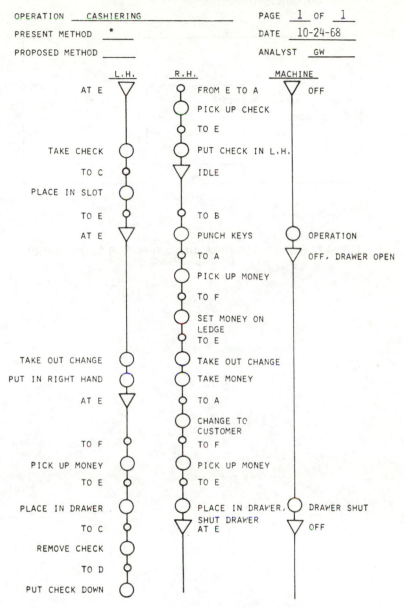

SUMMARY				
	L.H.	R.H.	BOTH	MACHINE
◯	8	10	18	2
o	6	9	15	-
▽	11	6	17	23
TOTALS	25	25	50	25

FIG. 14.6. WORKER-MACHINE OPERATION CHART FOR ORIGINAL METHOD
OF CASHIERING

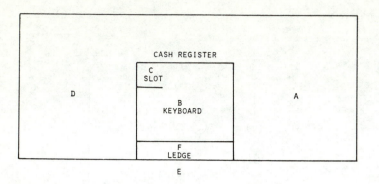

**FIG. 14.7. WORKPLACE ARRANGEMENT FOR ORIGINAL METHOD
OF CASHIERING**

Motion Analysis

INTRODUCTION

Motion analysis determines in considerable detail the actions of a worker's hands and fingers in accomplishing a task at one workplace. In one sense, motion analysis can be considered as the breakdown of the symbols on an operation chart similar to the way that the operation analysis was considered as the breakdown of the worker process chart symbols. Thus, the activities of workers can be studied at three levels of refinement. The worker may be analyzed by process analysis which gives a gross breakdown of activities; by operation analysis which gives an intermediate breakdown of activities; and by motion analysis which gives the greatest breakdown of activities. Because of its high level of refinement, motion analysis is primarily used to study highly repetitive tasks or tasks containing a large amount of manual effort. The task of tray assembly shown in Fig. 15.1 may be studied by motion analysis. Similar tasks that are performed by a large number of workers may also be studied by motion analysis.

The objective of motion analysis is to eliminate or reduce ineffective motions and to simplify and speed the effective motions of workers. Through motion study, easier methods of performing manual tasks can be developed. Motion study can also assist in training workers to do manual tasks requiring skill and finger dexterity. Very little motion analyses of tasks frequently done in hotels, institutions and restaurants have been carried out and considerable improvements could be made by using this technique.

Therbligs

Therbligs refer to fundamental hand motions as developed by the pioneer motion analysts. The therbligs, their symbols and color designations are shown in Table 15.1. The common symbol designation of the therbligs are letter abbreviations. The color designations may be used to simplify identification of the therbligs.

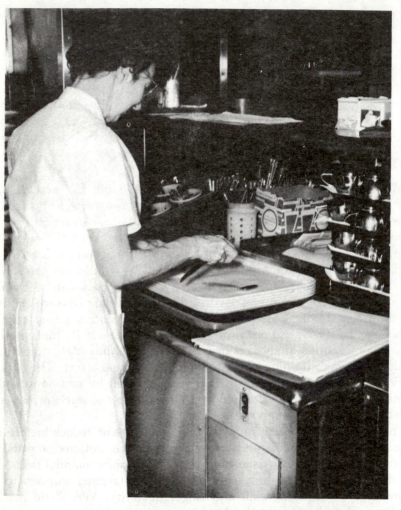

FIG. 15.1. THE HIGHLY REPETITIVE TASK OF ASSEMBLING FOOD TRAYS MAY BE STUDIED BY MOTION ANALYSIS

Therblig Definitions

The therblig definitions and an indication of their beginning and ending points are as follows:

1. **Grasp.**—Grasp is the motion of closing the fingers around an object to gain control of the object. Grasp begins when the fingers first touch

TABLE 15.1

SYMBOL AND COLOR DESIGNATIONS OF THERBLIGS

Therblig Name	Symbol	Color Designation
1. Grasp	G	Lake red
2. Position	P	Blue
3. Preposition	PP	Sky blue
4. Use	U	Purple
5. Assemble	A	Heavy violet
6. Disassemble	DA	Light violet
7. Release load	RL	Carmine red
8. Transport empty	TE	Olive green
9. Transport loaded	TL	Grass green
10. Search	SH	Black
11. Select	ST	Light gray
12. Hold	H	Gold ochre
13. Unavoidable delay	UD	Yellow ochre
14. Avoidable delay	AD	Lemon yellow
15. Rest	R	Orange
16. Plan	PN	Brown
17. Inspect	I	Burnt ochre

FIG. 15.2. WORKER GRASPING A GLASS WITH ONE HAND

The other hand is involved in a holding action.

the object and ends when the hand has control of the object. Example: Closing the finger around a glass prior to picking it up as shown in Fig. 15.2.

2. Position.—Position consists of turning or locating an object so it will be oriented in a particular way. Position begins when the hand or fingers begin to turn or locate the object and ends when the object has been positioned. Example: orienting a slice of ham prior to placing it on a slice of bread.

3. Preposition.—Preposition consists of orienting an object into a predetermined position so it will be ready for the next motion, usually a grasp. Preposition and position are similar except for the fact that preposition of objects takes place at a time prior to when it is needed. Prepositioning should eliminate the need for positioning at a later time. Example: turning the handles of cups so they are in the best position to be grasped.

4. Use.—Use consists of manipulating a tool or device in the manner which it was intended. Use begins when the hand starts manipulating the tool or device and ends when the manipulation stops. Example: manipulating a hand whip to stir food.

5. Assemble.—Assembly is the action of bringing two objects together to form one integrated object. One object may be placed into or on top of the other. Assembly begins when the hand starts to move the object into place and ends when the assembly is completed. Example: placing lettuce on a sandwich.

6. Disassemble.—Disassembly consists of separating one part of an integrated object from another part. Disassembly begins when the hand starts to remove the part and ends when the part is separated. Example: removing the cap from a jar of pickles.

7. Release Load.—This action consists of opening the fingers to lose control of an object. Release load begins when the fingers start to open and ends when the object has been separated from the fingers. Example: letting go of silverware into their containers.

8. Transport Empty.—Transport empty involves movement of the empty hand from one location to another. This action is usually associated with reaching for an object or returning the hand after placing an object. Transport empty begins when the hand starts its movement and ends when the movement ceases. Example: moving the empty hand to reach for a knife or other hand tool.

9. Transport Loaded.—Transport loaded consists of moving the hand while holding or pushing an object from one location to another. This action begins when the object starts to move and ends when the object stops moving. Example: sliding a form across the desk.

10. Search.—Search is the basic element used to locate an object. It involves the use of the hands or eyes in finding the desired object.

Search begins when the hands or eyes start their effort to locate the object and ends when the object is located.

11. Select.—Select consists of choosing one object from several similar objects. Search and select are very similar and some analysts suggest that they may be used interchangeably to simplify their use. Some analysts feel that both therbligs should be used for locating an object. Others feel that either one or the other should be used for locating the object: search when the object is among a mixed variety of objects and select when the object is one of a group of similar objects. This author favors the last criteria in the use of these therbligs. Select begins when the hands or eyes start to locate the object and ends when the object is located. Example: taking one spoon from a container of spoons.

12. Hold.—Hold consists of the hand maintaining an object in a fixed position. Hold frequently occurs in one hand while the other hand works on the object. Hold begins when the object is in the desired position and ends with the start of the next therblig. Example: holding an onion in one hand and peeling it with the other hand.

13. Unavoidable Delay.—Unavoidable delay is idleness of the hands beyond the control of the worker. Unavoidable delays occur because the nature of the task does not have things for both hands to do at the same time. Unavoidable delay begins with inactivity of the hand and ends when the hand starts an activity.

14. Avoidable Delay.—Avoidable delay is idleness of the hands which is within the control of the worker. Such delays may be avoided if the worker so desires. Avoidable delay begins with inactivity of the hands and ends when the hands become active. Example: stopping work to watch a person walk by.

15. Rest.—This inactivity occurs to recover from fatigue caused by the task. The amount of rest required will depend on the type of task and the endurance of the worker. Rest begins with inactivity of the hands and ends when the hands become active. It is extremely difficult to differentiate between avoidable delay and rest in some cases. Example: placing hands on table or at side to rest.

16. Plan.—Plan is a mental activity that usually precedes some physical activity of the hands. This therblig is frequently encountered in new employees. Plan begins and ends with the starting and completion of the mental activity. Example: sandwich maker plans procedure for assembling sandwiches.

17. Inspect.—Inspect involves examination of an object to compare the quality with a standard. The inspection can be made by sight, touch, odor or taste. Inspect frequently occurs simultaneously with other therbligs. Inspect begins when the worker starts the examination and ends when the examination is completed. Example: tasting soup for flavor or checking steaks for doneness.

Constructing Therblig Charts

Therblig charts are constructed in the same manner as operation charts except that therblig symbols instead of operation symbols are used. The data may be gathered by visual observation or by filming the operation. (Gathering data by filming and analyzing the film is referred to as micromotion analysis which is discussed in the next chapter.) Since some of the hand motions observed are similar, the analyst will have to make quick decisions as to the therblig to record on the chart. Some of these similar motions and suggested guides for therblig use are presented below.

Position and Preposition.—These two motions can be distinguished if the intent of the motion is determined. Position should be used when the hand orients an object for the benefit of the next therblig. Orienting a knife into the cutting position, or turning a spoon to obtain an ingredient are examples of this type of motion. The intent of the motion of orientation in both examples was for the benefit of the next therblig, i.e., use. Another situation where position should be used is when the intent of the orientation motion is to result in the immediate placement of an object in one particular location. Placing silverware at a banquet table involves position because each piece of silverware is intentionally put in a specified location.

The preposition therblig should be used when the orientation motion is for the benefit of a therblig that occurs later in the sequence. The waitress who turns a dinner plate on a tray before she picks it up, moves it and places it on the table is prepositioning. In this case the prepositioning was done so the plate could be put down with the meat toward the guest. The sequence of motions involved would be turning the plate (preposition); picking up the plate (grasp); moving the plate to the table (transport loaded); orienting the plate in the front of the guest (position); and putting down the plate (release load). The position and preposition therbligs should not follow one another in the therblig chart. If both motions are present in a sequence, they generally are separated by one or more other therbligs.

Assemble and Release Load.—Placing one object on top of another may be either assembly or release load. The intent of the action will determine which is the correct therblig to use. Putting the top slice on a sandwich should be considered an assembly because the intent is to have the sandwich consumed as a whole. In contrast, putting a slice of bread on a plate should be shown by release load because eventually the bread will be separated from the plate. Therefore, if the intent of placing one object on another is to have the two objects consumed, or used together, the assemble therblig is used. The release load therblig is used if the bringing together of two objects is for other purposes and the objects will be separated at a later time. The assemble and release load therbligs should not follow one another on a therblig chart.

Search and Select.—These two actions are so similar that many opinions regarding their use have been expressed. Probably the easiest procedure to follow for using the search or select therbligs is to make a choice between them based on the nature of the objects involved. Search should be used when the individual is attempting to find one object characterized by its shape, size or other specific identifying criterion. Looking for the pinkest sheet of paper, the biggest egg, the longest knife or the smallest potato are search activities.

Looking for an object whose characteristics are the same as other objects present, or where it does not matter which one of several objects is chosen should be charted by the select therblig. Taking an olive from a jar, the top sheet of paper from a stack, or the loaf of bread at the back of the shelf are examples of the select therblig. Search and select do not normally follow one another except for a few special situations. One exception occurs when an individual looking for an object has to first find the box, drawer or shelf containing the object. The activity in this case would be shown on the chart by the search therblig followed by the select therblig.

Therblig Chart Format

The therblig chart consists of left-hand and right-hand columns for the placement of the therbligs. Brief descriptions are included to describe each therblig. Therbligs occurring at the same time are placed on the same line.

Distances of the hand movements can be designated by using a number designation with the transport therbligs. For example, a movement of the empty hand over a distance of seven inches (178 mm) can be shown by the therblig designation TE 7. TL 18 represents moving an object with the hand a distance of 18 in. (457 mm).

The summary for the therblig chart should show the breakdown of therbligs used by each hand and the total number of therbligs for each hand. The total number of therbligs for each hand should be equal.

A workplace diagram should accompany all therblig charts. It is not necessary to break down the workplace into work areas as done with operation charts because all movements of the hands, regardless of length, are shown in the therblig chart.

Simo Charts

Simo (simultaneous motion) charts are therblig charts that are drawn to a time scale. In this sense the simo charts are made from the analysis of the filming of a procedure. Filming enables the analyst to carefully determine the therbligs involved. The film also serves to record the times since a timing device is frequently photographed along with the individual doing the work.

The simo chart includes the therblig, therblig description and therblig times for both hands. The times required for each motion are drawn to scale in a vertical column. The color designations of the therbligs may be shown in the time column.

Simo charts are only used for the most repetitive tasks because of the cost and time involved.

CHECK LIST FOR MOTION ANALYSIS

The analysis of motions should be guided by the principles of motion economy. The check list of motion analysis shown in Table 15.2 includes many of these principles.

TABLE 15.2

CHECK LIST FOR MOTION ANALYSIS

Can any motion be eliminated or simplified by:

I. Materials
    1. Reducing the weight
    2. Improving grasp characteristics of materials
    3. Using fewer materials
    4. Using interchangeable materials
    5. Prepositioning materials
    6. Sliding instead of picking up
    7. Changing shape of materials for easier assembly
    8. Standardizing materials to reduce searching and selecting
    9. Combining materials
    10. Better identification of materials

II. Process or Sequence
    1. Changing order to eliminate holds and delays
    2. Processing two items at one time
    3. Combining inspection with assembly
    4. Using machine inspection instead of visual inspection
    5. Combining movements
    6. Reducing transport empty movements

III. Method
    1. Balancing work of the hands
    2. Using uniform motion patterns
    3. Reducing hand to hand transfers
    4. Using chutes or conveyors

TABLE 15.2 *(Continued)*

  5. Using smooth motions, simultaneously and symmetrically
  6. Using gravity
  7. Reducing unavoidable delays
  8. Reducing positioning and prepositioning
  9. Using a holding device
 10. Shortening distances of transports
 11. Reducing regrasp
 12. Reducing bending or turning of body
 13. Reducing hand-eye coordination
 14. Reducing pickups and releases
 15. Placing grasp and release areas close together
 16. Proper training in motion economy

IV. Equipment, Workplace, Environment
  1. Prepositioning tools
  2. Using standardized tools
  3. Improving design of bins and containers
  4. Using jigs and fixtures for holding
  5. Using friction or gravity
  6. Using guides, funnels and templates
  7. Using a stacking device
  8. Using power tools
  9. Improving temperature, humidity, lighting
 10. Changing workplace height
 11. Rearranging materials at workplace
 12. Using special or combination tools
 13. Color coding or labeling
 14. Providing storage space for tools
 15. Arranging workplace for natural sequence of motions

V. Design of product
  1. Making product easier to pick up
  2. Reducing weight
  3. Using self-stacking products
  4. Using preprocessed products
  5. Changing shape of product
  6. Using unbreakable products
  7. Standardizing by using products requiring the same process
  8. Using dual-purpose products

ILLUSTRATIONS OF MOTION ANALYSIS CHARTS

A therblig chart of the original method of assembling tuna salads is shown in Fig. 15.3. The workplace of the method is shown in Fig. 15.4. The operation consists of a large number of complex hand motions. The therblig chart of the proposed method is shown in Fig. 15.5. Changes that were made in the arrangement of the workplace are shown in Fig. 15.6.

The therblig chart of an original method for making a ham sandwich is shown in Fig. 15.7. Figure 15.8 shows the workplace arrangement for the charted method. The method charted is representative of a cafeteria operation where sandwiches are made to order and can not be made up ahead of time or in batches.

THERBLIG CHART

Operation   Making Tuna Salad Plates

Present method   ✓   Date   10-11-65

Proposed method   Analyst   I.D.K.

Description	L.H.	R.H.	Description
Reach for the plate	TE	AD	Right hand waits
Grasp plate	G		
Return with plate	TL		
Position at left corner	P		
Release plate onto table	RL		
To lettuce	TE	TE	To lettuce
Grasp lettuce	G	G	Grasp lettuce
Return with lettuce	TL	TL	Return with lettuce
Position on table	P	P	Position on table
Hold lettuce	H	RL	Release lettuce
		TE	To various tool area
		SH	Search for knife
		G	Grasp knife
		TL	Return with knife
		P	Position to cut
		U	Chop lettuce into pieces
		RL	Drop knife at work area
Grasp lettuce	G	G	Grasp lettuce
Position lettuce on plate	P	P	Position lettuce on plate
Assemble	A	A	Assemble
Left hand waits	AD	TE	To various food area
		G	Obtain No. 10 scoop
		TL	To tuna area
		U	Fill scoop with salad
		TL	To work area
		P	Position salad on plate
		A	Assemble
		TL	Return to tool area
		RL	Release scoop in tool area
		TE	Return to work area
Reach for tomatoes	TE	AD	Right hand waits
Select tomato	ST		
Obtain tomato	G		
Return to work area	TL		
Position tomatoes	P		
Hold tomatoes	H	G	Grasp knife at work area
		P	Position knife
		U	Slice tomato
		RL	Drop knife
Grasp tomatoes	G	G	Grasp tomatoes
Position on left side	P	P	Position on left side
Assemble	A	A	Assemble
Grasp remaining slices	G	AD	Right hand waits
Return to tomatoes	TL		
Position in area	P		
Release slices	RL		
Return to work area	TE		
Left hand waits	AD	G	Grasp knife
		P	Position knife
		U	Scrape off work area
		TL	Return to previous position in work area
		RL	Release knife
		TE	To various tool area

FIG. 15.3.   THERBLIG CHART OF ORIGINAL METHOD OF PREPARING TUNA SALAD PLATES

Description	L.H.	R.H.	Description
		SH	Search for egg slicer
		G	Obtain egg slicer
Grasp slicer in motion	G	TL	Return to work area
Open slicer with left hand	DA	H	Hold slicer
Position slicer in work area	P	P	Position slicer
Release slicer	RL	RL	Release slicer
Left hand waits	AD	TE	To egg area
		ST	Select egg
		G	Grasp egg
		TL	To work area
		P	Position in slicer
		RL	Release egg
Grasp slicer handle	G	G	Grasp slicer handle
Slice egg	U	U	Slice egg
Withdraw wires from egg		H	Right hand holds slicer
Left hand waits	AD	G	Grasp slices
Grasp slices	G	H	Hold slices for separation
Separate slices	DA		
Position on right side of plate	P	AD	Right hand waits
Assemble	A		
Left hand waits	AD	G	Grasp egg slicer
		TL	To tool area
		RL	Release slicer
		TE	To olives and pickles
		ST	Select olives and pickles
		G	Obtain olives and pickles
		TL	To work area
		P	Position on plate
		A	Assemble
To souffle cup	TE	AD	Right hand waits
Grasp cup	G		
To celery seed dressing	TL		
Position over dressing	P		
Hold	H	TE	To celery seed dressing
		G	Grasp ladle
		U	Fill and pour into cup
		P	Replace ladle in dressing
		RL	Release ladle
Return with cup to work area	TL	TE	Return to work area
Position on plate	P	AD	Right hand waits
Assemble on plate	A		
Left hand waits	AD	G	Grasp plate
		TL	To portable cart
		P	Position on portable cart
		RL	Release plate
		TE	Return to work area

Summary	*L.H.*	*R.H.*	*Both Hands*
G	10	15	25
P	10	12	22
U	2	6	8
A	4	4	8
DA	2	—	2
RL	3	10	13
TE	5	10	15
TL	6	11	17
SH	—	2	2
ST	1	2	3
H	17	4	21
AD	39	23	62
Totals	99	99	198

SOUFFLE CUPS	LETTUCE	PICKLES, OLIVES	EGGS	TUNA SALAD	TOMATOES
PLATES		WORK AREA		HAND TOOLS	CELERY SEED DRESSING
					PORTABLE CART

FIG. 15.4. WORKPLACE ARRANGEMENT FOR ORIGINAL METHOD OF PREPARING TUNA SALAD PLATES

THERBLIG CHART

Operation Making Tuna Salad Plates

Present method _____   Date 10-13-65

Proposed method √   Analyst I.D.K.

Description	L.H.	R.H.	Description
Reach for plate	TE	TE	To lettuce
Grasp plate	G	G	Grasp lettuce
Return with plate	TL	TL	Return with lettuce
Position at left corner	P	P	Position on table
Release plate	RL	RL	Release lettuce
Grasp lettuce	G	TE	To various tools
Hold lettuce	H	SH	Search for knife
		G	Grasp knife
		TL	Return with knife
		U	Chop lettuce
		RL	Drop knife in work area
Grasp lettuce	G	G	Grasp lettuce
Position lettuce	P	P	Position lettuce
Assemble	A	A	Assemble
To olives	TE	TE	To tool area
Select olives and pickles	ST	SH	Search
Grasp olives and pickles	G	G	Grasp No. 10 scoop
To work area	TL	TL	To tuna salad area
Position plate	P	U	Fill scoop
Assemble	A	TL	To work area
Hand waits	AD	P	Position on center of plate
		A	Assemble
		TL	Return to tool area
		RL	Release scoop
		TE	To tomato area
		ST	Select tomato
		G	Grasp tomato
		TL	To work area
		P	Position on table
		RL	Release tomato

FIG. 15.5. THERBLIG CHART OF PROPOSED METHOD OF PREPARING TUNA SALAD PLATES

THERBLIG CHART—(*Continued*)

Description	L.H.	R.H.	Description
Grasp tomato	G	G	Grasp knife
Hold tomato	H	P	Position knife
		U	Slice tomato
		RL	Release knife
Grasp tomato	G	G	Grasp tomato
Position on left side	P	P	Position on left side
Assemble	A	A	Assemble
Hand waits	AD	G	Grasp remaining slices
		TL	Return to tomato area
		P	Position on tomato plate
		RL	Release slices
		TE	Return to work area
		G	Grasp knife
		U	Scrape off area
		P	Position knife
		RL	Release knife
To egg area	TE	TE	To tool area
Select egg	ST	SH	Search for egg slicer
Grasp egg	G	G	Grasp egg slicer
Return to work area	TL	TL	Return to work area
Release egg	RL	H	Hold slicer
Open slicer	DA		
Grasp egg	G		
Position in slicer	P		
Release egg	RL	RL	Release slicer
Grasp slicer handle	G	G	Grasp handle
Slice egg	U	U	Slice egg
Draws wires back		H	Hold slicer
Grasp egg slices	G	G	Grasp egg slices
Separate slices	DA	H	Hold slices
Position on plate	P	AD	Hand waits
Assemble	A	G	Grasp slicer
To souffle cups	TE	TL	To tool area
Grasp cup	G	RL	Release slicer
To dressing	TL	TE	To dressing
Position over dressing	P	G	Grasp ladle
Hold	H	U	Fill and pour into cup
		RL	Release ladle
Return to work area	TL	TE	To work area
Position on plate	P	AD	Hand waits
Release cup	RL	G	Grasp plate
Hand waits	AD	TL	To portable cart
		P	Position on cart
		RL	Release
		TE	Return to work area

Summary		*Present Method*			*Proposed Method*	
	L.H.	*R.H.*	*Both Hands*	*L.H.*	*R.H.*	*Both Hands*
G	10	15	25	11	15	26
P	10	12	22	8	9	17
U	2	6	8	2	6	8
A	4	4	8	4	3	7
DA	2	—	2	2	—	2
RL	3	10	13	4	11	15
TE	5	10	15	4	9	13
TL	6	11	17	5	10	15
SH	—	2	2	—	3	3
ST	1	2	3	2	1	3
H	17	4	21	10	6	16
AD	39	23	62	23	2	25
Totals	99	99	198	75	75	150

CELERY SEED DRESSING	LETTUCE	PICKLES, OLIVES	EGGS	TUNA SALAD	TOMATOES
PLATES	SOUFFLE CUPS	WORK AREA		HAND TOOLS	
				PORTABLE CART	

FIG. 15.6.   WORKPLACE ARRANGEMENT OF PROPOSED METHOD OF PREPARING TUNA SALAD PLATES

THERBLIG CHART

Operation Making single ham sandwich

Present method √   Date 11-7-62

Proposed method ___   Analyst G.W.

Description	L.H.	R.H.	Description
At side	AD	TE	To bread
		ST	Two slices
		G	Grasp bread
To working area	TE	TL	To working area
Take one slice	G	H	Hold bread
Place on table	P	P	Place on table
At working area	AD	RL	Release bread
		TE	To mayonnaise
		G	Grasp spoon
		U	Obtain mayonnaise
		TL	To working area
Hold bread	H	P	Position spoon
		U	Spread mayonnaise
At working area	AD	TL	To mayonnaise
		RL	Return spoon
To ham	TE	TE	To ham
Select slices	ST	ST	Select slices
Obtain ham	G	G	Obtain ham
To working area	TL	TL	To working area
Position on bread	P	P	Position on bread
	AD	TE	To lettuce
		ST	Select leaf
		G	Obtain lettuce
		TL	To working area
On ham	P	P	On ham

FIG. 15.7.   THERBLIG CHART OF ORIGINAL METHOD OF MAKING HAM SANDWICHES

THERBLIG CHART (*Continued*)

Description	L.H.	R.H.	Description
Place on ham	A	A	Place on ham
	AD	TE	To tomatoes
		ST	Select tomato
		G	Obtain tomato
		TL	To working area
On lettuce	P	P	On lettuce
Place on lettuce	A	A	Place on lettuce
Top slice		H	Hold sandwich
Hold sandwich	H	TE	To knife
		G	Obtain knife
		TL	To sandwich
		P	Position
		U	Cut sandwich
		TL	Return knife
		RL	Put knife down
To dishes	TE	AD	
Obtain dish	G		
To working area	TL		
Put on table	RL		
To sandwich	TE	TE	To sandwich
Pick up sandwich	G	G	Pick up sandwich
To dish	TL	TL	To dish
Position over dish	P	P	Position over dish
Place on dish	RL	RL	Place on dish
Grasp dish	G	AD	
To pickles	TL	TE	To pickles
Hold dish	H	ST	Select pickles
		G	Obtain
		P	Position over dish
		RL	Place on dish
To counter	TL	AD	
Place on counter	RL		

Summary	L.H.	R.H.	Both Hands
G	5	8	13
P	5	8	13
U	—	3	3
A	3	2	5
RL	3	5	8
TE	4	8	12
TL	5	9	14
ST	1	5	6
H	13	2	15
AD	18	7	25
Totals	57	57	114

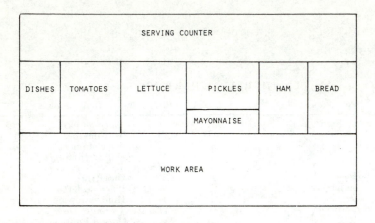

FIG. 15.8.   WORKPLACE ARRANGEMENT FOR METHOD OF MAKING
HAM SANDWICHES

Micromotion Analysis

INTRODUCTION

Micromotion analysis refers to the use of photographic techniques to make detailed studies of motions. The general procedure that is followed is to take motion pictures of an activity with a timing device in the pictures or to use a camera with a constant and known film speed. The film records both the activity and the time involved. Then the film is analyzed and the results are presented graphically.

FIG. 16.1. ASSEMBLING SALADS IS A HIGHLY REPETITIVE
TASK THAT MAY BE IMPROVED BY MICROMOTION ANALYSIS

257

Micromotion techniques can be used to analyze individual operators, work crews in a limited area or worker and machine systems. Highly repetitive tasks such as assembling salads (Fig. 16.1) or loading a dishwasher (Fig. 16.2) lend themselves to micromotion analysis. Although this technique provides a convenient and accurate method of work analysis, it is limited in its use for two reasons. One obvious reason is cost. Micromotion techniques are three to four times as costly as visual observation methods and are therefore used only where the results will be meaningful. The second reason for limiting the use of micromotion analysis is that other analysis techniques can be successfully and conveniently used to study the majority of the work systems found in hotels, restaurants or institutions. Micromotion techniques would therefore be used only in the most serious and detailed analysis.

FIG. 16.2. A FAST DISHMACHINE LOADER IS BEST STUDIED BY MICROMOTION ANALYSIS BECAUSE VISUAL OBSERVATION IS DIFFICULT

MICROMOTION ANALYSIS EQUIPMENT

Motion Picture Cameras

Moving pictures for micromotion analysis may be made with a 16-mm amateur camera. The camera should have a film capacity of 100 ft (30.5 m) which provides about 4 min of running time at 16 frames per second; a lens aperture of f.2.4 or larger; and adjustable focusing from 3 or 4 ft (0.914 to 1.22 m) to infinity. A variable speed spring motor giving speeds from 8 frames per second to 64 frames per second is desirable but not necessary. Spring-driven cameras are not constant speed and should not be used for timing purposes. Timing based on film speed can only be accomplished by using an electric motor driven camera.

When using a spring-driven camera, a timing device is placed in the picture so the time interval between frames appears on the film. An ordinary sweep-second hand electric clock can be used as the timing device to obtain the relative time of different activities. Accurate time readings are obtained by using a microchronometer which can be read to 1/2000 of a minute. The timing device should be placed so the entire face will show on the film and yet not obscure any of the motions to be photographed.

Auxiliary equipment needed for micromotion analysis includes a camera tripod, exposure meter, lights and a projector. The tripod should be used so the camera does not move while the pictures are being taken. The lights and exposure meter will assure the proper exposure of the film under any conditions. Any type of 16-mm projector can be used for viewing the film, however a hand cranked projector is best for analyzing the film.

Taking the Pictures

The workers who are to be filmed should be informed of the purpose of the study and their cooperation obtained. The choice of workers to film is important because some individuals may become self-conscious and not work in a normal manner when photographed. The activity to be filmed should be visually observed first so that unexpected activities will not occur.

The camera should be placed as close to the worker as possible, making sure that all activities performed will be photographed. Sometimes a grid background is used behind the worker so distances of movements can be obtained through film analysis. When a timing device is used, it should be located in such a manner that it will appear in the pictures but not interfere with the activities of the operation.

Lights should be placed so that all activities will be equally illuminated.

Care should be taken to prevent areas of glare. After checking the exposure and setting the camera to the proper aperture opening and focal length, the filming is begun. Several cycles of the operation may be filmed and the best one used for the analysis.

A written record of the filming should be kept to identify the film and the details of the filming procedure. A simple form that may be used to record the information is shown in Fig. 16.3.

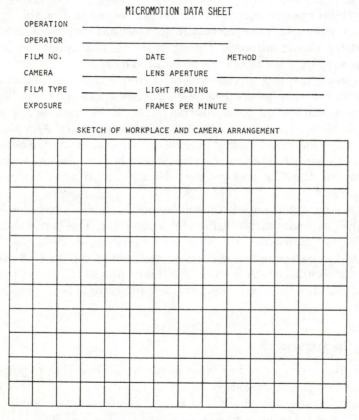

MICROMOTION DATA SHEET

OPERATION _____

OPERATOR _____

FILM NO. _____ DATE _____ METHOD _____

CAMERA _____ LENS APERTURE _____

FILM TYPE _____ LIGHT READING _____

EXPOSURE _____ FRAMES PER MINUTE _____

SKETCH OF WORKPLACE AND CAMERA ARRANGEMENT

FIG. 16.3. DATA SHEET FOR RECORDING FILMING
PROCEDURE

Analyzing the Film

Film analysis is a frame-by-frame procedure. The starting point of the operation is determined and the analysis proceeds from this point. The time indicated by the timing device is noted and the film is moved a frame at a time until a basic activity is identified. When the basic activity has been completed the time is again noted and recorded. A film analysis sheet used for recording the times and activities for a simo chart is shown in Fig. 16.4.

FILM ANALYSIS DATA SHEET

FILM NO. _____   SHEET ____ OF ____

OPERATION _____   DATE _____

DESCRIPTION _____   ANALYST _____

TIME READING	SUBTRACTED TIME	THERBLIG SYMBOL	L.H. DESC.	R.H. DESC.	TIME READING	SUBTRACTED TIME	THERBLIG SYMBOL

FIG. 16.4. FILM ANALYSIS DATA SHEET FOR RECORDING
TIMES AND ACTIVITIES

Memomotion Analysis

Memomotion refers to the technique of taking motion pictures at very slow speeds. This technique is also referred to as time-lapse photography. The film speed used in memomotion analysis is usually 1 frame per second and when the film is viewed at 16 frames per second the actions are sped up 16 times. Memomotion may be used to study workers, worker and machine systems or work crews. The information obtained by memomotion can be analyzed and graphically presented in many different ways. Memomotion is primarily suited for analyzing long or irregular cycles of work.

The memomotion pictures are taken with an electric motor driven camera. Since only one frame per second is taken, the film cost is considerably less than with normal film speeds. With the constant film speed, time is automatically recorded by the number of frames.

Memomotion is particularly helpful in the study of multi-worker activities and multi-worker and multi-machine activities. The technique eliminates all the problems of visual observation of the members of the crew. The frame-by-frame analysis of the memomotion pictures gives the exact relationships of the work elements performed by each member of the crew. Delays, bottlenecks and machine interference which may be difficult to observe visually are easily pinpointed by memomotion. The movements made by individuals for materials or between workplaces are emphasized by memomotion and therefore inefficient layouts are quickly spotted.

Memomotion techniques have been used to analyze the work of maids. A portable setup was used to follow the maids and film their activities (Mundel 1960). The memomotion film was analyzed and proposed improved methods were developed. The improved methods showed that 34% savings in time could be expected.

CYCLEGRAPHIC AND CHRONOCYCLEGRAPHIC ANALYSIS

Cyclegraphic and chronocyclegraphic analysis are used to study the motion paths of body members of individuals usually at one workplace. The technique involves placing small light bulbs on the body members and recording the motion paths on a time exposure picture. The cyclegraph and chronocyclegraph are limited to operations of relatively short cycle time and those requiring some skill.

The cyclegraphs are made by using a continuous light source on the body member. As the movements are made, the light source shows the paths as white lines on the photograph.

Chronocyclegraphs are made by using blinking lights attached to the body members. The motion paths appear as dashed white lines on the photographs. Chronocyclegraphs enable a speed determination to be made by measuring the distances between the dashes.

Cyclegraphs and chronocyclegraphs are usually used when more detail than an operation chart is desired without involving the taking of motion pictures. These graphs are also very helpful in training workers to do tasks involving some degree of skill.

Supplemental Analysis Techniques

INTRODUCTION

The preceding chapters have presented the most frequently used analysis techniques for studying existing work. Practically all types of activities encountered in hotels, restaurants and institutions can be studied by one or more of these techniques. In addition to these techniques, supplemental charts or other types of diagrammatic aids can be used to enhance or emphasize certain aspects of the analysis. This chapter presents some of the supplemental techniques that may be used either in combination with other techniques or by themselves.

ASSEMBLY CHARTS

Assembly charts are used to emphasize the order in which the various components or materials are put together to form a final product. Assembly charts only show the points where two or more materials are brought together. An assembly chart for a hospital tray makeup line is shown in Fig. 17.1.

The assembly chart only shows components or materials as they become a part of the final product. The circles on the chart do not represent operations or methods. The procedures used for the assembling may be studied by product process charting or by operation charting.

COMBINATION CHARTS

The technique of combining different analysis methods on one chart can provide additional information that may not appear on a single type of analysis chart. The resultant chart is referred to as a combination chart. For example, it is possible to combine paperwork analysis with operation analysis on one chart. This would be done when the method used by an individual to perform a particular operation has an important

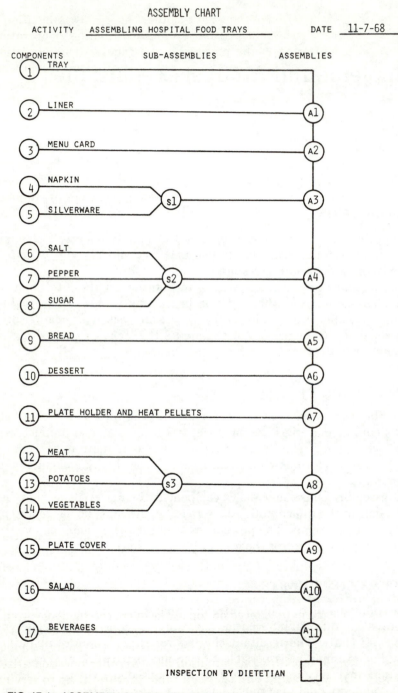

FIG. 17.1. ASSEMBLY CHART OF ASSEMBLING HOSPITAL FOOD TRAYS

bearing on the completion of the form. Another beneficial combination is the worker process and operation analysis. In this situation an operation or inspection appearing in the process chart is analyzed by operation analysis and the operation chart is placed directly after the process symbol. An example of a combined worker process and operation chart is shown in Fig. 17.2. The combination of the worker process and operation charts results in a more continuous analysis so the analyst can better understand the operation or inspection involved.

When two process analysis techniques are combined on one chart such as form process and worker process, the symbols can be placed on the chart to show the simultaneity of operations. Other process analysis combinations that could be made and presented on one chart are product and worker process, and product and paperwork process. These combinations are easily made if single products are involved.

More complex charts result when combinations include multi-activity analysis techniques. A three worker multi-worker, machine and product process chart would be difficult and time consuming to construct; however, a very complete picture of the relationships between the workers, machine and the products would be shown. Another combination of multi-activity analysis with other techniques may occur in analyzing a machine data processing system. In this case, a multi-worker, multi-machine and form process chart could possibly be constructed. Such a complex chart would only be made for highly repetitive activities.

SPECIAL SYMBOLS

The symbols presented for the various types of analysis charts in the earlier chapters are for general usage. The symbols were developed and have been primarily used by analysts in the manufacturing industries. Unfortunately, some of the activities and procedures encountered in the hotel, restaurant and institutional field can not be aptly described by these symbols. When process charting a food product through a kitchen, many decisions may have to be made between using the operation, delay or storage symbols. Consider the situation when veal cutlets are placed on a steam table to be kept warm until they are served. This obviously would call for using the storage symbol because the food is placed there to maintain a desired temperature. In contrast, when a cooked roast is taken out of the oven and placed on top of the oven, the tendency would be to use the delay symbol. But the purpose of placing the roast on top of the oven was to keep it warm, and to be consistent, the analyst should use the storage symbol for this situation also. Another question arises when cold turkey is placed on the steam table to warm it up to serving temperature. The use of the storage symbol might be indicated based on the reasoning presented above. However, this activity would be better represented by the operation symbol because a change in the temperature of the product is accomplished. Table 17.1 indicates some of the activities and procedures that cannot be easily associated with the commonly used symbols.

TABLE 17.1

ACTIVITIES AND PROCEDURES THAT ARE DIFFICULT TO ASSOCIATE WITH COMMONLY USED SYMBOLS

Activity	*Present Difficulty When Analyzing*
Yeast dough left on table to rise	Product
Frozen steaks left on table to thaw	Product
Pots in water in pot sink	Product
Forming meatballs	Motion
Kneading dough	Motion
Information slip in room rack	Paperwork

COMBINATION CHART

TYPE ___OPERATION AND WORKER PROCESS___   PAGE _1_ OF _2_

ACTIVITY ___CLEARING TABLES___   DATE _11-10-68_

PRESENT ___•___   PROPOSED _____   ANALYST _GW_

TO TABLE WITH CART
STACK SOILED TABLEWARE
TO CART
PLACE TABLEWARE IN BUS BOX
TO TABLE
PICK UP TRASH AND WIPE TABLE
TO CART
PLACE TRASH IN BUS BOX
WAIT FOR NEXT TABLE, REPEAT CYCLE
TO SOILED DISH TABLE IN DISHROOM

                              L.H.   R.H.
PICK UP BUS BOX   PICK UP BUS BOX
TO SHELF   TO SHELF
HOLD BUS BOX   PICK UP GLASSES
                                          TO GLASS RACK
                                          PLACE GLASSES IN RACK
                                          TO BUS BOX
                                          PICK UP CUPS
                                          TO OVERHEAD RACK

FIG. 17.2. COMBINATION OPERATION AND WORKER PROCESS CHART OF CLEARING DISHES

Special symbols may be used to overcome the difficulties encountered with the regular symbols. Special symbols usually are of a specific nature for a particular industry or organization. For example, a set of special symbols suitable for food service operations are shown in Table 17.2. These symbols are used to represent specific cooking processes and are beneficial in analyzing equipment utilization.

TABLE 17.2

SPECIAL SYMBOLS FOR COOKING PROCESSES

Cooking process	Symbol	Cooking process	Symbol
Bake		Fry	
Boil		Grill	
Broil		Steam	

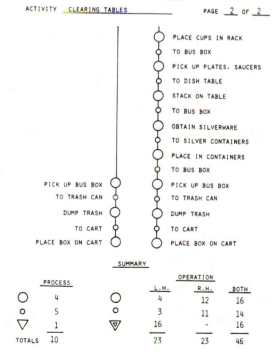

Another area where special symbols are helpful is the analysis of materials handling problems. Basic information about materials handling can be obtained from product process charts in most cases. However, in other cases additional information such as the type of handling equipment and storage containers would lead to more complete analysis. Special materials handling symbols to be used in a separate equipment column on a product process chart are shown in Table 17.3.

TABLE 17.3

MATERIALS HANDLING EQUIPMENT SYMBOLS FOR
PRODUCT PROCESS CHARTS

Equipment	Symbol	Equipment	Symbol
Belt conveyor	B	Bag	
Chute conveyor	C	Box	B
Flight conveyor	F	Basket	B
Roller conveyor	R	Carton	C
Slat conveyor	S	Crate	C
Wheel conveyor	W	Drum	
Hand platform truck		Tote box	T B
Hand truck		Skid	
Mobile cart		Man	
Pallet		Dolly	

The special symbols are placed on the same line as the regular symbols corresponding to the materials handling activity. Thus the special symbols that indicate how the material is moved are placed beside the movement and/or operation symbols. If the product is moved by a cart, then the special cart symbol is placed on the same line as the movement symbol. If the product is picked up or put down by a worker, the special worker symbol is placed on the same line as the operation symbol. The container symbols are usually placed on the same line as the storage symbols. A product process chart using the materials handling symbols is shown in Fig. 17.3.

PRODUCT PROCESS CHART

JOB   MAKING TABLE TOWELS   PAGE   1 OF 1

PRESENT PROCEDURE   *   DATE   12-17-68

PROPOSED PROCEDURE   ANALYST   IDK

DIST.	SYMBOL	DESCRIPTION	EQUIPMENT
	○	MATERIAL ISSUED, PLACED IN CART	X
100	○	TO CUTTING BENCH	▭
	○	PLACED ON BENCH	X
	▽	ON CUTTING BENCH	
	○	SPREAD OUT, CUT, PLACED IN CART	X
10	○	TO SEWING TABLE	▭
	○	STACKED ON TABLE	X
	▽	ON TABLE	
	○	HEMMED	X
	□	COUNTED INTO CART	X
50	○	TO LAUNDRY ROOM	▭
	○	REMOVED, MARKED, PLACED IN BASKET	X
20	○	TO WASHING MACHINE	⋈
	○	LAUNDERED, RETURNED TO BASKET	X
20	○	TO MANGLE	⋈
	○	MANGLED, STACKED ON TRUCK	X
60	○	TO STORAGE AREA	⌐
	□	INSPECTED	X
	○	PLACED ON SHELF	X

FIG. 17.3. PRODUCT PROCESS CHART USING MATERIALS
HANDLING SYMBOLS

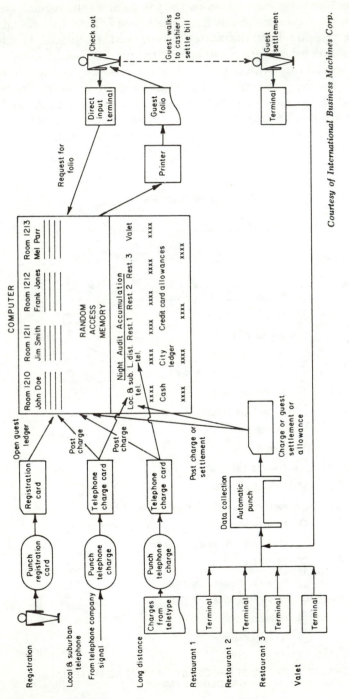

Courtesy of International Business Machines Corp.

FIG. 17.4.   DATA PROCESSING FLOW CHART OF HOTEL FRONT OFFICE
ACCOUNTING PROCEDURE

Special symbols are also used in charting data processing procedures. A front office accounting procedure using the data processing symbols is shown in Fig. 17.4. Figure 17.5 shows a hospital admission procedure charted with the data processing symbols.

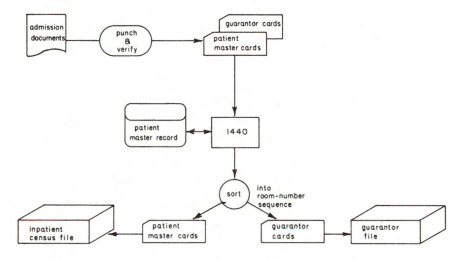

FIG. 17.5.   DATA PROCESSING FLOW CHART OF HOSPITAL
PATIENT ADMISSION PROCEDURE

Reprinted by permission from *General Information Manual, The IBM 1440 Data Processing System for Patient and General Accounting in Hospitals* by International Business Machines Corp.

PROCESS FLOW DIAGRAMS

Process flow diagrams are a variation of the simple flow diagrams discussed earlier. A process flow diagram is constructed by charting the process on a scaled layout drawing of the work areas. The process charting symbols are placed on the layout drawing to indicate where operations, inspections, delays and storages occur. The movements are shown by a line with the movement symbol placed in it. Numbers are usually placed within the symbols to indicate the sequence of the process and the direction of flow. Figure 17.6 shows a process flow diagram. The process flow diagrams are helpful when decisions regarding the rearrangement of workplaces are needed. The diagram quickly points out the process flow in the work area. Places where backtracking or cross traffic occur can be easily located and corrected. The identification of the locations of operations, inspections, storages and delays are also helpful because an overall picture of the procedure can be obtained. Areas where materials handling equipment may be used to eliminate delays or reduce storage time can also be indicated by the diagram.

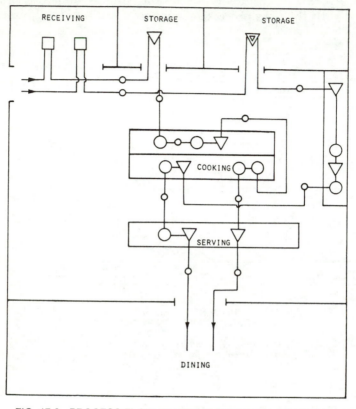

FIG. 17.6. PROCESS FLOW DIAGRAM SHOWING LOCATIONS
OF EACH COMPONENT IN THE PROCESS

Although process flow diagrams are usually made of products, they can also be used to show worker processes. If the number of products or workers to be diagrammed are great, different colors can be used to clarify the diagram.

STRING DIAGRAMS

String diagrams are used when regular flow diagrams cannot be easily drawn because the movements are too lengthy or too complex. String diagrams are constructed by using thread to indicate the movements. The thread is strung around pins which represent the workplaces on a scaled drawing of the entire work area. The string diagram is started by tying the string to the pin which corresponds to the first workplace identified on the process chart. As movements on the process chart are indicated, the string is strung to the next appropriate pin and this procedure is followed until the last movement is made. String diagrams can be used to show the movements of products or workers. If more than one product or worker is involved, using different colored strings will identify the movements of each product or worker.

The string diagram can also be used to determine the total distance of movements. In this case the diagram has to be made on an accurate scaled drawing and the strings must be strung along the exact paths of the movements. The total distance is determined by measuring the length of string used and computing the actual distance moved from the scale of the drawing. A scale of ¼ in. equals 1 ft is frequently used for string diagrams.

PRECEDENCE DIAGRAMS

In most work systems certain activities or tasks have to precede certain other activities or tasks. For example, in food service, measuring precedes combining; panning precedes baking; and portioning precedes serving. Precedence requirements may be illustrated by a precedence diagram. Precedence diagrams graphically portray the activities required to accomplish a given job and the precedence requirements that control the completion of the activities. The diagram is made by using circles to represent the activities and lines with arrows between the activities indicate the precedence requirements. A simple precedence diagram is illustrated in Fig. 17.7.

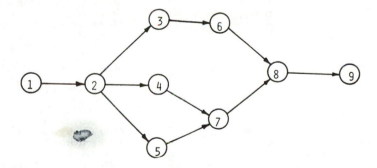

FIG. 17.7. A SIMPLE PRECEDENCE DIAGRAM SHOWING
PRECEDENCE REQUIREMENTS

It should be noted that the diagram is started on the left and proceeds to the right. This arrangement means that the activities on the left side

of the diagram have relatively few precedence requirements while activities on the right side of the diagram have a greater number of precedence requirements. It can also be seen that the number of lines
entering or leaving an activity is representative of the importance of the
activity. If an activity has three lines leaving, it indicates that three
other activities are dependent on its completion. Two lines entering an
activity means that it is dependent on the completion of two other
activities which are not dependent on each other.

Precedence diagrams that indicate the time required for each activity
are useful for balancing the activities of crews or determining the size of
crews to use.

Precedence Activity Charts

Precedence activity charts show the relationships between activities,
workers and the precedence requirements. This chart is drawn to a time
scale with the activities of each worker shown by rectangles placed on the
same line. The length of the rectangles are varied to correspond to the
time of the activity. The precedence and time requirements for a typical
job are given in Table 17.4.

TABLE 17.4

PRECEDENCE AND TIME REQUIREMENTS (Minutes)

Activity	Assigned to Worker	Time Required	Precedence Requirement
1	A	4	None
2	A	6	After activity 1 is completed
3	B	5	After activity 1 is completed
4	B	3	None
5	A	10	After activity 2 is completed
6	C	5	After activity 4 is completed
7	B	13	After activities 1 and 4 are completed
8	C	7	After activity 6 is completed
9	C	9	After activity 8 is completed
10	A	12	After activities 5 and 8 are completed
11	A	4	After activity 10 is completed
12	C	7	After activity 9 is completed
13	B	8	After activity 9 is completed
14	B	6	After activities 10 and 13 are completed
15	C	5	After activity 13 is completed

The precedence activity chart for the data from Table 17.4 is shown in
Fig. 17.8. The numbers in the rectangles identify the activities.

The chart can be used to determine the total time required to complete
the job as well as the amount of idle time for each worker. The total time

to complete the activities shown in Fig. 17.8 is 38 min. The idle times for each worker as charted are: worker A—2 min; worker B—3 min; and worker C—5 min.

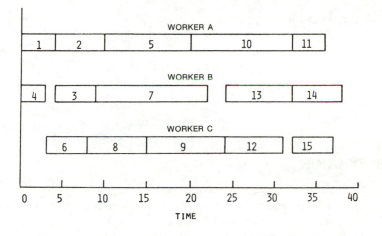

FIG. 17.8. THE PRECEDENCE ACTIVITY CHART PICTORIALLY
SHOWS THE IDLE TIME OF EACH WORKER

18

Time Study

INTRODUCTION

The analysis and design of work results in improvements in the processes, methods, equipment and workplaces required to complete a task. However, the creation of efficient work systems does not automatically result in reduced cost or increased profits. It is up to management to plan, direct and control the work systems so the benefits of the work analysis and design program can be fully attained. This is especially true of hotels, restaurants and institutions because the variable demand for their services requires variation in the output of the work systems. Work systems are normally designed to produce for the maximum demand. When the demand drops below the maximum level the system has to be adjusted accordingly. The adjustment in the work system is primarily made by decreasing the manpower. For example, a food production system may vary its output by using fewer personnel in the morning when the demand is light and more personnel in the afternoon when the demand is greater. The ability to successfully vary the work system to meet the anticipated demand is one of the major responsibilities of management.

A knowledge of the performance of a work system is necessary in order to effectively vary the output for different situations. The procedure for determining the output from a work system is referred to as work measurement. Work measurement should answer such questions as how many front desk clerks, nurses, waiters, dishwashers, etc., are required for a given period of time. In brief, work measurement provides the information for effective staffing of work systems to meet varying situations.

One of the techniques used in work measurement is time study. Time study is a procedure for measuring the amount of time required to accomplish a task under a given set of conditions. The main purpose of time study is to develop standard times. Standard time is defined as the time required to complete a task using standard materials, processes, methods, equipment and environment, with due consideration given to personal performance and allowances. This infers that the task has undergone work analysis and design to the extent that it is performed in the same way each time it occurs.

Time study, as referred to in this chapter, is a work measurement technique and not a work analysis technique. The recording of time during analysis of work (also referred to as time study) is for the benefit of the analysis and should not be used in the development of standard times.

Standard times are one of the most important measures of work and can be used in several different ways. The use of standard times will permit more effective scheduling of the activities required to accomplish a given function. For example, the many activities in catering a banquet such as purchasing, food preparation, set up, serving and cleanup can be planned to make optimum use of human and physical resources. This problem is greatly simplified when the standard times for completing the activities for various sized banquets with various menu offerings and types of service are known.

Standard times can also be used to set performance standards for workers. Performance standards are primarily used for fairly routine or repetitive activities such as dishwashing, salad preparation, making up rooms or maintenance activities. The standard times used in this situation should be based on the performance expected from average workers. Performance standards are beneficial to both management and labor because they set a level of satisfactory activity and protect the interest of both groups. Using performance standards also result in better employer-employee relationships.

Another use of standard times is to determine the task assignments for each member of a crew or to determine the size of crew to use. The productivity of crews is dependent on the activities assigned to each member and the length of time required to complete each activity. Standard times will aid planning crew activities so the amount of idle time is minimized.

Standard times may also be used to compare different methods of doing work. If two or more different methods of accomplishing the same task are being considered, and the other factors involved are constant, the choice should be based on the standard times.

TIME STUDY PROCEDURE

The procedure used in conducting time studies for determining standard times include recording the standard conditions; measuring and recording the times; adjusting the data based on worker performance; and determining the allowances for rest and other personal needs. The difference between simply measuring the time to do a task and determining standard times should be emphasized. Measuring the time for a given task is just one step in the development of the standard time, but it may also be used for other purposes as well. Time is frequently measured to determine where analysis should be applied, or to get an idea of the length of time required to do certain activities. Such time measurements are used primarily for informative purposes and cannot be used in the development of standard times. Standard times must represent the time required to perform a given task under realistic conditions. This means that the standard time must consider the differences between individuals, possible delays that may be encountered, the effects of fatigue and the environmental factors present during prolonged working periods.

Recording the Standard Conditions

The first step in conducting time studies for determining standard times is to identify properly the standard conditions of the task. This means a specific description of the materials used including shape, size, type, packaging and weight which should be recorded. Next, the process or method of accomplishing the task should be determined from instruction sheets or by visual observation of the task. The process or method is recorded by elements that can be easily identified. A sketch of the workplace and information regarding capacity and operating characteristics of the equipment used should be included. Finally, any extreme environmental conditions such as high humidity, excessive noise or hot temperatures should be noted. Recording the standard conditions is important from the standpoint of evaluating any changes that may occur after the time standards have been determined.

The task to be timed is broken down into elements which are listed chronologically. The element breakdown facilitates the timing and subsequent evaluation of the data. It also gives the time study analyst a chance to determine unusual occurrences that may occur during the task. The elements should be chosen so they can be easily detected during the timing. Beginning and ending points which can be anticipated are indicators of elements that can be easily detected. The action of starting to fill in a form is a better beginning point for an element (because it can be anticipated easier) than the action of picking up the form. In the same sense, the action of putting down a stirrer is a better ending point for an element than trying to determine when the stirring action ends.

Elements should also be chosen so they can be accurately timed. If manual timing devices are used the elements chosen should not be much shorter than 0.10 min or 6 sec. This limit should be used because the time study analyst must read the timing device and record the time readings. The elements can be shorter if automatic timing and recording devices are used.

Consideration should be given to the type of actions or motions involved in the task. The actions or motions that pertain to working on an object, running a machine or conducting an inspection can be logically grouped into separate elements. For example, actions and motions of reaching, grasping, moving and placing an object would be combined into one element; or the actions and motions required to adjust a chopper would be combined into one element.

Measuring and Recording the Times

Time values for time studies are usually measured by a stop watch or by using motion pictures taken at a known and constant film speed. Various types of time study machines and equipment have been developed recently, however, they would not be suitable or economical for the types of tasks found in the hospitality field. The use of the stop watch represents the simplest and most economical method for measuring time values. Most stop watches used for time study are graduated in decimal parts of a minute or an hour. Stop watches graduated into seconds may be used for timing if this unit of measurement is more desirable.

Two methods of operating the stop watch may be used: continuous timing or repetitive timing. In the continuous method of timing the watch runs continuously throughout the entire study. The watch is started at the beginning of the first element. At the end point of the first element, the time study analyst quickly reads the watch and records the time reading on the data sheet. The procedure is repeated at the end of each succeeding element. The time for each element is later found by subtracting the times recorded for successive elements.

The repetitive method of timing requires the analyst to "snap back" the stop watch to zero at each reading. The stop watch is started at the beginning of the first element and simultaneously read and "snapped back" at the end point of the first element. This procedure is continued for all the elements in the study. The repetitive method of timing eliminates the need for subtracting values since the actual time of each element is measured and recorded directly. The constant manipulation of the stop watch in the repetitive method of timing can lead to errors especially if the elements are of short duration.

Both methods of timing require some practice so the stop watch can be read with a quick glance. A form such as the one shown in Fig. 18.1 can be used to record the timings from either method. The readings from the continuous method are entered under the reading (R) column and the resultant times from the subtraction procedure are entered in the time (T) column. Under the repetitive timing method, the readings are entered directly in the (T) column. If desirable, a form with only time columns may be used.

Timing can also be accomplished by using motion pictures. Taking motion pictures at a known film speed or including a timing device in the picture are frequently used. The motion picture technique simplifies the observation process and provides a permanent record of the timing. The

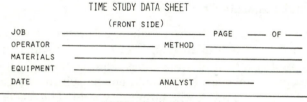

TIME STUDY DATA SHEET
(FRONT SIDE)

JOB _____ PAGE ___ OF ___
OPERATOR _____ METHOD _____
MATERIALS _____
EQUIPMENT _____
DATE _____ ANALYST _____

WORKPLACE DIAGRAM

ELEMENT	ELEMENT DESCRIPTION	ELEMENT TIME	REMARKS

FIG. 18.1. PART I—TIME STUDY FORM

element times are obtained by viewing the films. determining the beginning and ending points of the elements, and recording the times on a suitable form.

Determining the Number of Cycles to Time

Time study is similar to statistical sampling since a single timing of an element is really a single sample of the time required to do the element. As more and more cycles of the same element are timed, the accuracy of the time study increases. The determination of the number of cycles to time is based on statistics. The statistical method requires that some preliminary timings be obtained. Table 18.1 can be used to determine the number of preliminary timings to take depending on the total element time.

TIME STUDY DATA SHEET

(BACK SIDE)   CYCLES

ELEMENTS		1		2		3		4		5		6		7		8		9		10	
NO.	DESCRIPTION	R	T	R	T	R	T	R	T	R	T	R	T	R	T	R	T	R	T	R	T
1																					
2																					
3																					
4																					
5																					
6																					
7																					
8																					
9																					
10																					
11																					
12																					
13																					
14																					
15																					
16																					
17																					

SUMMARY AND CALCULATIONS

ELEMENTS	1	2	3	4	5	6	7	8	9	10	11	12	13	14
TOTAL TIME														
NO. OF CYCLES														
AVG. TIME														
RATING FACTOR														
RATED TIME														
ALLOWANCE														
ALLOWED TIME														
STANDARD TIME														

FIG. 18.1. PART II

TABLE 18.1

PRELIMINARY TIMINGS TO OBTAIN FOR TIME STUDIES

Element Time (Min)	Number of Cycles to Time
0.10 to 0.25	100
0.25 to 0.50	50
0.50 to 0.75	40
0.75 to 1.0	30
1.0 to 2.0	20
2.0 to 4.0	15
4.0 to 8.0	10
8.0 to 16.0	8
16.0 to 32.0	5
32.0 to 64.0	3

The results of the preliminary timings are analyzed to see if sufficient timings were obtained. The equation to determine the number of timings required for ± 5% accuracy and 95% confidence limits is:

$$N' = \left(\frac{40\sqrt{N\Sigma X - (\Sigma X)^2}}{\Sigma X} \right)^2$$

where N′ = required number of timings
N = number of preliminary timings
X = time readings of an element

The equation is suitable for machine computation of the required number of timings since ΣX and ΣX^2 can be obtained simultaneously. The required number of timings as calculated by the equation are then compared to the number of preliminary timings. If the required number (N′) is equal to or less than the preliminary number (N), then the average value of the preliminary timings is within ± 5% accuracy with 95% confidence limits. If the required number of timings is greater than the preliminary number of timings taken, the statistical criteria have not been met and additional timings have to be taken. The number of additional timings to take is the difference between the computed required number (N′) and the preliminary number (N). The results of the preliminary timings are not discarded.

When the additional timings are completed, the same procedure is again used to see if the statistical requirements of the time study have been achieved.

To illustrate the procedure, assume that the following preliminary timings were obtained; 6, 4, 5, 7, 8, 5, 6, 5, 8 and 4 min. In this example

$N = 10$, $\Sigma X = 58$ and $\Sigma X^2 = 356$. Substituting these values into the equation gives:

$$N' = \left(\frac{40\sqrt{10(356) - (58)^2}}{58}\right)^2$$

$$N' = \left(\frac{40\sqrt{196}}{58}\right)^2$$

$$N' = \left(\frac{40(14)}{58}\right)^2$$

$$N' = 93.1$$

The calculation of N' indicates that the 10 preliminary timings were not enough and 83 additional timings should be taken.

Equations for the frequently used accuracies and confidence limits in time study are given below.

$$N' = \left(\frac{20\sqrt{N\Sigma X^2 - (\Sigma X)^2}}{\Sigma X}\right)^2 \text{ for } \pm 5\% \text{ accuracy, } 68\% \text{ confidence limits}$$

$$N' = \left(\frac{30\sqrt{N\Sigma X^2 - (\Sigma X)^2}}{\Sigma X}\right)^2 \text{ for } \pm 5\% \text{ accuracy, } 87.5\% \text{ confidence limits}$$

$$N' = \left(\frac{40\sqrt{N\Sigma X^2 - (\Sigma X)^2}}{\Sigma X}\right)^2 \text{ for } \pm 5\% \text{ accuracy, } 95\% \text{ confidence limits}$$

Time Study Rating

The average time obtained from several timings of a given element or task is the basis for developing standard times. Since the individual being observed and timed is seldom working at a standard pace or under conditions that are standard, the measured time values should be adjusted to account for these discrepancies. Individuals being timed usually work slower or faster than their normal pace for a number of reasons. If an individual being timed thinks the time study is to measure his or her performance for possible personal reward, he or she will probably work faster than his or her normal pace. Individuals who think the time study is to be used to set standards or quotas will usually work slower than their normal pace. Many individuals become self-conscious when they are being timed and may work faster or slower than normal because of this feeling. Therefore, the measured time values are adjusted to account for these variations from the normal pace. This adjustment is referred to as pace rating.

Differences in skill and effort may also call for an adjustment in the measured time values. When a highly skilled individual is used in the time study, the measured time values will have to be adjusted if a meaningful standard time is to be developed. Many other factors such as attitudes, working environment, coordination or speed of movements may also be justification for adjusting the measured times.

Time study rating is a matter of judgment on the part of the analyst. Before the actual timing takes place the analyst should become familiar with the task to be studied and develop a mental concept of the standard performance. This is not always easy, however experience will improve the analyst's ability to visualize what the standard performance should be. Actually performing the task to be studied for several times will provide information regarding difficult elements or other problems that may not be easily seen. Another thing that helps an analyst in developing the concept of standard performance is to observe several different people perform the task.

After the concept of standard performance is determined, the analyst will judge the performance of the individual during the timing. The judgment is indicated on the time study form as a percentage of the conceptualized standard performance. A rating of 100% indicates that the individual performed the task at the pace, skill level, etc., that the analyst considered standard. Ratings over 100% indicate the individual performed better than standard while ratings under 100% indicate substandard performance. For example, an individual judged at working 20% better than standard would be given a rating of 120%. An individual judged at working 20% lower than standard would be given a rating of 80%.

The measured time values are adjusted by multiplying them by the rating. This is done in the summary portion of the time study data form shown in Fig. 18.1. The adjusted measured times are referred to as rated times or normal times.

Time Study Allowances

In order to develop realistic standard times, allowances for personal needs or other work interruptions should be made. If workers did not have to rest, go to the bathroom, wait for materials or other workers, and clean up, the rated times could be used as the standard time. Unfortunately this does not happen and such interruptions of work and the personal needs of the workers are anticipated and the rated times are adjusted to allow for them. Thus the standard time for a task includes the rated time for the regular work plus additional time to allow for other occurrences during the work day.

Determining the allowances is frequently a matter of judgement or company policy. Allowances for unavoidable delays and other interruptions of work are usually determined by the analyst. Sometimes the analyst may undertake a separate study to determine what interruptions may be expected, how often they occur and how long they last.

The allowances for personal time are usually set by company policy. The working environment usually plays an important part in setting personal allowances. Persons working in extremely hot or cold conditions are given greater personal allowances. Personal allowances of 20 to 40 min per 8 hr work shift are common. The allowances for interruptions and personal needs are expressed as a percentage of the rated time.

The equation for the standard time using the rating and allowance percentage is given as:

$$Ts = fTa\,(1 + A)$$

where Ts = standard time in minutes
f = per cent rating factor expressed as a decimal
Ta = average measured time in minutes
A = per cent allowance expressed as a decimal

The calculation of the standard time is also done on the time study data sheet shown in Fig. 18.1.

Standard Time Data

INTRODUCTION

The time study procedure of work measurement can be a lengthy and costly method of obtaining the information required to develop standard times. An alternative to direct time studies is to use standard time data. Standard time data are the collection of times required to do certain identified activities. The data are presented for units of work small enough that they can be used to determine the time to do a wide variety of tasks. Of course the tasks have to be broken down into the particular standard work units for which times are available. The standard time data are the result of many direct time studies of activities containing these standard work units.

Standard time data can be used to develop standard times for a particular task in less time than direct time study. Another advantage of standard time data is that it can be used to determine and set standards for future work. Using standard time data also eliminates some of the human relations problems encountered in direct time study.

Standard time data have been developed for two different types of work units. The standard time data developed by the Methods-Time-Measurement Association are primarily based on therblig breakdown of motions and are referred to as basic motion time data. The second type of standard time data is based on elements or groups of therbligs and represent larger work units. This second type of data is referred to as elemental time data. Elemental time data are frequently developed within an organization to fit their needs.

BASIC MOTION TIME DATA

The basic motion time data include times for reach, move, turn and apply pressure, grasp, position, release load, disengage, eye travel time and eye focus, and body, leg and foot motions. The relations for simultaneous motions are also given in the data. The basic motion times are shown in Fig. 19.1. The time unit used for the basic motion time data is the T.M.U. One T.M.U. is equal to 0.00001 hr or 0.0006 min. The time values given in the table are normal performance times without any allowance for personal needs, delays or other interruptions.

The procedure followed in using the basic motion time data is fairly simple. First the task is broken down into the motions required by the left and right hand and other body members. Then the time required for each motion is selected from the appropriate time data table. The non-limiting motion times are deleted in determining the normal time for the task. For example, if the left hand and right hand are performing simultaneously, but the time required to complete the motion with the left hand is shorter, it is deleted since it is nonlimiting. The right hand motion time is the limiting factor in this case and is used in determining the total time of the task.

Considerable data regarding the type of basic motion is given in the tables and this information should be used to properly identify and classify the motions.

Reach

Reach is the motion used when the primary purpose is to move the hand to a given destination. One variable affecting the time required for reach is the length of movement. Reach times for movements from ¾ to 30 in. (1.9 to 76.2 cm) in length are provided in the table. This distance is the actual distance that the hand moves and not the straight line between the point of origination and the point of termination.

Another variable affecting reach times is the amount of control required to successfully complete the reach movement. More time is logically needed in reaching for an object mixed among other objects than if the object were by itself. Generally the factors that affect grasp motions such as size, shape and location of the object also affect the reach motion preceding the grasp. The amount of control required for reach is identified by four different types as described in the reach table.

In breaking down the task it is necessary to indicate the length and type of reach involved. This can be done by using a system of symbols. The symbol for reach (R) is followed by the numerical value of the distance traveled and the letter designation of the type of reach. For example, a reach of 12 in. (30.5 cm) for an object in a fixed location is identified by R12A.

TABLE I—REACH—R

Distance Moved Inches	Time TMU				Hand In Motion		CASE AND DESCRIPTION
	A	B	C or D	E	A	B	
¾ or less	2.0	2.0	2.0	2.0	1.6	1.6	**A** Reach to object in fixed location, or to object in other hand or on which other hand rests.
1	2.5	2.5	3.6	2.4	2.3	2.3	
2	4.0	4.0	5.9	3.8	3.5	2.7	
3	5.3	5.3	7.3	5.3	4.5	3.6	**B** Reach to single object in location which may vary slightly from cycle to cycle.
4	6.1	6.4	8.4	6.8	4.9	4.3	
5	6.5	7.8	9.4	7.4	5.3	5.0	
6	7.0	8.6	10.1	8.0	5.7	5.7	
7	7.4	9.3	10.8	8.7	6.1	6.5	
8	7.9	10.1	11.5	9.3	6.5	7.2	**C** Reach to object jumbled with other objects in a group so that search and select occur.
9	8.3	10.8	12.2	9.9	6.9	7.9	
10	8.7	11.5	12.9	10.5	7.3	8.6	
12	9.6	12.9	14.2	11.8	8.1	10.1	
14	10.5	14.4	15.6	13.0	8.9	11.5	**D** Reach to a very small object or where accurate grasp is required.
16	11.4	15.8	17.0	14.2	9.7	12.9	
18	12.3	17.2	18.4	15.5	10.5	14.4	
20	13.1	18.6	19.8	16.7	11.3	15.8	
22	14.0	20.1	21.2	18.0	12.1	17.3	**E** Reach to indefinite location to get hand in position for body balance or next motion or out of way.
24	14.9	21.5	22.5	19.2	12.9	18.8	
26	15.8	22.9	23.9	20.4	13.7	20.2	
28	16.7	24.4	25.3	21.7	14.5	21.7	
30	17.5	25.8	26.7	22.9	15.3	23.2	

TABLE II—MOVE—M

Distance Moved Inches	Time TMU			Hand in Motion B	Wt. Allowance			CASE AND DESCRIPTION
	A	B	C		Wt. (lb.) Up to	Factor	Constant TMU	
¾ or less	2.0	2.0	2.0	1.7	2.5	1.00	0	
1	2.5	2.9	3.4	2.3				
2	3.6	4.6	5.2	2.9	7.5	1.06	2.2	**A** Move object to other hand or against stop.
3	4.9	5.7	6.7	3.6				
4	6.1	6.9	8.0	4.3				
5	7.3	8.0	9.2	5.0	12.5	1.11	3.9	
6	8.1	8.9	10.3	5.7				
7	8.9	9.7	11.1	6.5	17.5	1.17	5.6	
8	9.7	10.6	11.8	7.2				
9	10.5	11.5	12.7	7.9	22.5	1.22	7.4	
10	11.3	12.2	13.5	8.6				**B** Move object to approximate or indefinite location.
12	12.9	13.4	15.2	10.0	27.5	1.28	9.1	
14	14.4	14.6	16.9	11.4				
16	16.0	15.8	18.7	12.8	32.5	1.33	10.8	
18	17.6	17.0	20.4	14.2				
20	19.2	18.2	22.1	15.6				
22	20.8	19.4	23.8	17.0	37.5	1.39	12.5	
24	22.4	20.6	25.5	18.4				**C** Move object to exact location.
26	24.0	21.8	27.3	19.8	42.5	1.44	14.3	
28	25.5	23.1	29.0	21.2				
30	27.1	24.3	30.7	22.7	47.5	1.50	16.0	

TABLE III—TURN AND APPLY PRESSURE—T AND AP

Weight	Time TMU for Degrees Turned										
	30°	45°	60°	75°	90°	105°	120°	135°	150°	165°	180°
Small— 0 to 2 Pounds	2.8	3.5	4.1	4.8	5.4	6.1	6.8	7.4	8.1	8.7	9.4
Medium—2.1 to 10 Pounds	4.4	5.5	6.5	7.5	8.5	9.6	10.6	11.6	12.7	13.7	14.8
Large— 10.1 to 35 Pounds	8.4	10.5	12.3	14.4	16.2	18.3	20.4	22.2	24.3	26.1	28.2

APPLY PRESSURE CASE 1—16.2 TMU.   APPLY PRESSURE CASE 2—10.6 TMU

FIG. 19.1. BASIC MOTION TIMES
Reprinted with permission from MTM Association for Standards and Research, Ann Arbor, Mich.

TABLE IV—GRASP—G

Case	Time TMU	DESCRIPTION
1A	2.0	**Pick Up Grasp**—Small, medium or large object by itself, easily grasped.
1B	3.5	Very small object or object lying close against a flat surface.
1C1	7.3	Interference with grasp on bottom and one side of nearly cylindrical object. Diameter larger than ½″.
1C2	8.7	Interference with grasp on bottom and one side of nearly cylindrical object. Diameter ¼″ to ½″.
1C3	10.8	Interference with grasp on bottom and one side of nearly cylindrical object. Diameter less than ¼″.
2	5.6	Regrasp.
3	5.6	Transfer Grasp.
4A	7.3	Object jumbled with other objects so search and select occur. Larger than 1″ x 1″ x 1″.
4B	9.1	Object jumbled with other objects so search and select occur. ¼″ x ¼″ x ⅛″ to 1″ x 1″ x 1″.
4C	12.9	Object jumbled with other objects so search and select occur. Smaller than ¼″ x ¼″ x ⅛″.
5	0	Contact, sliding or hook grasp.

TABLE V—POSITION*—P

CLASS OF FIT		Symmetry	Easy To Handle	Difficult To Handle
1—Loose	No pressure required	S	5.6	11.2
		SS	9.1	14.7
		NS	10.4	16.0
2—Close	Light pressure required	S	16.2	21.8
		SS	19.7	25.3
		NS	21.0	26.6
3—Exact	Heavy pressure required.	S	43.0	48.6
		SS	46.5	52.1
		NS	47.8	53.4

*Distance moved to engage—1″ or less.

TABLE VI—RELEASE—RL

Case	Time TMU	DESCRIPTION
1	2.0	Normal release performed by opening fingers as independent motion.
2	0	Contact Release.

TABLE VII—DISENGAGE—D

CLASS OF FIT	Easy to Handle	Difficult to Handle
1—Loose—Very slight effort, blends with subsequent move.	4.0	5.7
2—Close — Normal effort, slight recoil.	7.5	11.8
3—Tight — Considerable effort, hand recoils markedly.	22.9	34.7

TABLE VIII—EYE TRAVEL TIME AND EYE FOCUS—ET AND EF

Eye Travel Time $= 15.2 \times \dfrac{T}{D}$ TMU, with a maximum value of 20 TMU.

where T = the distance between points from and to which the eye travels.
D = the perpendicular distance from the eye to the line of travel T.

Eye Focus Time = 7.3 TMU.

TABLE IX—BODY, LEG AND FOOT MOTIONS

DESCRIPTION	SYMBOL	DISTANCE	TIME TMU
Foot Motion—Hinged at Ankle.	FM	Up to 4″	8.5
With heavy pressure.	FMP		19.1
Leg or Foreleg Motion.	LM —	Up to 6″	7.1
		Each add'l. inch	1.2
Sidestep—Case 1—Complete when lead-ing leg contacts floor.	SS-C1	Less than 12″	Use REACH or MOVE Time
		12″	17.0
		Each add'l. inch	.6
Case 2—Lagging leg must contact floor before next motion can be made.	SS-C2	12″	34.1
		Each add'l. inch	1.1
Bend, Stoop, or Kneel on One Knee.	B,S,KOK		29.0
Arise.	AB,AS,AKOK		31.9
Kneel on Floor—Both Knees.	KBK		69.4
Arise.	AKBK		76.7
Sit.	SIT		34.7
Stand from Sitting Position.	STD		43.4
Turn Body 45 to 90 degrees—			
Case 1—Complete when leading leg contacts floor.	TBC1		18.6
Case 2—Lagging leg must contact floor before next motion can be made.	TBC2		37.2
Walk.	W-FT.	Per Foot	5.3
Walk.	W-P	Per Pace	15.0

TABLE X—SIMULTANEOUS MOTIONS

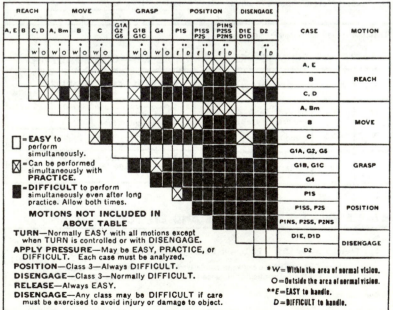

SUPPLEMENTARY MTM DATA

> Tables 1 and 2 are supplementary data. For proper explanation and usage, refer to MTM Application Training Supplements No. 8 and No. 9.

TABLE 1 —POSITION—P (SUPPLEMENTARY DATA)

Class of Fit and Clearance	Case of† Symmetry	Align Only	Depth of Insertion (per ¼')			
			0	2	4	6
21 .150'—.350'	S	3.0	3.4	6.6	7.7	8.8
	SS	3.0	10.3	13.5	14.6	15.7
	NS	4.8	15.5	18.7	19.8	20.9
22 .025'—.149'	S	7.2	7.2	11.9	13.0	14.2
	SS	8.0	14.9	19.6	20.7	21.9
	NS	9.5	20.2	24.9	26.0	27.2
23* .005'—.024'	S	9.5	9.5	16.3	18.7	21.0
	SS	10.4	17.3	24.1	26.5	28.8
	NS	12.2	22.9	29.7	32.1	34.4

*BINDING—Add observed number of Apply Pressure
DIFFICULT HANDLING—Add observed number of G2.

†Determine symmetry by geometric properties, except use S case when object is oriented **prior to** preceding Move.

TABLE 2—APPLY PRESSURE—AP (SUPPLEMENTARY DATA)

Apply Force (AF) =1.0+(0.3×lbs.). TMU for up to 10 lb. =4.0 TMU max. for 10 lb. and over	
Dwell, Minimum (DM) =4.2 TMU	Release Force (RLF) =3.0 TMU
AP = AF+Dwell+RLF	APB = AP+G2

Move

Move is the action used to transport an object. The variables affecting the move times are distance, type of movement and weight of the object. The three types of movements are: (A) movement of the object against a stop or to the other hand such as closing a door or transferring a knife from one hand to the other; (B) movement of the object to an approximate or indefinite location such as lifting a tray or moving ingredients to a pan; and (C) movement of the object to an exact location such as moving a slice of ham to the bread or moving the cap to the jar.

The weight of the object is used to determine a multiplying factor for the times given in the table. For example, moving a 10-lb (4.5-kg) weight requires multiplying the move time by 1.11 and adding the constant given in the tables.

The designation of a move is similar to the reach motion. Thus M8B12 indicates an 8-in. (20.3-cm) type B move where the object weighs 12 lb (5.4-kg).

Turn and Apply Pressure

The turn motion refers to rotating the empty or loaded hand. This motion involves the muscles of the hand, wrist and forearm. Turn times are given for various amounts of rotation and three ranges of weights. A designation of T60° represents a rotation of the empty hand of 60°.

Exerting a force by the fingers or hand is designated by the apply pressure motion. Two types of apply pressure are considered. Type 1 apply pressure requires regrasping or adjusting the muscles to apply the force such as required when turning a valve. Type 2 apply pressure does not involve regrasping or adjusting the muscles. An example of the type 2 apply pressure is pushing a button or lever. The apply pressure is designated as either AP1 or AP2.

TABLE 19.1

GRASP MOTIONS

Type	Description	Example
1A	The simple grasp of a single object	Grasping a spoon, dish or lever
1B	The action of pinching a small object or an object lying against a flat surface	Grasping a piece of paper, string or a coin
1C	Type of grasp where interference is present on the bottom and one side of the object	Grasping a pencil from a box of pencils
2	A regrasp requiring the shifting of the position of the fingers	Shifting a fork in the hand prior to using
3	Transferring the grasp of an object from one hand to the other	Moving a knife from the left hand to the right hand
4	Grasping an object from a group of objects so search or select are required	Getting a tomato from the basket
5	The action of touching an object without picking it up	Touching a coin to slide it

Grasp

Grasp is the motion involved when the purpose is to gain control of an object. Several types of grasp are considered depending upon the size of the object and the finger actions involved. The types, descriptions and examples of the grasp motion are shown in Table 19.1.

Position

The position motion is used to align, orient and engage one object with another. The factors affecting the position motion are the class of fit, symmetry and difficulty of handling. Three classes of fit are used: (1) loose—which requires no pressure; (2) close—which requires light pressure; and (3) exact—which requires heavy pressure.

Symmetry refers to the shape of the objects that are to be engaged. Putting a round plug in a round hole is considered to be symmetrical because the plug may be put into the hole in an infinite number of ways. If a limited number of ways of engaging one object to another is involved, such as a square plug in a square hole, the classification is referred to as semisymmetrical. If only one method of engaging is available such as putting a key in the keyhole, the classification is referred to as nonsymmetrical.

The difficulty of handling the object to be positioned is broken down into two classes: easy and difficult. Most position motions are in the easy to handle classification. Only when very large, heavy or flexible objects are involved would the difficult to handle classification be used.

A designation of P2SSD would mean positioning a close fit, semisymmetrical object that is difficult to handle.

Release

Only two types of release motions are considered. The type 1 normal release consists of opening the fingers or hand to lose control of an object. Type 2 is a contact release which consists of removing the fingers from the contact grasp of an object.

Disengage

The disengage motion is the action of separating one object from another. Times are related to classes of fit and the ease or difficulty of handling the object to be disengaged. Thus a D2E designation indicates disengaging a close fit object which is easy to handle.

Simultaneous Motions

The table of simultaneous motions identifies those motions that can be easily accomplished at the same time. Such questions as can a type 1A grasp be performed by one hand while a type 4B grasp is performed by the other hand, or can a type 1 release and a type 2 apply pressure be performed simultaneously are indicated in the table. The table of simultaneous motions is also useful when planning a sequence of motions for each hand for future work.

Illustrations

Illustration of using the basic motion time data are shown in Fig. 19.2 and 19.3. Figure 19.2 shows the basic motion analysis of a ladling operation. The basic motion analysis of a broiling activity is depicted in Fig. 19.3.

ELEMENTAL TIME DATA

Elemental time data are similar to basic motion time data except that gross motions or motions involving a logical grouping of therbligs are considered. The elemental time data is best used for long cycle activities. The procedure for using elemental time data is similar to that for basic motion data. The motions required to do a task are identified and each motion is assigned a symbol and time. Unlike basic motion data where many different types of motion are indicated, elemental time data offer a limited number of motions to choose from.

The elemental time data consist of the elements *Obtain, Place, Rotate, Use, Finger Shift, Exert Force* and *Body Motions* as shown in Fig.19.4. The times for the elements are given in T.M.U.'s. The following descriptions of each element will clarify their use.

Obtain

The element *obtain* is characterized by the distance, degree of control and the number of *obtains* involved. The symbol for *obtain* is O and the distance involved is indicated directly after the symbol. Thus O12 represents *obtain* with a 12-in. (30.5 cm) reach.

The degree of control refers to the method that an individual uses to bring the object under control. Two alternatives are used: some control or high control. Some control is used when the object can be obtained by contact or simply closing the fingers. All other methods are considered as high control. The degree of control is indicated after the distance so that O12S means *obtain*, 12-in. (30.5 cm) reach, some control.

OBTAIN—O

Distance in Inches	Degree of Control			
	Some—S		High—H	
	1	2	1	2
2	8	8	17	30
6	13	13	21	34
12	17	17	25	38
18	21	21	30	42

PLACE—P

Distance in Inches	Other Hand O	Location				
		General G	Exact			
			Loose—L		Close—C	
			1	2	1	2
2	7	5	11	26	21	47
6	11	9	16	31	27	52
12	15	13	21	36	31	57
18	19	17	26	41	37	62

ROTATE R			USE U		FINGER SHIFT		BODY MOTIONS B		
H	F	9	V	4	FS	6	A	Arise-Sit	108
	W	15	L	8	EXERT		F	Foot	9
C	S	17	M	13	FORCE		V	Vertical	61
	L	19	H	17	EF	11	W	Walk	17

FIG. 19.4. ELEMENTAL TIME DATA

Reprinted with permission from R.M. Crossan and H.W. Nance, *Master Standard Data*, McGraw-Hill Book Co., New York.

The number of *obtains* is broken down into two types. Obtaining one object with one hand is designated by the number 1 placed after the degree of control designation. Obtaining one object with both hands, or two objects, one with each hand is designated by the number 2. If a handful of objects is obtained, this is indicated in the description of the element.

Place

The element *place* designates the movement of an object to an immediate destination. Important factors affecting the *place* element are distance, destination, number of alignments and the accuracy of final placement. The distance of the *place* element is indicated after the symbol P. The other variables and the symbols used to represent them are summarized in Table 19.2.

A designation of P6C2 means that 2 objects were moved 6 in. (15.2 cm) and placed in separate exact locations or that 2 alignments of a single object were made.

Operation: ladling soup. Ladle is in soup container; bowls are stacked at left. Top bowl is to be filled and placed on counter[1]

| LEFT HAND | | TIME CONSUMED | | RIGHT HAND |
Description of Motion	M.T.M. Definition of Motion	T.M.U.[2]	Description of Motion	M.T.M. Definition of Motion
		First Method		
		11.5	reach to ladle	reach to object in general location
		1.7	grasp ladle	pick-up grasp, single object, easily grasped
		5.6	regrasp ladle	regrasp for better control
		5.6	regrasp ladle	regrasp for better control
		10.6	lift filled ladle to clear container	move object to approximate location
		18.7	move filled ladle to bowl	move object to exact location
		5.6	position ladle over bowl	position—loose, symmetrical, easy to handle
		9.4	turn ladle to pour liquid	turn 180°
		10.0	pour liquid	estimated—*not* an M.T.M. time
		18.2	move ladle back to container	move object to approximate location
		3.5	turn ladle into liquid	turn 45°
		1.7	release ladle	normal release
		10.5	return arm to side	reach to indefinite location for body balance
Reach for bowl	reach to object in approximate location	11.5		
Grasp bowl	grasp object lying close against flat surface	3.5		
Regrasp bowl	regrasp for better control	5.6		
Regrasp bowl	regrasp for better control	5.6		
Move bowl to counter	move object to exact location	16.9		
Place bowl on counter	position—close, symmetrical, easy to handle	16.2		
Release bowl	normal release	1.7		
Return arm to side	reach to indefinite location for body balance	14.2		
Total		187.8[3]		

Second Method

Left hand — operation	Description	T.M.U.[2]	Right hand — operation	Description
Reach for bowl	reach to object in general location	11.5	reach for ladle	reach to object in general location pick-up grasp, single object, easily grasped
Grasp bowl	grasp object lying close against flat surface	3.5	grasp ladle	
Regrasp bowl	regrasp for better control	5.6		move object to exact location
Move bowl over container	move object to approximate location	13.5	move filled ladle to bowl	
		5.6	position ladle over bowl	position—loose, symmetrical, easy to handle turn $135°$
Move bowl to counter	move object to exact location	7.4	turn ladle to pour	
		10.0	pour liquid	estimated—*not* an M.T.M. time
Place bowl on counter	position—close, symmetrical, easy to handle	13.5	move ladle back to container	move object to approximate location
		16.2	return ladle into liquid	turn $45°$
Release bowl	normal release	1.7	release ladle	normal release
Return arm to side	reach to indefinite location for body balance	14.2	return arm to side	reach to indefinite location for body balance
Total		102.7[4]		

[1] This should not be considered a time standard for all ladling operations and should not be used as such. Variations in type of bowl, ladle, work place, layout, distances involved, and so on, will cause the times for individual ladling operations to vary considerably. Separate analyses of each situation should be made.
[2] T.M.U. = 0.036 sec.
[3] 6.8 sec.
[4] 3.7 sec.

FIG. 19.2.   BASIC MOTION ANALYSIS OF PERFORMING A LADLING OPERATION

Reprinted from "Methods Analysis," by J. Ronald Frazer, J. Am. Dietet. Assoc.

METHODS ANALYSIS CHART

Reference No. ————
Date ———— Study No. ————
Analyst ———— Sheet ———— of ———— Sheets

Part ———— Conventional Table Top Range
Operation ———— Broil Steak

Description—Left Hand	No.	L.H.	TMU	R.H.	No.	Description—Right Hand
(A) OPEN BROILER DOOR						
Reach for door handle		R-B	29.0	S		Stoop to reach door handle
Grasp door handle		G1A	2.0			
Overcome spring		AP2	10.6			
Open door		M12A	12.9	R-B		Reach toward rack
			54.5			
(B) ADJUST RACK POSITION						
Release door handle		RL1	6.4	R4B		Reach to rack
			2.0	G1A		Grasp rack
Reach to side of rack		R-B	12.2	M10B		Move rack out
Grasp side of rack		G1A				
Move rack to stop		M14A	14.4	RL1		Release front of rack
				R6B		Reach to side of rack
				G1A		Grasp side of rack
				M-A		Move rack to stop
Move rack to clear stop		M2B	4.6	M2B		Move rack to clear stop
Move rack out of groove		M2B	4.6	M2B		Move rack out of groove

(Steps Not Depicting Basic Motion Are Not Shown)

Description—Left Hand	No.	L.H.	TMU	R.H.	No.	Description—Right Hand
(J) REMOVE STEAK						
Move fork to steak		M8B	10.6			
Turn fork to secure steak		T90M	8.5			
Move steak to platter		M8B	10.6	M.B.		Move platter toward steak
Turn fork to release steak		T90M	8.5			
			38.2			

No.	Element Description	Element Time TMU	Conversion Factor 0.00001 Leveled Time	% Allowance	Element Time Allowed	Occurrences Per Piece or Cycle	Total Time Allowed
A	OPEN BROILER DOOR	54.5	0.000545				0.000545
B	ADJUST RACK POSITION	67.6	0.000676				0.000676
	(Steps Not Depicting Basic Motion Are Not Shown)						
J	REMOVE STEAK	38.2	0.000382				0.000382
						Total	0.009744

FIG. 19.3. A PORTION OF BASIC MOTION ANALYSIS OF A METHOD OF BROILING

Reprinted with permission from H.B. Maynard, *Industrial Engineering Handbook*, McGraw-Hill Book Co., New York.

TABLE 19.2

VARIABLES AND SYMBOLS FOR THE ELEMENT PLACE

Variable Symbol	Description
O	Objects placed in other hand
G	General destination; no visual control required
L	Exact destination; loose (no noticeable hesitation)
C	Exact destination; close, (noticeable hesitation)
1	Single alignment, one object, one hand
2	Eyes travel between two alignments, (two alignments of single object or two objects placed in separate, exact locations)

Rotate

The *rotate* element is employed to turn an object about an axis parallel to that of the forearm. The *rotate* element is similar to the turn motion described in the basic motion time data. *Rotate* is broken down into two general types: *Rotate Hand* (RH) where the individual performs the rotation of an object by grasping it with the fingers; and *Rotate Crank* (RC) where the rotation is accomplished by a cranking motion.

Rotate by hand may be of two types. The first type is rotation where the fingers are primarily used (RHF) and there is little resistance to turning. When the resistance to turning increases so that the fingers alone cannot turn, then the second type where the wrist has to be used is indicated (RHW).

The *rotate* by crank is also of two types depending on the diameter of the hand motion. RCL denotes a path diameter of over six in. (15.2 cm). RCS denotes a path diameter of between 2 to 6 in. (5 to 15.2 cm).

Use

The element *use* denotes a back and forth motion such as wiping a table or cutting. The *use* elements are typed according to the distance of the body member motions. The four types are:

UV—Performed by the fingers or hand, movement is less than one in. (2.54 cm).

UL—Performed by wrist, movement is about two inches (5.08 cm).

UM—Movement is about four in. (10.2 cm), some force is involved.

UH—Movement of about six in. (15.2 cm), considerable force involved.

Finger Shift and Exert Force

Finger shift is the element describing the movements of the fingers in prepositioning an object. This element is the same as "regrasp" described in basic motion data.

Exert force is the same as the basic motion described as "apply pressure." The element is defined as the application of force to overcome initial resistance or for pushing one object against or into another.

Body Motions

The motions of the human body are broadly classified as those that take place in the horizontal and vertical planes. Horizontal body motions are accomplished by moving the feet. The primary horizontal body motion is walking designated by the symbol W.

Vertical body motions are body arise (and sit) designated by BA, and bending, stooping and kneeling designated by BV. The movement of the foot hinged at the ankle is designated by BF.

Illustration

The use of elemental time data is illustrated by the analysis of a measuring operation as depicted in Fig. 19.5.

The basic motion and/or elemental motion time data may be profitably used to develop standard times for tasks with minimum cost. The standard time data is also useful for designing work methods, comparing different methods or evaluating complex worker-machine activities.

Basic Elements	Symbol	Time Measurement Unit	Process Time (Sec)
Obtain measure (R.H.)	O12H1	25	
Transfer measure to L.H.	P20	7	
Finger shift measure	FS	6	
Pick up vessel from table	O12H1	25	
Finger shift vessel	FS	6	
Bring near measure	P12C1	31	
Rotate hand to pour	RHW	15	
Process Time			7.0
Visual pause	VP	7	
Rotate vessel	RHW	15	
Place vessel on table	P12C1	31	
Pour measured amount	RHW	15	
Process Time			4.2
Transfer measure to R.H.	P20	7	
Place measure on work tray	P12G	13	
Total		203	11.2

FIG. 19.5. ELEMENTAL MOTION ANALYSIS OF MEASURING OPERATION

Reprinted with permission from G.M. Montag, M.M. McKinley and A.C. Klinschmidt, "Predetermined Motion Times—A Tool in Food Production Management," J. Am Dietet. Assoc.

20

Effective Use of Work Analysis and Design

INTRODUCTION

The results of work analysis and design and particularly the development of standard times provide the information required for efficient management. The basic uses of the information that enable management to economically achieve the objective and goals of the organization will be summarized. Two relatively new techniques, *Critical Path Scheduling* and *Linear Programming,* will be presented in greater detail to illustrate the use of such information.

USING WORK ANALYSIS AND DESIGN RESULTS

Product Design

Work analysis and design will provide the information required to evaluate the products produced by the organization from the standpoint of cost, customer appeal, ease of production and maintenance of quality. The effects of using different processes or alternate materials on the cost of the product can also be quickly evaluated.

Layout

The layouts of departments, work areas or workplaces should be evaluated on the basis of material flow or employee movements. Work analysis and design information also suggests possible uses of materials handling and other labor saving equipment.

Manpower

The effective use of manpower is probably the most important area that work analysis and design can provide information for. The information can be used to determine: (1) productivity levels; (2) number of employees needed; (3) skills required; (4) training requirements and costs; (5) proper work methods; and (6) turnover costs.

Scheduling

Scheduling of the various activities encountered to produce a product or provide a service is simplified when the details of the activities and the time required to do each activity is known. The Critical Path Method of scheduling will be presented later in this chapter.

Equipment Design

The design of equipment can be evaluated from the standpoint of ease of operation, cost, effect on methods of work and suitability for worker-machine systems by utilizing the results of work analysis and design programs. Human engineering knowledge should be applied to critically evaluate the controls and displays used on the equipment.

Selection of New Equipment

When new equipment is being considered either for replacement or for expansion of facilities, work analysis and design data will help determine or help compare: (1) cost of operation; (2) capacity required; (3) skill of operator; (4) number of operators required; (5) adaptability of different materials and processes; (6) compatibility with existing equipment; and (7) flexibility to changes in demand.

Cost Control

Work analysis and design provides the best information for determining direct and indirect labor costs. The very nature of the procedures used to break down various tasks and activities and the measurement of times results in more accurate costs than gross cost estimating techniques. Material, equipment, operating and overhead costs can also be accurately obtained.

Forecasting

The data gathered during work analysis and design automatically provide a basis for forecasting customer demand, work loads, peaks and valleys and potential sales. Such information is also used to develop staffing patterns and procedures.

Employer-employee Relations

The day-to-day contact between supervisors and employees can be improved through work analysis and design by setting equitable work performance standards and thus providing some measures of worker performance. The creation of improved physical environmental conditions, social conditions and information flow will also aid employer-employee relations.

Job Design and Evaluation

Work analysis and design can be used to evaluate job content and prepare adequate job descriptions. This in turn will aid the development of departments and the entire organizational structure.

New Management Techniques

The quantitative information needed for the scientific management techniques that have been and are being developed can be obtained by work analysis and design. Of the many techniques available, the Critical Path Method of scheduling and Linear Programming were selected to show their dependence on work analysis and design. In both techniques, the standard time or cost required to perform activities is used.

CRITICAL PATH SCHEDULING

The *Critical Path* method (CPM) is a basic technique for planning and scheduling activities for projects where precedence requirements exist. The *Critical Path* method utilizes a graphic presentation to show the relationships between the activities required to accomplish a given project. Each activity and the time to complete it are shown in a diagram similar to the precedence diagram. The precedence requirements are indicated by arrows connecting the activities presented in the diagram.

The *Critical Path* method of planning and scheduling can be applied to all projects that are expected to be completed at a specified time. Planning and scheduling the activities for catering a banquet, setting up for a convention, operating a tray assembly line in hospitals and cleaning or maintenance projects are examples of situations where CPM can be used. The CPM technique provides the following information about the project: (1) the expected duration of the project; (2) the activities which are critical or may delay the project; (3) the points in time when activities should begin and end; and (4) the amount of leeway available for scheduling activities.

With this information, CPM helps management and supervisors to understand the sequencing of activities and the necessity of emphasizing and pushing those that are critical to the satisfactory completion of the project. The critical activities define the *"critical path"* which determines the minimum time of completion for the project.

Constructing the CPM Diagram

The CPM diagram is a network presentation of the activities or tasks within a project. Each activity or task is represented by an arrow with circles at the head and tail. The arrows depict the direction of time flow and are not drawn to scale. The circles are referred to as events and indicate the points in time that the activity or task begins and ends. The time duration (any unit of time may be used) is indicated by the numbers placed above the arrows as shown in Fig. 20.1. The events are numbered and are used to identify the activities or tasks. For example, the activity designation of 1−3 identifies the activity that starts at event 1 and ends at event 3. Activity descriptions may also be placed on the network diagram.

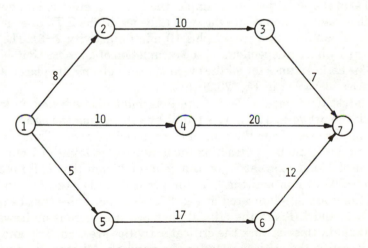

FIG. 20.1. A SIMPLE CPM NETWORK DIAGRAM

The network diagram is developed by first determining the activities that make up the project. In order to determine the sequence of the activities the following questions are asked: (1) What immediately precedes the activity? (2) What immediately follows the activity? (3) What other activities can be done at the same time?

Table 20.1 gives the answers to these questions for the activities making up the network shown in Fig. 20.1. Concurrent activities do not have to start and end at the same time but can be overlapping. The concurrent activities may be determined by drawing the activity arrows to a time scale.

TABLE 20.1

ACTIVITY INFORMATION FOR NETWORK CONSTRUCTION

Activity	Immediately Preceding Activity	Immediately Following Activity	Other Concurrent Activities
1-2	..	2-3	1-4, 1-5, 5-6
1-4	..	4-7	1-2, 1-5, 2-3, 5-6
1-5	..	5-6	1-2, 1-4
2-3	1-2	3-7	1-4, 4-7, 5-6
4-7	1-4	..	2-3, 3-7, 5-6, 6-7
5-6	1-5	6-7	1-2, 1-4, 2-3, 3-7, 4-7
3-7	2-3	..	4-7, 5-6, 6-7
6-7	5-6	..	3-7, 4-7

After the network has been constructed, the earliest and latest completion times for each event are determined. The earliest time (E.T.) and the latest time (L.T.) are determined by analyzing the sequence and duration of the activities. For example, the E.T. of completion for event 2 is 8 min assuming minutes are the time units used. The E.T. for event 3 is 18 min (8 min for activity 1−2 plus 10 min for activity 2−3). The E.T. for event 7 which is dependent on the completion of all the activities is 34 min. The earliest times for all the events in the network are placed above the circles as shown in Fig. 20.2.

The latest times for each event are determined by working backward through the network. The L.T. is found by subtracting the activity time following the event from the time of the succeeding event. Thus the L.T. for event 3 is found by subtracting the activity (3−7) time of 7 min from the time of 34 min of event 7, giving a value of 27 min. The L.T. for event 4 is (34−20) 14 min and the L.T. for event 6 is (34−12) 22 min. The latest times are also indicated in Fig. 20.2. The activities that have the same E.T. and L.T. are the critical ones because there is no leeway or slack time. In this network the critical activities are 1−5, 5−6 and 6−7 which describe the *critical path* for the network. All other activities in the network have slack time indicating that they can be delayed without changing the time of completion of the project. The slack time is determined by subtracting the E.T. from the L.T. and indicates the amount of delay that can occur. For example, activity 2–3 has a slack time of (27–18) 9 min meaning it could be delayed for that length of time (if activity 1–2 were completed at the E.T. indicated) without affecting the completion time of the project.

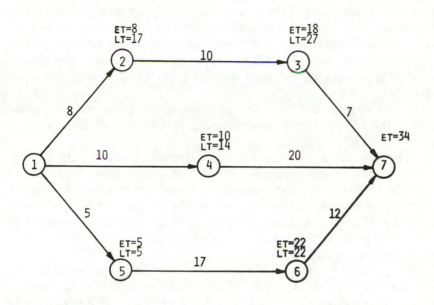

FIG. 20.2. NETWORK DIAGRAM SHOWING EARLIEST
AND LATEST TIMES OF COMPLETION FOR EACH EVENT

The example presented is relatively simple and the critical activities can be easily seen. In real situations the networks may involve many activities and become quite complex and the critical activities may not be easily foreseen.

USING THE CPM NETWORK

The obvious reason for constructing the CPM network is to identify the critical activities so management and supervisors can concentrate on them so the project can be completed on time. When projects are not running smoothly the greatest savings in time, money and confusion are obtained by working with the critical activities. The CPM network can also indicate where reporting procedures are needed to assure adequate control of the project.

LINEAR PROGRAMMING

Linear programming is a recently developed quantitative technique that may be used to solve certain types of allocation problems. The presentation of linear programming will be limited to two methods of solution for special problems related to work analysis and design. The first method presented is used to solve "assignment" type problems which are special cases of the general linear programming problems. The second method presented is an approximation technique that can be used to solve the "assignment" and "transportation" type problems. Both methods can be easily used without a formal mathematical background in linear programming therefore making them valuable tools for management.

The first step in applying linear programming is to identify the problems to be solved. Linear programming problems have the following characteristics.

1. The problem has many solutions, several of which may be satisfactory, but at least one will be the best or optimum solution. For example, there may be many satisfactory methods of accomplishing the activities of a work system by altering the assignment of workers to activities. However, at least one particular assignment of workers to activities may be the best from the standpoint of least time, least cost or some other measurable criteria.

2. The problem has certain demands that must be met. These demands are referred to as requirements of the problem. In the assignment of workers to activities, the requirement may state that each activity has to be done by two persons. In this case, assigning three workers to an activity would violate the requirements of the problem.

3. The problem has certain restrictions or limits which must not be exceeded. For the "workers to activity assignment problem", a restriction could be imposed upon the number of activities that could be assigned to each worker.

4. The alternative solutions to the linear programming problem should have significant differences between them. This is important so that solving for the optimum will be worthwhile.

5. The criteria for evaluating the problem must be in quantitative form. This last point is where the results of work analysis and design can provide the information for the problem. In the "workers to activities assignment," the time required or the cost of having each worker doing each activity would have to be known.

The Assignment Problem

The assignment problem is a special case of general linear programming problems that involve the simplest requirements and restrictions. To illustrate the assignment problem, consider the situation where 4 different workers are to be assigned to 4 different activities. The statement that several different solutions must be present indicates that each worker can perform each of the different activities. The requirements and restrictions of the assignment problem indicate that only a one-to-one assignment is permitted. That is, only one worker can be assigned to any one activity. In order to evaluate all possible assignments, the criteria of assigning the different workers to the different activities must be known. If time of completion of the activity were the criterion of evaluation, then the time for all possible combinations of workers and activities must be known. The statement that there must be significant differences between the solutions indicates that the times required for each worker to do each activity are considerably different.

TABLE 20.2

POSSIBLE ASSIGNMENTS OF FOUR WORKERS (A, B, C, D) TO FOUR ACTIVITIES (1, 2, 3, 4)

A-1 B-2 C-3 D-4	A-1 B-2 C-4 D-3	A-1 B-3 C-2 D-4	A-1 B-3 C-4 D-2	A-1 B-4 C-2 D-3	A-1 B-4 C-3 D-2
A-2 B-1 C-3 D-4	A-2 B-1 C-4 D-3	A-2 B-3 C-1 D-4	A-2 B-3 C-4 D-1	A-2 B-4 C-1 D-3	A-2 B-4 C-3 D-1
A-3 B-1 C-2 D-4	A-3 B-1 C-4 D-2	A-3 B-2 C-1 D-4	A-3 B-2 C-4 D-1	A-3 B-4 C-1 D-2	A-3 B-4 C-2 D-1
A-4 B-1 C-2 D-3	A-4 B-1 C-3 D-2	A-4 B-2 C-1 D-3	A-4 B-2 C-3 D-1	A-4 B-3 C-1 D-2	A-4 B-3 C-2 D-1

There are 24 possible solutions to the assignment of 4 workers to 4 activities. Indicating the workers by the letters A, B, C, D and the activities by the numbers 1, 2, 3, 4; the 24 possible solutions are shown in Table 20.2. The designation A-1 means A is assigned to activity 1. The possible number of solutions is determined by the factorial (!) of the things to be assigned. If 6 things were to be assigned, the possible solutions would be 720 ($6! = 6 \times 5 \times 4 \times 3 \times 2 \times 1 = 720$).

The objective of the linear programming problem should be stated in terms of the criteria used such as finding the least time assignment or least cost assignment. Although most linear programming problems are set up to minimize the criteria, maximizing problems can also be formulated.

The problems to be solved by linear programming are usually arranged in a matrix. The matrix for the assignment of four workers to four activities is shown below. The data within the cells indicate the criteria of assignments such as time. The restrictions show that only one activity can be assigned to each worker. The requirements call for assigning one worker to each activity.

		Activities				
		1	2	3	4	Restrictions
	A	10	18	19	16	1
	B	15	17	21	14	1
Workers	C	13	10	24	20	1
	D	19	19	17	23	1
Requirements		1	1	1	1	

The assignment type problem can be solved by using the "Hungarian Method" (Kuhn 1955). The Hungarian method uses a number of manipulative steps to arrive at the optimum solution. The steps for finding the minimum optimum value of assignment problems are:

Step 1.—Subtract the smallest number in the first row from all the numbers in the first row. Continue for each succeeding row.

Step 2.—Subtract the smallest number in the first column from all the numbers in the first column. Continue for each succeeding column. (If zeros exist in any column, this step is not necessary for that column.)

Step 3.—Make assignments to positions where single zeros exist. In the optimum solution, only one zero in each row and column will be assigned. This is to satisfy the requirements and restrictions of the problem. If assignments cannot be made because: (a) there are too many zeros, or (b) there are not enough zeros, proceed as follows.

Step 4.—To solve situations 3a (where there are too many zeros) find the rows where only one zero exists, mark this zero and cross out all other zeros in the same column as the marked zero. Next find the columns where only a single unmarked zero appears, mark this zero and cross out all other zeros in the same row as the marked zero. Repeat this procedure until 1 of 2 things happen.

1. There are no zeros left unmarked (which may give the desired solution, or we may have to proceed under situation 3b) or

2. The remaining zeros lie at least two in each row and column (which indicates that there may be more than one optimal solution).

Step 5.—If situation 3b occurs (where there are not enough zeros) proceed as follows:

Cover all zeros with the minimum number of straight lines. Next subtract the smallest number not covered by a line from all numbers not covered, and add it to all numbers that are covered by the intersection of two lines. Numbers that are covered by only one line are not changed. Repeat the procedure from step 1, until the desired solution is obtained.

To illustrate the procedure, the problem previously discussed and shown will be solved. The original matrix is shown below.

	1	2	3	4
A	10	18	19	16
B	15	17	21	14
C	13	10	24	20
D	19	19	17	23

Step 1.—The results of subtracting the smallest number in each row from the numbers in each row are:

	1	2	3	4
A	0	8	9	6
B	1	3	7	0
C	3	0	14	10
D	2	2	0	6

Step 2.—Since a zero exists in each column of the matrix, step 2 does not change the matrix.

Step 3.—Making the assignments where zeros exist is indicated by boxing the zeros as shown below.

	1	2	3	4
A	[0]	8	9	6
B	1	3	7	[0]
C	3	[0]	14	10
D	2	2	[0]	6

Since a single zero in each row and column were assigned, the optimum solution has been found. The solution indicates the following assignments:

Assign worker A to activity 1
Assign worker B to activity 4
Assign worker C to activity 2
Assign worker D to activity 3

The numerical value of the solution is obtained by referring to the original matrix and summing the times for the assignments made. The numerical solution to the problem is shown below.

Assignment	Time
A-1	10
B-4	14
C-2	10
D-3	17
Total	51 min

In this case the solution to the problem was obtained very simply. In fact the solution could have been obtained by selecting the best time (minimum) for each worker or activity without following the Hungarian Method because the solution was quite obvious.

A second example will be presented to illustrate the procedure when the solution may not be quite as obvious. Consider the assignment of workers to activities as shown in the following matrix.

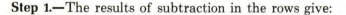

	Activities					
	1	2	3	4	5	Restrictions
A	20	18	14	19	17	1
B	18	30	19	17	14	1
Workers C	14	17	12	20	16	1
D	8	14	16	15	9	1
E	5	9	13	15	14	1
Requirements	1	1	1	1	1	

Step 1.—The results of subtraction in the rows give:

	1	2	3	4	5
A	6	4	0	5	3
B	4	16	5	3	0
C	2	5	0	8	4
D	0	6	8	7	1
E	0	4	8	10	9

Step 2.—The results of subtraction in the columns give:

	1	2	3	4	5
A	6	0	0	2	3
B	4	12	5	0	0
C	2	1	0	5	4
D	0	2	8	4	1
E	0	0	8	7	9

Step 3.—It appears that step 3 cannot be completed because too many zeros exist in row A, B and E, and columns 1, 2 and 3 (situation 3a). Proceed to step 4.

Step 4.—The procedure followed is indicated by the index numbers placed by the rows or columns. For example, the first single zero was found in row C; it was marked and the other zero in column 3 crossed out because only one zero can be assigned in any column. Crossed out zeros can not be used for assignments.

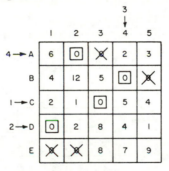

Step 4 could not be completed because there were not enough zeros in row E and column 5 (situation 3b). Proceed to step 5.

Step 5.—It is important that the minimum number of lines be used to cover all the zeros. The purpose of this step is to create additional zeros in the rows and columns where assignments could not be made. One system of lines covering all the zeros is shown below. There may be several systems of lines that can be used.

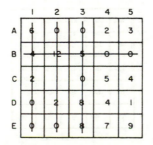

The smallest number not covered by a line is the value 1 found in row D, column 5. This value is subtracted from those numbers not covered by a line and added to those numbers covered by the intersection of two lines. This procedure results in the modified matrix shown below.

	1	2	3	4	5
A	6	0	0	1	2
B	5	13	6	0	0
C	2	1	0	4	3
D	0	2	8	3	0
E	0	0	8	6	8

Next the procedure is repeated from step 1 until the desired solution is found. In most cases, step 1 and step 2 will not have to be done because zeros will probably exist in all rows and columns. Repeating steps 3 and 4 for the modified matrix results in the following solution. The index shows the sequence of assignments made starting with row C.

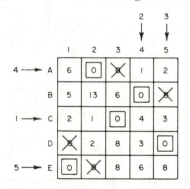

The assignments and the numerical values (taken from the original matrix) of the solution are shown in matrix form below.

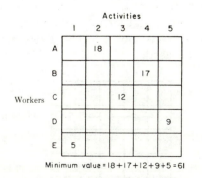

		Activities				
		1	2	3	4	5
	A		18			
	B				17	
Workers	C			12		
	D					9
	E	5				

Minimum value = 18+17+12+9+5 = 61

Some of the steps indicated in the Hungarian Method may be interchanged without affecting the solution. For example, step 2 could have been done before step 1, or assignments could have been made by columns first instead of by rows.

Nonsquare Assignment Problems

The Hungarian Method can only be used for a square matrix, that is, it must have the same number of rows and columns. Certain problems may be encountered where the matrix is not square and applying the Hungarian Method may result in a suboptimum solution. Nonsquare matrices should be converted to square matrices by the addition of dummy rows or columns. The entries for the dummy rows or columns will be zeros because each entry should have an equal chance of being assigned. The solution to the nonsquare problem is illustrated by the following example.

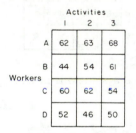

The original matrix for the problem is shown above. The problem of assigning workers to activities is again used but in this case one of the workers will not be assigned. (One worker will be assigned to the dummy activity.)

The addition of the dummy activity modifies the matrix as follows:

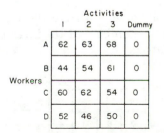

The solution of the problem can now proceed as before and is given as follows:

Step 1. Does not have to be done because zeros exist in every row.

Step 2.

	1	2	3	Dummy
A	18	17	18	0
B	0	8	11	0
C	16	16	4	0
D	8	0	0	0

Step 3. Cannot be completed.
Step 4.

	1	2	3	Dummy
A	18	17	18	☒
B	⊡0	8	11	☒
C	16	16	4	⊡0
D	8	⊡0	☒	☒

Since step 4 does not give a solution, proceed as shown.
Step 5.

	1	2	3	Dummy
A	18	17	18	0
B	0	8	11	0
C	16	16	4	0
D	8	0	0	0

Subtracting the numerical value of 4 from those numbers not covered by a line and adding it to the numbers at the intersections of lines gives the following adjusted matrix.

	1	2	3	Dummy
A	14	13	14	0
B	0	8	11	4
C	12	12	0	0
D	8	0	0	4

The assignments are made as indicated.

	1	2	3	Dummy
A	14	13	14	[0]
B	[0]	8	11	4
C	12	12	[0]	✗
D	8	[0]	✗	4

The desired solution is shown on the matrix below and indicates that worker A is not assigned to an activity.

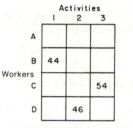

Activities

Workers		1	2	3
	A			
	B	44		
	C			54
	D		46	

Minimum value = 44+54+46 =144

Prohibiting Assignments

In some circumstances assignments may not be desirable and can be prohibited in the solution. Some reasons for prohibiting the assignment of workers to activities might be the following.

1. An individual may not have the skill required to do a good job.
2. A person may not like to do a particular activity.
3. An activity may call for certain personality characteristics.
4. An activity may be too fatiguing for older individuals.

When assignments are to be prohibited, the value of the entry in the matrix is arbitrarily made high so that the assignment will not appear in the solution. It is normal to use infinity (∞) as the value for prohibited assignments as shown in the matrix that follows on pg. 318. In this case, worker B will not be assigned to activity 2.

Using infinity in the matrix does not alter the procedure for solving the problem. Adding or subtracting from infinity still results in infinity.

Although all the examples presented were to find the minimum value, the Hungarian Method can be used to find maximum values as well. The only modification that has to be made is to multiply the entries in the

	Activity			
	1	2	3	4
A	86	72	63	79
B	68	∞	52	74
C	59	46	51	62
D	48	62	39	56

Workers

original matrix by −1. This has the effect of changing the largest values in the matrix to the smallest values so the procedure outlined can be followed.

THE TRANSPORTATION PROBLEM

The transportation type problems represent the largest group of all presently known applications of linear programming. The transportation problems involve requirements and restrictions that are different than the one-to-one allocation described for the assignment problem. The requirements may call for different allocations to be made to each category under consideration. For example, 6 items may be allocated to 1 individual while 5 items may be allocated to another individual. In the same sense, the restrictions in the transportation problem may place different limits on the allocations allowed in each category.

Several methods of finding the optimum solution to transportation problems are available, however, they all require a large amount of manipulation and calculation (Reinfeld and Vogel 1958). Since the primary purpose of presenting linear programming is to show how the results of work analysis and design can be used by management, an approximation method of solving the transportation problem will be presented. The method is referred to as Vogel's Approximation Method and gives a very good approximation to the optimum solution and in many instances gives the optimum solution itself. The approximation method will be illustrated by solving a typical transportation problem.

Assume that a large food service company prepares meals at three commissary locations to be delivered to five different outlets. The production capacity of the commissaries in terms of truckloads is given in Table 20.3.

TABLE 20.3

PRODUCTION CAPACITY OF COMMISSARIES

Commissary	Production Capacity (Truckloads)
A	6
B	4
C	7

The requirements of each of the five outlets are also stated in terms of truckloads as given in Table 20.4.

TABLE 20.4

REQUIREMENTS OF OUTLETS

Outlet	Requirement (Truckloads)
1	2
2	4
3	3
4	3
5	5

The cost per truckload associated with transporting the food from the commissaries to the outlets is shown in Table 20.5.

TABLE 20.5

COST OF TRANSPORTING FROM COMMISSARIES TO OUTLETS

From	To	Cost/Truckload ($)
A	1	8
A	2	10
A	3	9
A	4	17
A	5	21
B	1	11
B	2	18
B	3	23
B	4	7
B	5	25
C	1	21
C	2	9
C	3	17
C	4	12
C	5	20

The problem is to determine the number of truckloads that should be sent from each commissary to each outlet so the total cost of transportation is minimized. The problem is presented in matrix form as follows:

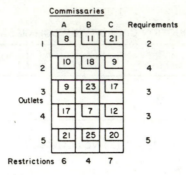

The matrix indicates the commissaries by the columns and the outlets by the rows. The number of truckloads available (restrictions) at each of the commissaries is shown at the bottom of each column. The number of truckloads needed (requirements) at each outlet is shown on the right end of each row. The numbers in the upper right hand corner of each cell are the costs associated with transporting from the various commissaries to the outlets.

The approximation method allocates the truckloads in a step-by-step process until a complete solution is obtained. The allocations are made in rows or columns where the greatest difference between the smallest and next smallest costs are found.

Approximation Method

The first step in the approximation method is to find the differences between the smallest and next smallest costs for each row and each column. These differences are indicated in a difference column and row as shown in the matrix below. For example, the difference for row 1 is 3, $(11-8)$ and the difference for row 2 is 1, $(10-9)$.

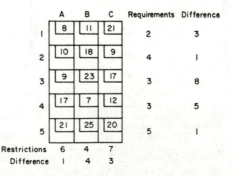

The next step is to allocate the maximum possible truckloads to the cell with the smallest cost in that row or column having the greatest difference. The greatest difference (a value of 8) occurs in row 3 of the matrix. The smallest cell in row 3 is in the first column and has a value of 9. Thus the maximum allocation should be made to cell A−3. The allocations have to conform to the requirements and restrictions as indicated in the matrix. For example, a maximum of 3 truckloads are required by outlet 3, thus a value of 3 is entered in cell A−3. Since three truckloads satisfy the requirements of outlet 3, the other cells in row 3 are crossed out indicating that allocations can not be made to them and the number of truckloads available at commissary A is reduced from 6 to 3. These changes are shown in the matrix given below.

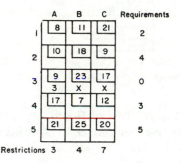

After the first allocation is made and the matrix adjusted, the procedure is repeated again. The difference computations are made only for those rows and columns where allocations can be made. This means that the difference for row 3 is not required. The difference computations for the second cycle are shown in the matrix below.

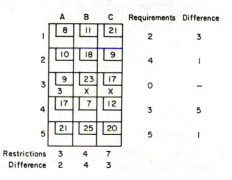

The greatest difference (a value of 5) for the second cycle is found to be in row 4. Therefore, the maximum possible allocation is made to the center cell in row 4 because it contains the smallest cost. Since 3 truckloads are needed at outlet 4, the value of 3 is placed in the cell. The adjustments to the matrix as indicated earlier are again made. The result of the adjustments after the second cycle and the difference computations for the third cycle are shown in the following matrix.

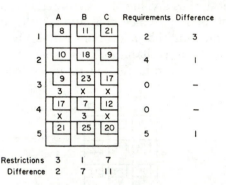

For the third cycle, the greatest difference is in the third column, and the smallest cell in the third column is C−2. A maximum of four truckloads are assigned to the cell. The allocation and adjustments for the third cycle are shown below.

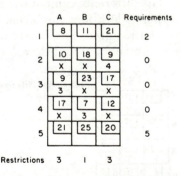

This procedure is repeated until all the allocations are made. The remaining allocations are given on page 323.

The results of the approximation method are interpreted in Table 20.6.

The costs for the solution are also summarized. Since the cost indicated in the matrix is the cost per truckload, the number of truckloads allocated is multiplied by this figure. The total cost for the allocation as shown is $205.00.

	A	B	C	4th Cycle req.	4th Cycle diff.	5th Cycle req.	5th Cycle diff.	6th Cycle req.	6th Cycle diff.
1	8 / I	11 / I	21 / X	2	3	I	13	0	—
2	10 / X	18 / X	9 / 4	0	—	0	—	0	—
3	9 / 3	23 / X	17 / X	0	—	0	—	0	—
4	17 / X	7 / 3	12 / X	0	—	0	—	0	—
5	21 / 2	25 / X	20 / 3	5	I	5	I	5	

4th Cycle	restr.	3	I	3
	diff.	13	14	I
5th Cycle	restr.	3	0	3
	diff.	13	—	I
6th Cycle	restr.	2	0	3
	diff.		—	

TABLE 20.6

RESULTS OF THE APPROXIMATION METHOD OF SOLVING THE TRANSPORTATION TYPE PROBLEM

Number of Truckloads	From	To	Cost (Dollars)
1	A	1	8
1	B	1	11
4	C	2	36
3	A	3	27
3	B	4	21
2	A	5	42
3	C	5	60
			$205 Total

Vogel's approximation method gives management a simple technique to solve the transportation type problems. The technique can also be used to maximize by using the differences between the two largest values in the rows and columns.

Although only two examples of linear programming problems were presented, any problem that will fit the format of the assignment or transportation type problem can be solved by these techniques.

Task Sequencing

INTRODUCTION

The sequencing or scheduling of various tasks that have to be performed for a given situation represents a significant problem for management. Satisfactory solutions to these types of problems are necessary in order to assure efficient operation of the business or institution. Of the many types of sequencing and scheduling problems that may be encountered, the case of scheduling several tasks through each of two pieces of equipment or through two work areas will be used to illustrate a solution procedure. The solution procedure will then be expanded to the problem of scheduling of several tasks through three pieces of equipment or three work areas. A necessary prerequisite to the solution of these types of problems is to know the times required to process each task on each piece of equipment or through each work area. Only those problems that involve tasks which are to be processed in the same order can be solved. This means that each task must first be processed on one piece of equipment before being processed on a second piece of equipment.

There are many examples of tasks in the hotel, restaurant and institutional field that have to be processed through two pieces of equipment in the same order. One example would be the preparation of raw vegetables in a large food service operation or in a commissary operation that must first be processed through a mechanical vegetable peeler before being processed through a vegetable chopper. Depending on the quantities of different vegetables to be prepared in a given time, each type of vegetable may take different amounts of time to process through each of the two pieces of equipment. For example, a large quantity of potatoes will take a longer time to peel than smaller quantities of carrots or beets. In some cases, identical quantities of different vegetables may require different processing times because of physical differences.

A slight variation in sequencing problems can occur when the tasks require processing at a work place before processing through a piece of equipment or vice versa. For example, some food items may be washed at a sink before being processed on a piece of equipment, while other food items must be processed on a piece of equipment first before being processed at a work place. The slicing of cooked meats or other items with a mechanical slicer prior to making sandwiches at a sandwich table is an example of the latter situation.

To simplify the presentation of the solution procedure, the term "equipment" will be used in all example problems with the understanding that it can represent a work place or a work area as well as a piece of equipment.

Sequencing for Two Pieces of Equipment

The general case of sequencing will be illustrated by the following problem. Six tasks involving two pieces of equipment, A and B, are to be scheduled so that they are completed in the shortest possible time. All the tasks must first be processed through equipment A and then through Equipment B. There is no restriction on the order in which the tasks may be done. The processing times for each task on each piece of equipment are given in Table 21.1.

TABLE 21.1

PROCESSING TIMES FOR TASKS

Task Number	Equipment A	Equipment B
1	5	7
2	9	4
3	4	8
4	7	3
5	8	9
6	7	6

One feasible solution to this problem is to perform the tasks in the given sequence of 1, 2, 3, 4, 5 and 6. This sequence will be used merely to show the computations required to determine the total elapsed time to complete all the tasks in the sequence.

The computations involve determining the starting and finishing times for each task on both pieces of equipment. The task starting times for each piece of equipment is dependent upon the finishing time of the task preceeding it. Task number 1 can be started on equipment A at time 0 because it is the first task in the sequence. The finishing time for task number 1 on equipment A is time 5 based on its processing time of 5.

Task number 2 can not start on Equipment A until time 5 which is the finishing time of the task preceeding it. Similarly, task number 3 can not be started until time 14 which is the finishing time for task number 2.

Since each task has to be processed first on equipment A and then on equipment B, the starting times of tasks on equipment B are also dependent on the finishing times on equipment A. Thus task number 1 can not start on equipment B until time 5 which represents the finishing time for task number 1 on equipment A. This may be considered as an idle period of 5 time units for equipment B. The starting times for the remaining tasks on equipment B have to be the latest time of the following:

1. The finishing time of the same task on equipment A, or
2. The finishing time of the preceeding task on equipment B.

Thus even though task number 1 is finished on equipment B by time 12, task number 2 cannot be started on equipment B until time 14 which is the finishing time for task number 2 on equipment A. This represents an idle period of 2 time units for equipment B at this point in the sequence.

The remaining starting and finishing times for this example are summarized in Table 21.2. The total elapsed time to complete the tasks for this sequence is 48 time units.

TABLE 21.2

STARTING AND FINISHING TIMES FOR TASKS PERFORMED IN
THE SEQUENCE 1, 2, 3, 4, 5, 6.

| | *Equipment A* | | *Equipment B* | |
Task Number	*Start*	*Finish*	*Start*	*Finish*
1	0	5	5	12
2	5	14	14	18
3	14	18	18	26
4	18	25	26	29
5	25	33	33	42
6	33	40	42	48

The same computations for this problem are shown graphically in Fig. 21.1. This is only one of 6 possible sequences for performing the tasks. The objective in solving this problem is to find the sequence of tasks that results in the minimum elapsed time. Some problems may have more than one sequence that results in the minimum elapsed time. If this occurs, other factors can be taken into consideration in order to select the optimum sequence.

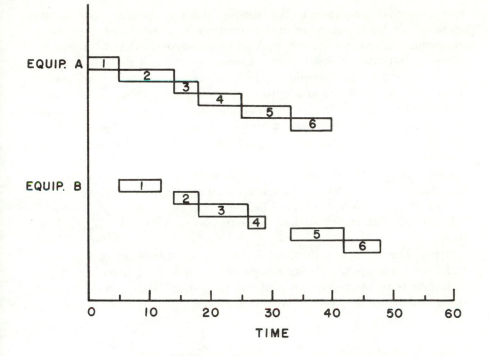

FIG. 21.1. STARTING AND FINISHING TIMES FOR EACH
TASK PERFORMED IN THE SEQUENCE 1, 2, 3, 4, 5, 6

Solution Procedure for Sequencing
With Two Pieces of Equipment

The following steps will indicate the procedure for solving the two
equipment problems for the minimum elapsed time. The solution will be
indicated by a six number sequence identifying the order in which the
tasks are to be done.

1. Search all the task times under both pieces of equipment for the
smallest time value.

2. If the smallest time value appears under equipment A (the first piece
of equipment in the processing order); the task having this smallest time value is placed first in the sequence.

3. If the smallest time value appears under equipment B (the second
piece of equipment in the processing order); the task is placed last in the
sequence.

4. If there are equal minimum time values for different tasks appearing
under both equipment A and equipment B, place first and last in the
sequence accordingly. The time value appearing under equipment A
identifies the task to place first in the sequence and the time value

appearing under equipment B identifies the task to place last in the sequence. If there are equal minimum time values for the same task appearing under both equipment A and equipment B, that task may be placed either first or last in the sequence.

5. If there are equal minimum time values for different tasks under equipment A, select the task with the smallest time value under equipment B and place it first in the sequence. If there are equal minimum time values for different tasks under equipment B, select the task with the smallest time value under equipment A and place it last in the sequence.

6. Eliminate the task and its time values from the data and continue the procedure above by placing the remaining tasks next to first or next to last until all tasks are placed in the sequence.

The solution procedure applied to the problem shown in Table 21.1 is as follows:

Step 1. The smallest time value of 3 is found for task number 4. Since this time value appears under equipment B, task 4 is placed last in the sequence as dictated by step 3 of the procedure. This is shown below using underlines as positions in the sequence.

_____   _____   _____   _____   _____   Task 4

Since the task is placed in the sequence, proceed to step 6.

Step 6. Task number 4 and its time values are eliminated from the data and the procedure is repeated for the remaining tasks.

Step 1 (Repeated). The next smallest time value of 4 is found for both task number 2 and task number 3. Since the minimum equal time value for task 3 is found under equipment A and the other equal time value for task 2 is found under equipment B; task number 3 is placed first in the sequence and task number 2 is placed second to last as dictated by step 4 of the procedure. The sequence thus far is shown below.

Task 3   _____   _____   _____   Task 2   Task 4

Step 6 (Repeated). Tasks 2 and 3 and their time values are eliminated from the data and the procedure is again repeated for the remaining tasks.

Step 1 (Repeated for the second time). The next smallest time value of 5 is found for task number 1. Since this value appears under equipment A, it is placed second to first in the sequence as dictated by step 2. The sequence developed at this point in the procedure is shown below.

Task 3	Task 1			Task 2	Task 4

Step 6 (Repeated for the second time). Task 1 and its time values are eliminated from the data and the procedure is continued.

Step 1 (Repeated for the third time). The next smallest time value of 6 is found for task number 6. Since this time value appears under equipment B, it is placed third to last in the sequence. The sequence now has 5 of the 6 tasks placed and is shown as follows.

Task 3	Task 1		Task 6	Task 2	Task 4

At this point the only task that is left (Task 5) has to be placed in the sequence and takes the last vacant position. The final sequence for this problem is shown below.

Task 3	Task 1	Task 5	Task 6	Task 2	Task 4

The computations for the starting and finishing times for this sequence are shown in Table 21.3. The minimum elapsed time for completing all the tasks is 41 time units and represents the optimum solution to the problem. The graphical presentation of this solution is shown in Fig. 21.2. This solution represents a reduction of 7 time units compared to the initial feasible solution shown earlier.

TABLE 21.3

STARTING AND FINISHING TIMES FOR TASKS PERFORMED IN THE SEQUENCE
3, 1, 5, 6, 2, 4

	Equipment A		Equipment B	
Task Number	Start	Finish	Start	Finish
3	0	4	4	12
1	4	9	12	19
5	9	17	19	28
6	17	24	28	34
2	24	33	34	38
4	33	40	38	41

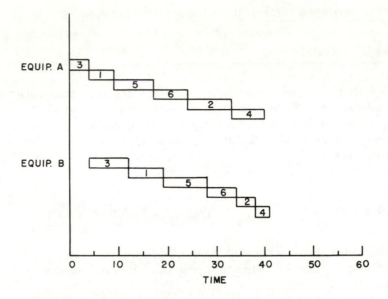

FIG. 21.2. STARTING AND FINISHING TIMES FOR EACH TASK
PERFORMED IN THE SEQUENCE 3, 1, 5, 6, 2, 4

A second example of the problem involving two pieces of equipment is given by the data appearing in Table 21.4. The solution procedure applied to this problem is outlined below.

TABLE 21.4

PROCESSING TIMES FOR TASKS

Task Number	Equipment A	Equipment B
1	7	4
2	10	8
3	2	12
4	5	11
5	9	10
6	9	4
7	11	10

The smallest time value of 2 for task number 3 appears under equipment A. Task 3 is placed first in the sequence as shown on pg. 331 and eliminated from the data.

Task 3
_____ _____ _____ _____ _____ _____

The next smallest time value of 4 is found for both tasks number 1 and number 6. Since both time values are under equipment B, the task with the smallest time value under equipment A must be placed last in the sequence (see step 5 of the solution procedure). Task number 1 has the smallest time value of 7 under equipment A and therefore is the task that is placed last in the sequence as indicated below.

Task 3   Task 1
_____ _____ _____ _____ _____ _____ _____

After task number 1 is placed in the sequence, task number 6 is placed second to last as follows.

Task 3   Task 6   Task 1
_____ _____ _____ _____ _____ _____ _____

Now with tasks 1 and 6 eliminated from the data, the next smallest time value of 5 is found for task number 4. This time value appears under equipment A so task 4 is placed second to first in the sequence as shown below.

Task 3   Task 4   Task 6   Task 1
_____ _____ _____ _____ _____ _____ _____

When task 4 is eliminated, the next smallest time value of 8 appears for task number 2, and since it appears under equipment B, it is placed third to last in the sequence. The sequence now appears as:

Task 3   Task 4   Task 2   Task 6   Task 1

_____ _____ _____ _____ _____ _____ _____

The next smallest value after task 2 is eliminated from the data is the value of 9 for task number 5. Since the time value appears under equipment A, it is placed third to first in the sequence as shown below.

Task 3   Task 4   Task 5   Task 2   Task 6   Task 1
_____ _____ _____ _____ _____ _____ _____

The last task to enter the sequence is task number 7 and it is placed in the vacant slot. The completed sequence for this problem is indicated below.

Task 3   Task 4   Task 5   Task 7   Task 2   Task 6   Task 1
_____ _____ _____ _____ _____ _____ _____

TABLE 21.5

STARTING AND FINISHING TIMES FOR TASKS PERFORMED IN THE SEQUENCE
3, 4, 5, 7, 2, 6, 1

Task Number	Equipment A		Equipment B	
	Start	Finish	Start	Finish
3	0	2	2	14
4	2	7	14	25
5	7	16	25	35
7	16	27	35	45
2	27	37	45	53
6	37	46	53	57
1	46	53	57	61

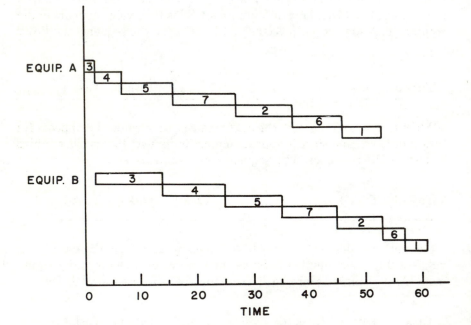

FIG. 21.3. STARTING AND FINISHING TIMES FOR EACH
TASK PERFORMED IN THE SEQUENCE 3, 4, 5, 7, 2, 6, 1

The starting and finishing times for the tasks are shown in Table 21.5. The minimum elapsed time to complete all the tasks is 61 time units. The graphical presentation of this solution to the sequencing problem is shown in Fig. 21.3.

SEQUENCING FOR THREE PIECES OF EQUIPMENT

For the situation where tasks have to be processed through three pieces of equipment, a similar solution technique for determining the minimum elapsed time can be used if the following constraints can be imposed on the problem.

A. No passing of the tasks is permitted. This means that all the tasks have to be processed in the same order on all three pieces of equipment.

B. One of the following conditions must be satisfied by the task times involved in the problem:

1. The minimum time to process any task on the first piece of equipment has to be greater than or equal to the maximum time to process any of the tasks on the second piece of equipment. If the first piece of equipment is A and the second piece of equipment is B, this condition states that the smallest time value for any of the tasks under equipment A has to be greater than or equal to the largest time value for any of the tasks under equipment B, or

2. The minimum time to process any task on the last piece of equipment has to be greater than or equal to the maximum time to process any task on the second piece of equipment. This condition states that the smallest time value for any of the tasks under equipment C (the third piece of equipment in the process) has to be greater than or equal to the largest time value for any of the tasks under equipment B.

If neither of the above conditions is present in a given problem, the solution technique cannot be used to find the optimum sequence.

TABLE 21.6

PROCESSING TIMES FOR TASKS

Task Number	Equipment A	Equipment B	Equipment C
1	7	4	2
2	9	5	8
3	6	2	7
4	8	2	5
5	10	4	4

An example of a problem that does satisfy the above conditions is shown by the data in Table 21.6. Note that the problem does contain data that satisfies condition 1 because the smallest time value of 6 under equipment A is greater than the largest value of 5 found under equipment B. This problem will be used to illustrate the solution procedure for three pieces of equipment.

Solution Procedure for Three Pieces of Equipment

The following steps can be used to find the optimum sequence of tasks involving three pieces of equipment as long as the aforementioned conditions for the problem are satisfied.

1. Total the processing times for the first and second pieces of equipment for each task shown in the problem. These total times will be used to represent the times for one piece of equipment.

2. Total the processing times for the second and third pieces of equipment for each task shown in the problem. These totals will be used to represent the times of a second piece of equipment.

3. Since the data has now been reduced to a problem involving only two pieces of equipment, the solution procedure shown for two pieces of equipment can be used to obtain the optimum sequence.

Applying the first two steps of the above procedure to the data shown in Table 21.6 results in the reduction of the problem to that shown in Table 21.7.

TABLE 21.7

TOTALED PROCESSING TIMES FOR TASKS

	Total Time Values	
Task Number	Equipment A and B	Equipment B and C
1	11	6
2	14	13
3	8	9
4	10	7
5	14	8

Solving now as a problem involving two pieces of equipment shows that the smallest time value of 6 for task number 1 appears under the second piece of equipment, and thus is placed last in the sequence. The beginning of the development of the sequence is shown on pg. 335.

Task 1
_____   _____   _____   _____

The next smallest time value of 7 for task number 4 also appears under the second piece of equipment and therefore is placed second to last in the sequence. The sequence now is:

Task 4   Task 1
_____   _____   _____

The next smallest time value of 8 appears for both tasks 3 and 5 and since each appears under the first piece of equipment and the second piece of equipment respectively; task 3 is placed first in the sequence and task 5 is placed third to last in the sequence. The addition of these two tasks to the sequence is shown below.

Task 3   Task 5   Task 4   Task 1
_____   _____   _____

The only task left is task number 2 and it is entered into the vacant slot to complete the sequence as follows:

Task 3   Task 2   Task 5   Task 4   Task 1
_____   _____   _____

The interpretation of the optimum sequence for the three pieces of equipment along with the starting and finishing times for each task are given in Table 21.8. The total elapsed time for completing all the tasks is 46 time units. The graphical representation of this solution is shown in Fig. 21.4.

TABLE 21.8

STARTING AND FINISHING TIMES FOR TASKS PERFORMED IN THE SEQUENCE
3, 2, 5, 4, 1

Task Number	Equipment A		Equipment B		Equipment C	
	Start	Finish	Start	Finish	Start	Finish
3	0	6	6	8	8	15
2	6	15	15	20	20	28
5	15	25	25	29	29	33
4	25	33	33	35	35	40
1	33	40	40	44	44	46

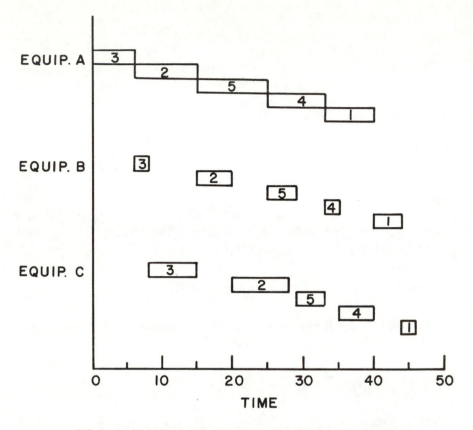

FIG. 21.4. STARTING AND FINISHING TIMES FOR EACH TASK
PERFORMED IN THE SEQUENCE 3, 2, 5, 4, 1

In addition to determining the elapsed time for completing all the tasks, an evaluation of the idle time of each piece of equipment can be made. This evaluation is made for the time period beginning with the start of the first task on the first piece of equipment until the last task has been processed on the last piece of equipment. The following idle times for each piece of equipment in this problem are identified as follows:

For equipment A:

> 4 time units which occur during the processing of task 1 on equipment B.
> 2 time units which occur during the processing of task 1 on equipment C.

Total of 6 units of idle time for equipment A.

For equipment B:

6 time units which occur during the processing of task 3 on equipment A.

7 time units which occur between the finish of task 3 and the start of task 2 on equipment B.

5 time units which occur between the finish of task 2 and the start of task 5 on equipment B.

4 time units which occur between the finish of task 5 and the start of task 4 on equipment B.

5 time units which occur between the finish of task 4 and the start of task 1 on equipment B.

2 time units which occur during the processing of task 1 on equipment C.

Total of 29 units of idle time for equipment B.

For equipment C:

6 time units which occur during the processing of task 3 on equipment A.

2 time units which occur during the processing of task 3 on equipment B.

5 time units which occur between the finish of task 3 and the start of task 2 on equipment C.

1 time unit which occur between the finish of task 2 and the start of task 5 on equipment C.

2 time units which occur between the finish of task 5 and the start of task 4 on equipment C.

4 time units which occur between the finish of task 4 and the start of task 1 on equipment C.

Total of 20 units of idle time for equipment C.

The total idle time for all three pieces of equipment is 55 time units.

Even though the solution technique presented in this chapter is limited to scheduling tasks through 2 or 3 pieces of equipment, there are many possible applications of the technique in the hotel, restaurant and institutional field. Substantial increases in efficiency could be obtained in a given operation if the technique is applied even with its limitations. Acceptance and utilization of these newer techniques will enable management to solve some of their ever increasing problems.

BIBLIOGRAPHY

ABDELLAH, F.G., and LEVINE, E. 1954. Work sampling applied to the study of nursing personnel. Nursing Res. 3, No. 1, 11-16.

ALLEN, A. 1957. Applying industrial methods in hospital laboratory operations. Hospital Topics 35, No. 10, 123-128, 134.

AMRINE, H.T., and NICHOLS, E.D. 1959. A physiological appraisal of selected principles of motion economy. J. Ind. Eng. 10, 373-378.

ANON. 1958. Work injuries and work injury rates in school lunchrooms. Bur. Labor Statistics Rept. 159.

ANON. 1962. Hotels and Motels. U.S. Dept. Labor, Washington, D.C.

ANON. 1963. Color standards. Does industry want them? Mill and Factory 73, No. 3, 64-66.

ASCHHEIM, C. 1959. How a laundry methods study raised productivity 70 per cent. Hospitals 33, No. 6, 99, 102.

ASHE, B.B. 1962. Time studies help make every minute count. Mod. Hospital 98, 96, 98.

AVE'LALLEMANT, C. 1965. Work measurement: first step to better manpower management. Hospitals 39, 67-71.

AVERY, A. (No date). Human Engineering in Kitchen Design. U.S. Naval Supply Res. and Develop. Facility Rept., Dept. Navy, Washington.

AVERY, A. 1961. Let's make kitchens workable. Food Serv. Mag. 23, 17-19, 54.

AVERY, A. 1965. Human engineering; the institutional kitchen. Cornell Hotel Restaurant Admin. Quart. 6, No. 1, 74-83.

BARISH, N.N. 1951. Systems Analysis for Effective Administration. Funk & Wagnalls Co., New York.

BARNES, R.M. 1957. Work Sampling, 2nd Edition. John Wiley & Sons, New York.

BARNES, R.M. 1958. Motion and Time Study. John Wiley & Sons, New York.

BATTERSBY, A. 1964. Network Analysis for Planning and Scheduling. Saint Martin Press, New York.

BECKWITH, R.E., and VASWANI, R. 1957. The assignment problem—a special case of linear programming. J. Ind. Eng. 8, 167-172.

BELLOWS, R. 1961. Psychology of Personnel in Business and Industry. Prentice-Hall, Englewood, Cliffs, N.J.

BENDER, F.E., KRAMER, A. and KAHAN, G. 1976. Systems Analysis for the Food Industry. AVI Publishing Co., Inc., Westport, Conn.

BENDER, W., Jr. 1964. Industrial engineers seek better methods. Mod. Hospital 102, No. 4, 91-95, 160.

BENNETT, A.C. 1957. Work simplification techniques make easy methods not so hard to find. Hospitals 31, No. 3, 45-47.

BENNETT, A.C. 1964. Methods Improvement in Hospitals. J.B. Lippin-cott Co., Philadelphia.

BLAKER, G. 1965. Facilitating motion economy through well designed equipment. Hospitals *39*, No. 6, 104-107, 110.

CAMERON, D.C. 1952. Travel charts—a tool for analyzing material move-ment problems. Mod. Mater. Handling *7*, No. 1, 37-40.

CARROLL, P. 1957. Cost control through time study. J. Ind. Eng. *8*, 229-232.

CHANE, G.W. 1942. Motion and Time Study. Harper & Brothers, New York.

CHAPANIS, A. 1965. Man-Machine Engineering. Wadsworth Publishing Co., Belmont, Calif.

CHAPANIS, A., GARNER, W.R., and MORGAN, C.T. 1949. Applied Experi-mental Psychology. John Wiley & Sons, New York.

CLOSE, G.C., Jr. 1960. Work Improvement. John Wiley & Sons, New York.

COFFEY, C.A., SPRAGG, D., McCUNE, E., and GORDON, R. 1964. Contin-uous time study shows how scheduled time is spent. Hospitals *38*, 96, 103-107.

CONNOR, R.J. 1961. A work sampling study of variations in nursing work load. Hospitals *35*, 40-41, 111.

CONNOR, R.J. 1961. Hospital work sampling with associated measures of production. J. Ind. Eng. *12*, No. 2, 105-107.

CROSSAN, R.M., and NANCE, H.W. 1962. Master Standard Data. Mc-Graw-Hill Book Co., New York.

DANA, A.W. 1961. Method and motion studies. Cornell Hotel Restaurant Admin. Quart. *2*, No. 1, 71-75.

DAVIDSON, H.O. 1960. Work sampling—eleven fallacies. J. Ind. Eng. *11*, 367-371.

DICKIE, R. 1961. Routing traffic through a kitchen. Volume Feeding Man-agement *16*, 28.

DONALDSON, B. 1961. Work sampling simplifies work scheduling. Mod. Hospital *96*, 144.

ELLIS, D.S. 1951. Speed of manipulative performance as a function of work surface height. J. Appl. Psychol. *35*, No. 4, 289-296.

FERGUSON, S.A., and WOMER, C.B. 1956. Putting work simplification to work. Mod. Hospital *87*, No. 3, 76-78.

FRAZER, J.R. 1953. Methods analysis. J. Am. Dietet. Assoc. *29*, 786-790.

FREDERICK, E.J. 1963. Work sampling in the laundry. Hospitals *37*, No. 10, 68-73.

FREDERICK, W.S. 1959. Human energy in manual lifting. Mod. Mater. Handling *14*, No. 3, 74-76.

FRENCH, C.E. 1957. Fast and simple method for checking labor perform-ance. Food Eng. *29*, No. 4, 63-65.

FRISBY, C.B. 1950. Human factors in the design of machinery and work-ing methods. Occupational Psychology *24*, 168-173.

FUHRO, W.J. 1963. Work Measurement and Production Control with the F-A-S-T System. Prentice-Hall, Englewood Cliffs, N.J.

GAMORAN, A.C. 1952. Time and motion studies appraise aide training. Hospitals 26, 63-64.

GANONG, W.L. 1961. Work simplification and measurement. J. Am. Dietet. Assoc. 38, 122-127.

GOLD, B. 1955. Foundations of Productivity Analysis. Univ. Pittsburgh Press. Pittsburgh, Pa.

GUNTER, J.F. 1958. Work organization and simplification. Hospital Management 86, No. 10, 93.

HAAS, S.J., and GELTMAN, L. 1958. How work simplification can simplify purchasing. Hospitals 32, 65.

HANSEN, B.L. 1960. Work Sampling for Modern Management. Prentice-Hall, Englewood Cliffs, N.J.

HANSEN, K.E. 1963. Work sampling can cut dietary costs. Mod. Hospital 100, No. 5, 86-88, 183.

HARTMAN, J. 1960. Flow charts led to efficient operation. Mod. Hospital 95, No. 11, 124-125.

HEILAND, R.E., and RICHARDSON, J. 1957. Work Sampling. McGraw-Hill Book Co., New York.

HELSON, H. 1949. Design of equipment and optimal human operation. Am. J. Psychol. 62, 473-497.

HOLMES, D.S. 1958. Notes on work sampling sample size. J. Ind. Eng. 9, 242-243.

HUDSON, W.R. 1956. Comments on the analysis of the less repetitive types of work. J. Ind. Eng. 7, No. 2, 66-70.

IGEL, A.A. 1961. Improved work methods. Hospital Management 91, No. 1, 67-69.

INDERDOHNEN, J.F. 1960. Boosting Productivity in Small Shops. Small Business Admin., Washington, D.C.

IRESON, W.G., and GRANT, E.L. (Editors). 1955. Handbook of Industrial Engineering and Management. Prentice-Hall, Englewood Cliffs, N.J.

ISHERWOOD, T.D. 1960. Labor cost analysis by work sampling in the small business. J. Ind. Eng. 11, 417-420.

JAVITZ, A.E. 1961. Engineering psychology and human factors in design. Electro-Technology 67, No. 5, 107-130.

JOHNSON, S.M. 1954. Optimal two- and three-stage production schedules with setup time included. Naval Res. Logistics Quart. 1, No. 1, 61-68.

KELLEY, J.E., Jr. 1959. Critical-Path Planning and Scheduling: An Introduction. Mauchly Associates, Ambler, Pa.

KIRIKOS, N. 1961. Cutting waste motion through kitchen layout. Restaurant Management 88, No. 6, 72, 96.

KOTSCHEVAR, L.H. 1957. The human body, how to increase its efficiency. Institutions Mag. *40*, No. 4, 14, 56.

KOTSCHEVAR, L.H. 1962. Work Simplification, 2nd Edition. Institutions Magazine, Chicago, Ill.

KOTSCHEVAR, L.H., and TERRELL, M.E. 1961. Food Service Planning. John Wiley & Sons, New York.

KRUSHAK, P.T. 1944. Time and Motion Studies in Salad Preparation. M.S. Thesis, Mich. State Univ., East Lansing.

KUHN, H.W. 1955. The Hungarian method for the assignment problem. Naval Res. Logistics Quart. *2*, No. 1 and 2, 83-87.

LEHRER, R.N. 1957. Work Simplification—Creative Thinking about Work Problems. Prentice-Hall, Englewood Cliffs, N.J.

LESPERANCE, J.P. 1954. Economics and Techniques of Motion and Time Study. Wm. C. Brown Co., Dubuque, Iowa.

LEWIS, B.T., and PEARSON, W.W. 1961. Management Guide for Work Simplification. John F. Rider Publishers, New York.

LLEWELLYN, R.W. 1958. Travel charting with realistic criteria. J. Ind. Eng. *6*, 217-220.

LUNDBERG, D. 1953. Time, motion study makes for less effort but more work. Institutions Mag. *33*, No. 3, 42-44.

MACKWORTH, N.H. 1946. Effect of heat on wireless telegraph operators hearing and recording Morse messages. Brit. J. Ind. Med. *3*, 143-158.

MARTENEY, A.L., and OHLSON, M.A. 1964. Work sampling of a dietary staff. J. Am. Dietet. Assoc. *45*, 212-217.

MASTIN, J.P., and FERRELL, E.S. 1964. Applications of work sampling in a hospital cafeteria. Hospitals *38*, No. 5, 93-100.

MAYNARD, H.B. (Editor). 1956. Industrial Engineering Handbook. McGraw-Hill Book Co., New York.

MAYNARD, H.B., STEGEMERTEN, G.J., and SCHWAB, J.L. 1962. Methods Time Measurement. McGraw-Hill Book Co., New York.

McCORMICK, E.J. 1964. Human Factor Engineering. McGraw-Hill Book Co., New York.

MELLARD, H. 1962. Methods improvement study. Hospital Management *94*, No. 10, 84-85.

MELLIN, W.R. 1959. What is an organized methods improvement program? J. Ind. Eng., *10*, 426-432.

MILLER, R.J., and PHILLIP, C.R. 1964. Project Management with CPM and PERT. Reinhold Publishing Co., New York.

MONTAG, G.M., McKINLEY, M.M., and KLINSCHMIDT, A.C. 1964. Predetermined motion times—a tool in food production management. J. Am. Dietet. Assoc. *45*, 206-211.

MOORE, J.M. 1961. Plant Layout and Design. Macmillan Co., New York.

MUNDEL, M.E. 1956. Motion study in food service. J. Am. Dietet. Assoc. *32*, 546-547.

MUNDEL, M.E. 1960. Motion and Time Study; Principles and Practice. Prentice-Hall, Englewood Cliffs, N.J.

MURRELL, K.F.H. 1957. Data on human performance for engineering designers, Engineering *184*, No. 4771, 194-198.

NADLER, G. 1955. Motion and Time Study. McGraw-Hill Book Co., New York.

NADLER, G. 1957. Work Simplification. McGraw-Hill Book Co., New York.

NADLER, G. 1959. Work design; a philosophy for applying work principles. J. Ind. Eng. *10*, No. 3, 185-192.

NADLER, G. 1963. Work Design. Richard D. Irwin, Homewood, Ill.

NIEBEL, B.W. 1962. Motion and Time Study. Richard D. Irwin, Homewood, Ill.

OPTNER, S.L. 1965. Systems Analysis for Business and Industrial Problem Solving. Prentice-Hall, Englewood Cliffs, N.J.

PEDDERSEN, R.B., AVERY, A.C., RICHARD, R.D., OSENTON, J.R., and POPE, H.H. 1973. Increasing Productivity in Foodservice. Cahners Books, Boston.

PETERS, G.A., Jr. 1956. Human engineering—a new approach to operational design. Mech. Eng. *78*, 926.

POPE, H.H. 1956. Use of time studies in club food preparation. Club Management *35*, No. 2, 58, 60.

POPE, H.H. 1962. Work measurement standards. Restaurant Management *91*, No. 8, 53-55.

REED, R., Jr. 1960. How to staff an efficient tray line system. Mod. Hospital *94*, No. 5, 138, 140, 142.

REED, R., Jr. 1960. Menu processing takes to methods engineering. Mod. Hospital *94*, No. 4, 150-152, 154, 156, 158.

REED, R.M. 1964. Methods improvement and the status quo. Hospitals *38*, No. 6, 109-112.

REINFIELD, N.V., and VOGEL, W.R. 1958. Mathematical Programming. Prentice Hall, Englewood Cliffs, N.J.

ROPER, D.E. 1964. Critical-path scheduling. J. Ind. Eng. *15*, No. 2, 51-59.

ROSS, L.N. 1972. Work Simplification in Food Service: Individualized Instruction. The Iowa State Univ. Press, Ames, Iowa.

RUTHERFORD, R., and HOOD, M.P. 1953. Method of determining size and shape requirements of work surface for preparing products for baking. J. Home Econ. *45*, No. 3, 158-160.

SANFORD, J., and CUTLAR, K. 1964. Work sampling of activities of food service managers. J. Am. Dietet. Assoc. *44*, 182-184.

SCHELL, M.L. 1962. Work sampling—an approach to a problem. J. Am. Dietet. Assoc. *41*, 456-458.

SCHELL, M.L., and KORSTAD, P.J. 1964. Work sampling study shows division of labor time. Hospitals *38*, No. 2, 99-102.

SCHNORR, C.G. 1958. Human engineering. J. Ind. Eng. *9*, No. 6, 506-512.

SCHUMACHER, W.A., and ZIEMBA, J.V. 1963. Incentive technique in work simplification. Food Eng. *35*, No. 11, 41-43.

SHAW, A.G. 1952. The Purpose and Practice of Motion Study. Harlequin Press Co., Manchester, England.

SHOWALTER, C.L. 1962. Methods improvement in the clinical laboratory. Hospitals *36*, 72-80.

SIMERSON, F.W. 1958. Work simplification. J. Am. Dietet. Assoc. *34*, 57.

SLEIGHT, R.B. 1948. The effect of instrument dial shape on legibility. J. Appl. Psychol. *32*, 170-178.

SMALLEY, H.E. 1958. Industrial engineering in hospitals. J. Ind. Eng. *10*, No. 3, 171-175.

SMALLEY, H.E., and FREEMAN, J.R. 1966. Hospital Industrial Engineering. Reinhold Publishing Corp., New York.

SMITH, W.P. 1955. Travel charting—first aid for plant layout. J. Ind. Eng. *6*, No. 1, 13-15, 26.

STOCKTON, R.S. 1963. Introduction to Linear Programming. Allyn and Bacon, Boston.

STOKES, J.W. 1970. How to Manage a Restaurant or Institutional Food Service. Wm. C. Brown Co. Publishers, Dubuque, Iowa.

SUTERMEISTER, R.A. 1963. People and Productivity. McGraw-Hill Book Co., New York.

THIELMANN, C.F. 1961. Four departments, One aim: find a better way. Hospitals *35*, No. 11, 40-43.

THORNER, M. 1973. Convenience and Fast Food Handbook. AVI Publishing Co., Inc., Westport, Conn.

TORGERSEN, P.E. 1959. An example of work sampling in the hospital. J. Ind. Eng., *10*, 197-202.

WEBER, E.S. 1963. How to step up employee productivity. Cornell Hotel Restaurant Admin. Quart. *4*, No. 1, 13-19.

WILSON, W. 1962. Supervision and work simplification. Mass Prod. *38*, No. 9, 80-85.

WISE, B.I., and DONALDSON, B. 1961. Work sampling in the dietary department. J. Am. Dietet. Assoc. *39*, 327-329.

WITSKY, H.K. 1970. Practical Hotel-Motel Cost Reduction Handbook. Ahrens, N.Y.

WOLNEZ, G.T. 1966. Accident prevention in the plant kitchen. Natl. Safety News *93*, No. 4, 26-31.

WOODSON, W.E. 1964. Human Engineering Guide for Equipment Designers. Univ. Calif. Press, Berkeley, Calif.

ZIEMBA, J.V. 1963. Work simplification. Food Eng. *35*, No. 11, 413-416.

GLOSSARY[1]

Abnormal time The elapsed time for any element recorded during a time study which, being excessively longer or shorter than the majority or median of the elapsed times, is judged at the time of a study to be not representative for the element, and which may be excluded in determining the most typical elapsed time (or the average time) for the element.

Accumulative timing A time-study technique utilizing 2 stop watches connected so that when 1 is stopped the other is simultaneously started. Each watch is thus read alternatively while its hand is stationary.

Accuracy Degree of correctness, exactness, or precision. The relationship between the mean value of a large number of measurements and the objective true value of the quantity measured.

Activity 1. The identification of a certain phase or function of an organization. 2. The rate of sale or production of an item. 3. That part of operating or budget capacity actually spent on an operating basis.

Actual time The time taken by a workman to complete a task or an element of a task.

Allowance A time increment included in the standard time for an operation to compensate the workman for production lost due to fatigue and normally expected interruptions, such as for personal and unavoidable delays. It is usually applied as a percentage of the normal or leveled time.

Allowed time The leveled time plus allowances for fatigue and delays. *See Standard time.*

Aptitude The physical and psychological potentiality of an individual to perform a specific type of work.

Assemble (n.) The basic element employed when one or more objects are put on or into another object so that they fit or contact each other in a predetermined relation in order to form a unit.

Automaticity The ability to perform hand, arm, leg or body motions or motion patterns without apparent mental direction, as a result of practice.

Auxiliary department A department that provides services such as maintenance, material handling, warehousing and the like to the production departments. It rarely performs manufacturing operations on the product to be marketed.

Average time The arithmetical average of all the actual times, or of all except the abnormal times, taken by a workman to complete a task or an element of a task.

---

[1] Extracted from ASME Standard Industrial Engineering Terminology (ASME No. 106-1955), with the permission of the Publisher, The American Society of Mechanical Engineers, United Engineering Center, 345 East 47th Street, New York.

Avoidable delay Any time during an assigned work period which is within the control of the workman and which he uses for idling or for doing things unnecessary to the performance of the operation. Such time does not include allowance for personal requirements, fatigue and unavoidable delays.

Balance 1. That quality of a motion sequence which promotes the development of rhythm and automaticity. 2. As applied to progressive related operations, it is the condition in which the standard times required for each successive operation are approximately equal and the work flows steadily or at a desired rate from one operation to the next.

Balanced line A series of progressive related operations with approximately equal standard times for each, arranged so that work flows at a desired steady rate from one operation to the next.

Balancing motion pattern A motion sequence that promotes the development of rhythm and automaticity.

Balancing delay The delay which occurs when one body member performs its work faster than another body member because of different motions, due to the requirements of the layout or the required sequence of motions, and therefore, must wait for the slower member or must work more slowly so as to finish its work simultaneously with the slower body member.

Budget An organized statement of expected income and expenditures for a definite future period, usually a month or a year, made in order to assist in controlling expenditures and to provide a criterion for judging performance during that period.

Chronocyclegraph technique A special type of cyclegraph technique in which an interrupter is placed in the electric circuit with a light bulb, and the light is flashed on and off. The slow cooling of the filament causes the path of the bulb when photographed to appear to be pear-shaped dots which indicate the direction and the path of the motion. Since the spots of light are spaced according to the speed of the movements, being widely separated when the workman moves fast and close together when the workman's movement is slow, it is possible, from the photograph, to obtain an approximation of time, speed, acceleration, and retardation, and to show direction and path of motion.

Chronological study A time study usually done over a relatively long period such as a day which records events in the order in which they occur. Usually made on nonrepetitive and semirepetitive operations. Often used to secure an overall picture and to check frequency, nature, and duration of delays.

Color code Method of using colors to accentuate variances in a drawing or print. Used to identify piping, tote boxes, traveler tabs, etc., as to particular use or destination.

Conditions Both job evaluation and time study are working conditions which affect the operator during an operation but which do not directly affect the operation. Such factors as heat, light, and humidity are typical "condition" factors since they influence the fatigue, attitude, and therefore, the general performance of the operation.

Constant element 1. An element for which the leveled or normal time is always the same regardless of the characteristics of the parts being worked upon, as long as the method and the working conditions are unchanged. 2. An element for which, under a specified set of conditions, the standard time allowance should always be the same.

Continuous method The procedure of timing, used in making time studies, whereby the watch is permitted to run continuously throughout the period of study which the observer notes and records the reading of the watch at the end of each element, delay or any other occurrence happening in the study, regardless of whether or not it has a direct bearing on the job. The elapsed times are secured by subtracting the successive readings after the timing has been completed.

Cycle A sequence of elements in the performance of a task, in which after the last element is completed for one unit of production, the first element is again normally started for the succeeding unit of production with the other elements following in like order.

Cyclegraph technique The method devised by the Gilbreths and used in motion study by which a three-dimensional pattern of a motion path may be recorded by attaching a small electric light bulb to the finger, hand, or other part of the workman's body and photographing, with a stereoscopic camera, the path of the light as it moves through space.

Cycle timing 1. Observance of the total time required to complete a cycle. 2. A time-study technique used to time work elements that are too short to time in the usual manner. It consists of timing a cycle or periodically recurring series of elements, first including and then excluding the element for which the time is needed. The needed time for this element is then obtained by subtraction.

Decimal-hour stop watch A two-handed timing device whose movement may be started or stopped manually and whose large outer dial is divided into 100 spaces each of which represents 0.0001 hr. The position of the large hand on the large dial indicates time in hours to four decimal places and the position of the small hand on a smaller, inner dial indicates time in hours to two decimal places.

Decimal-minute stop watch A two-handed timing device whose movement may be started or stopped manually and whose large outer dial is divided into 100 spaces each of which represents 0.01 min. The position of the large hand on the large dial indicates time in minutes to two decimal places and the position of the small hand on a smaller, inner dial indicates time in whole minutes.

Delay A period during which conditions (except those which intentionally change the physical or chemical characteristics of an object) do not permit or require immediate performance of the next planned action.

Delay allowance 1. A time increment included in a time standard to allow for contingencies and minor delays beyond the control of the workman. 2. A separate credit (in time or money) to compensate the workman on incentive for a specific instance of delay not covered by the piece rate or standard.

Department An organizational unit established to operate in and be responsible for a specified activity or physical or functional area.

Direct labor Work which alters the composition, condition, conformation or construction of the product, the cost of which can be identified with and assessed against a particular part, product or group of parts or products accurately and without undue effort and expense.

Direct-labor standard A specified output or a time allowance established for a direct-labor operation.

Direct material All material that enters into and becomes part of the finished product (including waste), the cost of which can be identified with and assessed against a particular part, product or group of parts or products accurately and without undue effort and expense.

Disassemble (n.) The basic element denoting the removal of a part of a unit or assembly.

Do (n.) The basic element that accomplishes in full or in part the purpose of the operation. It includes the basic elements of use and assemble and may sometimes be expressed in terms of other basic elements.

Drop delivery 1. Method of introducing an object to the workplace by gravity. 2. a. A method whereby a chute or container is so placed that when work on a part in question is finished it will fall or drop into a chute or container or onto a conveyor with little or no "transport" by the workman. b. The laying aside of a part by releasing it so that it falls or moves away from the work area either through the force of gravity or by mechanical or other means.

Efficiency 1. The ratio of standard performance time to actual performance time, usually expressed as a percentage. 2. The ratio of actual performance numbers (e.g., number of pieces) to standard performance numbers, usually expressed as a percentage.

Effort 1. The evidence of the will to work as manifested by a workman performing an operation. 2. The sum total of the mental absorption and physical participation which may be required by a workman on a given operation.

Elapsed time 1. The actual time taken by a workman to complete a task, an operation or an element of an operation. 2. The total time interval from the beginning to the end of a time study.

Element A subdivision of the work cycle composed of a sequence of one or several fundamental motions and/or machine or process activities, which are distinct, describable and measurable.

Element breakdown The subdivision of an operation each of which is composed of a distinct, describable and measurable sequence of one or several fundamental motions and/or machine or process activities.

Element time The term used to indicate either the actual, observed, selected, normal or standard time to perform an element of an operation.

Fatigue A physical and/or mental weariness, real or imaginary, existing in a person, adversely affecting the ability to perform work.

Fatigue allowance Time included in the production standard to allow for decreases or losses in production which might be attributed to fatigue. (Usually applied as a percentage of the leveled, normal or adjusted time.)

Film analysis A frame-by-frame study of a motion picture of an operation to determine the motions used, their sequence, and the time taken for each. See *Micromotion study definition 2.*

Film-analysis chart A graphical representation of the activities of the various body members as determined by film analysis. Often referred to as a right- and left-hand or simo chart.

Film-analysis record A tabular record of the data obtained from a film analysis.

Find (n.) The basic element, following the search element, which denotes the mental recognition of the desired part or object for which one is searching.

Flow diagram A graphical representation on a floor plan of the work area involved, the locations of work stations and the paths of movement of men and/or materials.

Flow process chart A graphic representation of the sequence of all operations, transportations, inspections, delays and storages occurring during a process or procedure. It includes information considered desirable for analysis such as time required and distance moved.

Frequency 1. The number of times an element occurs during an operation cycle. 2. The number of times a specific value occurs within a sample of several measurements of the same dimension or characteristic of several similar items.

Frequency study A study made to determine the number of occurrences of elements during a given period.

Gantt chart A graphic representation on a time scale of the current relationship between actual and planned performance.

Grasp The basic element employed when the predominant purpose is to secure sufficient control of one or more objects with the fingers or the hand to permit the performance of the next required basic element.

Gravity feed A method of supplying materials into a machine or to a work station by the force of gravity. Generally, a hopper and/or a chute is used to store and to guide the materials to the point of use.

Handling time   1. The time required to perform the manual portion of an operation.   2. The time required to move materials, or parts, to and/or from a work station.

Hold   The basic element employed when the hand maintains static control of an object while work is being performed on it.

Idle time   1. A time interval during which either the workman, the equipment, or both do not perform useful work.

Indirect labor   1. Work which is performed rendering services necessary to production, the cost of which cannot be assessed against any part, product, or group of parts or products accurately or without undue effort and expense.   2. Necessary work which does not alter the composition, condition, conformation, or construction of the product.

Indirect material   Material consumed in the process of production or manufacture that does not become a part of the finished product and/or cannot be readily identified with or charged to a particular part, product, or group of parts or products.

Industrial engineering   The art and science of utilizing and coordinating men, equipment, and materials to attain a desired quantity and quality of output at a specified time and at an optimum cost. This may include gathering, analyzing, and acting upon facts pertaining to building and facilities, layouts, personnel organization, operating procedures, methods, processes, schedules, time standards, wage rates, wage-payment plans, costs, and systems for controlling the quality and quantity of goods and services.

Industrial relations   The management function that deals with all phases of employee-management relationships. Its objective is to devise and administer plans and procedures that engender and stimulate employee productive effort, cooperation, and job satisfaction.

Inspect   Often an element included in an operation in order to assure acceptable quality through a regular check by the employee performing the operation.

Inspection   Examining an object for identification or checking it for verification of quality or quantity for any of its characteristics.

Interference time   A period of time during which one or more machines are not operating because the workman or workmen assigned to operate them are busy operating other machines in their assignment or are performing necessary duties related to operating such other machines such as making repairs, cleaning the machines, or inspecting completed work.

Jig   A device which holds a piece of work in a desired position and guides the tool or tools which perform the necessary operations.

Job 1. A position or post of employment. 2. A group of tasks assigned to an employee or group of employees.

Job analysis A detailed examination of a job to determine the duties, responsibilities, and specialized requirements necessary for its performance.

Job breakdown A description of a task in terms of its elements.

Job content The duties, function, and responsibilities comprising a given job.

Job description A written statement covering the essential features of a job including its purpose, duties, skill requirements, effort and responsibility, working conditions, and relation to other jobs.

Job evaluation 1. A systematic procedure following job analysis for comparing (for wage and salary determination) the relative worth to the employer of two or more jobs or positions. 2. A weighing of all the factors in the various jobs or positions in an enterprise so that directly or indirectly an objective scale may be established whereby commensurate pay or pay rates may be assigned on the basis of job content.

Job factor Any characteristic of a job which influences its relative worth or value and provides a basis for the selection, training, placement and compensation of workmen. Major job characteristics or factors are skill required, responsibility exercised, physical and mental effort involved, working conditions, and experience and education required.

Job specification A detailed, written statement of the physical and mental attributes required of a person to perform a specific job competently.

Job standardization The establishment of a prescribed method for performing an operation or procedure and the specifying of its minimum requirements.

Labor 1. (n.) The mental and/or physical effort and energy expended by humans to produce and distribute materials, goods, and services. 2. (n.) Employees with little or no supervisory responsibility whose sole or main task is to aid in the production of materials, goods or services. 3. (v.) To work or toil.

Labor cost That part of the cost of goods, services, and the like attributable to wages. It commonly refers only to direct workmen, but may include indirect workmen as well.

Labor productivity The rate of output of a workman or group of workmen per unit of time, usually compared to an established standard or expected rate of output.

Layout (n.) The arrangement of items within an area. The items may include roads, railroads, buildings, offices, departments, warehouses, equipment, machinery, furniture, facilities, parts, aisles, and so on. *See also Plant layout.*

Leveling A method of performance rating in which the causes for the observed performance, considered to be skill, effort, conditions, and consistency, are evaluated. The algebraic sum of the point values assigned to each factor is used in adjusting the time taken by the workman being time studied to the time required by a workman working at the average performance level under the usually prevailing conditions.

Machine controlled time That part of a work cycle that is entirely controlled by a machine and therefore, is not influenced by the skill or effort of the workman.

Machine idle time That portion of a regular working period during which a machine that is capable of operating is not being used.

Management 1. The art and science of directing and controlling human effort so that the established objectives of an enterprise may be attained in accordance with accepted policies. 2. The group of people who direct and control human effort toward the attainment of the objectives of an enterprise.

Management engineering The application of engineering principles to all phases of planning, organizing, and controlling a project or enterprise.

Man and machine chart See Multiple-activity process chart.

Man-hour A unit for measuring work. It is equivalent to one man working at normal pace for 60 min, 2 men working at normal pace for 30 min, or some similar combination of men working at normal pace for a period of time.

Manit A contraction for man-minute.

Man-minute A unit used for measuring work. It is equivalent to 1 man working at normal pace for 1 minute, 2 men working at normal pace for 30 sec, or an equivalent combination of men working at normal pace for a period of time. *See Manit.*

Manual element A distinct, describable, and measurable subdivision of a work cycle or operation performed by one or more human motions that are not controlled by process or machine.

Mass production A method of quantity production in which a high degree of planning, specialization of equipment and labor, and integrated utilization of all productive factors are the outstanding characteristics.

Material flow The progressive movement of material, parts, or products toward the completion of a production process between stations, storage areas, machines, departments, and the like. *See Flow process chart and Flow diagram.*

Material handling The movement of materials, parts, subassemblies, or assemblies either manually or through the use of powered equipment.

Maximum working area 1. (Horizontal plane) The area at the work place which is bounded by the imaginary arc drawn by the workman's finger tips moving the horizontal plane with the arm fully extended and moving about the shoulder as a pivot. The section where the maximum areas of the right and left hands overlap constitutes the maximum working areas for the two hands. 2. (Vertical plane) The space on the surface of the imaginary sphere which would be generated by rotating, about the workman's body as an axis, the arc traced by the workman's finger tips of the right or the left hand when the arm is fully extended and is moved vertically about the shoulder as a pivot. 3. (Three-dimensional) The space within reach of a workman's finger tips as they develop arcs of revolution when the workman's hands are extended and moving about the shoulder as a pivot.

Memo-motion study A motion-study technique that utilizes a motion-picture camera operating at slower-than-normal speeds such as 1 frame per sec or 1 frame per $\frac{1}{100}$ min.

Merit rating An organized and systematic evaluation of an employee's ability and job performance in terms of such factors as quality and quantity of work, knowledge, initiative, and dependability. The rating is made periodically in order to determine if the employee's services are better or poorer than the accepted norm.

Method 1. The procedure or sequence of motions used by one or more individuals to accomplish a given operation or work task. 2. The sequence of operations and/or processes used to produce a given product or accomplish a given job. 3. A specific combination of layout and working conditions; materials, equipment, and tools; and the motion pattern involved in accomplishing a given operation or task.

Methods engineering The technique that subjects each operation of a given piece of work to close analysis in order to eliminate every unnecessary element or operation in order to approach the quickest and best method of performing each necessary element or operation. It includes the improvement and standardization of methods, equipment, and working conditions; operator training; the determination of standard times; and occasionally devising and administering various incentive plans.

Methods study The analysis of the sequence of motions used or proposed for use in performing an operation and of the tools, equipment, and work station layout used or proposed for use.

Methods-time measurement A system of predetermined motion-time standards. It is a procedure which analyzes any operation into certain classifications of human motions required to perform it and assigns to each motion controlling only the individual performing it a predetermined time standard which is determined by the nature of the motion and the conditions under which it is made. Abbreviated as MTM.

Microchronometer 1. A two-handed clock whose dial is divided into 100 divisions; the large hand of the clock is usually geared to make 20 revolutions in 1 min and the small hand to make two revolutions each minute. 2. A clock, devised by Frank B. Gilbreth, which is used in micromotion study by placing it in foreground when photographing an operation so that the time is recorded on the film. 3. An accurate time-piece which measures time in units of 1/2,000 of a minute and fractions thereof.

Micromotion study 1. That phase of motion study which divides manual work into fundamental elements, often called therbligs or Gilbreth basic elements, analyzes these elements separately and relatively, and from this analysis, establishes more efficient methods. 2. The analysis of elements of motions too short or rapid for the eye to distinguish, by the use of motion pictures, sometimes in combination with an adequate time-indicating device. (Since the motion-picture camera itself can indicate time intervals, an additional timing device is often dispensed with in micromotion study.)

Minimum time The shortest elapsed time recorded for a particular element of a time study excepting those known to be incorrect.

Motion A movement of the human body or any of the body members.

Motion cycle A complete series of motion elements involved in performing an operation, beginning with a motion connected with the production of the unit and ending when the same motion is about to be repeated with the next unit.

Motion study The analysis of the manual and the eye movements occurring in an operation or work cycle for the purpose of eliminating wasted movements and establishing a better sequence and coordination of movements.

Move The basic element employed when the predominant purpose is to transport an object to a destination. *See Transport loaded.*

Multiple-activity process chart A synchronized graphic representation of operations performed simultaneously by 2 or more men, 2 or more machines, or a combination of men and machines.

Nonrepetitive A descriptive term applied to a type of work, operation, part, or the like that does not recur frequently or in a reasonable, regular sequence.

Normal elemental time The selected or average elemental time adjusted by leveling and/or other methods of adjustment to obtain the time required by a qualified workman to perform a single element of an operation.

Normal pace The work rate usually used by workmen performing under capable supervision but without the stimulus of an incentive-wage-payment plan. This pace can easily be maintained day in and day out without undue physical or mental fatigue and is characterized by the fairly steady exertion of reasonable effort.

Normal time 1. The time required by a qualified workman, working at a pace which is ordinarily used by workmen when capably supervised to complete an element, cycle, or operation when following the prescribed method. 2. The sum of all the normal elemental times which constitute a cycle or operation.

Normal working area 1. (Horizontal plane) The area at the workplace which is bounded by the imaginary arc drawn by the workman's finger tips moving in the horizontal plane with the elbow as a pivot when the workman is standing or is seated in the normal working position and when the upper arm is hanging from the shoulder in a relaxed position. The section where the normal areas of the right and left hands overlap in front of the workman constitutes the optimum normal working area for the two hands. 2. (Vertical plane) The space on the surface of the imaginary sphere which would be generated by rotating, about the workman's body as an axis, the arc traced by the workman's finger tips of the right or the left hand when the forearm is moved vertically about the elbow as a pivot. 3. (Three-dimensional) The space within reach of a workman's finger tips as they develop arcs of revolution, the elbow acting as a pivot when the workman is standing or is seated in the normal working position and when the upper arm is hanging from the shoulder in a relaxed position.

Observation 1. In time study, the act of noting and recording the time taken by a workman performing an operation or an element of an operation. 2. In motion study, the act of noting and recording the motions used by a workman to perform an operation or an element of an operation. 3. In work sampling, the act of noting and recording what a workman is doing at a specific instant.

Observation form A sheet of paper used to record data taken during time studies, methods studies, or work-sampling studies, specifically ruled into titled lines, columns, and spaces to suit the specific requirements of the study.

Operation The intentional changing of an object in any of its physical or chemical characteristics; the assembly or disassembly of parts or objects; the preparation of an object for another operation, transportation, inspection, or storage; planning, calculating, or the giving or receiving of information.

Operation analysis 1. A study of the factors which affect the performance of an operation, such as purpose of the operation, other operations on the part, inspection requirements, materials used, manner of handling material, setup and tool equipment, existing working conditions, and methods employed. 2. A procedure employed in studying the major factors which affect the general method of performing a given operation.

Operation-analysis chart A form that lists all the important factors affecting the effectiveness of an operation and is used to guide the progress and insure the completeness of an operation analysis.

Operation-process chart A graphic representation of the points at which materials are introduced into the process and of the sequence of inspections and all operations except those involved in material handling. It may include other information considered desirable for analysis such as time required and location.

Organization 1. The process of determining the necessary activities and positions within an enterprise, department, or group arranging them into the best functional relationships; clearly defining the authority, responsibilities, and duties of each; and assigning them to individuals so that the available effort can be effectively and systematically applied and coordinated. 2. The group of people which has been brought together to conduct a business or enterprise.

Organization chart A graphical representation of the formal organizational structure of an enterprise showing lines of authority, responsibility, and coordination.

Overhead Costs or expenses which are not directly identifiable with or chargeable to the manufacture of a particular part or product. For example, items such as taxes, insurance, supplies, supervisory and clerical charges, and the like. Synonyms: burden, indirect manufacturing expense.

Pace rating See Speed rating.

Performance The degree with which a workman applies his skill and effort to an operation under the conditions prevailing. This degree is expressed in terms of a performance efficiency or defined bench marks such as good, average, and poor.

Performance rating The act of comparing an actual performance by a workman against a defined concept of a normal performance. Various methods of performance rating are in use differing primarily as to the basis on which comparison is made.

Performance standard A criterion or bench mark with which actual performance is compared.

Personal allowance Time included in the production standard to permit the workman to attend to personal necessities, as obtaining drinks of water, making trips to the rest room, and the like. (Usually applied as a percentage of the leveled, normal, or adjusted time.)

Plan The basic element which denotes the mental act, previous to the physical movement, of determining a method of proceeding with the work.

Plant layout The physical arrangement, either existing or in plans, of industrial facilities.

Position   1. (Time-study usage) The element which consists of aligning, orienting, or locating one object in relation to another.   2. (Motion-study usage) The basic element which consists of aligning, orienting, and engaging one object with another where the motions used are so minor that they do not justify classification as other basic elements.

Predetermined motion-time system   A procedure in which (a) all manual motions are analytically subdivided into the basic elements required for their performance and (b) predetermined time values are assigned to the basic elements.

Preposition   The basic element employed when the transporting device or the object transported is prepared for the next basic element, which is usually position. (Note the difference between the basic element, preposition, and the prepositioning of tools and materials in laying out the work station. The latter term, denoting a function of general planning, involves a number of basic elements.)

Principles of motion economy   The rules and their corollaries applying to human motions, which guide toward development of the optimum way of accomplishing a given job.

Process   1. A planned series of actions or operations which advances a material or procedure from one stage of completion to another.   2. A planned and controlled treatment that subjects materials to the influence of one or more types of energy for the time required to bring about the desired reactions or results. Examples include the curing of rubber, mixing of compounds, heat-treating of metals, machining of metals, and the like.

Process chart   A graphic representation of events occurring during a series of actions or operations and of information pertaining to those events.

Process time   1. The time required to complete a specified series of progressive actions or operations on one unit of production.   2. That portion of a work cycle during which the material or part is being machined or treated according to a specification or recipe designed to produce the desired reaction or result. The time required is controlled by the machine, specification, or recipe, and not by the workman.

Production control   The procedure of planning, routing, scheduling, dispatching, and expediting the flow of materials, parts, subassemblies, and assemblies within the plant from the raw state to the finished product in an orderly and efficient manner.

Production planning   1. The systematic scheduling of men, materials, and machines by using lead times, time standards, delivery dates, work loads, and similar data for the purpose of producing products efficiently and economically and meeting desired delivery dates.   2. Routing and scheduling.

Production study A detailed record, often in the form of a time study or work-sampling study, kept of an activity, operation, or group of activities or operations, for a period of time in order to obtain reliable data concerning working time, idle time, downtime, personal time, machine breakdowns, amount produced, and so on.

Productive time 1. Elapsed time during which useful work is performed in a manufacturing process. 2. That portion of an operation cycle during which the workman's time is utilized effectively. The remainder of his time is considered idle or unproductive.

Productivity The actual rate of output or production per unit of time worked.

Rating See Merit rating and Performance rating.

Ratio delay study See Work-sampling study.

Reach The basic element employed when the predominant purpose is to move the hand to a destination or general location. *See Transport empty.*

Release (Abbreviated term for "release load.") The basic element employed when the hand or body member relinquishes control of an object.

Repetitive The general term used when referring to processes, operations, elements of operations, or the products resulting from there that occur or are produced over and over again with negligible variation. The term must be qualified or explained when it is used in order to have a concrete meaning.

Rest to overcome fatigue An allowance or delay allowed workmen for the purpose of recovering from the effects of exertion or sustained mental or visual attention. It is usually included in the general allowance, but on work of a particularly exhausting nature it may be included in the job-time standard as a separate allowance or element.

Right- and left-hand chart A form of operator process chart on which the motions made by one hand in relation to those made by the other hand are recorded, using standard operation-chart symbols or basic therblig abbreviations or symbols.

Sampling The practice of selecting a small portion (usually determined statistically) of the total group under consideration for the purpose of inferring the value of one or several characteristics of the group.

Scheduling 1. The prescribing of when and where each operation necessary to the manufacture of a product is to be performed. 2. The establishing of times at which to begin and/or complete each event or operation comprising a procedure.

Search The basic element employed to locate an object with the eyes or fingers.

Simo chart (Simultaneous motion-cycle chart) A graphical representation of an operation, usually, although not necessarily, made from a motion-picture film, in which the basic motions, such as therbligs, used to perform the operation by the right- and left-hand members of the body are separately plotted in columns scaled to time, using standard symbols for the elements.

Skill   The ability to use one's knowledge, technical proficiency, developed and/or acquired ability, in devising an efficient method of accomplishing a given objective.

Snapback method   The procedure of timing, used in making time studies, whereby the stop watch is read and the watch hand returned to zero at the termination of each element or work cycle.

Speed rating   A method of performance rating that compares the speed or tempo with which a workman performs the motions necessary to execute an operation against the observer's concept of standard or normal tempo.

Standard allowance   The established or accepted amount by which the normal time for an operation is increased within an area, plant, or industry to compensate for the usual amount of fatigue and/or personal and/or unavoidable delays.

Standard cost   The normal expected cost of an operation, process, or product including labor, material, and overhead charges, computed on the basis of past performance cost, estimates, or work measurement.

Standard elemental time   The normal elemental time plus allowances for fatigue and delays.

Standardization   A management-sponsored program to establish criteria or policies that will promote uniform practices and conditions within the company and permit their control through comparisons. It deals with such areas as work quality and quantity, working conditions, wage rates, and production methods.

Standard performance   The performance which must be given by a workman to accomplish his work in the standard time allowed.

Standard practice   The established or accepted procedure used within an area, plant, or industry for carrying out a specified task or assignment.

Standard time   1. The time which is determined to be necessary for a qualified workman, working at a pace which is ordinarily used under capable supervision and experiencing normal fatigue and delays, to do a defined amount of work of specified quality when following the prescribed method. 2. The normal or leveled time plus allowances for fatigue and delays.

Standard-time data   A compilation of all the elements that are used for performing a given class of work with normal elemental time values for each element. The data are used as a basis for determining time standards on work similar to that from which the data were determined without making actual time studies.

Storage Keeping and protecting an object against unauthorized removal.

Subassembly Two or more parts joined together to form a unit which is only a part of a complete machine, structure, or other article.

Subtracted time On a time study conducted using the continuous-timing method, the elapsed time obtained for an element of an operation by subtracting the watch reading recorded at the beginning of an element from the watch reading recorded at the end of that element during the same cycle.

Synthesis of elemental times 1. The act of selecting and combining the proper elemental times obtained from time studies or predetermined elemental motion-time studies of actual operations in order to obtain the normal or standard time for an operation without making a study of it. 2. In time-formula development, the combining and simplifying of the mathematical or graphical expressions for determining individual elemental times.

Synthetic time standard A time standard developed for an operation by utilizing predetermined elemental time data or standard data rather than by making a time study.

Task 1. The amount of work established as standard in any particular instance. 2. A specifically assigned amount of work.

Therblig 1. The name of the basic work elements which are used in varying sequence and combinations to perform all manual and/or mental work. 2. The term, coined by Frank B. Gilbreth to designate subdivisions of work in his classification of physical motions and associated mental processes. Synonym: Gilbreth basic element.

Time standard See Standard time.

Time study The procedure by which the actual elapsed time for performing an operation or subdivisions or elements thereof is determined by the use of a suitable timing device and recorded. The procedure usually but not always includes the adjustment of the actual time as the result of performance rating to derive the time which should be required to perform the task by a workman working at a standard pace and following a standard method under standard conditions.

Transportation The moving of an object from one place to another, except when such movements are a part of the operation or are caused by the workman at the work station during an operation or inspection.

Transport empty The basic element employed when the hand or a transporting device held in the hand is moved from one point or object to another, unresisted and without load. *See Reach.*

Transport loaded The basic element employed to move a part or object with the hand or other transporting device to a desired location. *See Move.*

Trunk movement Any motion made by that portion of the human body located above the hips and below the neck but excepting the arms, hands, and fingers.

Unavoidable delay An occurrence which is essentially outside the workman's control or responsibility, that prevents him from doing productive work.

Unavoidable-delay allowance Time included in the production standard to allow for time lost which is essentially outside the workman's control; as interruption by supervision for instruction, waits for crane, or minor adjustments to machines or tools. (Usually applied as a percentage of the leveled, normal, or adjusted time.)

Use The basic element employed to perform the activity which is the purpose of the operation other than assembly. The time required for use is usually, but not necessarily, markedly controlled by the requirements of the activity rather than by the workman.

Wink A unit of time equal to $1/2000$ min which the Gilbreths developed and used in motion and time study.

Wink counter An electrically or mechanically driven timing device indicating time in winks.

Work cycle 1. A pattern of motions and/or processes that is repeated with negligible variation each time an operation is performed. 2. A succession of operations and/or processes that is repeated with negligible variation each time a unit of production is completed.

Work-factor A system of predetermined motion-time standards employing the Work-Factor as an index of motion difficulty (that is, demonstrating that time is proportional to specific factors in work, such as body member, distance, direction, weight, control, and the like and that the relationship is consistent and interchangeable). The system is used for determining efficient methods and setting performance time standards.

Working area See Maximum work area, Normal working area.

Working conditions Factors such as light, temperature, smoke, safety, hazards, noise, dust, and the like that affect the performance of a job or the general well-being of the employee.

Workplace See Work station.

Work-sampling study A statistical sampling technique employed to determine the proportion of delays or other classifications of activity present in the total work cycle.

Work simplification See Methods engineering.

Work station That section of a production center where the workman performs his assigned tasks including the space required for his auxiliary equipment, as tools, a work-bench or a machine with any stands, containers, conveyors, etc., for the material being worked on.

Written standard practice   A standard practice that has been recorded and approved by the proper authority or authorities. *See Standard practice.*

Appendix A

PROBLEMS AND EXERCISES

Chapter 1

1.1. Indicate several measures of productivity that could be used in various areas of the hotel, restaurant and institutional field. Identify the basic data that would be needed and the computations involved.

1.2. Using the data shown in lecture 1, prepare a graph by plotting annual sales volume versus sales per employee. Use averages for plotting purposes. What conclusions could be drawn from the plotted graph?

1.3. Visit a local hotel, motel or restaurant and identify which of the items shown in Table 1.2 would apply to the operation. What type of general efficiency rating would you give the operation based on your observations?

1.4. A restaurant employs 15 full time and 10 part time (4 hours/day) people. During a 6 month period, 6 full time and 5 part time employees resigned and were replaced. Assuming the resignations and replacements continue at the same pace, determine the annual labor turnover rate for the restaurant.

1.5. Obtain wage data for a hotel, restaurant or hospital and make a graph showing labor costs for the last 5 years. Show actual dollars and percentage labor cost of total sales. Time should be shown on the horizontal axis of the graph.

1.6. Determine the peak customer service rate for a fast food operation by plotting the meals served per minute versus time of day. This is best done for several different days.

Chapter 2

2.1. Using direct observation, estimate the productivity (in percentage of productive time out of total time spent on the job) for any or all of the following:
   a. Front desk clerk
   b. Waiter or waitress
   c. Salad maker

362

    d. Accountant
    e. Dishwasher

2.2. Interview several managers or operators to determine what types of work analysis or design projects have been accomplished in the hospitality industry.

2.3. Identify 5 concepts such as new foods, equipment, techniques, procedures, etc., that will probably require the design of a new work system for food service operations.

2.4. Obtain an organization chart for a large hotel or hospital and show how a work analysis and design manager would fit into the organization.

2.5. Develop a list of reasons why employees might not accept a work analysis and design program. Indicate how management should handle each of the reasons identified.

Chapter 3

3.1. Select a task that you have performed or are familiar with and identify several factors that affect the output or end result of the task. What changes or improvements might be made in order to do the task more efficiently?

3.2. Evaluate the main cooking area in an existing operation from the standpoint of the physical environment commenting on temperature, relative humidity, ventilation, lighting, sound and color. What recommendations would you make to improve the physical environment?

3.3. Make a list of all the functions that are performed by the food and beverage department of a large hotel.

3.4. Develop a standard written procedure for a routine maintenance task that you are familiar with.

Chapter 4

4.1. Plan a materials handling system for moving tableware for a large dormitory cafeteria. Identify the type of equipment that would be used in the system.

4.2. Observe a worker doing a repetitive task and determine what percentage of the hand movements are:
    a. Simultaneous
    b. Symmetrical

4.3. Evaluate the design and layout of any work place from the standpoint of conformance to the principles of motion economy.

4.4. Identify several pieces of equipment whose design is based upon a principle of materials handling or a principle of motion economy.

4.5. Evaluate the layout of a food service operation noting any aspects that reflect a principle of layout.

Chapter 5

5.1. Determine the effective temperatures for the following conditions:
   a. 80°F dry-bulb and 50% R.H.
   b. 80°F dry-bulb and 90% R.H.
   c. 65°F dry-bulb and 50% R.H.

5.2. Evaluate the illumination level at several different work areas or work places to determine if they are in accordance with the recommended levels given in Table 5.3.

5.3. Indicate where color coding is used (forms, equipment, etc.) in hotels or restaurants.

5.4. Evaluate several different types of food service equipment from the standpoint of location and legibility of displays and ease of use of controls.

Chapter 6

6.1. Identify several pieces of equipment that have potential safety hazards and indicate how they might be modified to make them safer.

6.2. Use the safety check list given in Table 6.2 to inspect a food service operation for hazards.

6.3. Indicate what steps can be taken to prevent the following types of accidents:
   a. Falls
   b. Snagging
   c. Cuts
   d. Burns
   e. Electrical shock

Chapter 7

7.1. Prepare a function analysis form for the catering department of a hotel. Use the check list shown in Table 7.1 as a guide.

7.2. Draw a function flow chart showing the flow of paperwork for a motel or hotel.

7.3. Perform an activity analysis for any of the following:
   a. Night auditor
   b. Catering manager
   c. Housekeeper

    d. Maid
    e. Hostess

7.4. Gather data and prepare a work distribution chart for the front office or the accounting office of a large motel or hotel.

7.5. Prepare a relationship chart for the kitchen equipment of a table service restaurant.

Chapter 8

8.1. Develop a random sampling time table for a sampling study requiring 20 daily observations for a 5 day period.

8.2. Conduct a sampling study of equipment usage in a food service operation to determine the percentage of time a particular piece of equipment is used. The study should be carried out over a period of several days.

8.3. Develop a data sheet for conducting a sampling study of a hotel manager. Include categories of productive activities that may be expected to be observed.

8.4. How many samples would be needed for a work sampling study if the desired accuracy is ±4% and the estimated value of P is 35%. Assume a confidence level of 95%.

8.5. Assume that the first sampling at 95% confidence level to determine the idle time of a worker has been completed. Out of a total of 800 samples, the worker was found to be idle for 320 of them. Determine the relative accuracy of the sampling study.

Chapter 9

9.1. The following steps were observed in preparing lamb stew:

The cook filled out one requisition in the office for lamb and another for frozen peas. He went to the meat cooler storage room, waited, obtained the lamb, went to the meat cutting table and trimmed and cubed the lamb. He then removed the cubed lamb to a refrigerator where it was stored overnight. In the morning he picked up the cubed lamb, went to his work table, placed the lamb on the table, went to the dry goods storage and picked up some flour, returned to the work table and floured the cubed lamb, moved the product to the oven where it was browned.

He removed the product, moved and placed it in a steam-jacketed kettle and slowly simmered it. While the product was simmering he proceeded to the vegetable storage area, picked up onions, moved to the vegetable table and peeled the onions by hand; then took the peeled onions to the range and placed the onions in a kettle on the range for cooking. He went back to the vegetable storage area, picked up carrots and potatoes, moved to the steamer area, placed the carrots and potatoes in separate steamer baskets for partial cooking. He went back to the storage area for more flour and then to the work table where he placed the flour in a pan, measured out water and mixed the flour and water. He picked up some salt at the work table and the pan containing the mixture of flour and water, went to the steamers and picked up the potatoes and carrots, went to the range and picked up the cooked onions, and then to the steam-jacketed kettle where the mentioned products were mixed with the cubed lamb. The stew was cooked until thickened then transferred to pots and the pots moved to the range. Frozen peas obtained from the issue room were then taken to a steam-jacketed kettle and cooked, then transferred to the cook's table, awaiting demand. Counter pans were then filled with the stew, moved to the cook's table and topped with peas, then moved to the dumb-waiter, then to the service room from the dumb-waiter by a cook's helper on the next floor.

Construct a product process chart for the lamb stew. What improvements could be made in this procedure?

9.2.   The procedure for making potato salad is given below. Construct a product process chart for the procedure described. What changes can be made to simplify the process?

The salad girl, at her work table, filled out a requisition for the necessary ingredients. The ingredients are: potatoes, mayonnaise, sour cream, onions, celery, salt, pepper, and celery seed. The girl then got a pan from the pot rack, filled it with water from her work sink and placed it on the range to boil. She then picked up another pan from the pot rack, took it with her to the storeroom and filled it with the potatoes. These were taken to the work sink, peeled, washed, drained and placed back in the pan. Then she took them to the range and placed them in the boiling water. Carrying the same pan that served to transport the potatoes, the girl went directly from the range to the storeroom and got the onions and celery. She took these to her work table and chopped them up. These ingredients were then put back in the pan and placed into the salad reach-in for storage while the potatoes cooked. When the potatoes were cooked, the girl got a colander from the pot rack and placed it in her work sink. Next, she went to the range, got the potatoes, took them to her work sink and placed them in the colander to drain and cool. When this was done, she took them to her work table and diced them. Then she got a large container from the pot rack, brought this to her work area and put the potatoes in it. Next she got her chopped onions and celery from her reach-in box and placed them in with the potatoes. Then she went to the storeroom and got the mayonnaise, sour cream, salt, pepper, and celery seed, all in their respective containers, and took them to her work area. These were all measured and then placed into the large container. All the ingredients were then mixed. This done, the potato salad was then placed in her reach-in box to be available for future use.

9.3. Make a product process chart of a proposed procedure for preparing a food item using a recipe as a guide. Select a recipe with at least five different ingredients.

Chapter 10

10.1. Construct a form process chart for the following procedure.

The menus for a particular restaurant chain are prepared at the central home office. There, a month before they are to be used, the menus are determined by a committee consisting of the two district managers, the head dietician, the executive chef and the purchasing director. Their decisions are placed on form M-A and placed in the secretarial mail box. Later, a mail boy picks up the form and delivers it to the secretarial pool mail box. There, when a girl gets a chance, she takes form M-A and types the information from it onto form M-B which is in 7 copies. The original form M-A together with M-B is placed in the out mail box for delivery to the head dietician.

Sometime later, a mail boy brings the forms to the head dietician's mail box along with her other mail. When she comes to the forms, she compares M-A with M-B, and if there are no errors, she initials it and takes copy 1 for her files. The remaining copies are placed in her mail box to be distributed. Form M-A is destroyed.

On his rounds, the mail boy picks up the copies and places them in his cart. Copies 2, 3, 4, and 5 are brought to the regional manager's office and copies 6 and 7 to the office of the executive chef. In his course of work, the regional manager reads form M-B, initials it and makes out 5 copies of requisition R-M, which is an order form for the printing of the menus. The forms are separated and then stapled as follows—copy 2 M-B with copy 1 R-M, copy 3 M-B with copy 2 R-M, copy 4 M-B with copy 3 R-M, and copy 5 M-B with copy 4 R-M. The first set (2 and 1) is placed in his file and all others in his mail box. Sets 2 and 3 (3 and 2, 4 and 3) will eventually be mailed to the two district managers. Set 4 (5 and 4) is taken to the printing department and copy 5 R-M to the accounting department.

In the printing department, two invoices with 3 copies each are prepared and separated. The three copies of the first invoice 1 I-M are distributed as follows—copy 1 goes with the menus to the 1st district manager, copy 2 to the accounting office and copy 3 is stapled to the combined M-B and R-M. The second invoice 2 I-M is distributed in the same manner except that copy 1 goes to the 2nd district manager. When the accounting department gets the two invoice copies, it staples them to copy 5 R-M and files them.

10.2. Prepare a form process chart for a paper work procedure that you are familiar with. After completing the chart, indicate where improvements can be made using the check list given in Table 10.2.

10.3. Construct a work distribution chart for the accounting office of a large hotel.

Chapter 11

11.1. Construct a worker process chart for the procedure followed by the cook in problem 9.1.

11.2. Construct a worker process chart for the procedure followed by the salad girl in problem 9.2. Devise an improved procedure by using the check list given in Table 11.2.

Chapter 12

12.1. An analysis of a cook's movements during a typical work period shows the following:

Movement From	Movement To	Frequency
Refrigerator	Table	10
Refrigerator	Sink	2
Refrigerator	Oven	2
Table	Refrigerator	10
Table	Sink	16
Table	Range	4
Table	Oven	8
Sink	Refrigerator	2
Sink	Table	6
Sink	Range	10
Range	Table	14
Range	Oven	4
Oven	Refrigerator	2
Oven	Table	6
Oven	Range	4

Arrange the five pieces of equipment in a straight line so that the total distance traveled by the cook is minimized. Assume the distance moved between adjacent pieces of equipment is equal.

12.2. An analysis of several recipes shows the following frequency of movements between five work places designated as A, B, C, D and E.

Movements Between	Frequency
A and B	10
A and C	13
A and E	10
B and C	12
B and D	8
B and E	9
C and D	3
D and E	7

Assuming that the work places are to be placed equidistant in a straight line and that C must be placed adjacent to E, arrange the work places to minimize the total distance traveled.

12.3. The quantity of materials and the sequence of movements for four different products are shown below:

Product No.	Quantity (lbs)	Sequence of Movements
1	200	B D A B C D
2	100	F E A E B D C
3	400	A C A F D C B
4	200	D A B C D B

The departments through which the materials move and their dimensions are:

Department	Dimensions
A	10 ft. × 10 ft.
B	10 ft. × 10 ft.
C	10 ft. × 10 ft.

D	10 ft. × 20 ft.
E	10 ft. × 10 ft.
F	10 ft. × 20 ft.

Arrange the departments to fit into a 20 ft. x 40 ft. rectangular configuration so that the material flow is minimized. Distances of movements are to be measured from the centers of departments over the shortest horizontal and/or vertical routes.

12.4. Using the data given in problem 12.3., arrange the departments to minimize flow given the restriction that department D must be placed at the right hand end of the configuration.

Chapter 13

13.1. The actions required for a particular operation are shown below. Meeting the hand and precedence requirements, develop a method of performing the operation that would minimize the number of delays. All actions take the same time to perform, therefore, any blank spaces in the procedure must be shown as delays. Show your method in the form of an operation chart identifying the actions by number and symbol.

Action No.	Symbol	Hand Requirement	Precedence Requirement
1.	Operation	R.H.	None
2.	Operation	EITHER	None
3.	Operation	L.H.	Anytime after 1 and 2 are done
4.	Operation	R.H.	Same time as 14
5.	Operation	R.H.	Anytime after 14 is done
6.	Hold	EITHER	Anytime after 5 is done
7.	Operation	R.H.	Same time as 6
8.	Movement	L.H.	Anytime before 16
9.	Operation	R.H.	None
10.	Movement	L.H.	After 2 is done
11.	Operation	R.H.	After 10 is done
12.	Movement	EITHER	None

13.	Operation	L.H.	After 3 and 10 are done
14.	Hold	L.H.	After 9
15.	Movement	R.H.	After 13 and 14 are done
16.	Operation	L.H.	After 15 is done

13.2. The data showing movements of a worker's hands is given as follows:

Movements From −To		Frequency L.H	R.H.	Movements From −To		Frequency L.H.	R.H.
A	B	4	7	E	A		8
A	C	7	3	E	B	5	
A	D	3		E	C	3	3
A	E	9		E	D		
A	F		6	E	F	1	4
A	G	6		E	G	6	
A	H	5		E	H	3	9
B	A	1	4	F	A		8
B	C	4		F	B	4	1
B	D	7	1	F	C		
B	E			F	D	1	5
B	F	6		F	E	1	2
B	G		8	F	G		
B	H	5		F	H	4	8
C	A		7	G	A		
C	B	4		G	B	3	8
C	D		3	G	C		
C	E	2	1	G	D	6	1
C	F			G	E	1	

Movements		Frequency		Movements		Frequency	
C	G	1		G	F		
C	H		8	G	H		4
D	A	1	3	H	A	2	
D	B	9	9	H	B		
D	C	7	7	H	C	5	8
D	E			H	D	1	2
D	F	3	1	H	E		
D	G		3	H	F	9	1
D	H	1		H	G	3	

The work place is 2 ft. x 4 ft. consisting of 8 sub-work areas as shown below:

Design the work place (arrange the sub-work areas)

a. So the total distance traveled by both hands is a minimum. Measure distances over the shortest horizontal and/or vertical routes.

b. So the most frequently used sub-work areas for the left hand are arranged in the following priority: 6, 2, 5 and 1; and the most frequently used sub-work areas for the right hand are arranged in the priority of 7, 3, 8 and 4.

c. So the total distance traveled for each hand is equal or near equal.

Chapter 14

14.1. Give an example from the hotel, restaurant or institutional field of each of the multi-activities shown in Table 14.1. Indicate the time controlling element for each example.

14.2. Devise an improved method for the cashiering task shown in Fig. 14.6. Show your method by a worker-machine operation chart.

Chapter 15

15.1. Devise an improved method for making a ham sandwich as shown in Fig. 15.7. Show your improved method by a therblig chart.

15.2. The following procedure was established for a person making shrimp salad plates. A sketch of the salad table is shown below.

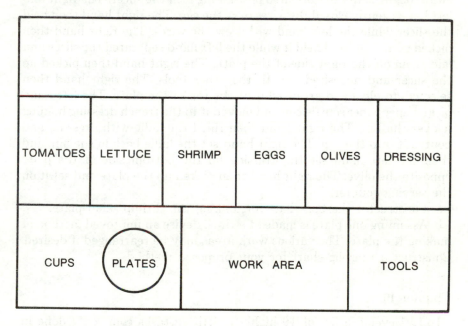

The left hand obtained a dinner plate from the lowerator and set it on the left corner of the work area. Several pieces of lettuce were then obtained by both the right and left hands, and returned to the work area. The right hand picked up the knife from amongst the other various hand tools, and proceeded to chop the lettuce, held by the left hand, into smaller pieces. When completed, the knife was set down in the work area. Both hands then lifted the lettuce onto the plate and spread it out to form a bed. The right hand picked up the #10 scoop and filled it with shrimp salad. The right hand brought the full scoop to the center of the plate and released the contents to form a circular mound. The left hand moved to the tomatoes, selected one and brought it to the work area. The tomato was placed so that the center section ran horizontally. Held in this position by the left hand, the tomato was then sliced by the knife picked up with the right hand. When completed, the right hand set down the knife, and then with the left hand selected two slices of tomato. These were picked up by the left hand and placed with the help of the right hand on the left side of the plate. The left hand picked up the remaining slices and returned them to the tomato bin. The right hand then picked up the knife and with the back end of the blade scraped the work area clean. The knife was returned to its previous position by the right hand which then brought the egg slicer to the work area, opening it with the left hand while in motion. The right hand then selected an egg and brought it to the work area positioning it in the slicer. The right and left hands gently closed the wires over the egg. The right hand then held the slicer while the left hand withdrew the wires. The right hand then picked up the egg and held it while the left hand separated the slices and laid them on the right side of the plate. The right hand then picked up the slicer and deposited it with the other tools. The right hand then selected an olive and arranged it at the top of the plate. The left hand picked up a paper souffle cup and moved it to the french dressing holding it over the bin. The right hand then filled the ladle with dressing and poured it into the cup. The right hand set the ladle back in the bin, and then the left hand set the dressing on the bottom side of the plate opposite the olive. The right hand then picked up the plate and set it on the serving counter.

a. Construct a therblig chart for making the shrimp salad plate.

b. Assuming one plate is made at a time, devise an improved method of making the plate. The various work areas may be rearranged if desired. Construct a therblig chart for your proposed method.

Chapter 16

16.1. Develop a list of 10 highly repetitive tasks commonly done in hotels, restaurants or institutions that could be studied and analyzed by micromotion techniques.

16.2. Identify 5 examples of multi-activities that could be easily analyzed by memomotion techniques.

Chapter 17

17.1. Develop an assembly chart for the preparation of banquet meals for 300 persons.

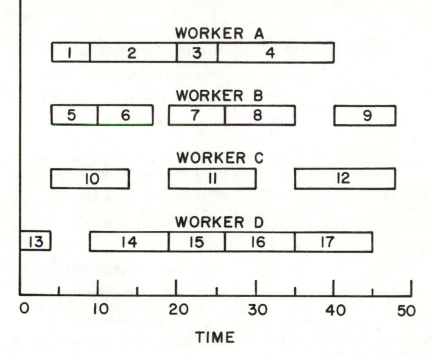

WORKER A

| 1 | 2 | 3 | 4 |

WORKER B

| 5 | 6 | 7 | 8 | 9 |

WORKER C

| 10 | 11 | 12 |

WORKER D

| 13 | 14 | 15 | 16 | 17 |

0   10   20   30   40   50

TIME

17.2. Draw a process flow diagram for the procedure shown in Fig. 9.5.

17.3. Make a string diagram showing the movements of the employee cleaning a bathroom as described in Fig. 11.2.

17.4. Refer to the precedence activity chart shown above to determine the following:

    a. Minimum time to complete all activities.

    b. Total idle time of all workers.

17.5. Construct a precedence activity chart from the following data for a 3 worker crew.

Task	Time (min)	Limitations or restrictions
1.	6	None
2.	7	After task 1 is completed
3.	4	After task 1 is completed

Task	Time (min)	Limitations or restrictions
4.	5	None
5.	9	None
6.	10	After task 3 is completed
7.	14	After task 6 is completed
8.	10	Has to start same time as task 9
9.	8	After task 6 is completed
10.	13	None
11.	8	After task 9 is completed
12.	6	After task 9 is completed
13.	3	After task 10 is completed
14.	7	None
15.	4	After task 14 is completed
16.	10	After task 13 is completed

Determine the minimum time to complete the above tasks and the idle time for each worker.

Chapter 18

18.1.   The results of 5 preliminary timings for a direct time study of a task were 6, 4, 5, 7 and 8 minutes. What is the required number of timings for ±5% accuracy and 68% confidence limits.

18.2.   What is the required number of timings for the data in problem 18.1 for ±5% accuracy and 95% confidence limits.

18.3.   The following procedure and related times have been observed in the baking of peanut butter cookies.

Worker Number	Task	Time–min/100 doz cookies
1	Obtain, measure and sift granulated sugar	.30
1	Obtain, measure and sift brown sugar	.20
1	Obtain, measure and blend flour and sugar	.50
1	Mix remaining ingredients and unload mixer	13.00
2	Transport and unload dough at shaper	2.00
2	Set up cookie shaper (done only once)	6.00
2	Shape cookies	24.00
3	Grease 40 baking sheets	18.00
3	Place cookies on baking sheets (30 cookies/sheet)	30.00
4	Place 40 baking sheets on mobile rack	8.00
4	Transport to oven	2.00
4	Load into oven, bake, unload	32.00
5	Transport from oven to package table	4.00
5	Remove cookies from sheets and package	20.00
5	Wash baking sheets	10.00

The quantity and price of the raw materials for making 100 dozen cookies is as follows:

Material	Quantity	Price/lb
Granulated sugar	13.0#	.20
Brown sugar	10.0#	.20
Crisco	11.5#	.40
Salt	0.1#	.03
Peanut butter	13.0#	.60
Mixed eggs	5.0#	.50
Water	2.2#	—
Soda	0.3#	.08
Flour	16.0#	.15
Baking powder	0.2#	.30
Crisco (greasing sheets)	2.0#	.40

The hourly wages of the 5 workers are:

Worker Number	Wage
1	$5.00
2	$4.00
3	$3.00
4	$4.00
5	$3.00

a. Determine the total production time to make 1, 2 and 3 batches (100 doz cookies).

b. Determine the total material and direct labor cost for making 1 batch of cookies.

c. If overhead cost is assumed to be 150% of the direct labor cost, and the selling price desired is to be 110% of the production cost, how much would you sell one dozen cookies for?

Chapter 19

19.1. Using the MTM actions and time data, determine the rated time for the task shown in Fig. 15.6.

19.2. Using the elemental time data system, determine the time to do the task described in Fig. 13.6.

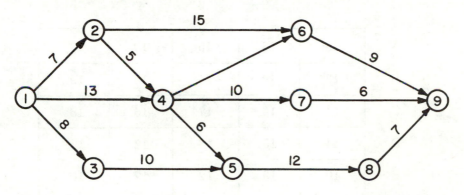

Chapter 20

20.1. Shown above is the CPM diagram for a set of activities. Determine the earliest and latest times for each of the events.

20.2. Determine the earliest, latest and slack times for each event in the following CPM diagram.

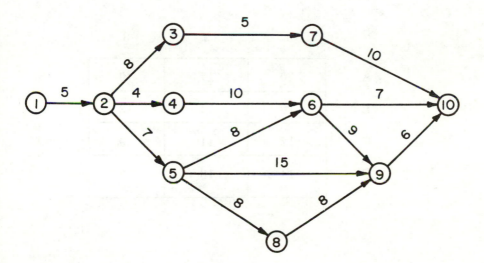

20.3. Use the Hungarian method to find the solution to the following assignment problem that gives the minimum value.

	1	2	3	4	5
A	18	16	15	19	17
B	13	19	14	18	19
C	14	16	17	15	18
D	14	15	18	12	17
E	10	13	12	17	16

20.4. Solve the following assignment problem for the maximum value.

	1	2	3
A	20	17	19
B	10	14	13
C	12	11	9
D	14	18	13

20.5. Solve the following transportation problem for the minimum value using Vogel's method.

Commissaries

		A	B	C	Requirements
	1	8	7	6	3
	2	5	10	9	2
Outlets	3	4	8	3	4
	4	5	6	7	1
	5	7	6	10	2
Restrictions		5	4	3	

20.6. Solve the following assignment problem for minimum value using Vogel's method. Compare Vogel's solution to the solution obtained by the Hungarian method.

	1	2	3	4	5	6
A	10	8	7	11	14	13
B	20	18	16	14	12	17
C	19	17	15	19	21	24
D	14	17	19	15	20	18
E	10	12	14	16	17	12
F	17	23	19	25	14	20

Chapter 21

21.1. Schedule the tasks shown below so they are done in the minimum elapsed time.

| | *Processing Times* | |
Task Number	*Equipment A*	*Equipment B*
1	6	8
2	8	4
3	9	7
4	7	6
5	5	9
6	3	4
7	8	7

21.2. Obtain the optimal schedule for the following tasks.

| | *Processing Times* | | |
Task Number	*Equipment A*	*Equipment B*	*Equipment C*
1	8	7	10
2	10	6	12
3	14	4	6
4	9	7	7
5	10	3	9
6	15	4	14
7	11	6	20
8	16	5	13

21.3. Determine the sequence that minimizes the total elapsed time to complete the following tasks.

Task Number	Equipment A	Equipment B
1	4	8
2	8	9
3	10	6
4	11	10
5	5	12
6	9	10
7	13	9
8	7	14

21.4. Determine the sequence that minimizes the total elapsed time to complete the followng tasks.

Task Number	Equipment A	Equipment B	Equipment C
1	10	6	2
2	7	2	7
3	9	4	5
4	12	3	8
5	14	4	4
6	10	5	10

TEMPERATURE CONVERSION

The numbers in boldface type in the center column refer to the temperature, either in degree Celsius or Fahrenheit, which is to be converted to the other scale. If converting Fahrenheit to degree Celsius, the equivalent temperature will be found in the left column. If converting degree Celsius to Fahrenheit, the equivalent temperature will be found in the column on the right.

Temperature			Temperature			Temperature			Temperature		
Celsius	°C or F	Fahr	Celsius	°C or F	Fahr	Celsius	°C or F	Fahr	Celsius	°C or F	Fahr
-40.0	-40	-40.0	+1.7	+35	+95.0	+43.3	+110	+230.0	+85.0	+185	+365.0
-39.4	-39	-38.2	+2.2	+36	+96.8	+43.9	+111	+231.8	+85.6	+186	+366.8
-38.9	-38	-36.4	+2.8	+37	+98.6	+44.4	+112	+233.6	+86.1	+187	+368.6
-38.3	-37	-34.6	+3.3	+38	+100.4	+45.0	+113	+235.4	+86.7	+188	+370.4
-37.8	-36	-32.8	+3.9	+39	+102.2	+45.6	+114	+237.2	+87.2	+189	+372.2
-37.2	-35	-31.0	+4.4	+40	+104.0	+46.1	+115	+239.0	+87.8	+190	+374.0
-36.7	-34	-29.2	+5.0	+41	+105.8	+46.7	+116	+240.8	+88.3	+191	+375.8
-36.1	-33	-27.4	+5.5	+42	+107.6	+47.2	+117	+242.6	+88.9	+192	+377.6
-35.6	-32	-25.6	+6.1	+43	+109.4	+47.8	+118	+244.4	+89.4	+193	+379.4
-35.0	-31	-23.8	+6.7	+44	+111.2	+48.3	+119	+246.2	+90.0	+194	+381.2
-34.4	-30	-22.0	+7.2	+45	+113.0	+48.9	+120	+248.0	+90.6	+195	+383.0
-33.9	-29	-20.2	+7.8	+46	+114.8	+49.4	+121	+249.8	+91.1	+196	+384.8
-33.3	-28	-18.4	+8.3	+47	+116.6	+50.0	+122	+251.6	+91.7	+197	+386.6
-32.8	-27	-16.6	+8.9	+48	+118.4	+50.6	+123	+253.4	+92.2	+198	+388.4
-32.2	-26	-14.8	+9.4	+49	+120.2	+51.1	+124	+255.2	+92.8	+199	+390.2
-31.7	-25	-13.0	+10.0	+50	+122.0	+51.7	+125	+257.0	+93.3	+200	+392.0
-31.1	-24	-11.2	+10.6	+51	+123.8	+52.2	+126	+258.8	+93.9	+201	+393.8
-30.6	-23	-9.4	+11.1	+52	+125.6	+52.8	+127	+260.6	+94.4	+202	+395.6
-30.0	-22	-7.6	+11.7	+53	+127.4	+53.3	+128	+262.4	+95.0	+203	+397.4
-29.4	-21	-5.8	+12.2	+54	+129.2	+53.9	+129	+264.2	+95.6	+204	+399.2
-28.9	-20	-4.0	+12.8	+55	+131.0	+54.4	+130	+266.0	+96.1	+205	+401.0
-28.3	-19	-2.2	+13.3	+56	+132.8	+55.0	+131	+267.8	+96.7	+206	+402.8
-27.8	-18	-0.4	+13.9	+57	+134.6	+55.6	+132	+269.6	+97.2	+207	+404.6
-27.2	-17	+1.4	+14.4	+58	+136.4	+56.1	+133	+271.4	+97.8	+208	+406.4
-26.7	-16	+3.2	+15.0	+59	+138.2	+56.7	+134	+273.2	+98.3	+209	+408.2
-26.1	-15	+5.0	+15.6	+60	+140.0	+57.2	+135	+275.0	+98.9	+210	+410.0
-25.6	-14	+6.8	+16.1	+61	+141.8	+57.8	+136	+276.8	+99.4	+211	+411.8
-25.0	-13	+8.6	+16.7	+62	+143.6	+58.3	+137	+278.6	+100.0	+212	+413.6
-24.4	-12	+10.4	+17.2	+63	+145.4	+58.9	+138	+280.4	+100.6	+213	+415.4
-23.9	-11	+12.2	+17.8	+64	+147.2	+59.4	+139	+282.2	+101.1	+214	+417.2
-23.3	-10	+14.0	+18.3	+65	+149.0	+60.0	+140	+284.0	+101.7	+215	+419.0
-22.8	-9	+15.8	+18.9	+66	+150.8	+60.6	+141	+285.8	+102.2	+216	+420.8
-22.2	-8	+17.6	+19.4	+67	+152.6	+61.1	+142	+287.6	+102.8	+217	+422.6
-21.7	-7	+19.4	+20.0	+68	+154.4	+61.7	+143	+289.4	+103.3	+218	+424.4
-21.1	-6	+21.2	+20.6	+69	+156.2	+62.2	+144	+291.2	+103.9	+219	+426.2
-20.6	-5	+23.0	+21.1	+70	+158.0	+62.8	+145	+293.0	+104.4	+220	+428.0
-20.0	-4	+24.8	+21.7	+71	+159.8	+63.3	+146	+294.8	+105.6	+222	+431.6
-19.4	-3	+26.6	+22.2	+72	+161.6	+63.9	+147	+296.6	+106.7	+224	+435.2
-18.9	-2	+28.4	+22.8	+73	+163.4	+64.4	+148	+298.4	+107.8	+226	+438.8
-18.3	-1	+30.2	+23.3	+74	+165.2	+65.0	+149	+300.2	+108.9	+228	+442.4
-17.8	0	+32.0	+23.9	+75	+167.0	+65.6	+150	+302.0	+110.0	+230	+446.0
-17.2	+1	+33.8	+24.4	+76	+168.8	+66.1	+151	+303.8	+111.1	+232	+449.6
-16.7	+2	+35.6	+25.0	+77	+170.6	+66.7	+152	+305.6	+112.2	+234	+453.2
-16.1	+3	+37.4	+25.6	+78	+172.4	+67.2	+153	+307.4	+113.3	+236	+456.8
-15.6	+4	+39.2	+26.1	+79	+174.2	+67.8	+154	+309.2	+114.4	+238	+460.4
-15.0	+5	+41.0	+26.7	+80	+176.0	+68.3	+155	+311.0	+115.6	+240	+464.0
-14.4	+6	+42.8	+27.2	+81	+177.8	+68.9	+156	+312.8	+116.7	+242	+467.6
-13.9	+7	+44.6	+27.8	+82	+179.6	+69.4	+157	+314.6	+117.8	+244	+471.2
-13.3	+8	+46.4	+28.3	+83	+181.4	+70.0	+158	+316.4	+118.9	+246	+474.2
-12.8	+9	+48.2	+28.9	+84	+183.2	+70.6	+159	+318.2	+120.0	+248	+478.4
-12.2	+10	+50.0	+29.4	+85	+185.0	+71.1	+160	+320.0	+121.1	+250	+482.0
-11.7	+11	+51.8	+30.0	+86	+186.8	+71.7	+161	+321.8	+122.4	+252	+485.6
-11.1	+12	+53.6	+30.6	+87	+188.6	+72.2	+162	+323.6	+123.3	+254	+489.2
-10.6	+13	+55.4	+31.1	+88	+190.4	+72.8	+163	+325.4	+124.4	+256	+492.8
-10.0	+14	+57.2	+31.7	+89	+192.2	+73.3	+164	+327.2	+125.5	+258	+496.4
-9.4	+15	+59.0	+32.2	+90	+194.0	+73.9	+165	+329.0	+126.7	+260	+500.0
-8.9	+16	+60.8	+32.8	+91	+195.8	+74.4	+166	+330.8	+127.8	+262	+503.6
-8.3	+17	+62.6	+33.3	+92	+197.6	+75.0	+167	+332.6	+128.9	+264	+507.2
-7.8	+18	+64.4	+33.9	+93	+199.4	+75.6	+168	+334.4	+130.0	+266	+510.8
-7.2	+19	+66.2	+34.4	+94	+201.2	+76.1	+169	+336.2	+131.3	+268	+514.4
-6.7	+20	+68.0	+35.0	+95	+203.0	+76.7	+170	+338.0	+132.2	+270	+518.0
-6.1	+21	+69.8	+35.6	+96	+204.8	+77.2	+171	+339.8	+133.3	+272	+521.6
-5.5	+22	+71.6	+36.1	+97	+206.6	+77.8	+172	+341.6	+134.4	+274	+525.2
-5.0	+23	+73.4	+36.7	+98	+208.4	+78.3	+173	+343.4	+135.6	+276	+528.8
-4.4	+24	+75.2	+37.2	+99	+210.2	+78.9	+174	+345.2	+136.7	+278	+532.4
-3.9	+25	+77.0	+37.8	+100	+212.0	+79.4	+175	+347.0	+137.8	+280	+536.0
-3.3	+26	+78.8	+38.3	+101	+213.8	+80.0	+176	+348.8	+138.9	+282	+539.6
-2.8	+27	+80.6	+38.9	+102	+215.6	+80.6	+177	+350.6	+140.0	+284	+543.2
-2.2	+28	+82.4	+39.4	+103	+217.4	+81.1	+178	+352.4	+141.1	+286	+546.8
-1.7	+29	+84.2	+40.0	+104	+219.2	+81.7	+179	+354.2	+142.2	+288	+550.4
-1.1	+30	+86.0	+40.6	+105	+221.0	+82.2	+180	+356.0	+143.3	+290	+554.0
-0.6	+31	+87.8	+41.1	+106	+222.8	+82.8	+181	+357.8	+144.4	+292	+557.6
.0	+32	+89.6	+41.7	+107	+224.6	+83.3	+182	+359.6	+145.6	+294	+561.2
+0.6	+33	+91.4	+42.2	+108	+226.4	+83.9	+183	+361.4	+146.7	+296	+564.8
+1.1	+34	+93.2	+42.8	+109	+228.2	+84.4	+184	+363.2	+147.8	+298	+568.4

COMPARISON OF AVOIRDUPOIS AND METRIC UNITS OF WEIGHT

1 oz = 0.06 lb = 28.35 g	1 lb = 0.454 kg	1 g = 0.035 oz	1 kg = 2.205 lb
2 oz = 0.12 lb = 56.70 g	2 lb = 0.91 kg	2 g = 0.07 oz	2 kg = 4.41 lb
3 oz = 0.19 lb = 85.05 g	3 lb = 1.36 kg	3 g = 0.11 oz	3 kg = 6.61 lb
4 oz = 0.25 lb = 113.40 g	4 lb = 1.81 kg	4 g = 0.14 oz	4 kg = 8.82 lb
5 oz = 0.31 lb = 141.75 g	5 lb = 2.27 kg	5 g = 0.18 oz	5 kg = 11.02 lb
6 oz = 0.38 lb = 170.10 g	6 lb = 2.72 kg	6 g = 0.21 oz	6 kg = 13.23 lb
7 oz = 0.44 lb = 198.45 g	7 lb = 3.18 kg	7 g = 0.25 oz	7 kg = 15.43 lb
8 oz = 0.50 lb = 226.80 g	8 lb = 3.63 kg	8 g = 0.28 oz	8 kg = 17.64 lb
9 oz = 0.56 lb = 255.15 g	9 lb = 4.08 kg	9 g = 0.32 oz	9 kg = 19.84 lb
10 oz = 0.62 lb = 283.50 g	10 lb = 4.54 kg	10 g = 0.35 oz	10 kg = 22.05 lb
11 oz = 0.69 lb = 311.85 g	11 lb = 4.99 kg	11 g = 0.39 oz	11 kg = 24.26 lb
12 oz = 0.75 lb = 340.20 g	12 lb = 5.44 kg	12 g = 0.42 oz	12 kg = 26.46 lb
13 oz = 0.81 lb = 368.55 g	13 lb = 5.90 kg	13 g = 0.46 oz	13 kg = 28.67 lb
14 oz = 0.88 lb = 396.90 g	14 lb = 6.35 kg	14 g = 0.49 oz	14 kg = 30.87 lb
15 oz = 0.94 lb = 425.25 g	15 lb = 6.81 kg	15 g = 0.53 oz	15 kg = 33.08 lb
16 oz = 1.00 lb = 453.59 g	16 lb = 7.26 kg	16 g = 0.56 oz	16 kg = 35.28 lb

COMPARISON OF U.S. AND METRIC UNITS OF LIQUID MEASURE

1 fl oz = 29.573 ml	1 qt = 0.946 liter	1 gal. = 3.785 liters
2 fl oz = 59.15 ml	2 qt = 1.89 liters	2 gal. = 7.57 liters
3 fl oz = 88.72 ml	3 qt = 2.84 liters	3 gal. = 11.36 liters
4 fl oz = 118.30 ml	4 qt = 3.79 liters	4 gal. = 15.14 liters
5 fl oz = 147.87 ml	5 qt = 4.73 liters	5 gal. = 18.93 liters
6 fl oz = 177.44 ml	6 qt = 5.68 liters	6 gal. = 22.71 liters
7 fl oz = 207.02 ml	7 qt = 6.62 liters	7 gal. = 26.50 liters
8 fl oz = 236.59 ml	8 qt = 7.57 liters	8 gal. = 30.28 liters
9 fl oz = 266.16 ml	9 qt = 8.52 liters	9 gal. = 34.07 liters
10 fl oz = 295.73 ml	10 qt = 9.46 liters	10 gal. = 37.85 liters

1 ml = 0.034 fl oz	1 liter = 1.057 qt	1 liter = 0.264 gal.
2 ml = 0.07 fl oz	2 liters = 2.11 qt	2 liters = 0.53 gal.
3 ml = 0.10 fl oz	3 liters = 3.17 qt	3 liters = 0.79 gal.
4 ml = 0.14 fl oz	4 liters = 4.23 qt	4 liters = 1.06 gal.
5 ml = 0.17 fl oz	5 liters = 5.28 qt	5 liters = 1.32 gal.
6 ml = 0.20 fl oz	6 liters = 6.34 qt	6 liters = 1.59 gal.
7 ml = 0.24 fl oz	7 liters = 7.40 qt	7 liters = 1.85 gal.
8 ml = 0.27 fl oz	8 liters = 8.45 qt	8 liters = 2.11 gal.
9 ml = 0.30 fl oz	9 liters = 9.51 qt	9 liters = 2.38 gal.
10 ml = 0.34 fl oz	10 liters = 10.57 qt	10 liters = 2.64 gal.

CONVERSION OF OVEN TEMPERATURES

Conventional (Fahrenheit)		Metric (Celsius)
200 F		93 C
225 F		107 C
250 F	Very low	121 C
300 F	Low	149 C
325 F		163 C
350 F	Moderate	177 C
400 F	Hot	204 C
450 F	Very high	232 C
500 F	Extremely high	260 C

VOLUME CONVERSION DIFFERENCES
CONVENTIONAL VS. METRIC MEASUREMENTS

Utensil	Capacity (ml)	Tolerance (ml)
1 cup	236.6	11.8
½ cup	118.3	5.9
⅓ cup	78.9	3.9
¼ cup	59.2	3.0
1 tablespoon	14.79	0.73
1 teaspoon	4.93	0.24
½ teaspoon	2.46	0.12
¼ teaspoon	1.23	0.06

Index

Accidents, 31, 79, 97
 causes, 100
 frequency, 96
 prevention, 100
Accumulative timing, 344
Accuracy, 147, 156, 344
 determining, 146, 154
 sampling, 144
Activity, 344
 analysis, 117
  checklist, 125
  data form, 122
 charts, 122
 dummy, 316
 hotel, 132
 nonrepetitive, 29
 relationship charts, 130
 restaurant, 132
Air conditioning, 66−67
Air movement, 62, 66
Allocation, 309
Allowance, 344
Assembly charts, 263
Assignment problems, 308−315
 nonsquare, 315

Balance, 345
Basic motion time data, 286−288

Change, resistance to, 7, 20, 24
Charts, activity, 123−124
 activity relationship, 130
 assembly, 264
 combination, 263
 form process, 179
 function, 116
  flow, 117
 multiactivity, 233
 operation, 219
 precedence activity, 274
 procedure flow, 187
 product process, 164
 simo, 248, 357−358
 therblig, 246
 travel, 202, 210, 213
 work distribution, 128
 worker process, 189
Chronocyclegraph, 345
Chronocyclegraphic analysis, 262
Color, 32, 76
 association, 78
 code, 346
 coding, 101
 effect of light sources, 75

functional uses, 78
 perception, 74
Combination charts, 263
Comfort index, 64
Conditions, 346
Confidence level, 144, 147
Consultants, 22−23
 use, 25
Continuous timing, 281, 346
Contrast, 74, 77
 ratio, 74
Controls, 88
Costs, comparison, 37
 indirect, 37
 installation, 36
 labor, 3, 28, 36
 operating, 36−37
 turnover, 3
CPM diagram, 305−307
Critical path method, 304−305
Cyclegraph, 346
Cyclegraphic analysis, 262

Data collection, 33
 discussion, 33
 self analysis, 119
 time lapse photography, 122
Delay, 347
 symbol, 164, 179, 189
Design, 16
Dials, open-window, 86
 placement of numerals, 87, 89
 readability, 88
Displays, design, 84
 direction of movement, 89
 placement, 88
Distance charts, 209, 211, 215
Drop delivery, 347

Effective temperature, 62
Efficiency, 347
Element, 18, 33, 348
 breakdown, 348
 productive, 19
 unproductive, 19
Elemental time data, 298
Environment, 61
 nonphysical, 32, 36
 physical, 32, 35−36
Equipment, 31
 arrangement, 206
 design, 61, 83, 92, 303
 safe use, 98, 102
Events, 305

387